Probability Models of
Collective Decision Making

Merrill Political Science Series

Under the editorship of

John C. Wahlke

Department of Political Science
SUNY at Stony Brook

Probability Models of Collective Decision Making

Edited by

Richard G. Niemi
University of Rochester

Herbert F. Weisberg
University of Michigan

Charles E. Merrill Publishing Company
A Bell & Howell Company
Columbus, Ohio

Published by

Charles E. Merrill Publishing Company
A Bell & Howell Company
Columbus, Ohio 43216

ISBN: 0-675-09180-2

Library of Congress Catalog Card Number: 77-172268

1 2 3 4 5 6 7—77 76 75 74 73 72

Printed in the United States of America

CONTRIBUTORS

Peter H. Aranson

Department of Political Science
University of Minnesota

Wade W. Badger

Department of Physics and Astronomy
University of Rochester

Bo H. Bjurulf

Department of Political Science
University of Lund, Sweden

Bruce D. Bowen

Department of Political Science
University of Michigan

Steven J. Brams

Department of Politics
New York University

James S. Coleman

Department of Social Relations
Johns Hopkins University

Richard B. Curtis

Carnegie Commission on Higher Education
Berkeley, California

Otto A. Davis

School of Urban and Public Affairs
Carnegie-Mellon University

Melvin J. Hinich

School of Urban and Public Affairs
Carnegie-Mellon University

David H. Koehler   School of Government and Public
                            Administration
                          American University

Richard G. Niemi   Department of Political Science
                          University of Rochester

Peter C. Ordeshook   School of Urban and Public Affairs
                          Carnegie-Mellon University

Charles R. Plott   Division of the Humanities and Social Sciences
                          California Institute of Technology

David W. Rohde   Department of Political Science
                          Michigan State University

Norman J. Schofield   Department of Government
                          University of Essex, England

Kenneth A. Shepsle   Department of Political Science
                          Washington University, St. Louis

Herbert F. Weisberg   Department of Political Science
                          University of Michigan

CONTENTS

PREFACE

The past decade has seen considerable work in the formal modelling of collective decision making. Increasingly that work has been put into a probability framework, mainly because modellers found that the probabilistic formulation allowed the solution of problems which could not be handled by a completely deterministic approach. For this volume, we have solicited sixteen original papers which explore the frontiers of work on probability models of collective decision making. Our introduction reviews the main areas of work on this subject, placing the papers in this collection into the framework of the previous literature and suggesting possible lines of future development. Additionally, the conclusion examines the assumptions which are entailed by a probabilistic approach to formal modelling, along with the advantages and disadvantages of probability models.

The papers in this volume vary considerably in the complexity of mathematics which is used. While we would encourage the reader to examine the full range of material, some readers might appreciate an indication of the level of mathematics contained in specific pieces. Calculus is employed only in chapter 3 and in the papers on spatial modelling in the final section of the book. The other papers require much less formal mathematics, though some make considerable use of combinatorial procedures which are explained in standard statistics texts. The reader without a mathematical background is particularly encouraged to examine the applications articles by Koehler (chapter 7), Rohde (chapter 8), Bowen (chapter 9), and Weisberg and Niemi (chapter 10).

Finally, we would like to express our appreciation to our contributors, most of whom have labored through several drafts in order to produce chapters that are technically correct and yet eminently readable. Professors Bo Bjurulf, Lutz Erbring, Charles Plott, and Kenneth Shepsle provided valuable comments and suggestions on the introduction and conclusion. We would also like to thank Mrs. Sharon Stevenson, who provided us considerable clerical assistance in the preparation of the manuscript.

Rochester, New York
Ann Arbor, Michigan

Introduction: Substantive Applications of Collective Decision-Making Models

We begin this essay in the belief that formal models of collective decision making are assuming increasing importance in social science. Collective decision making—such as that done by committees, legislatures, courts, political parties, electorates, and societies—has long been a concern of political scientists. Lately, under the influence of economic analysis in particular (and the psychological decision-making literature to a lesser extent), many social scientists have come to recognize the need for formal models of such processes.[1] This has resulted in the collaboration of political scientists, economists, psychologists, sociologists, mathematicians, and other kindred spirits in the formation of the Public Choice Society, which publishes its own journal devoted largely to formal analyses of all types of nonmarket decision making. It has also resulted in the publication of a growing number of books devoted to formal models of political processes—by Arrow (1951, 1963), Downs (1957), Black (1958), Buchanan and Tullock (1962), Riker (1962), Olson (1965), Tullock (1967), Curry and Wade (1968), Farquharson (1969), Axelrod (1970), and others.

Our purpose in editing this collection of articles is to further this development of, interest in, and use of formal models by political scientists

---

[1] The nature and utility of such models, as well as their shortcomings, are discussed by Kaplan (1964, chap. 7). See also Davis (1969).

and by others interested in political and social processes. But we have another purpose as well—namely, to suggest that some of the most interesting models to be developed will be probabilistic in nature.[2] Probability models are far from rare in the social sciences.[3] Indeed if we include the models underlying quantitative data analysis—such varied and diverse procedures as statistical inference, cross-tabulations (with percentages within a given row or column of the table being treated as a conditional probability distribution), regression, variance, and covariance analysis (which explicitly include a probabilistic error term), latent structure analysis, factor analysis, models for cross-level inference, Markov chain models, and causal modelling—probability models are ubiquitous in political science as well as in all the social sciences. But the widespread application of formal probability models to collective decision-making processes is relatively recent.

For this volume we have solicited sixteen original articles that contain some of the most promising and exciting work in this area. The authors include not only political scientists and economists, but two physicists, a sociologist, and a statistician. The papers show in detail the many and varied uses of probability theory in the development of formal models of collective decision making. They also reveal the considerable potentiality and utility of probabilistic models and, like all models, illustrate the hazards and liabilities that attend this approach. These articles are all the better since they build on previous work in this area, and we are confident that they will spur further studies of this variety.

In the introductory and concluding comments, we undertake two tasks that go beyond the scope of any single article. In the introduction we consider the variety of substantive applications of models of collective decision making. Such work dates back at least as far as Condorcet's (1785) treatment of the "jury problem" (Black, 1958, pp. 163-73). It has included analysis of a large number of topics which are frequently related to one another on a tangential level at best. This material will be reviewed along with some attempt to categorize it, in the hope that this framework will be a useful stimulus to further investigations as well as providing an overview of where current efforts have been directed. The development of probability models out of deterministic theorizing will be a continuing theme. Thus the papers in this volume will be set into a common framework with previous writings in the area. Much of this material will

---

[2] The basis for this suggestion is found in the introduction, and especially in the conclusion, of this volume.

[3] Some people would distinguish between probability models and probabilistic models. The former would be models in which probabilities are the main variables, while the latter would be those in which probabilities are used only for random shock effects. While we deal mainly with the former type in this volume, we will use the terms interchangeably for stylistic purposes.

be familiar to readers, though the breadth of materials covered, its arrangement, and the commentary on it, should make it useful even to those who have worked in the area.

In the concluding essay we will turn to some of the issues involved in probabilistic modelling which have been treated only indirectly, unsystematically, and haphazardly heretofore. Advantages and disadvantages of probability models will be examined. Then the uses of probability in these models will be discussed, with emphasis on the various interpretations given to probabilities in probabilistic models. The conclusion weaves together issues involved in the uses of probability modelling throughout the collective decision-making field. It represents a conscious attempt to treat probability modelling as a field of study and to discuss it at that level. Undoubtedly further work in this area will go so far beyond present work as to make our discussion look incomplete, but we have tried to move to a theoretical framework which will be useful in stimulating and directing that future development. The conclusion should be understandable to anyone who is somewhat familiar with the literature. The greater the reader's familiarity with the literature, the more he should find it useful and the more he may be able to improve upon our initial effort.

Formal models have been used to deal with a variety of problems in collective decision making. We shall consider four basic topics which have been treated: constitutional design, coalition formation, the paradox of voting, and spatial modelling of competition. We briefly review the major work in each area, and indicate how the papers in this volume contribute to these areas. In each case emphasis is placed on the contributions made by probabilistic models.

I. CONSTITUTIONAL DESIGN

A basic problem for any society is the choice of a decision-making mechanism. For democratic societies in particular, the problem is to choose decision-rules which satisfy essential democratic requirements. The nature of such requirements has been discussed in the literature along with the degree to which common decision mechanisms (particularly majority rule) meet these criteria. Many different desiderata for decision-rules have been proposed. Arrow (1951, 1963) presented four basic conditions— the admissibility of all logically possible individual preference orderings, independence from other alternatives, a Pareto principle, and a non-dictatorship requirement—and then proceeded to demonstrate their inconsistency. We shall return to Arrow's result later in the context of the paradox of voting. May (1952) developed a different set of four conditions—that the rule be always decisive, an equality notion, a neutrality requirement, and a positive responsiveness criterion—and then proved that these are four independent, necessary, and sufficient conditions for majority rule.

Another approach to the constitutional design problem involves a cost-minimization strategy for the individual. Buchanan and Tullock (1962) consider the choice of a decision-rule from the perspective of an individual trying to minimize the costs imposed on him. These costs include so-called external costs resulting from collective actions with which the individual disagrees and decision-making costs resulting from participation in the decision process. The greater the proportion of the members of the decision-making body required to make a decision, the less the individual member needs to worry about external costs being imposed upon him, but the costs of reaching a decision in that body increase. The individual will favor that decision-rule which minimizes the sum of these two costs.

Rae (1969) has provided a probabilistic formulation of this problem focussing on the external costs discussed by Buchanan and Tullock. Rae seeks to minimize the probability that the voting will impose on the individual a result which differs from his preferences. Assuming that the probability that each member will support any proposal is exactly one-half and that the probability of one member supporting a proposal is independent of the probability of any other member supporting it, Rae demonstrates that majority rule is the optimal decision-rule. Taylor (1969) generalizes Rae's result, showing that majority rule is optimal if all members have any common probability (p) of supporting a proposal.

This formulation of the cost-minimization problem is particularly interesting because it suggests one way in which a probabilistic reinterpretation can aid a deterministic model. A knotty problem in the Buchanan-Tullock formulation is the seeming inability to measure external and decision-making costs. While we know generally the form of the relationship between these costs and the decision-rule, precise measurements are elusive to say the least. Thus while the individual is well-advised to support that decision-rule which minimizes the sum of these two costs, it is impossible to tell just where that minimum point is. With the probabilistic formulation (of external costs) we are able to specify exactly what decision-rule is optimal. And importantly, the probabilistic assumptions lend themselves to what we think is a meaningful interpretation. Thus the reformulation of the Buchanan-Tullock version moves us from an indeterminate situation to one in which specific results can be derived.

We should not be content with Rae's reformulation of the original problem, although we regard it as a major advance. In making this move to a probabilistic model, we noted that only Buchanan and Tullock's notion of external costs was retained. In this sense the reformulation is less general than the original model. It would be useful if the decision-making costs could also be translated into a probabilistic version and incorporated into Rae's model of external costs. Similarly, the reformulated model has lost some generality by Rae's assumption of independent voters. This assumption is common to many probability models since it simplifies their solution, but it is so unrealistic that attempts to relax it would be worthwhile.[4] Some of the groundwork for loosening the independence assumption in the context of Rae's model has been made by Badger in this volume, for he finds an analytic solution which makes it possible to solve for an optimal decision-rule when the legislative body is divided into groups (and/or isolated individuals), each of whom has a different probability of supporting a proposal. Thus the problem can conceivably be restored to its original generality, but with the probabilistic version providing the wherewithal for calculating specific results.

In this volume, four papers address themselves to the constitutional design problem. Curtis (chap. 1) generalizes Rae's model to the case of unequal probabilities of members voting yes, showing how the expected loss for the "average member" is minimized under majority rule. He is able to relax the assumption of a common probability of all members voting for a motion, but in doing so he must speak of the optimal decision-rule for the hypothetical average member rather than minimizing the expected costs for some individual member. Curtis also proves Rae's conjecture that the optimal decision-rule depends directly on the extent to which members weight the loss caused by the passage of a proposal they oppose more or less heavily than the loss associated with the defeat of a proposal they support. Majority rule is the optimal decision-rule only when these two losses are weighted equally.

Badger (chap. 2) retains Rae's objective of looking for the decision-rule which is optimal for a particular individual. Like Curtis, Badger does not require a common probability of all members voting for a motion, and he is able to obtain a general solution in which the optimal decision-rule depends on the individual's estimates of the frequency with which each of his colleagues and himself will favor future proposals. The general solution, however, is so general that any decision-rule could conceivably be optimal. So to get more useful results, Badger progressively narrows the assumptions, solving, for example, for the case in which the specific individual has one probability of favoring the motion while all the others have some other common probability. Badger also demonstrates the relevance of the weighting function mentioned previously in connection

---

[4] Fortunately some initial efforts at relaxing this assumption have been made by Bjurulf (chap. 11 in this volume) and Coleman (1970). (See the conclusion.)

with Curtis. Finally, he suggests that the decision-rule for a society should not be chosen by unanimity but by majority rule because it satisfies May's conditions referred to above. He further demonstrates that the choice of a decision-rule by majority vote is not susceptible to the paradox of voting.

Schofield (chap. 3) examines the effect of group size on the optimality of the decision-rule. He defines the marginal advantage of a decision-rule as the difference between the losses to the individual under that rule and the rule which is least advantageous for him. One interesting, and certainly nonobvious, result is that this marginal advantage disappears as the group becomes large for the Rae-Taylor single-issue model (i.e., a general, but common, p value). Paradoxically, when examining a continuous distribution of issues, with a common p value on a single issue for all individuals but possibly different p values for different issues, majority rule is still optimal but its marginal advantage remains significantly greater than zero as the group becomes large. Thus the optimality of majority rule cannot be dismissed as characterizing only very small groups.

Plott's paper on constitutional design (chap. 4) places the work of Buchanan and Tullock, Rae, Taylor, Curtis, Badger, and Schofield in a much broader perspective. It shows that their formulations can be viewed as part of a much larger model, which specifies in a highly general way the relationship between individual preferences and collective outcomes. In particular, Plott's formulation calls attention to a parameter handled only implicitly in previous models—the individual's preferences for the possible outcomes. Rather than employing the dichotomy of whether or not the individual favors a given outcome, it is possible to move toward a continuous measure of the extent to which the individual is satisfied (or dissatisfied) with a given outcome.[5]

Plott also points to two interesting dilemmas in the constitutional design literature. The individual is called upon to make judgments now about decision processes which will be in effect in the future. To have preferences now on mechanisms for making future decisions is paradoxical since one's policy preferences may change as may the policy arena itself. Since the problem seems to call for an evaluation, now, in terms of future preferences, Plott maintains that the "foundations of this procedure, in the current theory of preference, are not obvious" (p. 87). He then suggests an expected utility approach to the problem in cases where the individual knows now his attitude toward risk for all future preferences that he may have.

---

[5] As a first approximation for such an approach, Niemi and Weisberg (chap. 6 in this volume, footnote 10) suggest employing the individual's decisiveness; the more extreme the individual's probability of favoring a given alternative, the more dissatisfied he would be if it failed (and possibly the more satisfied he would be if it passed).

The second dilemma is that within the traditional approaches an individual's evaluation of various constitutions depends upon the "status quo" from which the constitutions are assumed to proceed. That is, an individual's evaluation of a political process cannot be separated from and depends directly upon his own position vis-à-vis that process. For example, a poor person may prefer majority rule whereas a rich person may prefer unanimity. Since no systematic way exists for specifying an individual's "position" *prior* to the constitution, the existing analyses are subject to a rather fundamental ambiguity.

Plott resolves this difficulty by making the "status quo" a random variable. The resulting formulation allows both dilemmas to be systematically eliminated simultaneously. Thus it seems that uncertainty about the future makes probabilistic models particularly apropos for the study of constitutional design. In fact the very nature of a constitution is similar to a statistical decision-rule (or pure strategy). If only a single social choice were needed, there would be no need for a constitution; with dynamics, uncertainty and thus probability follow immediately.

II. COALITION FORMATION

After a decision-rule is selected, concern shifts to the process of constructing a winning coalition. Work in this area has included studies of the process mechanisms involved in voting as well as the nature of the coalitions that form.

Process mechanisms have been modelled in the area of mass electoral behavior and elite legislative behavior. The classic model at the individual voter level is due to McPhee (McPhee and Smith, 1962). The McPhee electoral model consists of three stages—a stimulation phase in which an artificial population is generated by a probabilistic process, a discussion phase in which the individual contacts a friend and votes if they are in agreement or returns to the stimulation phase possibly to obtain a new preference if they disagree, and a learning phase in which the voter obtains his predispositions for voting at the next election as a function of his present vote and his past voting history. This model has been used to investigate political immunization in an electorate, the process by which an electorate becomes insensitive to certain classes of phenomena as it passes through a series of elections (McPhee and Ferguson, 1962).

Cherryholmes and Shapiro (1969) adapted the logic of the McPhee model to dealing with a fixed population of legislators. Theirs is a two-stage model of legislative voting. The first phase is a predisposition phase in which each legislator is given a predisposition on each bill according to the party, committee, region, state, and constituency effects of the bill as well as his voting behavior on similar bills in the preceding Congress.

Legislators strongly predisposed to vote for or against the bill are predicted to do so. Members with weak predispositions go through a probabilistic communications phase in which they are assigned probabilities of having conversations with the president and other legislators, and their predispositions are modified if the conversations occur. The communications phase is probabilistic because the circumstances causing the conversations are not fully known, and conversations depend to some extent on chance encounters which are inherently unpredictable. Cherryholmes and Shapiro used this model to predict voting in two issue areas in Congress, achieving a high level of predictive success.

The McPhee and Cherryholmes and Shapiro models are both presented as simulations, as are several other process models of voting among mass electorates and legislative elites. The Simulmatics project (Pool, Abelson, and Popkin, 1964) sought to predict state and national election results, but without a strong emphasis on the individual process mechanisms. Abelson and Bernstein (1963) have developed a complex model which may be particularly able to account for polarization in an electorate. A modular election simulation by Coombs, Fried, and Robinovitz (1968) includes a candidate decision model, a probabilistic information and communication model, and two alternative probabilistic voter decision models. Matthews and Stimson (1970) have provided a deterministic model of legislative voting in which the votes of a member in one session are determined by cues taken from the sources with which he voted most frequently in the previous session. However, a probabilistic model might yield better predictions, predicting the votes of a member by weighting the predispositions of the cue sources by the relative frequency with which the member voted with them in the previous session.

Computer simulation of individual process mechanisms is not the sole approach to their study. Another approach has been to derive from relatively formal models some implications for the behavior of aggregate populations, and then to test those implications with relevant empirical data. One such attempt has been to derive implications for aggregate historical election series from electoral theory developed at the individual level. Survey studies of the American electorate since the 1940s have pointed to long-term party identification as a major determinant of individual voting behavior, with short-term effects related to specific elections deflecting the vote in a given election from what would be expected on the basis of party identification alone (Campbell, *et al.*, 1960, 1966). This individual level theory has several aggregate level implications.

The postulated short-term forces permit victories by the party which is in the minority with respect to partisan affiliation. Stokes (1962) has used the historical variance in the two-party vote division to estimate the probability of a minority party election victory as a function of the party identification balance. This model demonstrates that minority party victories are in accord with the individual level theory, but finds that minority party victories will be the exception rather than the rule so long as the partisan balance is not too even. This model could also be applied to determine the probability of landslide elections as a function of the partisan balance.

The postulated long-term party identification force serves as a major restoring force, keeping the electoral system in equilibrium rather than allowing a landslide election to permanently shift the system to a level at which the minority party would die. In order to determine whether there is a basis for postulating such restoring forces, Stokes and Iversen (1962) constructed a symmetric random walk model which was free of restoring tendencies. They demonstrated that if such restoring forces were absent, it would be very unlikely that the historical division of the two-party vote would have remained within its actual historical bounds since the Civil War. The narrowness of the historical bounds constitutes evidence in support of the existence of restoring forces in the electoral system, forces such as long-term party identification.

Further testing of these models is feasible. For example, the relative magnitude of the restoring forces could be estimated by a nonsymmetric random walk. These same questions of deviating elections and restoring forces could be examined at subnational levels of aggregation. Finer tests of the fit of minority party victories can be devised. The number of alternations in office between the parties could be tested against chance expectations by means of the theory of runs. The number of elections prior to the nth victory of a party could be compared to the value which would be predicted on the basis of independent electoral trials.

The work that has already been done, however, is worthy of special emphasis on three grounds. First of all, these historical models involve probabilistic features at both the individual and aggregate levels. At the individual level, the probability of defection from partisanship in one's voting behavior is a critical component. At the aggregate level the probability of a "deviating" election, of keeping the electoral system in equilibrium, and potentially of other electoral features, are crucial concepts. A second feature of these models is that they involve a substantial interplay between individual level mechanisms and aggregate level behavior. In doing so they carry out the often cited but seldom followed dictum that studies of individual behavior (the micro level) are most useful to the extent that they can be related to systemic features and aggregate level activities (the macro level). Finally, these models accomplish that most difficult task of testing their implications against empirical data—in this case aggregate historical election series. Because of the success of these models which have been developed formally, it is our hope that major efforts will be devoted to formalizing other models that show comparable potential, for example, Campbell's surge and decline model (Campbell, *et al.*, 1966, chap. 3).

Another attempt to relate formal models to aggregate behavior is likewise noteworthy. Rabushka and Shepsle (1972) use a model of individual behavior under uncertainty to explain the conflict and strife regularly noted in plural (multi-ethnic) societies. They observe that because of the uncertainties generated by elite policies, it is possible for leaders temporarily to hold together a multi-ethnic coalition. Such coalitions tend to be short-lived, however, and it is in the self-interest of conflicting segments of the elite to employ strategies that reassert the division of society along ethnic or other lines, in the process making ethnicity the sole basis of political activity.

The formal model underlying the Rabushka-Shepsle analysis is similar to that utilized by Shepsle in two chapters of this book (chaps. 12 and 13). Additional comments on the approach are thus reserved for discussion of those papers. What should not be lost here, however, is that the comments about historical voter models apply equally well to the Rabushka and Shepsle study. It is particularly compelling that this study, like the electoral models, has been able to partly bridge the chasm between formal theories and empirical regularities. That each of these models employs probabilistic interpretations of selected aspects of individual and collective behavior may be more than incidental to that accomplishment.

Further work on coalition formation gives less emphasis to process mechanisms and more emphasis to the critical features of coalitions that form—the dynamics of their construction, the probability of their victory, and their likely size. Several examples of probabilistic work in this area are included in this volume.

Dynamic aspects of coalition formation are a basic concern in the collective decision-making literature. A considerable amount of research, both empirical and theoretical, falls under this rubric. For example, portions of Axelrod (1970) as well as many of the papers in the recent collection by Groennings, Kelley, and Leiserson (1970) deal with the process of coalition building. Recently a number of authors have begun to apply probability methods to the study of experimental games (Laing and Morrison, 1971) and coalition dynamics, although the latter work dates back to the power index developed by Shapley and Shubik (1954) and applications of that idea (e.g., Riker, 1959; Schubert, 1964). The probabilistic work includes two recent papers by Coleman (1968, 1970) in which the power of protocoalitions and the strength of inducements for uncommitted members to join them is a function of their probability of winning. These notions are closely related to the ideas used by Brams in his paper in this volume, a relationship which is spelled out in Brams and Riker (1972). Another important piece is Brams's and O'Leary's study of agreement in voting bodies (Brams and O'Leary, 1970, 1971; Mayer, 1971). The measures they propose, which are probabilistic in form, have the considerable virtue of being suitable where there are more than two voting alternatives (e.g., yea, nay, and abstain) and for bodies divided into any number of blocs. Vote-trading or logrolling has also come under initial probabilistic analysis in a paper by Haefele (1970).

Brams and Riker (1972) have developed several probabilistic models of the coalition formation process. They present the sizes of the relative inducements for uncommitted members to join one of two opposed protocoalitions as a function of the probability that each of these protocoalitions will win. The paper by Brams in the book (chap. 5) extends this work with a more complete cost-benefit analysis. He continues to focus on the process of coalition formation rather than just the final outcome. He generalizes the previous work by adding the possibility of defection from a protocoalition, comparing the exact advantages to a coalition of attracting an uncommitted individual as opposed to inducing a member of the opposing protocoalition to defect. One interesting aspect of the results is that the larger protocoalition is favored almost exclusively. This contrasts with Riker's earlier work (1962, chap. 6) using a deterministic model, in which smaller protocoalitions were more often advantaged (although the two analyses are not strictly comparable). To the extent that the two approaches do conflict, it is clear that they are not irreconcilable, for Brams (1972b) and Niemi (1970b) have further developed the probabilistic model, finding some circumstances under which uncommitted members may rationally decide to join the smaller protocoalition rather than the larger one.

The paper by Niemi and Weisberg (chap. 6) examines the likelihood of victory of a coalition assuming a probabilistic formulation of individual voting behavior. They begin by considering the probability of victory for a motion if all members share a common probability of voting for it. Then they detail the case of some members being committed to favor the proposal and others being committed to oppose it with the remaining members having a common probability of voting for it. This is followed by the general case of individuals or coalitions having any fixed probabilities of voting for the proposal. The probability of victory for the motion is shown to be a function of the probability of the individual members supporting the motion, the decision-rule employed, and the size of the decision-making group.

The relevance of group size is of particular interest in this work. Under the Niemi-Weisberg formulation, motions can pass in small groups when the same individual probability and decision-rule would make failure in large groups virtually certain. Conversely bills might fail in small groups which would be certain to pass in larger ones. Thus large groups may more accurately reflect the wishes of their members than would small ones. This dependence on size in the Niemi-Weisberg paper is a direct consequence of the probabilistic formulation. A similar size effect can be seen in other probabilistic work, such as the constitutional design literature, as we noted above, and Coleman (1970). Since it has frequently been pointed out that small groups differ in crucial ways from large ones, it is highly suggestive that formal models incorporating probabilistic elements contain this same feature.

A final topic in coalition formation is the size of the winning coalition. Riker's (1962) size principle predicts that winning coalitions will be of minimal size since they seek to minimize their costs and maximize the returns to their members. However, there are a large number of costs related to coalition building and some lead to larger coalitions. Adrian and Press (1968) list a total of eight distinct decision costs: information costs, responsibility costs, intergame costs, costs of division of payoffs, dissonance costs, inertia costs, time costs, and persuasion costs. Some of these costs are internal to the decision-making body; under appropriate zero- or constant-sum conditions these internal costs do lead to minimal winning coalitions in accord with Riker's size principle. However, other costs are external to the body. As the game is extended beyond the decision-making body, the constant-sum constraint on the game is frequently removed. There is a tendency toward unanimous coalitions in this instance since unanimity can bolster the decision-making body's position relative to other possibly antagonistic actors in the broader system.

Two papers in this volume examine the actual sizes of winning coalitions in decision-making bodies, both employing probabilistic approaches to determine the degree of fit with the size principle. Koehler (chap. 7) presents the first summarization in the literature of the size of winning coalitions in the U.S. House of Representatives. He employs the probabilistic indicator of voting behavior developed by Brams and O'Leary (1970). Koehler finds strong support for the size principle by comparing the size of winning coalitions to the size of the majority party, finding that winning coalition size is almost invariant with changes in party sizes. However the average vote is passed by a coalition of greater than minimal numbers. After demonstrating that a probabilistic model based on information costs is not sufficient to explain the amount of coalition padding which is found, Koehler suggests the novel view that the builder of a coalition in the House seeks to assemble a coalition making up a constitutional majority. Winning coalitions would be minimal if all members were present and voting; they may be larger than minimal if some members are absent, but the coalition builder has guaranteed himself victory in any case. Koehler realizes that he has not explained the number of virtually unanimous votes which do occur in House voting, though he suggests that a bandwagon effect may be responsible for them. The external costs and the unanimity on extreme goals discussed in the previous paragraph may also help explain these deviations from minimal winning coalitions.

Rohde (chap. 8) examines the sizes of winning coalitions in Supreme Court decisions on First Amendment cases. The size principle would predict minimal winning majorities on the Court since the Justices would have no need to compromise on the content of the majority decision in order to attract votes beyond a minimal winning majority. However Rohde argues that coalitions will be of greater than minimal size in cases where a threat to the Court is perceived—for example, a threat from Congress because of legislative attempts to overturn previous decisions on the same subject. This is a situation in which there are external costs and the game extends beyond the Court to other parts of the government. To test his theory, Rohde constructs a probability model of random voting on the Court. He then demonstrates that coalitions of larger than minimal winning size occur significantly more often in threat situations than would be expected on the basis of chance. Also he finds a significant difference in the frequency of minimal winning coalitions in threat and nonthreat situations. Thus, rather than just examining the size of winning coalitions to obtain a flat acceptance or rejection of the size principle, or simply listing alternative costs and principles, Rohde seeks identifiable conditions for minimal winning coalitions and specifies situations under which they would be expected to occur.

The size of winning coalitions is also discussed in the Niemi-Weisberg paper, with the emphasis on the differences between Riker's deterministic model and their probabilistic one. Under their formulation, minimal winning coalitions are more likely in large groups than in small ones. This paper also emphasizes the tension between maximizing the probability of victory for a coalition and keeping that coalition down to minimal winning size. This aspect of the model is further developed in Koehler's paper (chap. 7, footnote 8) where a probability model of coalition padding is sketched. Thus the same fundamental processes may be modelled in either a probabilistic or deterministic framework, but the two may yield quite different results with the probabilistic version containing some very real features (such as the possibility of a "majority" coalition losing) which are not present in the deterministic version.

III. PARADOX OF VOTING

The work discussed to this point has assumed the existence of winning alternatives and winning coalitions without giving attention to the conditions for their existence. A considerable body of literature on collective decision making addresses itself to the existence question.[6] In particular, the work on the paradox of voting treats the possibility that a decision-rule will not lead to a unique winning alternative. An intransitive social ordering may occur even when all individuals have completely transitive preference orderings.

Arrow (1951, 1963) proved that no decision-rule satisfying certain basic desiderata is invulnerable to the paradox. Subsequent work has focussed on the likelihood of the paradox, taking the position that a judgment as to its seriousness for collective decision making must rest on some notion of its relative frequency. However, it is very difficult to tell empirically just when the paradox has occurred, since the most common voting mechanisms do not yield the requisite information. Hence the only "known" instances of the paradox involve unusual voting procedures (Niemi, 1970a) or involve inferences made about particular legislative circumstances (Riker, 1958, 1965).

This difficulty in determining through a totally deterministic approach whether the paradox has actually occurred has led to probabilistic formulations of the problem. One popular means of ascertaining the likelihood of the paradox has been to assume that all possible individual preference orders are equally likely and then to evaluate the corresponding probability of the paradox. Simulation techniques have been used in this manner (Klahr, 1966; Campbell and Tullock, 1965; Pomeranz and Weil, 1970; Tullock and Campbell, 1970), and mathematical solutions have been developed recently (Niemi and Weisberg, 1968; Garman and Kamien, 1968; DeMeyer and Plott, 1970). This work has demonstrated that the probability of the paradox increases with the number of alternatives, while the number of individuals is basically irrelevant so long as it is not too small. Solutions have also been obtained for cases in which all individual preference orders are not equally likely; the probability of the paradox varies from zero to one depending on the initial probability assumptions (Niemi and Weisberg, 1967, 1968; Garman and Kamien, 1968; Gleser, 1969; May, 1971). Particular attention has been given in later work to conditions making the paradox more or less likely, as in Niemi's (1969) demonstration that the paradox is less likely as the individual preference orders are more unidimensional and in Weisberg and Niemi's (1971) classification of initial probability assumptions.

Papers in this volume by Bowen (chap. 9) and Weisberg and Niemi (chap. 10) investigate the paradox in legislative voting. Legislative rules do not permit enough votes to determine whether the paradox has occurred, but the votes which are taken provide some critical information. Both papers enlarge on results by Bowen (1969) to demonstrate that the

---

[6] A comprehensive summary of the literature on the theory of voting is provided by Plott (1971).

paradox can occur in the case of a single amendment to a bill only when the bill is defeated, a fact which considerably reduces the empirical frequency of the paradox in congressional voting. Weisberg and Niemi also show that in the case of two amendments there can be no paradox when either the unamended bill or the bill with only the first amendment added is passed. However, these deterministic conditions give no indication of the likelihood of the paradox when it can occur, so that probability estimation procedures are necessary.

In order to make estimates of the probability of the paradox empirically relevant, the legislative votes which are taken can be used to make inferences about those which are not taken. Using this information to its fullest, Bowen then employs a simulation approach for evaluation of the probability, whereas Weisberg and Niemi employ a mathematical solution. These two papers provide similar results for the case of a single amendment to a bill. However, they differ in their formulation of the problem and their interpretations of the actual voting patterns when there is more than a single amendment. Bowen examines actual votes during recent Senates, obtaining some instances in which the paradox is very probable and obtaining an indication of its relative frequency in Senate voting. Weisberg and Niemi derive some conditions which make the paradox particularly likely and cite the parameters of congressional voting in a recent year to suggest the overall likelihood of the paradox in Congress.

Juxtaposition of these two papers suggests strongly that one cannot rely solely on mechanical applications of the probability algorithms (see chap. 10, footnote 16). The probability procedures do, however, have the considerable virtue of making possible an exhaustive examination of legislative cases. Here might be an instance in which probabilistic and deterministic approaches can usefully complement one another, the first procedure sifting out likely instances of the paradox, which could then be subjected to a more thorough, essentially deterministic, analysis.

The paradox of voting has one further implication which increases its seriousness by an exponential factor. The possibility of the paradox allows legislators to distort their preferences in the voting, voting contrary to their true preferences in order to cause the paradox and thus preclude the loss of their favored alternative (Black, 1958, pp. 44-45). Such strategic voting gets more complicated in that other legislators might then choose not to follow their preferences in the voting as a means of preventing the first set from causing the paradox. Legislators themselves seem to be aware of these possibilities. It is no coincidence that many of the published examples of the paradox in legislative voting are caused by strategic voting (Riker, 1958, 1965).[7]

---

[7] The most complete discussion of strategic voting in the deterministic literature is that by Farquharson (1969).

The probability work on the paradox, including the papers by Bowen and Weisberg and Niemi, has assumed that strategic voting does not occur. However, this is a problem which might be built into probabilistic formulations of the paradox. For example, one might determine the proportion of cases in which strategic voting can lead to the paradox as a function of various initial probability assumptions. This would establish an upper limit on the probability of the paradox if strategic voting were used whenever possible.

The paper by Bjurulf (chap. 11) turns to the likelihood of the paradox in multiparty systems, a question which has not been previously examined. He treats such conditions as the relative sizes of the parties, the degree of conflict among their first choices, and the degree of overlap between two separate dimensions of conflict, showing how these factors increase or decrease the likelihood of the paradox. A major advance in this work is Bjurulf's treatment of parties as cohesive blocs which represents a rare attempt to relax the assumption of independent voting so common to probability work on collective decision making. In addition, his classification and analysis of systems of voting blocs represents an attempt to initiate a formal model of party divisions in multiparty legislatures.

One last question involving the paradox of voting relates to the effects of uncertainty. Zeckhauser (1969) allows lotteries on alternatives to compete as potential social choices, with the probability of obtaining a given outcome under the lottery affecting the individual choices, the social choice, and the occurrence of the paradox under majority rule. Shepsle (1970b) extends this analysis, and at the same time introduces some relevant political considerations.

A paper in this collection by Shepsle (chap. 12) considers the effects on the likelihood of the paradox of a choice between candidates who may take ambiguous stands on issues. He begins his consideration of the effects of uncertainty with the case of a risky challenger facing a certain incumbent, and later treats the case when both candidates are risky choices. Uncertainty is represented by viewing the candidate as a lottery with probabilities of taking different stands on an issue. He also examines the effect of constraining a candidate to a subset of the possible positions on an issue, the constraint being imposed when a candidate is restricted by the dominant image of his party. The use of probability calculations is, of course, a classical way of dealing with uncertainty. By making use of this approach, Shepsle is able to introduce some important aspects of uncertainty into the analysis of majority decision making. For additional comments on Shepsle's approach, see the section below on spatial modelling.

IV. SPATIAL MODELLING OF COMPETITION

The paradox of voting literature treats the quirk that a decision-rule may not yield a unique winning alternative. The literature on the spatial modelling of candidate and voter behavior treats the candidate's quest for a dominant strategy which can guarantee him victory. These two topics sound quite different and there are indeed some differences in the two strains of the literature, e.g., work on the paradox emphasizes discrete probability distributions while the spatial modelling literature generally uses continuous distributions. Actually, however, the two topics are equivalent problems.

Following the initial spatial modelling work by Hotelling (1929) and Smithies (1941), Downs (1957) provided the first extensive application in the arena of political competition. He showed that if all voters made their voting decisions between a pair of candidates on the basis of a single issue dimension, the candidates should converge in their position on that dimension if they are to maximize their votes. Indeed Black (1958) demonstrates that the optimal position on the dimension would correspond to the preference of the median voter. Garvey (1966) indicated that the dominance of the median position is dependent on the assumption of no abstentions and that different causes of abstention have different effects in the model.

The assumption of a unidimensional issue space was first relaxed in the work of Black and Newing (1951) and Plott (1967a) with the pessimistic conclusion that dominant points would only exist by accident. However, Davis and Hinich's (1966) introduction of the assumption of a continuum of people allowed the powerful tools of probability theory to be employed in the analysis. Using specific assumptions as to the shape of the individual loss functions, they were able to demonstrate conditions under which the multidimensional mean is the dominant candidate strategy. Subsequent work has varied the assumptions as to the individual loss functions (Davis and Hinich, 1967), examined the effects of abstention in the multidimensional case (Hinich and Ordeshook, 1969), and explored the implications for the responsible party doctrine (Ordeshook, 1970). This work has been summarized in an excellent review article by Davis, Hinich, and Ordeshook (1970). That article presents the conditions under which the mean is known to be dominant and indicates areas in which no general solution is yet available. Topics investigated in the spatial modelling area since the Davis, Hinich, and Ordeshook review article include the Pareto optimal qualities of electoral competition (Ordeshook, 1971) and the effects of the candidate's chances for victory (chaps. 13-16 in this volume; Aranson, 1972).

A dramatic new approach to the spatial modelling problem has been employed in a paper by Hinich, Ledyard, and Ordeshook (1971). They utilize work that has been done in n-person noncooperative game theory. A probabilistic interpretation of individual behavior is adopted. The probability of an individual's voting for a candidate is presumed to be related to his preferences for the issue positions of the candidate and his opponent. The assumptions used here are concave individual utility functions representing preference relations, a probability function based on the candidate's issue positions, a concave function relating the probability of voting for a candidate and the utility for his position, and a convex function relating the probability of voting for his opponent and the utility for his position. The authors demonstrate that an optimal position exists for each candidate under these assumptions. Furthermore, convergence of the candidates will occur if the functions relating probability and utility are identical for the two candidates. This formulation eliminated the assumptions of identical saliency for issues by all voters and radial symmetry of individual preferences, which have been basic to the previous work by Davis, Hinich, and Ordeshook. Hinich, Ledyard, and Ordeshook indicate that it may be necessary to reintroduce some of the previous assumptions in order to locate the dominant candidate strategies, but the existence problem can be solved under far weaker assumptions than were previously employed. Their adoption of a probabilistic formulation of individual choice behavior seems to promise considerable progress in the development of the spatial modelling approach.

A major critique of the spatial modelling work was provided by Stokes (1963), who spelled out several of its basic assumptions which do not match the empirical world very well. Some of the points raised by Stokes (especially unidimensionality) have been taken into account as the spatial modelling literature has developed, and we would concur that it is "extraordinarily premature" to judge whether spatial modelling of competition is "an unsatisfactory oversimplification of real world choice" (Aranson and Ordeshook, chap. 14, p. 298). Indeed the work in this volume provides a strong defense of this approach by demonstrating the ability of spatial modelling to handle real world complications which had previously been ignored in that literature.

Four of the papers in this collection are related to the spatial modelling area. A paper by Shepsle (chap. 13) for the first time introduces the effects of uncertainty into the spatial modelling of party competition. He examines the effects of ambiguity of a candidate's position on the existence of a dominant candidate strategy, beginning with the case of a risky challenger against an incumbent whose position is perceived with certainty and then generalizing to the case of two risky opponents. Different shapes for voter preference functions for risk are examined in terms of their implications for candidate strategy. Shepsle particularly emphasizes the question of how risky a strategy (how ambiguous a set of policy positions) a candidate should adopt in his quest for victory.

Shepsle's analysis is particularly interesting not only because he extends formal spatial analysis to include lotteries over alternatives, but also because he gives a meaningful interpretation to the existence of lotteries in a political context. His analysis yields a theoretical basis for understanding the ambiguity or fuzziness of issue positions often observed in election campaigns. Downs's (1957, pp. 135-37) original analysis suggested that party ideologies would be intentionally ambiguous, but that notion was not made an integral part of spatial theory. Shepsle has now provided a rigorous theoretical underpinning for this frequently observed phenomenon.

The papers by Aranson and Ordeshook (chap. 14) and Coleman (chap. 15) treat a new kind of problem for the spatial modelling literature—the need for a candidate to select a strategy which secures for him both the nomination of his party and victory in the general election.[8] Aranson and Ordeshook demonstrate the importance of the attitudes of the activists who control the nomination process in that they might demand a candidate who supports their ideological views, might seek a candidate with the maximum chance of victory in the final election regardless of his ideological views, or might adopt a mix of these two strategies. The existence of dominant strategies is discussed for these cases with various assumptions about the likely behavior of opposing candidates for the nomination and the final election.

Coleman incorporates Aranson and Ordeshook's cases (of activists' motives) into a single framework. He is able to do so by making assumptions which differ somewhat from those of Aranson and Ordeshook. For example, he assumes that the dimension on which the parties compete has the characteristics of a Guttman scale, and that voters assume that each party's candidates do not respond to changes in the positions of the other party's candidates. From this basis Coleman shows how a candidate might derive an optimal strategy for the entire election sequence. Coleman's approach also introduces a parameter representing each elector's probability that his party's candidate will be elected. In this respect his approach diverges from Aranson and Ordeshook's and much of the spatial modelling literature. It is significant, however, in light of the use of individual-level probability assumptions by Shepsle (chap. 13) and Hinich, Ledyard, and Ordeshook (1971). While in the present paper Coleman assumes that all individuals have the same probability,

---

[8] Actually this problem was introduced by Davis and Hinich (1967), but their treatment of it was quite limited.

this is not a necessary feature. In fact, the probability could be interpreted as a subjective measure which varied for individuals or classes of individuals. Variations in the distribution of parameter values might then yield significant advances in the subsequent development of this work.

It seems to us to be useful to have two different conceptualizations of the same problem, if for no other reason than that it suggests some consensus on what types of problems are of research interest. At the moment each approach has some "advantages"—Aranson and Ordeshook's seems to be a broader approach calling for less restrictive assumptions; but Coleman's seems to allow derivations of results when Aranson and Ordeshook's is indeterminate. Further development of both of these models is anticipated. One common point that should be noted is that both papers take note of an important political reality that has been treated only superficially in the spatial literature heretofore—namely, that candidates are not entirely free to move about the issue space. This same point is also a part of Shepsle's analysis, in that he points out that an incumbent in particular is constrained by prior positions taken by himself and his party.

This notion of constraints on parties' movements about the issue space is very similar to the notion underlying Davis and Hinich's contribution (chap. 16). They consider the effects on candidate strategy of events which preclude the adoption of certain policy alternatives. They examine the effects of such constraints on the preference distribution in the event of voters shifting their preference positions according to the minimal change which legitimizes their ideal preferences. Additional cases which may merit attention at a later date include candidate reaction to events precluding the adoption of certain policy alternatives when individual preferences remain fixed regardless of the impossibility of their attainment; and the instance of sharp (nonminimal) reversals of individual policy positions such as the vehement anti-Communist positions often taken by Communist sympathizers who convert. But the main point, as Davis and Hinich conclude, is that spatial analysis is flexible enough to incorporate such features of political reality as constraints on preference distributions.

Part 1

CONSTITUTIONAL DESIGN

1. Decision-Rules and Collective Values in Constitutional Choice

RICHARD B. CURTIS

Given a political body of n members who shall consider and vote upon a succession of proposals not known a priori, there is the constitutional problem of fixing ab initio the decision-rule by which the minimum number of yes votes (k) required for the adoption of any proposal is specified. In principle there are n different decision-rules which may be adopted ($k = 1, 2, 3, \ldots, n$). The basic question is which of these should be chosen and by what criterion.

In his recent paper Douglas W. Rae (1969) discussed a number of alternative criteria which have been suggested and proposes a normative criterion of his own. Only Rae's will be discussed here, since the criteria proposed here are modifications of his.

Basic to Rae's criterion is the individual voter, whom he names generically "Ego." Not only does Rae assume Ego to be independent of all other voters in that his vote on any particular issue is not conditioned on the vote of any of his colleagues, but Rae chooses to define the criterion which the decision-rule must obey on the basis of how the decision-rule will affect Ego, the generalized individual. He is able to maintain this criterion because of yet another assumption, namely that each voter, Ego included, is characterized by the same probability[1] of voting yes on any

---

[1] Rae, in fact, chooses this probability to be one-half. Taylor (1969) generalized the situation to an arbitrary but still common probability p.

given proposal. The result of this assumption is that all voters are essentially equivalent and that the decision-rule which optimizes the situation for Ego, an arbitrary individual, will simultaneously optimize the situation for everyone else.

As soon as we consider the members of the committee not to be identical, it is not possible to select a representative individual. In the place of a criterion, which is defined by the effect of the decision-rule on an individual, we must use a criterion which speaks in terms of the effect on the average voter. We therefore move subtly from a value assumption tied to the individual to a value assumption tied to the group. It is not the impact upon the individual which becomes determinative but the impact on the collection of individuals as measured by the average.

There does not seem to be any escape from this dilemma. As attractive as a criterion defined in terms of the individual might be, when we drop the assumption that the members of the committee behave identically, we must talk in terms of the entire committee. The situation becomes even less individual-oriented when we drop the assumption of independence of the voters. When a voter's decision on any particular proposal is conditioned upon the decisions made by others, a fabric of behavior is woven in which the thread representing a single voter cannot be isolated from the rest of the committee without unravelling the entire cloth. In this case we must again alter our criterion of choice of decision-rule from the effect on the average member to the effect upon the group as a whole. The criterion must now be expressed in terms of "the greatest good for the greatest number," a quite different value than Rae espouses.

To illustrate these comments more fully we shall prove Rae's conjectures, using his assumptions, and then generalize his model by dropping one or more assumptions. In so doing we shall prove again what Taylor has already done, but in a notation which will prove generalizable.

I. THE CRITERION OF CHOICE

For any individual there are six different outcomes to any vote involving a binary issue (yes or no).

A. He votes no and yet the motion passes.
B. He votes yes and yet the motion fails.
C. He votes yes and the motion passes.
D. He votes no and the motion fails.
E. He refrains from voting and the motion passes.
F. He refrains from voting and the motion fails.

For the purposes of this paper we shall define the outcome A and B to be "disappointing" without implying any more by that word than that outcome A or outcome B occurred. One could define outcomes C and D as being "happy" and E and F as being "indifferent," but we shall not need these definitions here. Initially we shall assume that A and B are equally disappointing, but this assumption will be relaxed in section 3.

The criterion which we adopt for determining the decision-rule will involve minimizing the frequency of outcomes A and B. Initially, following Rae, we will apply this to the individual, then as we drop assumptions to the average member, and finally to the group as a whole when we move to the most general situation.

II. THE INDEPENDENT VOTER MODEL

A. All Voters Identical

If we assume (as Rae does) that all voters are both independent and identical it is possible to define for each voter the same probability p that that voter will vote yes on any motion. Let us (with Rae) select one of these voters and call him Ego. If p is the probability of Ego's voting yes, then $q = 1 - p$ is the probability of Ego's voting no.

Now let us define $P_n(l)$ as the probability of there being exactly l yes votes on an arbitrary motion in a committee of size n. If we do not permit abstentions (outlawing outcomes E or F as Rae does), then

$$P_n(l) = \frac{n!}{l!\,(n-l)!}\,p^l q^{n-l}. \tag{1}$$

If k is the decision-rule, then the probability of passage of a motion is

$$P_{\text{pass}} = \sum_{l=k}^{n} P_n(l),$$

and the probability of failure of any motion is

$$P_{\text{fail}} = \sum_{l=0}^{k-1} P_n(l).$$

The conditional probability that the motion will pass, if Ego votes no, is

$$P_A = \sum_{l=k}^{n-1} P_{n-1}(l),$$

and the conditional probability that the motion will fail, if Ego votes yes, is

$$P_B = \sum_{l=0}^{k-2} P_{n-1}(l).$$

These results follow immediately by remembering that there must be at least k yes votes for the motion to pass, and conversely that there must be less than k votes for the motion to fail.

The probability that Ego will be disappointed is

$$P_k = qP_A + pP_B. \tag{2}$$

Rae's criterion for the decision-rule can be stated that P_k be a minimum, i.e., that the optimum decision-rule is that value of k which makes the possibility that Ego will be disappointed a minimum.

In Appendix I, it is shown that (2) can be rewritten after some algebraic manipulations as

$$P_k = \sum_{l=0}^{k-1} \frac{l}{n} P_n(l) + \sum_{l=k}^{n} \frac{n-l}{n} P_n(l). \tag{3}$$

At this point we prove an important lemma.

LEMMA: If $g(l)$ is any function of l with the property that

$$g(l) > 0 \quad \text{for } l = 0, 1, 2, \ldots, n \quad \text{and if } G_k \text{ is}$$

defined by

$$G_k = \sum_{l=0}^{k-1} lg(l) + \sum_{l=k}^{n} (n-l)g(l)$$

then G_k is minimum for $k = (n/2) + 1$ for n even and $k = (n+1)/2$ for n odd.

PROOF:

$$G_k = \sum_{l=0}^{k-1} lg(l) + \sum_{l=k}^{n} (n-l)g(l)$$

$$G_{k+1} = \sum_{l=0}^{k} lg(l) + \sum_{l=k+1}^{n} (n-l)g(l)$$

Thus $G_{k+1} - G_k = kg(k) - (n-k)g(k) = (2k-n)g(k)$. Since $g(k) > 0$, then

$$
\begin{aligned}
G_{k+1} - G_k &< 0 & \text{for } 2k < n \\
&= 0 & \text{for } 2k = n \\
&> 0 & \text{for } 2k > n.
\end{aligned}
$$

Thus if n is even and $n = 2m$:

$$G_1 > G_2 > \cdots > G_m = G_{m+1} < G_{m+2} < \cdots < G_{n-1} < G_n,$$

and if n is odd and $n = 2m + 1$:

$$G_1 > G_2 > \cdots > G_m > G_{m+1} < G_{m+2} < \cdots < G_{n-1} < G_n.$$

Therefore G_k is minimum for $k = m + 1 = (n/2) + 1$, if n is even, and for $k = m + 1 = (n + 1)/2$, if n is odd.

Q.E.D.

Going back to (1) we see that $(1/n)P_n(l)$ is positive for all l and thus P_k satisfies the conditions of the lemma. Therefore, that decision-rule which disappoints Ego least is majority rule.

B. Voters Not Identical

To this point we have merely duplicated Taylor's work and proven what Rae conjectured was true. Let us now generalize by dropping the requirement that all the voters be identical. To be specific let us suppose that the committee comprises n_L "liberals" and n_C "conservatives" where $n_L + n_C = n$. If the liberals have a probability p_L of voting yes ($q_L = 1 - p_L$) and the conservatives have the probability p_C of voting yes ($q_C = 1 - p_C$), then the probability of exactly l yes votes is

$$P(l \mid n_L, n_C) = \sum_j \frac{n_L!}{j!\,(n_L - j)!} \frac{n_C!}{(l - j)!\,(n_C - l + j)!} p_L^j q_L^{n_L - j} p_C^{l-j} q_C^{n_C - l + j}, \tag{4}$$

where the limits on the summation are set by the condition that there be no negative factorials.

There are now two different representative members of the committee, Ego_L and Ego_C each with their own probabilities for disappointment. The conditional probability of passage, if Ego_L votes no, is

$$P_{A_L} = \sum_{l=k}^{n-1} P(l \mid n_L - 1, n_C),$$

while the conditional probability of failure of the motion, if Ego_L votes yes is

$$P_{B_L} = \sum_{l=0}^{k-2} P(l \mid n_L - 1, n_C).$$

The corresponding probabilities for Ego_C are

$$P_{A_C} = \sum_{l=k}^{n-1} P(l \mid n_L, n_C - 1) \quad \text{and} \quad P_{B_C} = \sum_{l=0}^{k-2} P(l \mid n_L, n_C - 1).$$

Thus the probability of Ego_L's being disappointed is

$$P_{L_k} = q_L P_{A_L} + p_L P_{B_L},$$

while that for Ego_C is $P_{C_k} = q_C P_{A_C} + p_C P_{B_C}$.

Although Ego_L is indeed representative of all the liberals and Ego_C is representative of all the conservatives, neither is representative of the entire committee. The most obvious candidate for that role is the average member of the committee whose probability of disappointment is the weighted average of the probabilities for Ego_L and Ego_C:

$$P_k = \frac{1}{n}(n_L P_{L_k} + n_C P_{C_k}). \tag{5}$$

If we assume that this is the appropriate description of the representative member, then in Appendix B it is shown after some tedious algebra that

$$P_k = \sum_{l=0}^{k-1} \frac{l}{n} P(l \mid n_L, n_C) + \sum_{l=k}^{n} \frac{(n-l)}{n} P(l \mid n_L, n_C). \tag{6}$$

Since P_k satisfies the lemma, we find that the decision-rule which minimizes the probability of disappointment for the *average* member is majority rule.

Finally let us consider the generalized situation where the committee comprises m groups having $n_1, n_2, \ldots, n_m$ members respectively where $\sum_{i=1}^{m} n_i = n$. Let an arbitrary member of the ith group have the probability p_i of voting yes on a proposition ($q_i = 1 - p_i$). The probability of exactly l yes votes is

$$P(l \mid n_1, n_2, \ldots, n_m) = \sum_{j_1, j_2, \ldots, j_m} \frac{n_1!}{j_1!(n_1 - j_1)!} \cdots \frac{n_m!}{j_m!(n_m - j_m)!}$$
$$\times p_1^{j_1} q_1^{n_1 - j_1} \cdots p_m^{j_m} q_m^{n_m - j_m} \tag{7}$$

where the summation goes over all $j_1, j_2, \ldots, j_m$ subject to the conditions that $j_1 + j_2 + \cdots + j_m = l$ and that there be no negative factorials.

The conditional probability of passage of a motion when Ego_i (an arbitrary member of the ith group) votes no is

$$P_{A_i} = \sum_{l=k}^{n-1} P(l \mid n_1, n_2, \ldots, n_{i-1}, n_i - 1, n_{i+1}, \ldots, n_m)$$

and the conditional probability of failure of the motion when Ego votes yes is

$$P_{B_i} = \sum_{l=0}^{k-2} P(l \mid n_1, n_2, \ldots, n_{i-1}, n_i - 1, n_{i+1}, \ldots, n_m).$$

The probability that Ego_i will be disappointed is $P_{i_k} = q_i P_{A_i} + p_i P_{B_i}$

and the average probability of disappointment for the entire committee is

$$P_k = \frac{1}{n} \sum_{i=1}^{m} n_i P_{i_k}.$$

By a manipulation similar to (but much more complicated than) the liberal-conservative case, this expression can be written as

$$P_k = \sum_{l=0}^{k-1} \frac{l}{n} P(l \mid n_1, n_2, \ldots, n_m) + \sum_{l=k}^{n} \frac{(n-l)}{n} P(l \mid n_1, n_2, \ldots, n_m). \quad (8)$$

Again using the lemma, we have that the decision-rule which minimizes the probability of disappointment for the average member of the committee is majority rule. Since m, the number of subgroups was arbitrary, we include in this proof the case where every member of the committee is in a subgroup by himself, i.e., where the probability of voting yes differs for every member of the committee ($m = n$). Thus, regardless of the voting pattern of the individual members of the committee as long as they vote on every motion and vote independently of each other, the simple majority rule provides that *on the average* each member will be on the losing side of a motion less often than under any other decision-rule.

III. THE GENERAL MODEL

A. Equal Weighting of Disappointments

In all the above we have assumed that the members of the committee vote independently and that the disappointing outcomes of the vote are equally weighted. In this section we shall not make any assumptions about how individuals vote, or indeed about whether they refrain from voting. We require only that there exist a probability $P_n(l)$ that there be exactly l yes votes from among the committee of size n. In the sense of relative frequencies such a probability surely exists and except in pathological situations it is a positive and non-zero number for all $l = 0, 1, 2, \ldots, n$. If k is the decision-rule, let $N_k(l)$ be the number of disappointed voters when there are exactly l yes votes:

$$N_k(l) = l, \qquad \text{if the motion fails, i.e., } 0 \leq l \leq k - 1$$
$$= n - l, \quad \text{if the motion passes, i.e., } k \leq l \leq n.$$

The expectation of the number of disappointed voters is

$$\eta_k = \sum_{l=0}^{n} N_k(l) P_n(l)$$
$$= \sum_{l=0}^{k-1} l P_n(l) + \sum_{l=k}^{n} (n-l) P_n(l).$$

Since $P_n(l) > 0$ for all l, the η_k satisfies the lemma and is minimum for k corresponding to majority rule. In other words in this general situation, where we have made no assumptions about the behavior of the individual voters, majority rule minimizes the expected number of disappointed voters. The determination of the decision-rule is a result of requiring the least disappointment to the group as a whole, or conversely the greatest happiness to the committee taken together. This is a very different criterion than the one used by Rae, but it is the only applicable one under these unconstrained conditions.

B. Unequal Weighting of Disappointments

If we now relax the condition that the disappointments be equally weighted, we will have exploited to the fullest this class of models. Suppose that outcomes of type A (where the motion passes when Ego votes no) are given weight α $(0 \leq \alpha \leq 1)$ and that outcomes of type B (where the motion fails when Ego votes yes) are given the complementary weight $1 - \alpha$. The weighted number of disappointed voters when there are exactly l yes votes is

$$N'_k(l) = l(1 - \alpha) \quad \text{for } 0 \leq l \leq k - 1$$
$$= (n - l)\alpha \quad \text{for } k \leq l \leq n.$$

The expected number of disappointed voters with weighting is

$$\eta'_k = \sum_{l=0}^{n} N'_k(l)P_n(l)$$
$$= \sum_{l=0}^{k-1} l(1 - \alpha)P_n(l) + \sum_{l=k}^{n} (n - l)\alpha P_n(l).$$

Increasing the value of k to $k + 1$:

$$\eta'_{k+1} = \sum_{l=0}^{k} l(1 - \alpha)P_n(l) + \sum_{l=k+1}^{n} (n - l)\alpha P_n(l).$$

Subtracting:

$$\eta'_{k+1} - \eta'_k = k(1 - \alpha)P_n(k) - (n - k)\alpha P_n(k)$$
$$= (k - n\alpha)P_n(k)$$
$$\gtreqless 0 \quad \text{as } k \gtreqless n\alpha, \quad \text{if } P_n(k) > 0.$$

Thus, the decision-rule which minimizes the number of disappointed voters is $k = n\alpha$.

Majority rule follows from $\alpha = 1/2$. In that case $1 - \alpha = 1/2$ and the two disappointments are equally weighted. The two-thirds rule follows when $\alpha = 2/3$ and $1 - \alpha = 1/3$. In this case we weight passage of the motion when Ego votes no twice as heavily as failure of the motion when Ego votes yes, i.e., the outcome A is judged twice as disappointing as outcome B.

IV. CONCLUSIONS

We have then completed Rae's program, but at a price. To achieve complete generality it has been necessary to modify his criterion of choice for decision-rules from minimizing the disappointment of the individual voter to minimizing the disappointment of the group as a whole. Because of the generality of the treatment in section IIIB, all the previous work is subsumed in that result. The final criterion used reduces to Rae's as we reintroduce his limiting assumptions. What remains unclear, however, is whether another approach can restore the primacy of the individual when we drop the assumptions of independence and equivalent behavior of the members of the committee.

APPENDIX I

From expression (2), the definitions of P_A and P_B, and expression (1) we obtain

$$
\begin{aligned}
P_k &= qP_A + pP_B \\
&= q\sum_{l=k}^{n-1} P_{n-1}(l) + p\sum_{l=0}^{k-2} P_{n-1}(l) \\
&= q\sum_{l=k}^{n-1} \frac{(n-1)!}{l!\,(n-1-l)!} p^l q^{n-1-l} + p\sum_{l=0}^{k-2} \frac{(n-1)!}{l!\,(n-1-l)!} p^l q^{n-1-l} \\
&= \sum_{l=0}^{k-2} \frac{(n-1)!}{l!\,(n-1-l)!} p^{l+1} q^{n-l-1} + \sum_{l=k}^{n-1} \frac{(n-1)!}{l!\,(n-1-l)!} p^l q^{n-l} \\
&= \sum_{l=1}^{k-1} \frac{(n-1)!}{(l-1)!\,(n-l)!} p^l q^{n-l} + \sum_{l=k}^{n-1} \frac{(n-1)!}{l!\,(n-1-l)!} p^l q^{n-l} \\
&= \sum_{l=1}^{k-1} \frac{l}{n} \cdot \frac{n!}{l!\,(n-l)!} p^l q^{n-l} + \sum_{l=k}^{n-1} \frac{n-l}{n} \cdot \frac{n!}{l!\,(n-l)!} p^l q^{n-l} \\
&= \sum_{l=1}^{k-1} \frac{l}{n} P_n(l) + \sum_{l=k}^{n-1} \frac{(n-l)}{n} P_n(l) \quad \text{using (1)} \\
&= \sum_{l=0}^{k-1} \frac{l}{n} P_n(l) + \sum_{l=k}^{n} \frac{(n-l)}{n} P_n(l)
\end{aligned}
$$

since the two terms added both vanish.

This last expression is expression (3).

APPENDIX II

From expression (5) and the definitions of P_{L_k} and P_{C_k} we obtain

$$P_k = \frac{1}{n}[n_L P_{L_k} + n_C P_{C_k}]$$

$$= \frac{1}{n}[n_L(q_L P_{A_L} + p_L P_{B_L}) + n_C(q_C P_{A_C} + p_C P_{B_C})]$$

$$= \frac{1}{n}[(n_L q_L P_{A_L} + n_C q_C P_{A_C}) + (n_L p_L P_{B_L} + n_C p_C P_{B_C})]$$

Now using the definitions of P_{A_L}, P_{B_L}, P_{A_C}, P_{B_C} and the expression (4) we obtain:

$$(n_L q_L P_{A_L} + n_C q_C P_{A_C})$$

$$= \sum_{l=k}^{n-1} [n_L q_L P(l \mid n_L - 1, n_C) + n_C q_C P(l \mid n_L, n_C - 1)]$$

$$= \sum_{l=k}^{n-1} \sum_j \left[\frac{n_L!}{j!(n_L - 1 - j)!} \frac{n_C!}{(l-j)!(n_C - l + j)!} p_L^j q_L^{n_L-j} p_C^{l-j} q_C^{n_C-l+j} \right.$$

$$\left. + \frac{n_L!}{j!(n_L - j)!} \frac{n_C!}{(l-j)!(n_C - 1 - l + j)!} p_L^j q_L^{n_L-j} p_C^{l-j} q_C^{n_C-l+j} \right]$$

$$= \sum_{l=k}^{n-1} \sum_j \frac{n_L!}{j!(n_L - 1 - j)!} \frac{n_C!}{(l-j)!(n_C - 1 - l + j)!}$$

$$\times \left[\frac{1}{n_L - j} + \frac{1}{n_C - l + j} \right] p_L^j q_L^{n_L-j} p_C^{l-j} q_C^{n_C-l+j}$$

$$= \sum_{l=k}^{n-1} (n - l) \sum_j \frac{n_L!}{j!(n_L - j)!} \frac{n_C!}{(l-j)!(n - l + j)!} p_L^j q_L^{n_L-j} p_C^{l-j} q_C^{n_C-l+j}$$

$$= \sum_{l=k}^{n-1} (n - l) P(l \mid n_L, n_C)$$

$$= \sum_{l=k}^{n} (n - l) P(l \mid n_L, n_C) \quad \text{since the } l = n \text{ term vanishes.}$$

Also

$$(n_L p_L P_{B_L} + n_C p_C P_{B_C})$$

$$= \sum_{l=0}^{k-2} [n_L p_L P(l \mid n_L - 1, n_C) + n_C p_C P(l \mid n_L, n_C - 1)]$$

$$= \sum_{l=0}^{k-2} \sum_{j} \left[\frac{n_L!}{j!\,(n_L - 1 - j)!} \frac{n_C!}{(l - j)!\,(n_C - l + j)!} \right.$$
$$\times p_L^{j+1} q_L^{n_L - 1 - j} p_C^{l-j} q_C^{n_C - l + j}$$
$$\left. + \frac{n_L!}{j!\,(n_L - j)!} \frac{n_C!}{(l - j)!\,(n_C - 1 - l + j)!} p_L^{j} q_L^{n_L - j} p_C^{l - j + 1} q_C^{n_C - 1 - l + j} \right]$$

$$= \sum_{l=0}^{k-2} \sum_{j} \left[\frac{n_L!}{(j-1)!\,(n_L - j)!} \frac{n_C!}{(l - j + 1)!\,(n_C - 1 - l + j)!} \right.$$
$$\times p_L^{j} q_L^{n_L - j} p_C^{l - j + 1} q_C^{n_C - 1 - l + j}$$
$$\left. + \frac{n_L!}{j!\,(n_L - j)!} \frac{n_C!}{(l - j)!\,(n_C - 1 - l + j)!} p_L^{j} q_L^{n_L - j} p_C^{l - j + 1} q_C^{n_C - 1 - l + j} \right]$$

$$= \sum_{l=0}^{k-2} \sum_{j} \frac{n_L!}{(j-1)!\,(n_L - j)!} \frac{n_C!}{(l - j)!\,(n_C - 1 - l + j)!}$$
$$\times \left[\frac{1}{l - j + 1} + \frac{1}{j} \right] p_L^{j} q_L^{n_L - j} p_C^{l - j + 1} q_C^{n_C - 1 - l + j}$$

$$= \sum_{l=0}^{k-2} (l + 1) \sum_{j} \frac{n_L!}{j!\,(n_L - j)!} \frac{n_C!}{(l - j + 1)!\,(n_C - 1 - l + j)!}$$
$$\times p_L^{j} q_L^{n_L - j} p_C^{l - j + 1} q_C^{n_C - 1 - l + j}$$

$$= \sum_{l=0}^{k-2} (l + 1) P(l + 1 \mid n_L, n_C) \quad \text{using (4)}$$

$$= \sum_{l=1}^{k-1} l P(l \mid n_L, n_C)$$

$$= \sum_{l=0}^{k-1} l P(l \mid n_L, n_C) \quad \text{since the } l = 0 \text{ term vanishes.}$$

Thus

$$P_k = \sum_{l=0}^{k-1} \frac{l}{n} P(l \mid n_L, n_C) + \sum_{l=k}^{n} \frac{(n - l)}{n} P(l \mid n_L, n_C)$$

which is expression (6).

2. Political Individualism, Positional Preferences, and Optimal Decision-Rules

I. INTRODUCTION

How many individuals k out of a total of n should be required to support a proposal before it is adopted as collective policy? I would like to suggest that some valuable insight into the formal mechanics of collective decision making (in a committee, legislature, etc.) can be gained by concentrating our attention on the setting of "optimal" decision-rules. The individual legislator is assumed to be of primary importance. Whether or not a rule is "optimal" will therefore be based solely on each legislator's desire to minimize the frequency with which proposals he favors are rejected and proposals which he opposes pass anyway. Following the initial work on this subject done by Douglas Rae (1969), this optimality criterion will be termed "political individualism." It is assumed that each legislator faces a constitutional choice on a collective decision-rule while having only limited knowledge of the types of proposals to be considered and the way in which he and his colleagues will evaluate them. Given this high degree of future uncertainty, we shall assume that the most our legislator can reasonably estimate about himself and his colleagues is the overall

This research was partially supported by the Air Force Office of Scientific Research Grant No. AF-AFOSR-67-1314.

frequency or probability with which each can be expected to vote for or against future proposals. We shall also make the admittedly highly unrealistic assumption that the action each legislator takes on any given proposal is completely independent of the action taken by any other. This eliminates the consideration of factional disputes, logrolling, and the entire gamut of political and historical dynamics which are basic to the evolution of any real legislative structure. But then we shall not attempt to analyze such structures. By eliminating "interactive" political dynamics entirely, we hope to get a much narrower yet somwhat clearer view of the relationship between an individual legislative will and "optimal" collective policy. We should keep in mind that "optimal" is defined from the point of view of each legislator as that which allows him to "have his way" as frequently as possible.

It will be shown that the choice of an optimal decision-rule can be considered a trade off between an individual's desire to cast the pivotal vote as often as possible (which depends only on his estimation of the "other" legislators' behavior) and factors based solely on his own values and expected future behavior. The possibility of being the deciding voter is essential to a nonextreme result. On the basis of a slightly extended definition of political individualism, a nonvoting constitutor will prefer individual initiative, unanimity, or be indifferent between all possible rules.

I then consider the case of an individual who has a vote in the constituting body in more detail. Having ascertained $(n - 1)$ quantities characterizing the frequency with which he believes his legislative colleagues will vote affirmatively on future proposals, a similar prognostication about his own future behavior, and a value judgment (α) about the relative importance of minimizing the frequency with which proposals he favors are rejected vis-à-vis the frequency with which proposals he opposes pass anyway, it will be shown that each legislator's optimal decision-rule is implicitly determined by inequality (29). Any given legislator in general determines $n + 1$ different quantities which may or may not coincide with the corresponding evaluations made by any or all of his colleagues. The optimal decision-rule may turn out to be anywhere from one to n for each legislator depending on the values of the $n + 1$ quantities used in its determination. The rule is in theory sensitive to each of these $n + 1$ quantities. If any one of them is changed and the other n held constant, the choice of an optimal decision-rule may be affected. This situation should be contrasted with Rae's and Taylor's work (Rae, 1969; Taylor, 1969) in which the legislators are assumed identical and simple majority rule is therefore preferred by them all.

Although it is certainly possible to compute any individual's optimal decision-rule with the help of inequality (29), the most general case does not admit an explicit analytical result to which an intuitively meaningful interpretation can readily be attached. It is for this reason that I have chosen to deal at length with the special case in which all the "other" legislators are characterized by the same probability p_L of voting for future proposals. Our generic legislator characterizes himself by a comparable probability p which may or may not equal p_L. Under these conditions, the optimal decision-rule is specified by relation (32). I believe this result aptly demonstrates the significant theoretical properties of the most general case, and therefore deserves close attention. If we simplify this result further and assume $p = p_L$, the optimal decision will be given by the relation

$$(1 - \alpha)n < k < (1 - \alpha)n + 1.$$

This result reduces to a preference for simple majority rule when $\alpha = 1/2$ which in turn makes the connection with the work done by Rae (1969) and Taylor (1969).

Having determined which decision-rule is optimal for each legislator, there remains the important question of how these individual preferences will be synthesized to produce a constitutional choice. In Rae's case, the legislators were all assumed identical and so the problem did not arise. Curtis (chap. 1 in this volume) deals with this problem by assuming that the decision-rule chosen should be that preferred by the average voter. In this way he moves "from a value assumption tied to the individual to a value assumption tied to the group" (Curtis, p. 24). While this is certainly a valid approach, I think it more likely that a constituting body would settle the issue by means of a vote. While this approach maintains the primacy of the individual, it unfortunately leads us into the interminable sequence of asking how decisions are to be made about how decisions are to be made about how decisions are to be made . . . etc. I think it is clear that some sort of consensual agreement must be reached in order to extricate ourselves from this dilemma. It will be shown that, under quite reasonable assumptions about the basis of this consensus,[1] the decision-rule chosen will be that which receives a simple majority of the constituting legislators' votes when put against any other rule[2]—the so-called Condorcet criterion (see Black, p. 57). This result depends on the fact that each legislator can determine his most preferred decision-rule, his second choice, third choice, and indeed an entire preference schedule on the basis of political individualism. It is important to note that one rule (or, as noted below, perhaps two neighboring rules) can indeed always get a simple majority over all others. This follows immediately from the fact that each

---

[1] These assumptions are taken from May (1952). They are four in number and will be presented in detail later.

[2] At worst, this procedure will single out two neighboring rules (i.e., either k or $k + 1$ affirmative votes will be required to pass measures) as better than all others, but will not differentiate between them.

legislator's preference schedule is single-peaked (in the sense defined by Duncan Black), with the possible addition of a single-stepped plateau on top. The possibility of cycles (i.e., the possibility that decision-rule A will be preferred over decision-rule B, and B preferred over C, but that C will be preferred over A) does not therefore exist.[3] At the end of this section a comparison is also made between the assumptions necessary for individual preference formation and those necessary for group preference formation.

Finally, this whole scheme is briefly compared with a real constituting situation in order to get some idea of how well or how poorly it characterizes same.

II. POLITICAL INDIVIDUALISM AND POSITIONAL PREFERENCES

We have defined political individualism as the desire on the part of an individual legislator to minimize the frequency with which the proposals he favors fail to pass and the frequency with which proposals he opposes pass anyway. I shall denote these two frequency or probability "costs" by P_{FAIL} and P_{PASS}, respectively. P_{FAIL} is just the probability p with which a legislator expects to vote affirmatively times the conditional probability P^+_{FAIL} that there is insufficient support to pass a given measure even with his vote. Thus

$$P_{\text{FAIL}} = p(P^+_{\text{FAIL}}). \tag{1}$$

Correspondingly P_{PASS} is the probability $1 - p$ (the possibility of abstaining is excluded) with which a legislator expects to vote against proposals times the conditional probability P^-_{PASS} that a measure will pass without his vote.

$$P_{\text{PASS}} = (1 - p)(P^-_{\text{PASS}}) \tag{2}$$

P^+_{FAIL} and P^-_{PASS} will, of course, depend critically on the collective decision-rule adopted. Given that there are n legislators, P^+_{FAIL} and P^-_{PASS} are also functions of our generic legislator's estimate of the behavior of his n' $= n - 1$ colleagues. Assuming that each acts independently, it will be sufficient for him to make n' estimates of the probabilities with which they will vote affirmatively. In order to make this formally clear we should perhaps write

$$p = p_{it} [(1 \leq i \leq n), (0 < p < 1)] \tag{3}$$

---

[3] This line of reasoning implies, for example, that it is perfectly consistent for the initial organizational session of a legislative body to decide by a simple majority that the instigation of future procedural changes shall require the concurrence of a two-thirds majority.

for the ith legislator's estimate of his own probability of voting affirmatively, and

$$p_j = p_{ij}[(1 \leq i \leq n, 1 \leq j \leq n, i \neq j), (0 < p_j < 1)] \qquad (4)$$

for the ith legislator's estimate of the corresponding probability for each of his colleagues. Note that each of n legislators makes n estimates of the type (3) and (4), for a total of n^2 generally independent quantities. Much of the time we will not have to be this formal and will consider p the affirmative probability characterizing the generic individual whose position we adopt.

The question then arises as to how the two frequency "costs" under consideration should be added to produce a meaningful "total cost" function. Having accomplished this we can straightforwardly find the collective decision-rule which minimizes this total cost function. We must then make a value judgment as to the relative importance of these two kinds of costs. Certainly there is a precedent from the law for weighting them unequality. Commenting on the laws of England, Blackstone said: "It is better that ten guilty persons escape than that one innocent suffer" (1862, vol. 4, chap. 27, p. 358). Indeed a tenable connection will eventually emerge between this legal parallel and the unanimous agreement required for a juristic decision.

Instead of arbitrarily fixing these weighting factors, we shall consider them variables. Their importance will eventually become quite clear. In fact, I think this entire line of investigation can profitably be viewed as a correspondence between the initial value judgment inherent in these weightings and the optimal decision-rule which results. Let us first point out that we are really interested only in the relative magnitudes of these two weighting factors (i.e., their ratio). The decision-rule which minimizes our total cost function will be unchanged if both weighting factors are multiplied by an arbitrary constant. The magnitude of this minimum value *will* of course be changed, but this is of no consequence. Let us, therefore, define

$\alpha \equiv$ the relative importance of the frequency with which proposals that our generic legislator favors are rejected.

$(1 - \alpha) \equiv$ the relative importance of the frequency with which proposals that our generic legislator opposes are adopted.

The parameter α may take on any value between zero and one. A choice of α which is less than one-half implies that the individual in question is more concerned about proposals being adopted which he opposes than he is about proposals which he favors being rejected. For example, the choice of $\alpha = 1/3$ corresponds to the value judgment that not having legislation passed over a nay vote is twice as important as having legislation defeated in spite of an aye vote. It should be pointed out that a legislator's choice of α bears no necessary relation to the frequency with which he expects to vote affirmatively. Such a correspondence may, of course, exist but the frequency with which an individual expects to vote affirmatively does not necessarily tell us anything about the relative value which he puts on his aye and nay votes. A legislator may, for example, expect to vote for the great majority of proposals that come up, yet hold the defeat of propositions which he favors far less repugnant than the passage of those he opposes.

It is very important (and a problem which I will not consider) that the individual know what powers have been vested in the legislative body. Only then will he know what types of proposals can be entertained and consequently be able to weigh the relative importance of the two "costs" for the different types of legislation envisioned. Of course it may be desirable to consider the costs and consequent optimal decision-rules for certain types of legislation separately because of their importance and/or uniqueness. Constitutional amendments immediately come to mind as they expand or contract the types of proposals which can be considered.

I shall term the choice of α a "positional preference" following Douglas Rae (1969) and Samuel Huntington (1957). This choice is made along an inherently one-dimensional scale. We should like to suggest that it corresponds to "conservatism" (in Huntington's sense) for very low values of α and "radicalism" for very high values of α. Unlike "liberalism," "communism," or "democracy," we would like to think of both "conservative" and "radicalism" as having no substantive basis, no utopian ideal toward which a society's energies could be directed. They are, instead, diametrically opposite views on the desirability of the status quo or, looking at it from the other direction, the desirability of change without reference to the nature of that change.

> Radicalism is thus the opposite of conservatism, and, like conservatism, it denotes an attitude toward institutions rather than a belief in any particular ideals. Conservatism and radicalism derive from orientations toward the process of change rather than toward the purpose and direction of change. (Huntington, 1957, p. 458)

The conservative chooses a rather low value of α and therfore considers inappropriate legislative actions (i.e., those embodying change) much more dangerous than the defeat of desirable proposals. For the conservative, proposals are of real importance only if their passage is required for the continued viability of established institutions. Usually things work the other way around; the rejection of a proposal ensures the continuity of the status quo. The radical, on the other hand, chooses a rather high value of α and is therefore primarily interested in not being thwarted in his attempts to change the system. He is not particularly upset by the passage of those proposals which he opposes. This is a small price to pay for the possibility of changing the status quo easily.

Having defined α, we then wish to find the collective decision-rule which minimizes the weighted "total cost" function:

$$Q = \alpha[P_{\text{FAIL}}] + (1 - \alpha)[P_{\text{PASS}}]. \tag{5}$$

Using equations (1) and (2), this becomes

$$Q = \alpha p P_{\text{FAIL}}^{+} + (1 - \alpha)(1 - p)P_{\text{PASS}}^{-}. \tag{6}$$

It should be kept in mind that P_{FAIL}^{+} and P_{PASS}^{-} are, in general, functions of the as yet undecided optimal decision-rule and the probabilities p_{ij} defined in (4). Note that since P_{FAIL}^{+} and P_{PASS}^{-} are conditional probabilities, the development up to (6) is quite general; no use has so far been made of the probabilistic dependence or independence of the n legislators' voting behavior.

III. COMMITTEE OR UNICAMERAL LEGISLATURE

Let us assume that the legislative body in question is made up of $n \geq 2$ politically coequal members. By this we mean that the decision-rule can only depend on the number of legislators voting for or against a proposal. Let us restrict our attention to those rules which specify that a bill passes if k or more legislators vote for it and fails otherwise. Here k can take on any integral value from one (individual initiative) to n (unanimity). This class of rules is not particularly restrictive and probably includes all those of political interest. Our formulation precludes the possible difficulties arising from tie votes. It is felt that the special nature of this possibility does not merit general consideration. A more substantial objection can be raised about rules which allow k to be less than $n/2 + 1$ if n is even, or $(n + 1)/2$ if n is odd. Such rules allow the formation of more than one disjoint winning coalition. If these coalitions wish to impose mutually exclusive policies, then obviously we are reduced to collective decision-making chaos. There are, however, enough situations in which multiple policies can be implemented without contradicting one another that we feel justified in considering the entire range of possible k values. Agenda committees can allow an agenda to be augmented by individual initiative without incurring any substantive difficulties. Both houses of Congress are required to take and record roll call votes if one-fifth of those present so desire it (see the Federal Constitution of the United States, Article 1, Section 5). One of the best known situations in which something less than a simple majority initiates action is the "rule of four" followed by the Justices of the United States Supreme Court. Any four of them can require that a writ be granted and thus that a case be heard.

Since a value of k completely specifies a collective decision-making rule, we find that the probability of a proposal failing even though our generic legislator favors it is

$$P_{\text{FAIL}}^{+} = \sum_{j=0}^{k-2} P_j. \tag{7}$$

Here P_j is the probability of exactly j legislators voting for a proposal out of the $n' = n - 1$ "other" legislators, independently of how our generic legislator votes on the proposal.[4] P_{FAIL}^{+} is thus the probability that even with our generic legislator's vote, a proposal will receive somewhere between one and $k - 1$ votes, all losing combinations. Similarly,

$$P_{\text{PASS}}^{-} = \sum_{j=k}^{n-1} P_j \tag{8}$$

is the probability of a proposal passing without the support of our generic legislator. As our generic legislator is assumed to vote nay, the highest possible number of "other" votes a proposal can get is $n - 1$. We therefore conclude that

$$Q(k) = \alpha p \sum_{j=0}^{k-2} P_j + (1 - \alpha)(1 - p) \sum_{j=k}^{n-1} P_j. \tag{9}$$

Now our generic individual's $n - 1$ colleagues must as a group give any proposal somewhere between zero and $n - 1$ affirmative votes. Thus

$$\sum_{j=0}^{n-1} P_j = 1 \tag{10}$$

and

$$\sum_{j=0}^{k-2} P_j = 1 - \sum_{j=k-1}^{n-1} P_j \tag{11}$$

$$\sum_{j=k}^{n-1} P_j = 1 - \sum_{j=0}^{k-1} P_j. \tag{12}$$

Substituting equation (11) into equation (9) we get

$$Q(k) = \alpha p \left(1 - \sum_{j=k-1}^{n-1} P_j \right) + (1 - \alpha - p + \alpha p) \sum_{j=k}^{n-1} P_j$$

---

[4] Our assumption of mutual legislative independence is thus utilized for the first time. Note that if P_j was replaced by separate conditional probabilities in (7) and (8), (10) and the theoretical developments which follow would not in general be valid.

or

$$Q(k) = \alpha p - \alpha p P_{k-1} + (1 - \alpha - p) \sum_{j=k}^{n-1} P_j. \tag{13}$$

Substituting (12) into (9) we get an equivalent result

$$Q(k) = (1 - \alpha)(1 - p) - \alpha p P_{k-1} - (1 - \alpha - p) \sum_{j=0}^{k-1} P_j. \tag{14}$$

The second terms in both (13) and (14) are identical. P_{k-1} is just the probability that the $n - 1$ "other" legislators will be one vote short of passing a proposal and that our generic legislator will, therefore, have the deciding vote. I shall call expressions having such a pivotal nature "swing" terms. By itself, the swing term is minimized when P_{k-1} is largest. The maximization of P_{k-1} involves seeking out the mode of the distribution P_j, i.e., the most probable number of affirmative votes, and setting k one vote higher. Considered separately, the minimization of the third terms in both (13) and (14) depends critically on whether $\alpha + p$ is greater or less than one. If $\alpha + p > 1$, the third term in (13) will be negative. Minimization of this term alone then demands that the sum involved contain as many terms as possible or that $k = 1$. However, if $\alpha + p < 1$, then the third term in (13) is positive and its minimization demands that $k = n$ (which therefore eliminates it). Analogous statements hold for the third term in (14). It is for this reason that we shall call expressions embodying such all-or-nothing potentialities "critical" terms.

We may interpret the process of finding the optimal value of k as an interaction or trade off between the swing term and the critical term. The swing term usually tends to pull the optimum value of k toward the middle of the possible range of values, whereas the critical term always pulls the optimum toward one of the end points. Note that the all-or-nothing nature of the critical term depends on our generic legislator's own values (α) and behavior (p). In direct contrast, minimization of the swing term depends critically on his perception of the behavior of his fellow legislators.

The fact that our generic legislator has a chance of casting the deciding vote is absolutely essential to the existence of a nonextreme (i.e., $k = 1$ or $k = n$) result. We shall illustrate this by considering an individual who is charged with fixing an optimum decision-rule, but who expects to have no future role in the legislative body in question. He will, of course, employ only the criterion of political individualism in his deliberations. We will assume he is able to make a value judgment about α and estimate the probabilities of voting affirmatively for each of the legislators in exactly the same manner as did our generic legislator. He can also ascertain a value of p. It must, however, be slightly reinterpreted as the frequency with which he expects to favor proposals even though he never gets to vote on them. The real difference between the nonparticipating constitutor and our generic legislator shows up only in the revised expressions for P_{FAIL}^{+} and P_{PASS}^{-}. These will be

$$(P_{FAIL}^{+})_c = \sum_{j=0}^{k-1} P_j^{(n)} \qquad (15)$$

for a nonparticipating constitutor, only

$$(P_{PASS}^{-})_c = \sum_{j=k}^{n} P_j^{(n)} \qquad (16)$$

and, as I think should be evident, the plus and minus signs have lost their previous significance; the constitutor never gets to vote one way or the other. $P_j^{(n)}$ is just the probability of j legislators voting for a proposal out of a total of n. The revised "total cost" function then becomes

$$[Q(k)]_c = \alpha p \sum_{j=0}^{k-1} P_j^{(n)} + (1 - \alpha)(1 - p) \sum_{j=k}^{n} P_j^{(n)}. \qquad (17)$$

Certainly the n legislators must support any given proposal with somewhere between zero and n votes. Thus

$$\sum_{j=0}^{n} P_j^{(n)} = 1. \qquad (18)$$

We can therefore write that

$$[Q(k)]_c = \alpha p \left[1 - \sum_{j=k}^{n} P_j^{(n)} \right] + (1 - \alpha)(1 - p) \sum_{j=k}^{n} P_j^{(n)}$$

or

$$[Q(k)]_c = \alpha p + (1 - \alpha - p) \sum_{j=k}^{n} P_j^{(n)}. \qquad (19)$$

If $\alpha + p < 1$, $[Q(k)]_c$ will decrease monotonically and consequently attain a minimum when $k = n$. If $\alpha + p > 1$, $[Q(k)]_c$ will increase monotonically and consequently attain a minimum at $k = 1$. If $\alpha + p = 1$, $[Q(k)]_c$ remains constant and our nonparticipating constitutor will be indifferent to the value of k selected.

The nonparticipating constitutor's "all-or-nothing" preference brings into sharp focus the highly individual nature of an "optimal" decision-rule. Such a preference may at first seem highly unintuitive but makes good sense from the point of view of political individualism. As such this result is probably just as important to a basic understanding of the line of reasoning under investigation as are the "participatory" results which follow.

One can indirectly interpret an all-or-nothing preference as implying a basic hostility toward a decision-making process in which the individual has no part. If the rule of individual initiative is taken to its logical extreme, one approaches anarchy. On the other hand, if universal agreement is required on every issue (i.e., if unanimity is taken to its logical extreme), very few if any decisions will be made and the same end point may well be reached. In either case, the existence of a collective decision-making apparatus becomes meaningless.

In order to investigate the actual minimization of $Q(k)$, I shall first consider

$$\Delta Q(k) = \frac{Q(k+1) - Q(k)}{(k+1) - k} = Q(k+1) - Q(k). \tag{20}$$

Considering the fact that $Q(k)$ is only defined for integral values of k, $\Delta Q(k)$ is quite comparable to the first derivative of an absolutely continuous function which, for the sake of comparison, we shall call $f(k)$. In this latter case the standard procedure for finding the minimum value involves setting $[(d/dk)f(k)] = 0$ and solving for k. The function $f(k)$ must also be concave upwards in a small region about this point; the slope of $f(k)$ must be negative just before the minimum and positive just afterward. We shall require the value of k which minimizes $Q(k)$ to satisfy two inequalities.

$$Q(k-1) > Q(k) \tag{21}$$

$$Q(k) < Q(k+1). \tag{22}$$

$Q(k)$ decreases as the minimum value is reached and then increases at the next step. This is equivalent to requiring that

$$\Delta Q(k-1) = Q(k) - Q(k-1) < 0$$

$$\Delta Q(k) = Q(k+1) - Q(k) > 0$$

or

$$Q(k) - Q(k-1) < 0 < Q(k+1) - Q(k)$$

$$\Delta Q(k-1) < 0 < \Delta Q(k). \tag{23}$$

I think the analogy between these inequalities and the beforementioned derivative technique should be clear. I have chosen to call (23) a "three-point" criterion because the value of Q at $k-1$, k, and $k+1$ is involved. There is, of course, no *a priori* guarantee that there will be at most one value of k which satisfies our three-point criterion. The development in the appendix assures us, however, that this is indeed the case. There are three special cases in which no value of k satisfies (23). It may happen that two neighboring values of Q, say $Q(k)$ and $Q(k + 1)$, are equal and both less than all other values of Q. In this special case the three-point criterion will be replaced by a "four-point" criterion, namely

$$Q(k - 1) - Q(k - 2) < 0 < Q(k + 1) - Q(k) \qquad (24)$$

given that

$$Q(k) = Q(k - 1).$$

Consider the special case in which $Q(1) \leq Q(2) < Q(3)$. The minimum will then occur at $k = 1$ or jointly at $k = 1$ and $k = 2$ if the strict equality holds. Consider also the opposite extreme in which $Q(n) \leq Q(n - 1) < Q(n - 2)$. The minimum will then occur at $k = n$ or jointly at $k = n$, and $k = n - 1$ if the strict equality holds. The reader is asked to subsume the possibility of these three special cases whenever the three-point minimizing condition is under consideration.

The minimization of Q via the three-point criterion requires the calculation of

$$Q(k + 1) - Q(k) = \left[\alpha p - \alpha p P_k + (1 - \alpha - p) \sum_{j=k+1}^{n-1} P_j \right]$$
$$- \left[\alpha p - \alpha p P_{k-1} + (1 - \alpha - p) \sum_{j=k}^{n-1} P_j \right]$$
$$= - (1 - \alpha)(1 - p)P_k + \alpha p P_{k-1}.$$

Similarly,

$$Q(k) - Q(k - 1) = - (1 - \alpha)(1 - p)P_{k-1} + \alpha p P_{k-2}$$

and the three-point criterion therefore yields

$$- (1 - \alpha)(1 - p)P_{k-1} + \alpha p P_{k-2} < 0 < - (1 - \alpha)(1 - p)P_k + \alpha p P_{k-1}. \qquad (25)$$

Let us define the quantity

$$A = \left(\frac{1 - \alpha}{\alpha} \right)\left(\frac{1 - p}{p} \right) \qquad (26)$$

which, it will be noted, involves only estimates that our generic legislator makes about his own values and future behavior. Relation (25) is then equivalent to the two inequalities

$$A P_{k-1} > P_{k-2} \qquad (27)$$

$$A P_k < P_{k-1}. \qquad (28)$$

Multiplying both sides of inequality (28) by A and using (27), we can then write

$$P_{k-2} < AP_{k-1} > A^2 P_k. \tag{29}$$

This result demonstrates that minimizing $Q(k)$ is mathematically equivalent to maximizing a function which is basically an exponential transformation of $\{P_j\}$. The reader should satisfy himself that the maximum value $F(k)$ of $F(j) = A^{j-1} P_{j-1}$ (where $j = 1, 2, 3, \ldots, n$) also satisfies inequality (29).[5] Note that when $\alpha + p = 1$, $A = 1$ and inequality (29) reduces to finding the most probable value of P_{k-1}. Referring back to (13), we see that $\alpha + p = 1$ is just the condition under which the critical third term drops out. As we have already mentioned, the remaining swing term is minimized when k is set one vote higher than the most probable number of affirmative votes—just the condition demanded by (29) when $A = 1$. When $A \neq 1$ the interaction between the critical and swing terms is spelled out by inequality (29), although the explicit result of this interaction and its political interpretation are not yet clear.

In order to proceed further, we must specify P_j as a function of the values p_{ij} (see [4]) assigned to the $n - 1$ "other" legislators. Let us first assume that our generic ith legislator considers his colleagues an undifferentiated group or at least one about which he knows very little. He might then well characterize them all by the same (perhaps average) value $p_{ij} = p_L$ (for all j, $1 < j < n$, $i \neq j$). This being the case, P_j can easily be found as the term involving $(p_L)^j (1 - p_L)^{(n-1)-j}$ in the binomial expansion of

$$\sum_{j=0}^{n-1} P_j = 1 = [p_L + (1 - p_L)]^{n-1}.$$

We have, of course, assumed that there will be no absences or abstentions. P_j is taken as the probability of j aye votes and $(n - 1) - j$ nay votes. Consulting any book on elementary probability and statistics, we conclude that

$$P_j = \frac{(n-1)!}{j!(n-1-j)!} (p_L)^j (1 - p_L)^{n-1-j} = \binom{n-1}{j} (p_L)^j (1 - p_L)^{n-1-j}. \tag{30}$$

The binomial coefficient $\binom{n-1}{j} \equiv (n-1)!/j!(n-1-j)!$ gives the number of ways in which the $n - 1$ "other" legislators can be divided into two

---

[5] Note that given the absolutely continuous functions $f(x)$ and $p(x)$ and the relation

$$f(x) = A^x p(x)$$

we can just as well write

$$f(x) = e^{x \log A} p(x)$$

which should explain why $F(j)$ is termed a basically exponential transformation of $\{P_j\}$.

groups, one having j members (those supporting a given proposal) and the other having $n - 1 - j$ members (those opposing a given proposal). As all the legislators vote independently, each grouping is equally likely and indeed each occurs with probability $(p_L)^j(1-p_L)^{n-1-j}$. Thus P_j is composed of $(n-1)!/j!(n-1-j)!$ contributions, each having magnitude $(p_L)^j$ $\cdot(1-p_L)^{n-1-j}$.

Using (30), inequalities (27) and (28) become

$$\left(\frac{1-\alpha}{\alpha}\right)\left(\frac{1-p}{p}\right)\frac{(n-1)!}{[n-1-(k-1)]!(k-1)!}(p_L)^{k-1}(1-p_L)^{n-1-(k-1)}$$
$$> \frac{(n-1)!}{[n-1-(k-2)]!(k-2)!}(p_L)^{k-2}(1-p_L)^{n-1-(k-2)}$$

and

$$\left(\frac{1-\alpha}{\alpha}\right)\left(\frac{1-p}{p}\right)\frac{(n-1)!}{(n-1-k)!k!}(p_L)^k(1-p_L)^{n-1-k}$$
$$< \frac{(n-1)!}{[n-1-(k-1)]!(k-1)!}(p_L)^{k-1}(1-p_L)^{n-1-(k-1)}.$$

Dividing both sides of each inequality by $\dfrac{(n-1)!}{[n-1-(k-1)]!(k-1)!}$. $(p_L)^{k-1}(1-p_L)^{n-k}$ it is found that

$$\left(\frac{1-\alpha}{\alpha}\right)\left(\frac{1-p}{p}\right) > \left(\frac{1-p_L}{p_L}\right)\left(\frac{k-1}{n-(k-1)}\right)$$

and

$$\left(\frac{1-\alpha}{\alpha}\right)\left(\frac{1-p}{p}\right)\left(\frac{n-k}{k}\right) < \left(\frac{1-p_L}{p_L}\right).$$

We shall for the sake of convenience set

$$B = \left(\frac{1-p}{p}\right)\Big/\left(\frac{1-p_L}{p_L}\right). \tag{31}$$

We then have that

$$(1-\alpha)B(n-k+1) > \alpha(k-1)$$
$$(1-\alpha)B(n-k) < \alpha k.$$

Algebraically manipulating until k stands alone in each expression, we find that

$$\frac{(1-\alpha)n}{1-\alpha(1-1/B)} + 1 > k$$

$$\frac{(1-\alpha)n}{1-\alpha(1-1/B)} < k.$$

Using (31) we find that

$$(1 - 1/B) = (p_L - p)/p_L(1 - p)$$

so that we can finally write

$$\frac{(1 - \alpha)n}{1 - \alpha\left[\dfrac{p_L - p}{p_L(1 - p)}\right]} < k < \frac{(1 - \alpha)n}{1 - \alpha\left[\dfrac{p_L - p}{p_L(1 - p)}\right]} + 1 \tag{32}$$

as the condition determining k. If $p = p_L$, then k will be determined by the relation

$$(1 - \alpha)n < k < (1 - \alpha)n + 1 \tag{33}$$

which we might well call the egalitarian case. Taking into account the special cases subsumed under the three-point criteria, it can be seen that the egalitarian case reduces to a preference for simple majority rule when $\alpha = 1/2$. This is exactly the relation proposed by Rae (1969) and proven by Taylor (1969). Relations (33), (32), and (29) are then successively broader generalizations of this line of reasoning.

Relation (32) demonstrates that an optimal decision-rule will tend to be greater or less than it would under egalitarian conditions, depending on whether p_L is greater or less than p. This effect is obviously related to each legislator's desire to be the pivotal voter, which in itself would dictate that the optimal decision-rule be set one vote higher than the most likely number of affirmative votes. In the most general case we would expect the same sort of effect dependent on whether the mode of $\{P_j\}$ is greater or less than p.

The egalitarian case, I think, deserves further attention. So long as our generic individual is of the opinion that his future voting behavior will be basically similar to that of his colleagues (in the very weak sense that he will in general support proposals just as frequently as they will), his choice of a decision-rule will depend solely on his positional preference. This is not too untoward an assumption to make in the face of the many uncertainties embodied in constitutional choice. Putting this another way, the egalitarian case presupposes that over the long run you will support your fellow legislator as often as he supports you. I think this could be considered quite reasonable give and take, although it should be remembered that our model has specifically ruled out the interdependence of legislative voting patterns. Optimistically we could hope that an optimal decision-rule based on a consensually determined positional preference and a universally accepted pattern of egalitarian voting (i.e., an egalitarian pattern is accepted by each legislator) would provide an "unbiased" framework upon which the considered merits or demerits of future proposals and the interactions of the individual legislators could only improve.

If for the egalitarian case we define a fraction f via the relation $k = fn$, we can rewrite (33) as

$$(1 - \alpha) < f < (1 - \alpha) + \frac{1}{n}. \tag{34}$$

The fraction f is then very nearly independent of n. A legislative body will never be more than one vote away from the optimal value of k, whatever size it grows to be, if it requires *at least* an f-sized majority to pass legislation, e.g., a two-thirds or three-quarters majority. Relation (34) then shows that a group of egalitarian constitutors who consensually agree that the rejection of bad initiatives is twice as important as the passage of good ones ($\alpha = 1/3$) should choose a two-thirds majority for the passage of legislation. A group feeling that the rejection of bad initiatives is three times as important as the passage of good ones ($\alpha = 1/4$) should choose a three-quarters majority.

The prevalence of simple majority, two-thirds, and at times three-quarters majorities, may possibly be indicative of a basic inability to specify positional preferences very exactly. Constitutors then tend to choose between the simplest (perhaps one could say most natural) ratios of the two "costs" involved, i.e., 1:1, 2:1, or 3:1. (Not incidentally, these are also the ratios of yea to nay votes required to pass legislation by simple majority, two-thirds, and three-quarters majorities, respectively.) Note that for a one hundred-member legislature, a constitutor's ability to choose between $k = 51$ and $k = 52$ is in the egalitarian case dependent on whether he characterizes himself by a value of α between 0.49 and 0.50, or one between 0.48 and 0.49. And the width of these ranges becomes proportionally smaller as n increases.

Certainly $\alpha = 1/2$, implying the optimality of simple majority rule in the egalitarian case, has a priori the most to recommend it over any other assumption. Rae (1969) first treated the egalitarian case in which $\alpha = 1/2$ and $p = 1/2$. Given these particular assumptions, the critical term in (13) drops out and the minimization of $Q(k)$ depends on the swing term

$$-\alpha p P_{k-1} = -\left(\frac{1}{4}\right)\left[\frac{(n-1)!}{(k-1)!(n-k)!}\right]\left(\frac{1}{2}\right)^{n-1}.$$

Its minimization depends only on the maximization of the binomial coefficient. Under these conditions the optimality of simple majority rule hinges on the fact that there are more ways that n legislators can be divided into two groups of $n/2$ (for even n) or one group of $(n-1)/2$ and one group of $(n + 1)/2$ (for odd n) than in any other way. The above groupings give each individual the maximum probability of being (or of considering himself to have been) the deciding voter.

IV. TRANSITIVITY AND OTHER THEORETICAL QUESTIONS

In the most general case, each P_j can be explicitly written out in terms of the $n - 1$ quantities p_{ij}.[6] Inequality (29) will then yield the optimal decision-rule for the ith legislator. As indicated by the results of the simpler case given in (32), it will depend on $p = p_{ii}$, the quantities p_{ij}, and his choice of α. There consequently appears to be little basis for further simplification and little motivation for carrying through the myriad of possible cases.

I would, however, like to put this whole situation in a more general context. The criterion of political individualism allows each legislator to determine not only his most preferred or optimal decision-rule, but also his relative preferences for all n decision-rules. He can easily set up an entire preference schedule by comparing the various values of $Q(k)$ where $1 \leq k \leq n$. Our constituting legislators are therefore faced with a special case of the relationship between individual preferences and group choice dealt with at length by Kenneth Arrow (1963) and others. They have to collectively determine a decision-rule for the passage of future legislation, given only their individual preferences on the matter. In another sense the legislators are also faced with the interminable sequence of deciding how they will decide on how they will decide on how they will decide . . . , etc. This sequence can be quite naturally terminated at the second stage by the consensual acceptance of several very reasonable conditions which the constituting rule "ought" to satisfy. In order to specify these assumptions clearly, let us first consider the method by which the group shall choose between any two of the n possible rules. Let one of these choices be L (l or more votes are needed to pass a proposition) and the other M (m or more votes are needed to pass a proposition). Each of the n constituting

---

[6] In general:

$$P_{n'} = p_{i1} p_{i2} \dots p_{i,i-1} p_{i,i+1} \dots p_{in}$$

$$P_{n'-1} = P_{n'} \left[\frac{1 - p_{i1}}{p_{i1}} + \frac{1 - p_{i2}}{p_{i2}} + \cdots + \frac{1 - p_{i,i-1}}{p_{i,i-1}} + \frac{1 - p_{i,i+1}}{p_{i,i+1}} + \cdots + \frac{1 - p_{in}}{p_{in}} \right]$$

$$= P_{n'} \sum_{j=1}^{n} {}^{(\prime)} \left(\frac{1 - p_{ij}}{p_{ij}} \right).$$

Here the prime on the last summation denotes the deletion of the term in which $i = j$. Then

$$P_{n'-2} = P_{n'} \sum_{j=1}^{n-1} {}^{(\prime)} \sum_{k>j} {}^{(\prime)} \left(\frac{1 - p_{ij}}{p_{ij}} \right) \left(\frac{1 - p_{ik}}{p_{ik}} \right)$$

where the primes denote deletion of terms in which $i = j$ or $i = k$.

$$P_{n'-3} = P_{n'} \sum_{j=1}^{n-2} {}^{(\prime)} \sum_{k>j} {}^{(\prime)} \sum_{l>k} {}^{(\prime)} \left(\frac{1 - p_{ij}}{p_{ij}} \right) \left(\frac{1 - p_{ik}}{p_{ik}} \right) \left(\frac{1 - p_{il}}{p_{il}} \right), \text{ etc.}$$

legislators will therefore either prefer L to M, M to L, or be indifferent between them. We may, therefore, define a variable $X_{LM}(j)$ which takes on the values 1, 0, or -1, depending on whether the jth legislator ($1 \leq j \leq n$) prefers L or M, is indifferent between L and M, or prefers M over L. Following Kenneth May (1952), we shall define a *group decision function* f via

$$X_{LM} = f[X_{LM}(1), X_{LM}(2), \ldots X_{LM}(n)].$$

This function synthesizes the preferences of the n constituting legislators to form a group preference.

It is quite natural to require that this function be well defined, i.e., that X_{LM}, the group preference, take on one and only one of the values 1, 0, or -1 for any given set $\{X_{ML}(j)\}$. May calls this being *always decisive*. It also seems quite natural to assume that each constituting legislator should have an equal voice in deciding the rule to be adopted. The group decision function should be unchanged if the positions of any two values $X_{ML}(j)$ and $X_{ML}(j')$ are interchanged. The group decision function must then depend only on the number of votes cast for rule L [$N(1)$] and the number case for rule M [$N(-1)$]. May quite appropriately calls this property *equality*. The third condition for which we would ask consensual acceptance involves the a priori *neutrality* with which the group decision-rule shall treat all n possible rules and thus any pair. We do not want the method by which individual preferences are synthesized to favor any one rule over any other. Given that L is preferred over M, it should make no difference whether we let $X_{LM}(j)$ be 1 or -1 as long as we assign the alternate value whenever M is preferred over L. Formally we require that

$$f[-X_{LM}(1), -X_{LM}(2), \ldots, -X_{LM}(n)]$$
$$= -f[X_{LM}(1), X_{LM}(2), \ldots, X_{LM}(n)].$$

Our last condition effectively eliminates all rules except those which require *k or more* affirmative votes for the passage of legislation. It will be termed *positive responsiveness* and is formally stated as follows: If a group is indifferent between rules L and M (i.e., $X_{LM} = 0$) or prefers L over M (i.e., $X_{LM} = 1$), then the switch of a single legislator who had preferred M to L's cause should result in a group decision favoring L. These four conditions are then necessary and sufficient for the adoption of simple majority rule as the method of pairwise choice.

Theorem: A group decision function is the method of simple majority rule if and only if it is always decisive, egalitarian, neutral, and positively responsive. (May, 1952, p. 682)

Finally, as $N(1)$ is the number of votes cast for rule L while $N(-1)$ is the number case for rule M, we should formally state that simple majority rule is defined by the following relations:

$$X_{LM} = 0 \qquad \text{if and only if} \qquad N(-1) = N(1).$$
$$X_{LM} = 1 \qquad \text{if and only if} \qquad N(1) > N(-1).$$
$$X_{LM} = -1 \qquad \text{if and only if} \qquad N(-1) > N(1).$$

The proposal receiving the most votes is adopted. If both receive the same number, the result is a tie.

So far, so good, but this still does not assure us that one of the n rules will be able to get a simple majority over all the others. In fact, Arrow's work (1963) demonstrates that under very general conditions, none of which have been violated in the present development, this type of "uniqueness" cannot be guaranteed. Group decision-rules will not necessarily be transitive so that, for example, the group's preference for proposition A over proposition B, and proposition B over proposition C, will not guarantee their preference of A over C. It is of some theoretical interest, therefore, that simple majority rule will always yield transitive results among "political individualists." There will be one or, at most, two neighboring rules k and $k + 1$ which will be able to secure a simple majority over all others.

In order to prove these statements, it is first necessary to switch our attention from the minimization of a "total cost" function to the maximization of a "total utility" function. In our present context, these are alternative ways of looking at the same phenomenon. The value of k which minimizes $Q(k)$ will also maximize

$$C(k) = 1 - Q(k) \tag{35}$$

as $Q(k) \leq 1$ by the nature of its definition. The full plot of $C(k)$ as a function of k ($1 \leq k \leq n$) can then be considered a "preference curve" of the type considered by Duncan Black (1958). $C(k)$ is only defined for integral values of k, but, by connecting these pointwise values, we obtain the type of "curve" exemplified in figure 1.

The transitivity of collective choice using simple majority rule follows under the most general conditions of "non-interactive" political individualism (i.e., α arbitrary, p_{ii} and all the p_{ij}'s independent and, in general, different for each individual) because the preference curve of any such individual is "single-peaked" with the possible addition of a single-stepped "plateau" on top. "A single-peaked curve is one which changes its direction at most once, from up to down" (Black, 1958, p. 7). A single-peaked plateau would modify this slightly. Having increased to its maximum

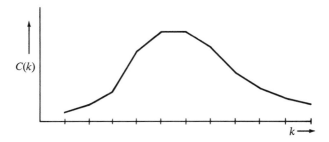

FIGURE 1

value, the preference curve would take one horizontal step $[C(k) = C(k + 1)]$ and then turn downwards. Such a situation is depicted in figure 1.

In order to demonstrate the universality of this modified single-peaked shape, we need an explicit expression for $C(k)$. Making use of (13) and (35), we find that

$$C(k) = 1 - \alpha p + \alpha p P_{k-1} - (1 - \alpha - p) \sum_{j=k}^{n-1} P_j.$$

Therefore,

$$\Delta C(k) = C(k + 1) - C(k) = (1 - \alpha)(1 - p)P_k - \alpha p P_{k-1}.$$

Remembering that

$$A = \left(\frac{1 - \alpha}{\alpha}\right)\left(\frac{1 - p}{p}\right),$$

this can be written as

$$\Delta C(k) = \alpha p[AP_k - P_{k-1}]$$
$$= \alpha p P_k[(A - 1) + (P_k - P_{k-1})/P_k]. \tag{36}$$

The sign of $\Delta C(k)$, which of course indicates whether $C(k)$ is increasing or decreasing, is determined by the sign of the quantity $[(A - 1) + (P_k - P_{k-1})/P_k]$. As A is not a function of k, this quantity will change sign at most once from positive to negative if $(P_k - P_{k-1})/P_k$ is a monotonically decreasing function of k. This condition will then guarantee a single-peaked preference curve with the possible addition of a single-stepped plateau on top if and only if $[(A - 1) + (P_k - P_{k-1})/P_k] = 0$ for the optimum value(s) of k. $(P_k - P_{k-1})/P_k$ will be monotonically decreasing if the following set of inequalities is satisfied

$$(P_k - P_{k-1})/P_k > (P_{k+1} - P_k)/P_{k+1} \qquad \text{(for all } k, 0 \leq k \leq n')$$

or, equivalently,

$$P_k^2 > P_{k-1}P_{k+1} \qquad \text{(for all } k, 0 < k < n') \qquad (37)$$

where $n' = n - 1$, the number of "other" legislators. The verification of these inequalities involves a fair amount of mathematical detail and is therefore left to the appendix in order to maintain a certain degree of continuity.

The transitivity of collective choice using simple majority rule then follows immediately from the work of Duncan Black.

> For a group of curves, all of which are either single-peaked or single-peaked with plateaus on top, if a_1 can defeat a_2 in a vote, and a_2 can defeat a_3, then a_1 can defeat a_3 .... The extension of the transitive property will also hold, namely, that if a_1 can defeat a_2, a_2 can defeat a_3 ..., and a_{r-1} can defeat a_r, then a_1 can defeat a_r. (Black, 1958, p. 31)

Duncan Black has also shown that, given a collection of single-peaked curves and single-peaked curves with plateaus on top, "at most there is a single range of values, each of which is able to get a majority against all other points lying outside that range" (Black, 1958, p. 30). Because our preference curves will at most have single-stepped plateaus, it follows that our "single range of values" will contain a maximum of two values and usually reduce to a single point. The possible indeterminancy in our scheme is quite comparable to that arising from a tie vote which indeed is one of its possible origins. This type of possible indeterminancy is not felt to be a great drawback as special mechanisms can in general be introduced to resolve such situations.

We have, therefore, been able to exhibit a satisfactory intellectual scheme for terminating the sequences of questions which ask how constitutors will make decisions about how they will make decisions about how they will make decisions, . . . , etc. It is simply an intellectual scheme, however, and should not be taken any more seriously than the assumptions upon which it is built. It is therefore of particular interest to examine these assumptions, particularly the relationship between those made about the formation of individual preferences, and those made about the method of group preference formation. Each individual forms his own preferences on the basis of political individualism and related assumptions while all the individuals must consensually agree on May's four assumptions before simple majority rule can be established as the method by which these preferences shall be synthesized. Having (I hope) clearly established the difference between the two stages of this development, let us look at their similarities. The rules considered by political individualists are inherently decisive and positively responsive, assuming these concepts are modified slightly to eliminate the possibility of a tie. Thus two of the four assumptions made at the second stage are implicitly present at the first stage. Analogs of the other two assumptions are present only in special cases. Political equality implies that the group decision function will be unchanged if any voter changes places with any other. We require the group decision function to be a symmetric function of its arguments. Now assume that each political individualist is egalitarian ($p_{ii} = p_{ij}$ for all j) and prefers the same value of α. Each such individual then considers himself on a par with every other individual inasmuch as he is assured that "changing places" with any one of them (i.e., taking on the other fellow's assumptions) would in no way affect his choice of an optimal decision-rule. Such a situation would, of course, produce consensual agreement and eliminate the necessity of a group decision-rule. Finally, the neutrality of a group decision function is mirrored at the level of individual preference formation only if $\alpha = 1/2$. Neutrality implies that a group decision function will not a priori favor one alternative over another. Setting $\alpha = 1/2$ implies that one considers bad actions to be equally as harmful as bad inactions; one is not prejudiced either for or against future proposals. When the four assumptions made at the second level of our development are rigorously applied in the context of political individualism, the latter reduces to a universal preference for simple majority rule. In this one quite narrow sense then, the adoption of simple majority rule on the basis of May's assumptions is equivalent to a particularly symmetric instance of the use of political individualism.

V.   A CURSORY COMPARISON WITH "REALITY"

It is rather interesting, I think, to compare the theoretical scheme at hand with an example of the type of situation it purports to describe. I will refer to a section of James Madison's *Journal of the Federal Constitution* (1893, pp. 714-16) in which the delegates decided whether a two-thirds or three-quarters majority of both Houses of Congress should be required to overrule the "negative" of the president. The legislative structure here is admittedly quite a bit more complex than the one considered theoretically, but there are a number of parallels. The decision between a two-thirds or three-quarters majority was made on the consensually accepted basis of "the greater number of these [states] which shall be fully represented" (1893, p. 56), i.e., simple majority rule with each state having one vote. Arguments which are clearly related to positional preferences are found intertwined with factional considerations. Clearly Gouverneur Morris, who "dwelt on the danger to the public interest from the instability of laws, as the most to be guarded against" (1893, p. 715), would be considered more conservative (and, hence, be characterized by a lower value of α) than Mr. Williamson who was "most of all, afraid that the repeal of bad laws might be rendered too difficult by requiring three-fourths to overcome the dissent of the President" (1893, p. 715). Both are talking about their attitudes toward change and both arguments can be couched in terms of the relative "costs" defined in our model. Colonel Mason even pointed out the relative nature of these costs (i.e., relative to each individual) when he said, "The example of New York depended on the real merits of the laws. The gentlemen citing it had no doubt given their own opinion. But perhaps there were others of opposite opinion, who could equally paint the abuses on the other side" (1893, p. 715).

On the other hand, the Convention's delegates discussed the decision-rules under consideration in terms of the factional dangers to be incurred from one or the other. They feared popular "majority tyranny" on the one hand and the impedance of orderly government by the president (representing the minority of status, wealth, and power) and a small group of senators on the other. "The latent causes of factions are thus sown in the nature of man" (Madison, 1922, p. 42), and Madison deemed insufficient even the extensive system of checks and balances which were expressly instituted to control its effects. He suggested that these effects could be checked if the bases for the formation of factions and their ability to coalesce were minimized.

> Extend the sphere, and you take in a greater variety of parties and interests; you make it less probable that a majority of the whole will have a common motive to invade the rights of other citizens; or if such a common motive exists, it will be more difficult for all who feel it to discover their own strength, and to act in unison with each other. (Madison, 1922, p. 47)

We might then characterize Madison as favorably predisposed toward the type of legislative independence assumed in our model. He does not, of course, believe it is humanly possible or that it should be imposed— "Liberty is to faction what air is to fire; an ailment without which it instantly expires . . ." (1922, p. 42). All in all, the type of mutual legislative independence assumed in our model is certainly *not* a justifiable assumption. However, the alternative is the introduction of the full range of political interactions, something which the author admits he is not capable of handling. I would therefore tentatively justify mutual legislative independence as a reasonable first step—something which can really only be done upon the successful completion of several succeeding steps.

APPENDIX

Arguments establishing the veracity of the inequalities

$$P_k^2 > P_{k-1}P_{k+1} \qquad \text{(for all } k, 0 \leq k \leq n') \qquad (37)$$

will be divided into two groups. First a direct inductive proof will be outlined which the more mathematically-minded reader will easily see how to formalize. Second, several quite sophisticated results will be given from a paper by Kielson and Gerber which establish inequalities (37) quite elegantly and succinctly.

Let $P_k^{(n')}$ be the probability of k affirmative votes out of n' "other" legislators. Consider first the case in which $n' = 1$, implying possible k values of zero and one. The two pertinent inequalities, $[P_0^{(1)}]^2 > P_{-1}^{(1)}P_1^{(1)}$ and $[P_1^{(1)}]^2 > P_0^{(1)}P_2^{(1)}$, are trivially satisfied as $P_{-1}^{(1)}$ and $P_2^{(1)}$ are zero on a priori grounds. This same sort of reasoning suffices to establish comparable inequalities for $k = 0$ and $k = n'$, i.e., the "endpoints" of the range of k values, whatever the value of n'.

Now consider the case in which $n' = 2$, implying k values of zero, one, and two. In order to facilitate the mathematical development, this case can be considered the $n' = 1$ case (or, in general, the $n' - 1$ case) augmented by another legislator. We can then write

$$P_0^{(2)} = (1 - q)P_0^{(1)}$$
$$P_1^{(2)} = (1 - q)P_1^{(1)} + qP_0^{(1)}$$
$$P_2^{(2)} = qP_1^{(1)}$$

where q is the probability that the added legislator will vote for future proposals. Formally these equations are an example of the convolution of two independent random variables. Note that the assumption of mutual legislative independence is necessary to assure their validity. Again the "endpoint" inequalities, $[P_0^{(2)}]^2 > P_{-1}^{(2)}P_1^{(2)}$ and $[P_2^{(2)}]^2 > P_1^{(2)}P_3^{(2)}$, are considered established. The quantities

$$[P_1^{(2)}]^2 = (1 - q)^2[P_1^{(1)}]^2 + 2q(1 - q)P_0^{(1)}P_1^{(1)} + q^2[P_0^{(1)}]^2$$

and

$$P_0^{(2)}P_2^{(2)} = q(1 - q)P_0^{(1)}P_1^{(1)}$$

are then calculated, from which the validity of the inequality

$$[P_1^{(2)}]^2 > P_0^{(2)}P_2^{(2)}$$

is immediately apparent.

The next case ($n' = 3$) is handled as a group of two "other" legislators which is augmented by a third. Thus

$$P_0^{(3)} = (1 - q)P_0^{(2)}$$
$$P_1^{(3)} = (1 - q)P_1^{(2)} + qP_0^{(2)}$$
$$P_2^{(3)} = (1 - q)P_2^{(2)} + qP_1^{(2)}$$
$$P_3^{(3)} = qP_2^{(2)}.$$

As the "endpoint" inequalities are once again considered established, it remains to show that $[P_1^{(3)}]^2 > P_0^{(3)}P_2^{(3)}$ and $[P_2^{(3)}]^2 > P_1^{(3)}P_3^{(3)}$. Dealing with the first of these, we find that

$$[P_1^{(3)}]^2 = (1 - q)^2[P_1^{(2)}]^2 + 2q(1 - q)P_1^{(2)}P_0^{(2)} + q^2[P_0^{(2)}]^2$$

and

$$P_0^{(3)}P_2^{(3)} = (1 - q)^2P_0^{(2)}P_2^{(2)} + (1 - q)qP_0^{(2)}P_1^{(2)}.$$

Subtracting $(1 - q)qP_0^{(2)}P_1^{(2)}$ from both these quantities and dividing the results by $(1 - q)^2$, it can be seen that the validity of the relation

$$[P_1^{(2)}]^2 + \frac{q}{1 - q}P_1^{(2)}P_0^{(2)} + \frac{q^2}{(1 - q)^2}[P_0^{(2)}]^2 > P_0^{(2)}P_2^{(2)}$$

would immediately verify the inequality in question. This is easily established using the main result obtained in the previous stage of this development, namely $[P_1^{(2)}]^2 > P_0^{(2)}P_2^{(2)}$. Indeed

$$[P_1^{(2)}]^2 + \frac{q}{1 - q}P_0^{(2)}P_1^{(2)} + \frac{q^2}{(1 - q)^2}[P_0^{(2)}]^2 > [P_1^{(2)}]^2 > P_0^{(2)}P_2^{(2)}.$$

The other inequality in question, $[P_2^{(3)}]^2 > P_1^{(3)}P_3^{(3)}$, can be established in exactly the same way.

This procedure can then be iterated indefinitely to any arbitrary value of n'. Inequalities established at any stage $n' - 1$ can be used in conjunction with equations of the form

$$P_0^{(n')} = (1 - q)P_0^{(n'-1)}$$
$$P_1^{(n')} = (1 - q)P_1^{(n'-1)} + qP_0^{(n'-1)}$$
$$\cdot$$
$$\cdot$$
$$\cdot$$
$$P_{n'-1}^{(n')} = (1 - q)P_{n'-1}^{(n'-1)} + qP_{n'-2}^{(n'-1)}$$
$$P_n^{(n')} = qP_{n'-1}^{(n'-1)}$$

to establish the desired inequalities at the n' stage.

At the more sophisticated level mentioned earlier, I would like to quote a definition, a theorem, and some accompanying commentary taken from a recent paper on discrete unimodality (Keilson and Gerber, 1971, p. 388).

Definition. A lattice distribution $\{p_n\}$ having $p_n > 0$ for all n on a lattice interval $I_p = \{n: n_1 < n < n_2\}$, finite or infinite, and no support elsewhere will be said to be log-concave (LC) if $p_n^2 \geq p_{n+1}p_{n-1}$ for all $n \in I_p$. A log-concave lattice distribution will be said to be strictly log-concave (SLC) if $p_n^2 > p_{n+1}p_{n-1}$ for all $n \in I_p$.

We note that singular distributions with all mass at a fixed value of n are strictly log-concave and that all lattice distributions with mass concentrated on two adjacent points are SLC . . . .

The basic theorem we present is the following:

Theorem **4**. The convolution of two SLC lattice distributions is itself SLC.

Now each of the "other" legislators is characterized by a "lattice distribution with mass concentrated on two adjacent points." That is, the possible number of votes which each legislator may cast for a future proposal is either zero or one. As $\{P_k\}$ is an n'-fold convolution of such SLC distributions, it follows that $\{P_k\}$ is itself SLC. Inequalities (37) then follow directly from the definition of a SLC distribution.

3. Is Majority Rule Special?

NORMAN J. SCHOFIELD

Majority rule has enjoyed a rather special place in the ideological tradition from which contemporary liberal democracy draws its rationale. Figures as dissimilar as Locke and Rousseau agreed in their own ways that majority decision enjoyed a special status among the infinity of ways in which collective policies might be chosen, and a sizeable technical literature has grown up in economics and politics analyzing the merits and liabilities of majority rule. Moreover, the issue is alive in a number of important political arenas during the present era; one thinks, for example, of the new Europe, the United Nations General Assembly, and the American Senate.

In this paper, we extend one line of argument on the relative merits of majority rule. Our thesis will be that majority decision is, under a variety of assumptions about the nature of political disputes in voting bodies, not only optimal but importantly so. We will argue that: (1) majority rule is an optimizing strategy for the generic individual who wants, so far as possible, to have his way in policy disputes, and (2) that, for some important models of opinion formation, its optimality does not

I am grateful to Douglas Rae, whose earlier paper *Decision Rules and Individual Values in Constitutional Choice* (1969), brought to my notice the problems that this paper attempts in part to solve. In addition he was kind enough to give me useful advice in writing this paper.

vanish with increasing group size. Our own contribution belongs to a specialized tradition in the technical literature, but the argument itself is part of a much broader dispute in political theory. We may begin, then, by setting our problem in the context of the more diffuse argument about majority rule and its alternatives.

I. THE GENERAL ARGUMENT

There are two classes of alternatives to majority decision making: those which give special (perhaps dictatorial) power to a specific set of members, and those which retain a formal equality of authority among all members but require the assent of more than a majority for the imposition of new policies. The first group of alternatives may be called *hierarchical* decision procedures, the second *restrictivist* decision procedures. Hierarchy gives special authority to specific individuals, be they yea-sayers or nay-sayers, while restrictivism gives special authority to individuals who happen to be nay-sayers. Thus, for example, a two-thirds decision-rule allows a minority of just over one-third to frustrate the wishes of a majority just under two-thirds, provided the former are nay-sayers, the latter yea-sayers.

Historically, of course, hierarchical procedures are more common than restrictivist ones, and unalloyed majority rule is in turn a very rare practice. It is indeed possible to interpret much of the important work done by social science in the past century—names like Mosca, Michels, Pareto, Weber, de Jouvenal, and Lasswell come quickly to mind—as arguments against the very *possibility* of majoritarian political decision making. And it would be heroically naïve to suggest that majority rule among equals is likely to become historically dominant as a means of collective policy making even in small polities such as the corporation, the university, or the interest association. And, even making due allowance for the technical efficiency of the sample survey and electronic communication, only a madman would seriously predict the emergence of direct majoritarian democracy in nation-states or even in their larger subunits.

Majority rule nevertheless remains a live issue for the political theorist on at least two counts. First, there are settings in which it is directly practicable; small voting bodies offer an example. Second, and equally important, it is useful to evaluate ideals, even if it is possible only to approximate them. It is no good saying we should not try to approximate an ideal on the ground that we cannot generally expect to attain a perfect fit between its strictures and actual practice. Such a retreat implies the naturalist fallacy—an unwarranted leap from *is* to *ought*—and leaves us without guidance for reform. We therefore proceed without further apology for the obduracy with which historical experience is apt to resist the reforms which would be implied by argument for majority rule.

If the majority rule argument is alive, it is also complex and quite often confused. One's assessment of majority decision depends on conjunctions between his normative criteria on the one hand and his assumptions about people and their disputes on the other. We will deal with one criterion (we call it "political individualism") and a variety of assumptions about the pattern of political disputes. We will begin, however, by outlining some important alternatives to this approach.

The best-known and most obvious arguments are those which begin with the criterion of political equality, by which we mean the requirement that individuals be counted equally in formal voting. Barring the logical possibility that nobody has *any* influence on outcomes, this means that proposals favored by more members of a group must dominate those preferred by fewer members. This rules out hierarchical procedures immediately, and, if one accepts the comparison between proponents of action and defenders of existing policies, political equality also precludes the recommendation of restrictive decision procedures, such as two-thirds voting. Indeed, a St. Louis lawyer, Paul Priesler, has recently brought a suit against a Missouri statute requiring two-thirds majorities for school bond plebicites on the grounds that it violates a closely related constitutional requirement—equal protection of the laws—by advantaging those who oppose bond issues. Thus, majority rule is left residually as the only permissible procedure for choosing collective policies, since it alone gives no *a priori* advantage to either specific sets of individuals or to sets of individuals who happen to seek retention of the status quo.

The major objection to this argument stems from its dispositional character. Members are equal up to the point of decision, at which time some members have their way and others don't. Equality of weights is one thing, equality of satisfactions another, and the former does not guarantee the latter. This is the basis for the very persuasive arguments —offered by theorists like Madison and Calhoun—which treat majority rule as an invitation to tyranny or a "licence to steal." But these arguments lead almost inevitably to the recommendation of restrictive decision procedures, and these open equally promising opportunities for oppressive behavior to the veto groups which they advantage. A vicious circle results, and one is apt to find himself unable to distinguish ethically among decision procedures once he enters into its logic. This suggests that another criterion—not instead of equality, but in addition to it—is required. Our criterion, political individualism, is a second-order criterion of the kind which seems to be required.

A very different (and generally not very helpful) criterion rests on the truth-value of policy outcomes. This criterion presumes that a transcendental criterion of truth exists quite apart from the opinions of the members in a group, then asks how likely each is to "see" this truth, and how likely a decision procedure is to allow these truth-seers to prevail over their misguided fellows. Three related lines of recommendation result. One is the unsophisticated notion that restrictive decision procedures should be adopted, a recommendation which implies that existing policies reflect a successful past effort to attain truthful (or just) policies and should, therefore, be retained unless a near unanimity of opinion gives testimony to the contrary. This line of thought led Rousseau to suggest restrictive decision procedures for serious decisions, and offered the apparent rationale for two-thirds decision in at least one medieval religious group, the Council of Ferrara. A second line of recommendation—exampled by Plato and perhaps by Lenin—runs toward the adoption of hierarchical decision with a cadre of well-schooled truth-seers in command. A third, and more sophisticated line of recommendation finds expression in Condorcet's well-known "jury theorem," which related the probability of a "just" outcome to the probability that each member will act justly and to the decision-rule by which their votes are aggregated. This theorem is interesting largely for the magnifying effect it assigns to the collectivization of choice: a just group is more apt to make just decisions than its individual members, an unjust one more apt to make unjust decisions than its members. And there is a nice conceptual relationship between the jury theorem and Rousseau's work, done at the same time by a kindred soul. Moreover, the theorem results from the first serious attempt to generate probabilistic models of voting bodies.

But this entire corpus of models and recommendations founders on a serious epistemological difficulty: who is to say which is a just or truthful outcome if we have already attributed only probable knowledge of these ideals to the people who make decisions? This question immediately reveals the historical gulf between our own basic assumptions about knowledge and those of our more optimistic forebearers. And the pursuit of these models would carry us quickly into the mouth of what the methodologists call "Mannheim's box," from which the only escape is an unwarranted claim to personal knowledge of transcendent truth. More serious still, from the view of political theory, is the implication that raw conflict of interest—between what one man wants and what another man wants in collective policy—represents mere error of judgment. No one alive in the contemporary world can accept this suggestion and no account of politics which mistakes conflict for error is apt to be at all persuasive.

For these reasons, our approach exfoliates the rationalist approach letting each individual be the judge of his own "truth"—his own wants, ideals, interests. The question about decision procedures is thus transformed from "How do we optimize the correspondence between policy and transcendental truth?" to "How do we optimize the correspondence between policies and individual preferences?" This new question recognizes conflict as a genuine element of political decision, even (in a sense) as its wellspring. And it allows us to consider political actors who are generous or churlish, honest or dishonest, sympathetic or antagonistic: we are able to take people as we find them.

This openness distinguishes our analysis from a third approach which is based on economic individualism. This approach, best known by the seminal work of Buchanan and Tullock (1962), treats politics as a mere extension of competitive market economics, and presumes that people are exclusively concerned with the self-interested maximization of utility in a narrowly economic sense—choosing "more" over "less." We recognize that people, including the members of voting bodies, may, and often do, treat politics as an extension of economic competition. But our analysis is not confined to this possibility, since it recognizes a plethora of other complex and competing forms of motivation, including motives which run counter to economic self-interest. We thus hope to escape an empirical error as well as an ideologically blinding view of political action.

These, then, are the three principle alternatives to our approach, and something is retained from each. The analysis from equality is reflected in our definition of the problem: we are interested in the preferences of a random individual, "ego," and he is equally apt to be any specific member of a group or voting body. This is not just a conceptual linkage, for it commits us to equality as a necessary though insufficient criterion for the choice of decision procedures. And we are interested in correspondence relations analogous to those found in the analysis from truth-value; it is just that we allow members to define their own preferences existentially, rather than imposing a template of truth transcendentally. And this implies an individualism of the kind expressed in the economists' approach to the question, except that we deny the confining assumption that men are driven by economic incentives alone. We turn now to an explanation of the presumptions which underlie the analytic results reported in our paper.

II. MAJORITY RULE AND INDIVIDUAL VALUES

The problem which interests us and our general approach to it, was first presented in Rae (1969, pp. 42-43) as follows:

> Let us suppose that the individual with whom we are concerned has some personal schedule of values. We know nothing about the specific content of his value schedule—its selfishness or altruism, its sophistication or naïvete, its generality or specificity—since this individual, whom we may

call "Ego," is a purely generic figure. We must, however, suppose that his schedule is complete enough that it leads Ego to like or dislike each proposal which comes before the committee. Accordingly, our major assertion is that Ego would like to optimize the correspondence between his preferences and the policies which are imposed by the committee: he wants to have his way by defeating proposals which his values lead him to dislike and by imposing those which they lead him to like. Our major normative assumption is then:

Value Assumption: Ego wishes to optimize the correspondence between his schedule of values and the list of policies which are imposed.

Now let us suppose that Ego looks ahead and contemplates four events which might occur:

A. Ego's value schedule leads him to support a proposal, but it is not imposed.

B. Ego's value schedule leads him to oppose a proposal, but it is imposed.

C. Ego's value schedule leads him to support a proposal, and it is imposed.

D. Ego's value schedule leads him to oppose a proposal, and it is not imposed.

Ego need not be much of a logician to see that our "Value Assumption" will be best served by the frequent occurrence of events *C* and *D*. Since it is also clear that the four classes of events are disjoint, Ego can be sure that a decision-rule which minimizes the summed frequencies of *A* and *B* will also maximize the summed frequences of *C* and *D*. Hence, Ego can see that the lower the frequency of events *A* and *B*, the higher the frequency of *C* and *D*, and the higher the degree of correspondence between his schedule of values and the list of policies imposed by the committee. This leads to a criterion by which Ego may evaluate decision-rules.

Criterion for Choice Between Decision-Rules: One should choose that decision-rule which minimizes the sum of the expected frequencies for (*A*) in which the committee does not impose a policy which his value schedule leads him to support, and (*B*) in which the committee imposes a policy which his value schedule leads him to oppose.

If decision procedures were chosen with certain knowledge about the issues to be decided and distributions of preference for and against change, the choice would be a simple strategic calculation for each individual and no general argument for or against procedures could be given. The choice would then be entirely determined by examining the altogether predictable outcomes of these predictable disputes. But such predictive knowledge cannot generally be assumed. As Buchanan (1966, p. 29) writes:

The center of attention becomes the mental calculus of the individual as he is confronted with a choice among alternative rules for reaching subsequent political decisions. The individual does not know, nor is he able to predict, what particular issues will be presented subsequent to the adoption of the rule. And, even if he [could] predict with some accuracy the sort of issues that may arise, he could hardly predict his own position vis-à-vis the other members of the group.

In what follows, let us assume uncertainty of this sort, and that we are dealing with a voting body, thus eliminating hierarchical alternatives and concentrating on the comparison between majority rule and its more restrictive alternatives. With a voting body of size n, we may define a decision-rule, k, which may take any value—from majority rule to the rule of consensus ($k = n$). We suppose that our voting body confronts an indeterminate sequence of binary choices, the acceptance or rejection of proposed policy changes over time. And, since the sequence of choices is indeterminate, so too are the preferences of the members, including our focal individual, Ego.

We now confront a guessing game about the sequence of disputes to come after a decision-rule has been adopted. And our recommendation of a decision-rule will depend on the guesses we make; but the work done so far on this problem has converged on a probabilistic recommendation of majority rule. These commendations amount to suggestions that this decision-rule is more likely than any other to optimize the correspondence between individual values and policy outcomes, as suggested by the criterion of choice.

The initial analysis began with the convenient though somewhat unconvincing assumption that each member could be assigned the same discrete probability (p) for favoring a given future proposal for policy change. From this, Rae developed the conjecture that majority rule minimized the expected frequencies of events A and B, maximized the correspondence between individual value schedules and policy outcomes. If, for example, each individual is assigned a probability of one-half for voting yes, probability curves of the kind shown in figure 1 result, and the minimum lies at majority rule. This is one not inconsiderable piece of testimony for the optimality of majority rule within the frame of values defined a moment ago. It suggests that this procedure offers the best expected fit between members' values and the policies which result from the aggregation of their preferences. In so far as this is the case, majority rule enjoys a special claim to recommendation.

Rae's conjecture was proved for general n and p by Taylor (1969), and may be taken as given—so far as it goes. But the conjecture is subject to two serious objections: (1) the assumption of identical discrete p's is brittle, and (2) it is not at all clear that the optimality of majority rule does not become trivial as n increases.

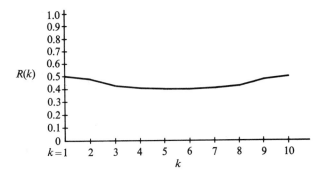

* If $p = 1/2$, then we have previously shown that $R(n) = p - p^n = 1/2 - 1/2^n$, and that $R(1) = (1-p)-(1-p)^n = 1/2 - 1/2^n$. As a representative example, the graph is shown for $n = 10$.

FIGURE 1[a]

The brittle assumption of identical discrete probabilities concerned Curtis (chap. 1 in this volume), who substituted a general array of p's. Curtis, that is, considered a model under which each member might have any given probability for supporting a proposed change of policy ($p_i = 0 \ldots 1$ for the ith member.) He began with a special case in which two factions—"liberal" and "conservative"—were assigned different probabilities of voting yes (p_L and p_C). Having demonstrated the optimality of majority rule for this case, he generalized his argument to a general array of p's ($p_1, \ldots, p_n$) and showed that majority rule remained optimal even for this much less brittle probability model. But, as he recognized, the price of this generalization was a change in the interpretation of the problem. Since no general p could be attributed to the member, no general individual (Ego) could be the object of attention. And, for the same reason, one could not hope to find a recommendation which would apply with equal force to all members. This required a shift from a generic individual to an average individual, from individual values to collective ones. Curtis's interesting paper explores the resulting difficulties.

But what interests us here is the second objection to the initial result. For the identical discrete p model, it is clear that size has a depressive effect on the marginal advantage offered by majority rule. Thus, for example, the difference in the expected frequencies of events A and B under majority rule and under the most restrictive alternative ($k = n$) declines as n increases, thus:[1]

---

[1] In computing the values in this table we have assumed that $p = 1/2$. These figures differ slightly from those given by Rae (1969); see section 3 below.

Size (n)	Expected frequency for majority rule	Expected frequency for rule of consensus ($k = n$)	Difference Marginal advantage of majority rule
3	.25	.375	.125
5	.31	.47	.16
7	.35	.50	.15
9	.37	.50	.13
11	.39	.50	.11

From this table it appears that the difference between the expected frequency of disappointment for majority rule and the expected frequency for the rule of consensus decreases as n increases. In section 3 we suggest that this difference can be regarded as a measure of the advantage of majority rule. We formalize this notion, and show that the advantage does become vanishingly small as the size of the voting body increases, for any discrete and constant probability p.

In section 4 we consider a slightly different situation. Suppose as before that each member of the voting body has the same probability p of supporting an issue, but that the issues evoke responses such that the p's (across the issues) are distributed by a probability density function $f(p)$. For each issue majority rule will be optimal (as already shown in section 3). We wish then to examine the marginal advantage of majority rule over any other decision-rule. If the issues are presented to the voting body in a random fashion then the distribution of p's across the issues should resemble a normal distribution. As examples, two convex, symmetric density functions are chosen, both resembling the normal distribution, and it is shown that the marginal advantage does not approach zero for large n. We conjecture that the marginal advantage is significant for any continuous distribution of p, even one that is nonsymmetric, and for any size of voting body.

III. THE DECISION RULE WITH A DISCRETE PROBABILITY

The probability that Ego votes for a proposal that is not imposed is given by the sum of the probabilities that Ego, together with ($f - 1$) members of the voting body, votes for the proposal, where f is less than the decision-rule k. If p is the probability that a member votes for the proposal, then:

$$P(A) = \sum_{f=1}^{k-1} \binom{n-1}{f-1} p^f (1 - p)^{n-f}.$$

The probability that Ego votes against a proposal that is imposed, is given by the sum of the probabilities that f members of the voting body, excluding Ego, vote for the proposal, where f is greater than or equal to the decision-rule k. Then:

$$P(B) = \sum_{f=k}^{n-1} \binom{n-1}{f} p^f (1-p)^{n-f}.$$

To find the value of k that minimizes the probability that Ego will be disappointed, we write $P(A) + P(B)$ as a function of k, giving:

$$R(k) = \sum_{f=1}^{k-1} \binom{n-1}{f-1} p^f (1-p)^{n-f} + \sum_{f=k}^{n-1} \binom{n-1}{f} p^f (1-p)^{n-f}. \quad (1)$$

Rae evaluated $R(k)$ in the case $p = 1/2$, for small values of n. His function was slightly different in that the case in which no one votes for a proposal was ignored. We include this possibility in order to handle the general problem of $p \neq 1/2$. Rae's results indicated that $R(k)$ is in fact minimized when k was majority rule. Michael Taylor (1969) verified this formally for all discrete p and all n. We give an alternative proof of the lemma, and use the same method to explore the questions raised in the previous section.

LEMMA. The decision-rule that minimizes the disappointment to Ego, when the probability p is discrete, is given by majority rule, $k = (n/2) = \mathbf{k}$.

PROOF. If $R(k)$ is a minimum for some value of k, then $R(k) \leq R(k-1)$ and $R(k) \leq R(k+1)$.

$$R(k) = \sum_{f=1}^{k-1} \binom{n-1}{f-1} p^f (1-p)^{n-f} + \sum_{f=k}^{n-1} \binom{n-1}{f} p^f (1-p)^{n-f}.$$

$$R(k-1) = \sum_{f=1}^{k-2} \binom{n-1}{f-1} p^f (1-p)^{n-f} + \sum_{f=k-1}^{n-1} \binom{n-1}{f} p^f (1-p)^{n-f}.$$

Therefore

$$0 \geq R(k) - R(k-1) = p^{k-1}(1-p)^{n-k+1}\left[\binom{n-1}{k-2} - \binom{n-1}{k-1} \right].$$

Thus

$$\binom{n-1}{k-2} - \binom{n-1}{k-1} \leq 0,$$

so that

$$\frac{1}{k-1} \geq \frac{1}{n-k+1} \quad \text{or} \quad 2k \leq n+2.$$

$$R(k+1) = \sum_{f=1}^{k} \binom{n-1}{f-1} p^f (1-p)^{n-f} + \sum_{f=k+1}^{n-1} \binom{n-1}{f} p^f (1-p)^{n-f}.$$

Therefore

$$0 \geq R(k) - R(k+1) = p^k(1-p)^{n-k} \left(\begin{matrix} n-1 \\ k \end{matrix} \right) - \left(\begin{matrix} n-1 \\ k-1 \end{matrix} \right)$$

Thus

$$\left(\begin{matrix} n-1 \\ k-1 \end{matrix} \right) - \left(\begin{matrix} n-1 \\ k \end{matrix} \right) \geq 0,$$

so that

$$\frac{1}{k} \leq \frac{1}{n-k} \quad \text{or} \quad 2k \geq n.$$

$R(k)$ is therefore minimized for values of k such that $n \leq 2k \leq n+2$. If k satisfies these inequalities we will write $k = \mathbf{k}$.

If n is odd, take $\mathbf{k} = (n+1)/2$, so that $n < 2k < n+2$. In this case we have the strict inequalities $R(\mathbf{k}) < R(\mathbf{k}-1)$ and $R(\mathbf{k}) < R(\mathbf{k}+1)$, so that $R(k)$ is minimized for $k = \mathbf{k} = (n+1)/2$.

If n is even, take $\mathbf{k} = n/2$, so that $n = 2k < n+2$. In this case we have $R(\mathbf{k}) < R(\mathbf{k}-1)$ and $R(\mathbf{k}) = R(\mathbf{k}+1)$.

From now on, we will use $\mathbf{k}$ to represent the value of k such that $\mathbf{k} = (n+1)/2$ if n is odd, and $\mathbf{k} = n/2$ for n even. In other words $\mathbf{k} = (n/2)$ is the smallest integer equal to or greater than $n/2$.[2]

We have now demonstrated that majority rule is optimal in the sense that it gives the decision-rule with the lowest probability that a generic individual will be disappointed. However we will show that the advantage becomes negligible as the size of the voting body increases. To do this we must consider three possibilities for the value of p.

1. If $p = 1/2$, then the graph of $R(k)$ against k will be symmetric about $k = (n+1)/2$. An example is given in figure 1 for $n = 10$. From equation (1) taking $k = n$, we find that[3]

$$R(n) = \sum_{f=1}^{n-1} \left(\begin{matrix} n-1 \\ f-1 \end{matrix} \right) p^f (1-p)^{n-f} = p - p^n. \tag{2}$$

Similarly, if we put $k = 1$ in equation (1), we find that

---

[2] Note that the following analysis would give the same conclusions if we had taken $\mathbf{k} = (n/2) + 1$ for n even. We use $\mathbf{k} = n/2$ to simplify the presentation.

[3] Note that equation (2) is simply obtained as follows:

$$R(n) = \sum_{f=1}^{n-1} \left(\begin{matrix} n-1 \\ f-1 \end{matrix} \right) p^f (1-p)^{n-f} = p \sum_{f=1}^{n-1} \left(\begin{matrix} n-1 \\ f-1 \end{matrix} \right) p^{f-1} (1-p)^{n-f} = p\{1 - p^{n-1}\} = p - p^n.$$

Equation (3) is obtained in an analogous manner.

$$R(1) = \sum_{f=1}^{n-1} \binom{n-1}{f} p^f (1-p)^{n-f} = (1-p) - (1-p)^n. \tag{3}$$

Therefore

$$R(n) - R(1) = (2p-1) + (1-p)^n - p^n. \tag{4}$$

If $p = 1/2$, then $R(n) - R(1) = 0$.

Similarly, if $p = 1/2$, we can show that $R(n-r) = R(1+r)$ for r between 0 and $(n/2)$. Hence the graph of $R(k)$ against k will be symmetric for $p = 1/2$.

If we can show that $R(n) - R(\mathbf{k}) = R(1) - R(\mathbf{k})$ approaches zero as n increases, this will indicate that $R(k)$ is a constant for n infinite. In other words all decision-rules are identical in the disappointment they cause to Ego, as the size of the voting body increases.

We can therefore use $R(n) - R(\mathbf{k}) = R(1) - R(\mathbf{k})$ as an indication of the marginal advantage of the decision-rule $\mathbf{k}$, if $p = 1/2$.

2. If p is greater than 1/2, then from equation (4), $R(n) - R(1) = (2p-1) + (1-p)^n - p^n$ will be greater than 0, so that $R(1) < R(n)$. The graph of $R(k)$ against k will then be skew symmetric. An example is given in figure 2 for $n = 10$. If we can show that $R(1) - R(\mathbf{k})$ approaches zero as n increases, this will indicate that $R(k)$ is constant, for k between 1 and $\mathbf{k}$, for very large n. Thus as n increases, the advantage of majority rule over any decision-rule less than $\mathbf{k}$ becomes negligible.

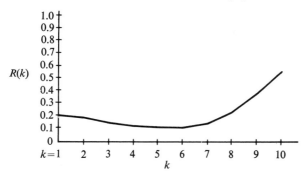

* If $p > 1/2$, then $R(n) > 1/2$, and $R(1) < 1/2$. For example, if $n = 10$ the graph is skew, and resembles the curve shown.

FIGURE 2[a]

3. If p is less than 1/2, then from equation (4), $R(n) - R(1) = (2p-1) + (1-p)^n - p^n < 0$, so that $R(n) < R(1)$. The graph of $R(k)$ against k will again be skew symmetric (cf. figure 3 for $n = 10$).

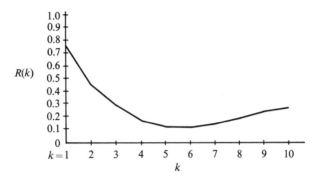

* If $p < 1/2$, then $R(n) < 1/2$, and $R(1) > 1/2$. For example, if $n = 10$ the graph is skew, and resembles the curve shown.

FIGURE 3[a]

If $R(n) - R(k)$ approaches zero, as n increases, then the advantage of majority rule over any decision-rule greater than **k** becomes negligible.

We will therefore take the value minimum $[R(n) - R(k), R(1) - R(k)]$ as an indication of the marginal advantage of majority rule **k**. Having evaluated this, we will give an approximation which allows us to study its behavior for large n.

LEMMA. Let **k** be the value of k corresponding to majority rule. Let the advantage to Ego of majority rule be $A(n) = $ minimum $[R(n) - R(k), R(1) - R(k)]$. Then this advantage approaches zero, for any discrete p, as n increases.

PROOF. From equations (1) and (2):

$$R(n) - R(k) = \sum_{f=1}^{n-1} \binom{n-1}{f-1} p^f(1-p)^{n-f} - \sum_{f=1}^{k-1} \binom{n-1}{f-1} p^f(1-p)^{n-f}$$

$$- \sum_{f=k}^{n-1} \binom{n-1}{f} p^f(1-p)^{n-f}$$

$$= \sum_{f=k}^{n-1} \left[\binom{n-1}{f-1} - \binom{n-1}{f} \right] p^f(1-p)^{n-f}$$

$$= p \sum_{f=k+1}^{n-1} \binom{n-1}{f-1} p^{f-1}(1-p)^{n-f} + \binom{n-1}{k-1} p^k(1-p)^{n-k}$$

$$- (1-p) \sum_{f=k}^{n-2} \binom{n-1}{f} p^f(1-p)^{n-f-1} - (1-p)p^{n-1}$$

$$R(n) - R(k) = (2p-1) \sum_{f=k}^{n-2} \binom{n-1}{f} p^f(1-p)^{n-f-1}$$

$$+ \binom{n-1}{k-1} p^k(1-p)^{n-k} - p^{n-1}(1-p). \tag{5}$$

Similarly from equations (1) and (3):

$$R(1) - R(k) = \sum_{f=1}^{n-1} \binom{n-1}{f} p^f (1-p)^{n-f} - \sum_{f=1}^{k-1} \binom{n-1}{f-1} p^f (1-p)^{n-f}$$

$$- \sum_{f=k}^{n-1} \binom{n-1}{f} p^f (1-p)^{n-f}$$

$$= \sum_{f=1}^{k-1} \left[\binom{n-1}{f} - \binom{n-1}{f-1} \right] p^f (1-p)^{n-f}$$

$$= (1-2p) \sum_{f=1}^{k-1} \binom{n-1}{f} p^f (1-p)^{n-f-1}$$

$$+ \binom{n-1}{k-1} p^{k-1}(1-p)^{n-k+1} - p(1-p)^{n-1}. \qquad (6)$$

If we take $p = 1/2$, then equation (5) becomes

$$R(n) - R(k) = \binom{n-1}{k-1} p^k (1-p)^{n-k} - p^{n-1}(1-p)$$

$$= \left(\frac{1}{2}\right)^n \left[\binom{n-1}{k-1} - 1 \right].$$

Similarly

$$R(1) - R(k) = \binom{n-1}{k-1} p^{k-1}(1-p)^{n-k+1} - p(1-p)^{n-1}$$

$$= \left(\frac{1}{2}\right)^n \left[\binom{n-1}{k-1} - 1 \right].$$

In both equations (5) and (6) the first term of the expression becomes zero if $p = 1/2$.

i) To prove the lemma for $p = 1/2$, we must take $k = \mathbf{k}$, and let n approach infinity. The advantage will then be

$$A(n) = R(n) - R(\mathbf{k}) = R(1) - R(\mathbf{k}) = \left(\frac{1}{2}\right)^n \left[\binom{n-1}{\mathbf{k}-1} - 1 \right],$$

and we must now evaluate $\underset{n\to\infty}{\text{Limit}} A(n)$. We use De Moivre's Theorem which states that

$$\binom{m}{r} p^r (1-p)^{m-r} \simeq \frac{1}{\sqrt{[2\pi m p(1-p)]}} \exp\left[-\frac{1}{2} \frac{(r-mp)^2}{mp(1-p)} \right] \quad \text{as } m \to \infty$$

If n is odd, then we substitute $m = n-1 = 2\mathbf{k} - 2$, $r = \mathbf{k} - 1$, $p = (1-p) = 1/2$, to obtain $A(n)$.

$$A(n) = \left(\frac{1}{2}\right)^n\left[\binom{n-1}{k-1} - 1\right]$$

$$\simeq \frac{\frac{1}{2}}{\sqrt{[2\pi(2k-2)\frac{1}{2}\frac{1}{2}]}}\left[\exp\left\{-\frac{1}{2}\frac{[(k-1)-\frac{1}{2}(2k-2)]^2}{(2k-2)\frac{1}{2}\frac{1}{2}}\right\}\right.$$

$$\left. - \exp\left\{-\frac{1}{2}\frac{[(2k-2)-\frac{1}{2}(2k-2)]^2}{(2k-2)\frac{1}{2}\frac{1}{2}}\right\}\right]$$

$$= \frac{\frac{1}{2}}{\sqrt{[\pi(k-1)]}}[1 - \exp(1-k)].$$

However the exponential term approaches zero very much faster than any geometric term, and we can therefore ignore it in the expression for $A(n)$ with n very large.

$$A(n) \simeq \frac{\frac{1}{2}}{\sqrt{[\pi\frac{1}{2}(n-1)]}} = 1/\sqrt{[2\pi(n-1)]}.$$

If n is even we can repeat this substitution with $m = n - 1 = 2k - 1$, $r = k - 1$, and $p = 1/2$. Hence

$$A(n) = \left(\frac{1}{2}\right)^n\left[\binom{n-1}{k-1} - 1\right]$$

$$\simeq \frac{\frac{1}{2}}{\sqrt{[2\pi(2k-1)\frac{1}{2}\frac{1}{2}]}}\left[\exp\left\{-\frac{1}{2}\frac{[(k-1)-\frac{1}{2}(2k-1)]^2}{(2k-1)\frac{1}{2}\frac{1}{2}}\right\}\right.$$

$$\left. - \exp\left\{-\frac{1}{2}\frac{[(2k-1)-\frac{1}{2}(2k-1)]^2}{(2k-2)\frac{1}{2}\frac{1}{2}}\right\}\right]$$

$$\simeq \frac{\frac{1}{2}}{\sqrt{[\pi\frac{1}{2}(n-1)]}}[\exp(-1/(4k-2)) - \exp(\frac{1}{2}-k)]$$

$$\simeq 1/\sqrt{[2\pi(n-1)]}$$

Here we use the fact that $\exp(-1/(4k-2))$ approaches 1 as n approaches infinity. Then for large n the marginal advantage of majority rule is given by $A(n) \simeq 1/\sqrt{[2\pi(n-1)]}$, if $p = 1/2$.

We have obtained an approximate value for the marginal advantage of the use of majority rule. This approximation is valid for large n, and in fact gives $A(n)$ to within one percent for n as low as ten. The expression for $A(n)$ obviously approaches zero as n approaches infinity. We can therefore say that for very large n and p equal to one-half, the marginal advantage of majority rule becomes negligible. Note that this bound on $A(n)$ can be regarded as the utility to each individual of the use of majority rule. If the individual utilities can be aggregated over the whole voting body then the total utility of the use of majority rule is of the order of

$$\frac{n}{\sqrt{[2\pi(n-1)]}} \simeq \frac{\sqrt{n}}{\sqrt{2\pi}}.$$

This is an increasing function of n, and suggests that majority rule is advantagous for large n in this sense.

ii) If $p > 1/2$, we wish to evaluate $R(1) - R(\mathbf{k})$. The first term in equation (6) will be negative. Consider $p^{k-1}(1 - p)^{n-k+1}$ in the second term. It can be shown that $p^r(1 - p)^{n-r}$ is maximal at $r = np$. Here we have $r = \mathbf{k} - 1$. If n is even, then $r = \mathbf{k} - 1 = \frac{1}{2}n - 1 = n(1/2 - 1/n)$. So the term $p^{k-1}(1 - p)^{n-k+1}$ is maximized at $p = 1/2 - 1/n$. But $p > 1/2$, so $p^{k-1}(1 - p)^{n-k+1} \leqq (1/2)^n$ if n is even. Similarly if n is odd, $r = \mathbf{k} - 1 = \frac{1}{2}(n + 1) - 1 = n(1/2 - 1/2n)$, so $p^{k-1}(1 - p)^{n-k+1}$ is maximized at $p = 1/2 - 1/2n$. For $p > 1/2$, $p^{k-1}(1 - p)^{n-k+1} \leqq (1/2)^n$. The third term $p(1 - p)^{n-1}$ will be small for large n, and can therefore be ignored. We have therefore shown that for large n, $R(1) - R(\mathbf{k}) \leqq \binom{n-1}{k-1}(1/2)^n$ if $p > 1/2$.

iii) Similarly, if $p < 1/2$, we wish to evaluate $R(n) - R(\mathbf{k})$. The first term in equation (5) will be negative. Consider $p^k(1 - p)^{n-k}$ in the second term. For n even, $\mathbf{k} = n/2$, so this expression is maximal at $p = 1/2$. But we have assumed that $p < 1/2$, so $p^k(1 - p)^{n-k} \leqq (1/2)^n$. For n odd, $\mathbf{k} = \frac{1}{2}(n + 1)$, so the expression is maximal at $p = 1/2 + 1/2n$. But $p < 1/2$, so that $p^k(1 - p)^{n-k} \leqq (1/2)^n$.

The third term $p^{n-1}(1 - p)$ will be small for large n, and we will ignore it. We have also shown that for large n, $R(n) - R(\mathbf{k}) \leqq \binom{n-1}{k-1}(1/2)^n$, if $p < 1/2$.

The marginal advantage of majority rule is thus given by $A(n) = \min [R(n) - R(\mathbf{k}), R(1) - R(\mathbf{k})]$, and we have established an upper bound on $A(n)$ and shown it to be $\binom{n-1}{k-1}(1/2)^n$. We can use the same approximation theorem as above to show that this bound is given approximately by $1/\sqrt{[2\pi(n - 1)]}$. This bound approaches zero, as n approaches infinity. For a large voting body, the marginal advantage of majority rule decreases as the size of the body increases, until, it becomes negligible. If p is greater than 1/2, then all decision-rules between 1 and $\mathbf{k}$ are equally optimal. Similarly if p is less than 1/2, all rules between $\mathbf{k}$ and n are equally optimal.

IV. THE DECISION-RULE WITH A PROBABILITY DENSITY FUNCTION ON THE SET OF ISSUES

In this section we assume that all the members of the voting body react with the same probability p of accepting the particular proposal that is before the voting body. However each proposal will provoke a different probability p from the body. These probabilities are assumed to be distributed by a probability density function $f(p)$. For each probability p, we can assume that the probability of disappointment to the generic individual Ego is given by the expression $R(k)$ in equation (1); k is the decision-rule that the voting body is using. If the issues are distributed by $f(p)$, then we can compute the expected value of the disappointment $R(k)$ caused by the decision-rule.

The expected value of the disappointment will be written as $R^*(k)$, and can be expressed as the integral of $R(k)f(p)$ between 0 and 1.

$$R^*(k) = \int_0^1 R(k)f(p)\,dp$$

We have already shown that $R(k)$ is minimized for the value of k corresponding to majority rule, i.e. $k = \mathbf{k}$. $R^*(k)$ will obviously be minimized for the same value of k. We have as yet made no assumptions on the type of density function involved. It must of course have total sum equal to 1. Therefore $\int_0^1 f(p)\,dp = 1$. It may be continuous or have a finite number of discontinuities. We take one of each type in the two examples we consider. If there are a finite number of discontinuities then the integral will be taken to mean a finite sum of integrals, each over a finite interval of p.

Then for any density function $f(p)$

$$R^*(k) = \int_0^1 \left[\sum_{f=1}^{k-1} \binom{n-1}{f-1} p^f (1-p)^{n-f} \right. $$
$$\left. + \sum_{f=k}^{n-1} \binom{n-1}{f} p^f (1-p)^{n-f} \right] f(p)\,dp. \quad (7)$$

We define the marginal advantage of majority rule, as we did in section 3, to be the function $A(n) = \text{minimum}\ [R^*(n) - R^*(\mathbf{k}),\ R^*(1) - R^*(\mathbf{k})]$. In this section we show that the advantage does not become negligible for large n. In other words we must show that $A(n)$ does not approach zero as n approaches infinity. We show this for two typical density functions, both of which are convex and symmetric about $p = 1/2$. They are therefore similar to the normal distribution in character.

The first representative density function is given by $f(p) = 6p(1-p)$, for p between 0 and 1, and zero outside. The integral of this function is $\int_0^1 f(p)\,dp = \int_0^1 6p(1-p)\,dp = 1$, as required. Its graph is presented in figure 4.

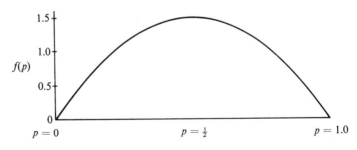

FIGURE 4. Graph of $f(p) = 6p(1-p)$.

LEMMA. If p is distributed by a density function $f(p) = 6p(1 - p)$, then the advantage to Ego of using majority rule is given by $A(n) = R^*(n) - R^*(k) = R^*(1) - R^*(k)$.

This advantage does not approach zero as n approaches infinity.

PROOF. From equation (7), we know that $R^*(k)$ is given by

$$R^*(k) = \int_0^1 \left[\sum_{f=1}^{k-1} \binom{n-1}{f-1} p^f(1-p)^{n-f} + \sum_{f=k}^{n-1} \binom{n-1}{f} p^f(1-p)^{n-f} \right] 6p(1-p) \, dp.$$

If $k = n$, then $R^*(n)$ is given by

$$R^*(n) = \int_0^1 \left[\sum_{f=1}^{n-1} \binom{n-1}{f-1} p^f(1-p)^{n-f} \right] 6p(1-p) \, dp.$$

Therefore

$$R^*(n) - R^*(k) = \int_0^1 \sum_{f=k}^{n-1} \left[\binom{n-1}{f-1} - \binom{n-1}{f} \right] p^f(1-p)^{n-f} 6p(1-p) \, dp.$$

But

$$\int_0^1 p^r(1-p)^s \, dp = \frac{r! \, s!}{(r+s+1)!}.$$

Also

$$\binom{n}{f} - \binom{n-1}{f-1} = \binom{n-1}{f-1}\left\{ \frac{n}{f} - 1 \right\} = \binom{n-1}{f}.$$

Therefore

$$\binom{n-1}{f-1} - \binom{n-1}{f} = \binom{n-1}{f-1} - \binom{n}{f} + \binom{n-1}{f-1} = 2\binom{n-1}{f-1} - \binom{n}{f}.$$

Putting this in the previous expression we obtain

$$R^*(n) - R^*(k) = 6 \sum_{f=k}^{n-1} \left[2\binom{n-1}{f-1} - \binom{n}{f} \right] \frac{(f+1)! \, (n-f+1)!}{(n+3)!}. \quad (8)$$

If $k = 1$, then from the above expression for $R^*(k)$, $R^*(1)$ is given by

$$R^*(1) = \int_0^1 \left[\sum_{f=1}^{n-1} \binom{n-1}{f} p^f(1-p)^{n-f} \right] 6p(1-p) \, dp.$$

Therefore

$$R^*(1) - R^*(k) = \int_0^1 \sum_{f=1}^{k-1} \left[\binom{n-1}{f} - \binom{n-1}{f-1} \right] p^f(1-p)^{n-f} 6p(1-p) \, dp$$

$$= 6 \sum_{f=1}^{k-1} \left[\binom{n}{f} - 2\binom{n-1}{f-1} \right] \frac{(f+1)! \, (n-f+1)!}{(n+3)!}. \quad (9)$$

If $k = \mathbf{k} = (n/2)$, then the expressions (8) and (9) are identical, so that $R^*(1) - R^*(\mathbf{k}) = R^*(n) - R^*(\mathbf{k})$. In appendix I we show that $A(n) = R^*(n) - R^*(\mathbf{k})$ approaches $6(1/2)^5 \simeq 0.19$, as n approaches infinity.

With this density function on the set of issues, the marginal advantage is always non-zero, for any size of voting body.

The second representative density function is given by taking $f(p)$ to be $\binom{m}{a}(1/2)^m$, for $p \in (a/(m+1), (a+1)/(m+1))$. Any integral value between 0 and m can be taken by a. Here m is a parameter which can be varied to change the function $f(p)$. The density function $f(p)$ has mean $p = 1/2$, and variance $\sigma = \frac{1}{2}\sqrt{m}$. As the parameter $m \to \infty$, then the distribution approaches that of a discrete $p = 1/2$. The marginal advantage should in this case approach zero, for large n, to agree with the conclusion of section 3.

If the parameter $m = 0$, then $f(p) = 1$, for all p. Therefore all values of p are equally likely. If m lies between 0 and ∞, then $f(p)$ is a step function. The graph of $f(p) = \binom{m}{a}(1/2)^m$, $a \in \{1, 2, \ldots, m\}$, for $m = 10$, is given in figure 5. As $f(p)$ is discontinuous at the values $p = a/(m+1)$, we have to sum the integrals over the continuous intervals in the expression for $R^*(k)$.

From equation (7) we now find that $R^*(k)$ is given by

$$R^*(k) = \sum_{a=0}^{m} \binom{m}{a}\left(\frac{1}{2}\right)^m \int_y^x \left[\sum_{f=1}^{k-1} \binom{n-1}{f-1}p^f(1-p)^{n-f}\right.$$
$$\left. + \sum_{f=k}^{n-1} \binom{n-1}{f}p^f(1-p)^{n-f}\right] dp \quad (10)$$

where $x = (a+1)/(m+1)$ and $y = a/(m+1)$. If we substitute $k = n$ in the above expression we can determine $R^*(n)$. Therefore

$$R^*(n) - R^*(k) = \sum_{a=0}^{m} \binom{m}{a}\left(\frac{1}{2}\right)^m \int_y^x \sum_{f=k}^{n-1} \left[\binom{n-1}{f-1}\right.$$
$$\left. - \binom{n-1}{f}\right]p^f(1-p)^{n-f}\, dp. \quad (11)$$

If we substitute $k = 1$ in equation 10, we can determine $R^*(1)$ and hence $R^*(1) - R^*(k)$. Therefore

$$R^*(1) - R^*(k) = \sum_{a=0}^{m} \binom{m}{a}\left(\frac{1}{2}\right)^m \int_y^x \sum_{f=1}^{n-1} \left[\binom{n-1}{f}\right.$$
$$\left. - \binom{n-1}{f-1}\right]p^f(1-p)^{n-f}\, dp. \quad (12)$$

LEMMA. If the probability p is distributed among the voting body by a density function $f(p) = \binom{m}{a}(1/2)^m$, for $p \in \{a/(m+1), (a+1)/(m+1)\}$,

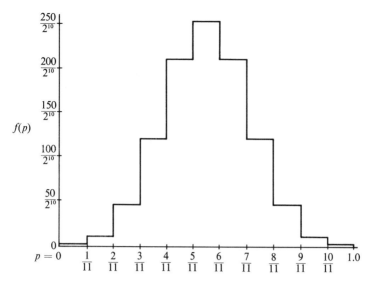

[a] To illustrate $f(p)$ we take m to be 10.

FIGURE 5. Graph of $f(p) = \binom{m}{a}(1/2)^m$ for p belonging to $\{a/m + 1,$ $(a + 1)/(m + 1)\}$.[a]

then the marginal advantage of majority rule is given by $A(n) = R^*(1) - R^*(k)$. As n approaches infinity the marginal advantage approaches $(1/2)^m\{(1/4) - m/[2(1 + m)^2]\}$. This expression is independent of n, and hence the marginal advantage does not become negligible for large n.

PROOF. In appendix II we evaluate equations (11) and (12) to determine $R^*(n) - R^*(k)$ and $R^*(1) - R^*(k)$, as n approaches infinity. There we show that

$$R^*(n) - R^*(k) \longrightarrow \left(\frac{1}{2}\right)^m\left[\frac{1}{4} + \frac{m}{2(1 + m)^2}\right] \quad \text{as } n \longrightarrow \infty$$

$$R^*(1) - R^*(k) \longrightarrow \left(\frac{1}{2}\right)^m\left[\frac{1}{4} - \frac{m}{2(1 + m)^2}\right] \quad \text{as } n \longrightarrow \infty. \quad (13)$$

We can therefore take our marginal advantage $A(n)$ to be $R^*(1) - R^*(k)$, and we have shown it to approach a value that is independent of n. The expression for $A(n)$ can be seen to be positive for all values of m not equal to infinity. If the parameter m is infinite, then the distribution described by $f(p)$ is that of a discrete $p = 1/2$. The expression for $A(n)$ given in (13) then becomes zero, which agrees with the previous result of section 3 that the marginal advantage for discrete p becomes negligible as n increases. If $m \neq \infty$, so that the density function describes a nondiscrete p, then the marginal advantage remains strictly positive. If $m = 0$, the marginal advantage attains its maximum possible value of 1/4. The density function then describes a completely heterogeneous set of issues on which the body must vote. All values of p, which we can regard as the responses of the voting body, are equally likely.[4] As m increases the variance of the density function approaches zero, so that the response of the voting body approaches the single value of $p = 1/2$. In this limiting condition we have shown that for a very large voting body the marginal advantage of majority rule becomes negligible.

V. CONCLUSION

We have shown that majority rule is optimal in that it minimizes a suitable measure of the disappointment caused by the decision-rule. We define the marginal advantage of the choice of the majority rule, and compute it for various possible behavior patterns of the voting body. If the voting body is homogeneous, so that every member responds with the same discrete probability p of accepting a proposal, then the marginal advantage becomes negligible for a large voting body. However, over a set of issues which evoke a probability distribution of p's the marginal advantage remains strictly positive, even when the size of the voting body becomes infinitely large. As the degree of heterogeneity of the issues increases, so that members more often display a probability p further away from one-half, then the marginal advantage increases to its maximal value of 0.25. We hope to consider in a further paper a class of density functions which are concave, with a minimum at $p = 1/2$, and also those density functions which are skew-symmetric. The concave function describes a voting body in which issues are polarized into two groups, one group which is highly supported and a second group which receives little support. We conjecture that any continuous distribution of p will give a marginal advantage that remains strictly positive as the size of the voting body becomes very large.

---

[4] The maximum marginal advantage for any distribution appears to be 0.25. If the distribution becomes more convex or more concave then the advantage decreases.

APPENDIX I

$$R^*(n) - R^*(k) = 6 \sum_{f=k}^{n-1} \left[2\binom{n-1}{f-1} - \binom{n}{f} \right] \frac{(f+1)!\,(n-f+1)!}{(n+3)!}$$

$$= 6 \frac{(n-1)!}{(n+3)!} \sum_{f=k}^{n-1} [(n-f+1)(f+1)f$$

$$- (f+1)(n-f+1)(n-f)]$$

$$= 6 \frac{(n-1)!}{(n+3)!} \sum_{f=k}^{n-1} [3nf(f+1) - 2(f+1)f$$

$$- n(n+1)(f+1)]$$

$$= 6 \frac{(n-1)!}{(n+3)!} \left[n^2(n^2-1) - nk(k^2-1) \right.$$

$$- \frac{1}{2}n(n-1)(n-2)(n+1) + \frac{1}{2}k(k-1)(k-2)(k+1)$$

$$\left. - \frac{1}{2}n^2(n+1)^2 + \frac{1}{2}n(n+1)k(k+1) \right].$$

For large n we can take **k** to be $n/2$. Therefore

$$R^*(n) - R^*(\mathbf{k}) \simeq 6\{n[n^3 - (\tfrac{1}{2}n)^3] - \tfrac{1}{2}[n^4 - (\tfrac{1}{2}n)^4] - \tfrac{1}{2}n^2[n^2 - (\tfrac{1}{2}n)^2]\}/n^4$$

$$= 6\{[1 - (\tfrac{1}{2})^3] - \tfrac{1}{2}[1 - (\tfrac{1}{2})^4] - \tfrac{1}{2}[1 - (\tfrac{1}{2})^2]\}$$

$$= 6/32 \simeq 0.19.$$

APPENDIX II

$$R^*(n) - R^*(k)$$

$$= \sum_{a=0}^{m} \binom{m}{a} \int_0^1 \sum_{f=k}^{n-1} \left[\binom{n-1}{f-1} - \binom{n-1}{f} \right] p^f (1-p)^{n-f} \, dp \left(\frac{1}{2} \right)^m$$

$$= \left(\frac{1}{2} \right)^m \sum_{a=0}^{m} \binom{m}{a} \int_{a/(m+1)}^{(a+1)/(m+1)} \sum_{f=k}^{n-1} \frac{(2f-n)}{n} \binom{n}{f} p^f (1-p)^{n-f} \, dp$$

$$= \sum_{a=0}^{m} \left(\frac{1}{2} \right)^m \binom{m}{a} \left[\sum_{f=k}^{n-1} \frac{(2f-n)}{n} \binom{n}{f} \right]$$

$$\times \sum_{r=0}^{n-f} \left[p^{f+r+1}(1-p)^{n-f-r} \frac{f!\,(n-f)!}{(n-f-r)!\,(f+r+1)!} \right] \Bigg|_{p=a/(m+1)}^{p=(a+1)/(m+1)}$$

$$= \sum_{f=k}^{n-1} \frac{2f-n}{n(n+1)} \left\{ 1 + \sum_{r=0}^{n-f} \binom{n+1}{f+r+1} \right.$$

$$\left. \times \sum_{a=1}^{m} \left[\binom{m}{a-1} - \binom{m}{a} \right] \left(\frac{a}{m+1} \right)^{f+r+1} \left(1 - \frac{a}{m+1} \right)^{n-f-r} \left(\frac{1}{2} \right)^m \right\}.$$

(Introduce the dummy variable $x = f + r + 1$)

$$(*) = \sum_{a=1}^{m} \left[\binom{m}{a-1} - \binom{m}{a} \right] \left(\frac{1}{2} \right)^m \sum_{f=k}^{n-1} \frac{2f-n}{n(n+1)}$$

$$\times \sum_{x=f+1}^{n+1} \binom{n+1}{x} \left(\frac{a}{m+1} \right)^x \left(1 - \frac{a}{m+1} \right)^{n+1-x} + \sum_{f=k}^{n-1} \frac{2f-n}{n(n+1)} \left(\frac{1}{2} \right)^m$$

$$= \left(\frac{1}{2} \right)^m \frac{(k-1)(n-k)}{n(n+1)} + \sum_{a=1}^{m} \left[\binom{m}{a-1} - \binom{m}{a} \right] \left(\frac{1}{2} \right)^m$$

$$\times \left\{ \sum_{x=k+1}^{n} \left[\frac{x(x-1) - nx + (k + kn - k^2)}{n(n+1)} \right] \right.$$

$$\times \binom{n+1}{x} \left(\frac{a}{m+1} \right)^x \left(1 - \frac{a}{m+1} \right)^{n+1-x} - \frac{n}{n+1} \left(\frac{a}{m+1} \right)^{n+1} \right\}$$

$$= \left(\frac{1}{2} \right)^m \frac{(k-1)(n-k)}{n(n+1)} + \sum_{a=1}^{m} \left[\binom{m}{a-1} - \binom{m}{a} \right] \left[\frac{1}{2} \left(\frac{a}{m+1} \right)^2 \right.$$

$$\left. - \frac{1}{2} \frac{a}{m+1} - \frac{n}{n+1} \left(\frac{a}{m+1} \right)^{n+1} + \frac{1}{2} \frac{(k + kn - k^2)}{n(n+1)} \right] \left(\frac{1}{2} \right)^m$$

$$= \left(\frac{1}{2} \right)^m \left[\frac{1}{4} + \frac{m}{2(1+m)^2} \right] \quad \text{if } n \to \infty, \text{ and } k = \mathbf{k} = n/2.$$

We can evaluate $R^*(1) - R^*(k)$ by the same procedure that leads to (*).

$$R^*(1) - R^*(k)$$

$$= \sum_{a=0}^{m} \binom{m}{a} \left(\frac{1}{2} \right)^m \int_{a/(m+1)}^{(a+1)/(m+1)} \sum_{f=1}^{k-1} \left[\binom{n-1}{f} - \binom{n-1}{f-1} \right] p^f (1-p)^{n-f} \, dp$$

$$= \sum_{a=1}^{m} \left[\binom{m}{a-1} - \binom{m}{a} \right] \left(\frac{1}{2} \right)^m \sum_{f=1}^{k-1} \frac{n-2f}{n(n+1)}$$

$$\times \sum_{x=f+1}^{n+1} \binom{n+1}{x} \left(\frac{a}{m+1} \right)^x \left(1 - \frac{a}{m+1} \right)^{n+1-x} + \frac{1}{2}^m \cdot \frac{(k-1)(n-k)}{n(n+1)}$$

$$= \sum_{a=1}^{m} \left[\binom{m}{a-1} - \binom{m}{a} \right] \left(\frac{1}{2} \right)^m \left[\frac{1}{2} \frac{a}{m+1} - \frac{1}{2} \left(\frac{a}{m+1} \right)^2 \right.$$

$$\left. - \frac{1}{2} \frac{n}{n(n+1)} + \frac{1}{2} \frac{(k-1)(n-k)}{n(n+1)} \right] + \left(\frac{1}{2} \right)^m \frac{(k-1)(n-k)}{n(n+1)}$$

$$= \left(\frac{1}{2} \right)^m \left\{ \frac{1}{4} - \frac{m}{2(1+m)^2} \right\} \quad \text{if } n \to \infty, \text{ and } k = \mathbf{k} = n/2.$$

4. Individual Choice of a Political-Economic Process

CHARLES R. PLOTT

INTRODUCTION

By what means does one determine a rule to use in determining a rule for the making of social decisions? This rather perplexing problem appropriately has the flavor of an infinite regress. Yet, several scholars have attempted to phrase the question in a manner which circumvents the problem. The essay here is a discussion of the broad settings in which the problem has been posed.

An examination of the question calls for the context of the question. Three separate contexts suggest themselves. The first context arises with the "justification" of "social actions" or "decisions." The second arises when one seeks advice on what type of rule he "should" support. The third involves a theory about the type of rules that are "likely" to be "agreed" upon by a group of people.

I

Frequently decisions are "justified" by appeal to the rule, or to the process by which the decision was made. "It's right because the judge says it is!" Naturally, this type of argument calls for a defense of the authority of the rule. "The judge's decision must be accepted because the constitution gives him authority to decide!" Even though this first context of the question has a natural motivation, the modern positivist point of view offers no foundation, unfortunately, for the ultimate justification of a rule. The constitution is simply accepted or rejected by each individual for reasons which are internal to himself. The discussion is simply ended by some practical means. "America! Love it or leave it!" Those who seek a "high authority," or "ultimate justification" free from their (or someone's) value system, are likely to be frustrated. In any case, in this paper the problem will not be addressed from that point of view.

One might seek advice as to the type of decision-making process he should support. An answer to the question from this (second) point of view would necessitate an investigation into his own preferences and motivation. These same variables are involved if a researcher wishes to *predict* the type of process an individual would support. Consequently, this point of view will not be investigated independent of an investigation into the possibility of predicting an individual's preference for processes.

If one is interested in the question from a predictive point of view, several contexts for the question arise. Is one interested in predicting the rules chosen by groups? Or, is one interested in predicting a given individual's attitude, or preference for various rules? An answer to the first appears to presuppose an answer to the second. If the second question is to be attacked, then what will be the parameters on the model? The setting for the individual's deliberations must be specified, together with his information about his environment, and the other individuals likely to be involved in the process. From this scientific point of view we proceed.

II

The first order of business is one of precisely identifying the situation with which an individual finds himself.[1] We suppose E is a universal set of mutually exclusive "social states." A "social state" is a primitive—that is, its interpretation depends upon the context of the problem. For some problems, a social state could be simply a set of bills passed and bills failed. For other problems, it could be a complete description of the amount of each type of commodity consumed by each individual as well as a complete specification of the outputs and inputs of each firm for an arbitrary period into the future. A social state can be just about anything one can imagine consistent with the concept of "the outcome" of a social decision process. In general, however, since the *rules* are used by society to choose from competing social states, the rules *themselves* are not to be included in the *description* of a social state.

---

[1] In developing the formal context for the problem, we follow the structures found in Plott (1971).

An "agenda" v, is a set of social states—a subset of E. The agenda can be considered as a set of "possible" social states. A "decision" must be made as to which member of the "agenda" will prevail. An "agenda" can be viewed as a "situation," or part of the context in which a decision is to be made. In a sense, a "decision," or application of a "decision-rule" is necessary in the first place because the agenda contains more than one element.

Along with the concept of "agenda" we consider the concept of "admissible agenda." We let a family $V = (v_1, \ldots, v_m)$ of agenda, denote the *set* of agenda which could possibly occur. The particular "agenda," v_i, may depend upon such diverse things (or parameters) as the weather, technology, wars, etc., outside the domain of the decision process. As an example, assume the universal set of social states is $E = \{x, y, z, w\}$ and assume $V = (\{x, y, z\}, \{x, z, w\}, \{y, z\})$. For a legislative model, we have assumed there are only four conceivable "legislative actions," x, y, z, w, of which the legislature can decide upon one and only one. Under these assumptions, however, the legislature will never face the four simultaneously. It will face either $\{x, y, z\}$ or $\{x, z, w\}$ or $\{y, z\}$ the particular set faced being, at this time, determined exogenously. I take this to be a proper formalization of the concept of "powers" of the legislature—the specific powers being contingent on "exogenous" factors. The importance of the concept has been recognized by Badger (chap. 2 of this volume) as well as others.

Now a "rule," or process, "picks" a single element from the agenda.[2] If we designate $C(v, \ldots)$ as the "outcome," we require for v in the admissible agenda V, $C(v, \ldots) \in v$. We suppose parameters on the choice are individuals' preference relations over E, $R_1, \ldots, R_n$, where R_i is the preference relation of individual i.[3] We have then, for all $v \in V$, and for all $R_1, \ldots, R_n$, $C(v, R_1, \ldots, R_n) \in v$.[4]

A rule is identified by its *outcomes*. In every possible "situation" the rule dictates a decision or choice. Suppose rule 1 is $C^1(v, R_1 \ldots R_n)$ and rule 2 is $C^2(v, R_1, \ldots, R_n)$, but, for all $v \in V$, and for all $R_1, \ldots, R_n$, we

---

[2] We could assume the result of the application of the rule is one *or more* elements of the agenda. The interpretation would be that the outcome is *any* one of the elements chosen. Models of this type are common (e.g. game theory) where laws governing the outcomes beyond a particular *set* have not been specified or isolated. This slight alteration in assumption would change things significantly and will not be done here.

[3] A "preference relation" is a binary relation R, such that for $\alpha, \beta \in E$ either $\alpha R \beta$ or $\beta R \alpha$, and for $\alpha, \beta, \gamma \in E$, if $\alpha R \beta$ and $\beta R \gamma$ then $\alpha R \gamma$. One can interpret $\alpha R_i \beta$ as "α is preferred or indifferent to β" by individual i. For a more descriptive exposition of "preferences" within the context of a closely related model see Arrow (1963).

[4] Sometimes a rule, together with the "situations" (admissible agenda and admissible individual preferences) in which it operates, is called a *constitution*. For the development of this concept again refer to Plott (1971).

have $C^1(v, R_1, \ldots, R_n) = C^2(v, R_1, \ldots, R_n)$. In this case, we claim they are the same rule. That is, even if "institutional features" of two rules are different, they are considered the same rule if, in every circumstance, they give identical results. The concept of a rule outlined here is very broad. In terms of institutional arrangements, a "rule" could be an organization with a decision-making procedure, or a judge with a specified "view" of the world, or a voting process.

We come now to the central problem to be addressed in this paper— the problem of predicting how an individual will evaluate various rules. Two different approaches can be identified in the literature dealing with political processes. The first is based on the "ethical" properties of the rule. The second is based on an individual's assessment of the "returns" to himself from various rules.

The "ethics approach" proceeds by identifying certain ethical properties of rules.[5] If the individual agrees with certain ethical postulates, then the theory predicts that his choice of rules will be restricted to an identifiable class of rules. For example, a set of necessary and sufficient conditions for simple majority decision has been isolated by May (1952). Murakami (1968) and Fishburn (forthcoming) have isolated necessary and sufficient conditions for a "representative system." DeMeyer and Plott (1971) identify the ethical properties of rules which involve certain weighting schemes.[6]

The fundamental idea behind the ethics approach is not so very different from the way some researchers view decision making under uncertainty. Faced with a problem with no "solution," the individual *resolves* the problem by reference to abstract propositions, together with rules for deduction. For example, while I really have no "preference" over rules, I agree with the abstract proposition "if $R_{f(1)}, \ldots, R_{f(n)}$ is a permutation of $R_1, \ldots, R_n$ then $C(v, R_1, \ldots, R_n)$ should equal $C(v, R_{f(1)}, \ldots, R_{f(n)})$." That is, if individuals "switch" preferences among themselves, choice (selection, outcome) remains the same. This seems to carry the property of "equality" and is, as a matter of fact, a property of majority rule. That is, if individuals "trade" preferences the *number* of people preferring one alternative over the other remains the same and so, under majority rule the outcome is unchanged. The property is labeled "equality" since it means the outcome is independent of "who" has "what" preferences.

The point of the example is that individuals may choose processes on the basis of "properties" of the process as opposed to choosing processes on the basis of a preference for the outcomes of the process. Most (if not all) of the results having a direct bearing on what I am calling the "ethics approach" to predicting choice were not deduced with choice prediction

---

[5] See Plott (1971) for a summary of the many ethical properties which have been isolated.

[6] The interested reader might refer to White (1970) for a very interesting survey of approaches to decision making.

as a purpose of the research. Rather, the problem has been viewed by writers as a somewhat more "purely mathematical" problem of decomposing rules into "component parts." Consequently a unified "theory" is not identifiable in the literature. However, hypotheses concerning preferences for abstract "properties" of processes can be distinguished from hypotheses concerning preferences for the objects of choice since many of the former are asserted to hold regardless of the objects of choice.

The second approach, which has its formal origins with Buchanan and Tullock (1962), views the individual as choosing among rules according to a direct calculation as to which rule affords him the best advantage. Buchanan and Tullock hypothesize the individual perceives a decision-making cost (which is an increasing function of the number of people required to "agree" before an action is taken), and a cost of being exploited by a larger group (which is a decreasing function of the number of people required to "agree" before action is taken). They assert the individual will choose the rule which minimizes the sum of the cost functions. People will always choose, they predict, the rule which affords themselves the greatest net gain.

A problem with the Buchanan-Tullock formulation is that it requires the existence of a well-defined status quo in terms of his own "belongs," his own attitudes and the attitudes of others. Before an individual can perceive himself as being exploited by a larger coalition, and calculating a value of that exploitation, he must have some idea of the things he has which can be taken from him, as well as his preferences regarding these things. At a constitutional stage, the rights and possessions of an individual, vis-à-vis the group, are not always so clear. Furthermore, since a decision-making rule is defined for situations when an individual's preferences are not what they are at the time of choosing the rule, the assumptions being made by Buchanan and Tullock about individuals' preferences are unclear.

An example may help make this last point clear. Suppose an individual's perferences are, at the time of choosing a rule, $R_i = [a \ P_i \ b \ P_i \ c \ P_i \ d]$. Now, given the current "situation," rule 1 chooses b and rule 2 chooses c. But, other things equal, if the individual's preference changes to $[d \ P_i \ c \ P_i \ b \ P_i \ a]$, rule 1 still chooses b but rule 2 chooses d. Which rule does he prefer? The procedure seems to call for a valuation in terms of current preferences of the various choices when one's preferences are something different than what they are currently. Valuations of this type, to my knowledge, have not been investigated, and the foundations of this procedure, in the current theory of preference, are not obvious.

III

The Curtis, Badger, and Schofield papers (chaps. 1-3 in this volume) pose the problem somewhat differently. However, the problems outlined above are not completely eliminated. We outline here a model for which their models are a very special case and in which at least a definite stand is taken on the issues raised above.

Assume both the agenda, v, and the vector of individuals' preferences $(R_1, \ldots, R_n)$, are random variables.[7] The individual, say α, is assumed to perceive a (perhaps subjective)[8] joint, multivariate distribution $P(v, R_1, \ldots, R_n)$. That is, $P(\hat{v}, \hat{R}_1, \ldots, \hat{R}_n)$ is the probability that the agenda will be $\hat{v}$, and individual 1 will have preference relation $\hat{R}_1$, and $\ldots$, and individual α will have preference relation $\hat{R}_\alpha$, and $\ldots$, and individual n will have preference relation $\hat{R}_n$. The individual views the agenda, his (future) preferences and the preferences of others as random variables.[9]

The starting point here is important. The distribution $P(v, R_1, \ldots, R_n)$ is our given individual's "view" of the world. He is postulated to have a view about the powers of the decision-making body and the actions he might expect others to take—how those powers may be used. This view of the world, together with his "preferences" are the foundations upon which his postulated behavior rests—i.e., the place where the theory begins. In order to make the nature of the model clear one can imagine a sequence of time periods. A single decision is to be made during each period. For each period the probability that the agenda will be $\hat{v}$ and the vector of individuals' preferences is $\hat{R}_1, \ldots, \hat{R}_n$ is given by $P(\hat{v}, \hat{R}_1, \ldots, \hat{R}_n)$. From this joint distribution we can deduce the marginal distributions for v and for $(R_1, \ldots, R_n)$.

The marginal distribution for v,

$$P(v) = \sum_{R_1 \in D} \sum_{R_2 \in D} \cdot \cdot \sum_{R_n \in D} P(v, R_1, \ldots, R_n)$$

$D =$ the set of all binary relations over E which have the properties of "preferences." That is, it is the set of all "conceivable" preference relations over E.

represents α's view of the "natural forces" which determine the "powers" of the legislature. This distribution indicates the probability (from the individual's view) that any particular agenda, v, will occur. While v may indicate the "powers" of the legislature, it is from the distribution $P(v)$

---

[7] In order to avoid notational problems and special assumptions, we will simply assume all variables are discrete.

[8] Whether the "probabilities" are subjective or objective makes little difference to the analysis. We are asserting a behavioral model. That an individual's feelings about "likeness" of various events conform to the laws of probability is simply one of the maintained hypotheses.

[9] There is no need to assume behavior is probabilistic at the time of choice. Choice and preference may be viewed as deterministic but at the time a rule is being chosen the values taken by the parameters dictating preference may be known only up to some probabilistic laws. Thus, since preferences are functions of random variables, they, themselves, are random variables.

that the individual must estimate the relative frequency with which certain "powers" occur. It is here that we record α's view of the relative frequency with which decisions over certain "sensitive" issues will be made.

The marginal distribution of $R_1, \ldots, R_n$ is deduced from $P(v, R_1, \ldots, R_n)$ as

$$P(R_1, \ldots, R_n) = \sum_{v \in V} P(v, R_1, \ldots, R_n).$$

This distribution $P(R_1, \ldots, R_n)$ indicates the probability that the preference relations of the individuals are $R_1, \ldots, R_n$. It is α's view of the *social* environment in which he is likely to find himself, This is his view of the preference he is likely to have, both absolutely, and relative to the preferences of all other individuals. Notice that the preference relation of individual α as well as the preference relations of the remaining individuals are possibly random. Of course, since the form of $P(R_1, \ldots, R_n)$ is not specified we have as a special possibility the case where α has a specific preference with certainty. We also have cases where α's preference is correlated with the preferences of others. In fact, the individual could view himself as always being in the "minority" and thus having preference for "rules" influenced by this point of view.

With these assumptions, a given rule induces a probability distribution over the elements of E. For $x \in E$ and for rule $C^i(\cdot, \ldots)$ we compute $P(x \,; i)$, the probability that social state x occurs given that the rule is $C^i(\cdot, \ldots)$, as

$$P(x; i) = \sum_{(v, R_1, \ldots, R_n) \in A} P(v, R_1, \ldots, R_n)$$
$$A = [(v, R_1, \ldots, R_n) : x \in C^i(v, R_1, \ldots, R_n)].$$

In a case where there are q rules being considered the procedure defines a family $F = \{P(\cdot \,; 1), P(\cdot \,; 2), \ldots, P(\cdot \,; q)\}$, of probability distributions over the elements of E. There is one probability distribution for each rule.

A preference relation over decision-rules corresponds, then, to a preference relation over $F = \{P(\cdot \,; 1), \ldots, P(\cdot \,; q)\}$. That is, for any preference relation, R, over rules there corresponds a preference relation over F given by $P(\cdot \,; i) \, R \, P(\cdot \,; j)$ if and only if $C^i(\cdot, \ldots) \, R \, C^j(\cdot, \ldots)$. Now, if the preference relation over the elements of F conform to von Neumann-Morgenstern utility theory,[10] we can assert the existence of numbers $u(x)$ such that

$$P(\cdot \,; i) \, R \, P(\cdot \,; j) \iff \sum_x P(x; i) \, u(x) \geq \sum_x P(x; j) \, u(x). \tag{1}$$

---

[10] See, for example, Luce and Raiffa (1957), or for a more advanced and complete discussion, see De Groot (1970).

That is, the individual orders the probability distributions (and thus decision-rules) as if he were ordering according to the expected value of utility. He prefers rule i to rule j if the expected utility under i is greater than the expected utility under j. At this point, we should take care to indicate that the numbers, $u(\cdot)$, are only used as a *numerical representation* of a preference relation. Any linear (affine) transformation of these numbers, $u'(x) = a + b\, u(x)$, will also be a representation. They need have no interpretation *at all* in terms of the "intensity" with which an object is preferred— if indeed this concept has meaning at all.

We now have a general model in which one can talk about the preference for "rules." Indeed we can talk about the "utility" of a rule by defining

$$U[C^i(\cdot, \ldots)] \equiv \sum_x [P(x; i)\, u(x)]. \tag{2}$$

Of course, this definition is subject to the qualifications above.

We are now in a position to overcome part of the difficulties raised in section 2, with the Buchanan and Tullock approach. The individual faces a task of choosing a rule which will be used to decide among alternative social states. The problem is that the individual may not know, at the time of choosing a rule, what his preference for the alternatives will be at the time the rule is applied. According to the Buchanan-Tullock theory the individual computes the loss due to various rules. But, how can "loss" be calculated when the preferences, which serve as a basis for the concept of "loss," are unspecified? This problem is addressed below while a second problem, relating to a problem of the status quo, is covered in the next section.

The first problem, that of specifying preference for rules in the absence of a knowledge of preference over the alternatives, is now addressed. The problem arises when we examine (1) above closely, We were willing to accept the assertion that a preference relation R exists over the probability distributions over E, i.e., we asserted that $P(\cdot; i)\, R\, P(\cdot; j)$ or $P(\cdot; j)\, R\, P(\cdot; i)$. Indeed any consistent choice over rules could be interpreted as the reflection of such a preference. But, in deducing the distribution $P(\cdot; i)$ we assumed the preference relation for α was *random*. What then might be the connection between α's random preferences for the alternatives and α's *fixed* preference over the various probability distributions over the alternatives?

The problem of making a connection between the preference relation over probability distributions over alternatives and the individual's random preference for alternatives will be done in a series of steps. We begin by calculating the conditional probabilities induced over the outcomes, given that the representative individual's (α) preferences are fixed. Let $[1, \ldots,$ $H(m)]$ be an index of the enumeration of all binary relations over E, having the properties of preferences—all conceivable preference relations.

That is, to one (arbitrary) of the conceivable preference relations over E we attach the index 1, to another we attach the number 2, etc., until all of them are indexed. If the number of alternatives in E is m, then we let the number of conceivable preference relations over E be $H(m)$.

We can then calculate the conditional probabilities $P(v, R_1, \ldots, R_n \mid R_\alpha = \gamma)$. That is, we calculate the conditional probability that the agenda is v and that the vector of preference relations is $(R_1, \ldots, R_n)$ *given that* individual α as the preference relation indexed by γ. We can then compute the conditional probability that the state x will be chosen given that the constitution is j *and* given that individual α has the preference relation γ. This conditional probability distribution will be denoted $P^\gamma(x; j)$ and is (notice since α is the only person whose preferences are fixed, there is only need for notation indicating which preference relation he has, γ, and no need for notation indicating it is the preference of α which is fixed) formally defined as

$$P^\gamma(\hat{x}; j) = \sum_{(v, R_1, \ldots, R_n) \in A} P(v, R_1, \ldots, R_n)$$

$$A = [(v, R_1, \ldots, R_{\alpha-1}, \gamma, R_{\alpha+1}, \ldots, R_n): \hat{x} = C^j(v, R_1,$$

$$\ldots, R_{\alpha-1}, \gamma, R_{\alpha+1}, \ldots, R_n)]. \tag{3}$$

This procedure yields a collection of families of probabilities $(B^1, \ldots, B^{H(m)})$ where $H(m)$ is the number of conceivable preference relations α might have, where q is the number of rules to be considered, and where

$$B^\gamma = \begin{bmatrix} b^\gamma_{11} & \cdots & b^\gamma_{1m} \\ \vdots & & \vdots \\ b^\gamma_{q1} & \cdots & b^\gamma_{qm} \end{bmatrix} = \begin{bmatrix} P^\gamma(1; 1) & \cdots & P^\gamma(m; 1) \\ \vdots & & \vdots \\ P^\gamma(1; q) & \cdots & P^\gamma(m; q) \end{bmatrix}. \tag{4}$$

That is B^γ ($\gamma = 1, \ldots, H(m)$) is simply a matrix of numbers. Each row indicates the probability of each of the m alternatives given that one of the q rules has been adopted and given that individual α has the preference relation γ. Each row of B^γ is a probability distribution over the m social states which would exist if the rule indexed by that row were adopted and conditional upon the fact that individual α has preference relation γ (of course γ can take $H(m)$ values so there are $H(m)$ such matrices).

We can now apply von Neumann-Morgenstern utility theory and obtain a family of "utilities" $(U_1, U_2, \ldots, U_{H(m)})$ with

$$U_\gamma = \begin{pmatrix} u_\gamma(1) \\ \vdots \\ u_\gamma(m) \end{pmatrix}, \quad \gamma = 1, 2, \ldots, H(m). \tag{5}$$

So $B^\gamma U_r$ becomes a q-dimensional column vector of expected utilities. Each of the q elements of $B^\gamma U_r$ indicates the expected utility which occurs to α if that rule were adopted and he had preference relation γ. The astute reader will recognize that this interpretation involves a very important assumption. The nature of the assumption will now be elaborated.

For a given ordering over alternative social states there are *many* "utilities" the expected value of which orders the degenerate probability distributions according to the given ordering. That is, a given preference relation over alternative social states under certainty conditions is compatible with many different preference relations over the *lotteries* involving those same alternatives. Stating the problem another way we notice that the fact that an individual has preference relation γ does not provide sufficient information to infer his preferences for lotteries, or probability distributions (except the degenerate ones) over the alternatives. Statement (5) assumes (or asserts) that for each preference relation over the alternatives there is a single, specified attitude toward lotteries over the alternatives. That is, we have asserted that if we know his preference for the objects then, due to an arbitrary restriction, we know the attitudes toward risk (or lotteries).

This admittedly strong assumption can be interpreted as follows. Even though the individual does not know, at the time of choosing a rule, his preference relation for objects, he does know his attitude toward risk. The sense in which this attitude is known is given by (5). Namely, he can compute, for each of his conceivable preferences, the expected "utility" of each of the rules given that he has the specific preference. Part of this problem can be removed by expanding the set of all possible preference relations to include the equivalence classes of von Neumann-Morgenstern utilities over the objects. That is, a preference relation would be a m-tuple of numbers and two m-tuples of numbers would be the same "preference" if they were connected by a positive linear (affine) transformation. If this is done, however, the formulation of the problem loses the attributes of finiteness (the domain of $P(R_1, \ldots, R_n)$ would no longer be finite[11]). This procedure would eliminate the arbitrary assumption under discussion but would complicate the argument, both from a technical and notational point of view, while adding little by way of substance.

We can now demand that (2) satisfy the relationship

$$\sum_x P(x; i)u(x) = \sum_\gamma \phi(\gamma) \sum_x P^\gamma(x; i)u_\gamma(x) \qquad i = 1, 2, \ldots, q \qquad (6)$$

---

[11] The size of the set of possible "preferences" would be nondenumerable. While the binary relation "x is a positive linear (affine) transformation of y" partitions the nonnegative orthant of Euclidian m-space, there is (for $m > 1$) a nondenumerable set of equivalence classes.

where $\phi(\gamma)$ is the probability individual α has preference relation γ,

i.e.,

$$\phi(\gamma) = \sum_{v} \sum_{R_1} \cdots \sum_{R_{\alpha-1}} \sum_{R_{\alpha+1}} \cdots \sum_{R_n} P(v, R_1, \ldots, R_{\alpha-1}, \gamma, R_{\alpha+1}, \ldots, R_n).$$

That is, the "utility function" defined by (2), can be viewed as the expected value of expected utility of the rule. We demand an individual's ordering of rules is based upon the sum, over all preferences, of the probability that preference will occur multiplied by the expected utility of the rule given that α has that particular preference relation. In the matrix notation developed in (4) and (5) equations (6) and (2) become

$$\begin{bmatrix} U(C^1(\cdot, \ldots)) \\ U(C^q(\cdot, \ldots)) \end{bmatrix} = \sum_{\gamma=1}^{H(m)} \phi(\gamma) B^\gamma U_\gamma. \tag{7}$$

From this we can see the "utility" of a rule is the expected value of expected utilities given the rule is adopted.

The relationship (6) is not without consequences. Suppose the set containing the $P(x; i)$ contained all of the probability distributions over the set of alternatives. That is, we assume that for any probability distribution of the alternatives there is a constitution which would induce it. Suppose further the functional $\sum_x P(x; i)u(x)$ represents a preference relation over these probabilities. In this case $u(x)$ would be unique to linear (affine) and *only* linear (affine) transformations[12] and the numerical functions, $u_\gamma(x)$, would be uniquely determined. That is, the functions $u_\gamma(x)$ are subject to no independent transformations at all. These utilities would have the properties of *absolute* utility. In our case, since there are only a finite set of proposed constitutions (a larger set is impossible since the set of social states is finite), we can say only that: (1) linear (affine) transformations of $u(x)$ preserve order; and, (2) both linear (affine) and scalar transformations of $u_\gamma(x)$ exist which alter order (that is, each u_γ would be subject to a different transformation).

While this is a framework for dealing with the problem posed by preference relations, we must still address the problem of the status quo.

IV

Even if an individual's preference relation over social states is known, his evaluation of rules depends upon the social state that exists at the time the rule is to be applied. If the social state is such that I control all resources, I think it safe to assert that I would feel differently about the relative merits of unanimity over majority rule than if the social state was

---

[12] For a proof of this proposition see DeGroot (1970, p. 108).

such that someone else controlled all of the resources. Notice, my opinion about rules differs according to the status quo even if my preference relation over social states remains the same. While I always prefer the state where I have everything to the state where I have nothing, my preference for unanimity over majority rule will depend upon whether the status quo is the first social state or the second. For some purposes this problem might cause no difficulties. If our theorizing is about choice at the constitutional stage, however (as are Buchanan and Tullock), the problem is critical.

In one sense we have already resolved the problem concerning the status quo. Recall we began the argument with a preference relation over the mutually exclusive "social states" or over lotteries involving these states. In the same way that one usually assumes a preference relation over the commodity space is independent of the budget constraint, we assume the preference relation for social states is independent of the existing social state. Since each rule induces (and is evaluated as) a probability distribution over social states, the preference relation for rules is independent of the status quo.

This approach somewhat begs the question, however, in that many rules are *defined* in terms of the status quo. Frequently it is the status quo which prevails in the event of a deadlock. For rules requiring more than a majority, the status quo dominates in the event that neither alternative receives the requisite vote. Any concept of domination, in the binary sense, involves some problem with the status quo in the event the binary relation is not total.

One's imagination, concerning the definition of decision-rules in terms of the status quo, need not stop with binary rules, such as majority, two-thirds, etc. Any choice, of which binary choice is a special case, can be conditioned upon the status quo. In order to see this we simply expand the agenda as follows. Suppose the agenda v_i has elements $\{x_1, x_2, \ldots, x_m\}$. From v_i we generate m new agenda

$$v_{i1} = \{\hat{x}_1, x_2, \ldots, x_m\}, v_{i2} = \{x_1, \hat{x}_2, \ldots, x_m\}, \ldots,$$
$$v_{im} = \{x_1, x_2, \ldots, \hat{x}_m\}.$$

The "hat" indicates that variable designated as the "status quo." In terms of this variable certain "rules" can be defined. Once the status quo is identified, the rule indicates what one must do in order to "get away" from it. For example, consider $v_j = \{x_1, x_2\}$ and $v_{1j} = \{\hat{x}_1, x_2\}$ and $v_{2j} = \{x_1, \hat{x}_2\}$. A "Pareto Rule" could be defined as $C(v_{1j}, R_1, \ldots, R_n) = x_1$ unless $x_2 P_i x_1$ for all i, and $C(v_{2j}, R_1, \ldots, R_n) = x_2$ unless $x_1 P_i x_2$ for all i. We need only notice that the expansion of the admissible agenda, as outlined here, does not change the structure or form of the theory exposited above. The status quo thus becomes an integral part of the analysis.

V

We turn now to a discussion of models which are special cases of the general model outlined here. These models are deduced from the general model by the application of a series of special assumptions.

First assume the admissible agenda is $V = (v = \{x, y\})$. That is, assume there are only two possible social states. We can consider x as the status quo. Assume next that the set of *admissible rules* are those for which the number of people who prefer x to y is the only variable determining whether x is chosen over y.[13]

We now turn to the preference relations. Assume there are only two possible preference relations. Preference 1 is xPy and preference 2 is yPx (indifference is excluded by assumption). From the model we know rule i will be "preferred" to rule j in case, by expression (7)

$$\phi(1)[P^1(x; i)u^1(x) + P^1(y; i)u^1(y)] +$$
$$\phi(2)[P^2(x; i)u^2(x) + P^2(y; i)u^2(y)] \geq$$
$$\phi(1)[P^1(x; j)u^1(x) + P^1(y; j)u^1(y)] +$$
$$\phi(2)[P^2(x; j)u^2(x) + P^2(y; j)u^2(y)] \tag{8}$$

where $u^1(\cdot)$ and $u^2(\cdot)$ are the von Neumann-Morgenstern utilities when the individual has preference relations 1 and 2 respectively.

We now assume with Curtis, Badger, and Schofield (chaps. 1-3 in this volume) that relationship (8) holds if and only if

$$\phi(1)P^1(y; i) + \phi(2)P^2(x; i) \leq \phi(1)P^1(y; j) + \phi(2)P^2(x; j). \tag{9}$$

They assume the individual "prefers" the rule for which the probability of "loss" is least. That is, they assume an individual chooses rules in order to minimize the probability of losing. A sufficient condition for (8) to imply (9) is that $u^1(x) = u^2(y) = 0$ and $u^1(y) = u^2(x) < 0$. The individual gets zero utility from winning and equal negative utility from losing. If one doesn't like the idea of negative utilities, any linear (affine) transformation of these assigned values will do as long as both $u^1(\cdot)$ and $u^2(\cdot)$ are subject to the *same* transformation.

---

[13] Logically speaking this restriction is severe, especially if the admissible agenda is enlarged. Whether it includes all rules of "political interest" or not, as Badger asserts, should be investigated. Wilson (forthcoming) calls, more or less, this class of rules "simple voting games."

With respect to "powers" of the legislature and the "social structure" we assume that the agenda and individuals' preferences are independent random variables,

$$P(v, R_1, \ldots, R_n) = P(v) \prod_{i=1} P(R_i) \text{ with } P(R_i) = P(R_j) \qquad \text{for all } i, j.$$

We can now state a very important result. Under the above assumptions the individual will always choose majority rule. Clearly, this is a testable proposition.

The model can be used to characterize another interesting idea. Both Rae (1969) and Badger discuss the concept of "positional preferences." The idea is that some people want change for the sake of change. In their model, however, since the status quo is specified in advance (even though preferences are random the status quo is not), one cannot disassociate a preference for change (to y) from a preference for y, and a preference for "no change" cannot be distinguished from a preference for x, the alternative which is the status quo.

By recalling the more general characterization of the status quo outlined above we can more precisely characterize the concepts "conservatism" and "radicalism." Conservatism is intended to mean opposition to change—regardless of the status quo. Radicalism is intended to denote a preference for change simply for the sake of change. Allow the admissible agenda V to be expanded to include sets with a finer index such as

$$v_{i1} = \{\hat{x}_1, x_2, \ldots, x_m\}, v_{i2} = \{x_1, \hat{x}_2, \ldots, x_m\}, \ldots,$$
$$v_{im} = \{x_1, x_2, \ldots, \hat{x}_m\}$$

when the "hat" indicates an element designated as the status quo. The concepts we seek to characterize are captured, now, in the form of the function $P(v, R_1, \ldots, R_n)$. Certain individuals' preferences may not be independent (in a statistical sense) of the agenda. If an individual tends to have a "high preference" for x_o, given that x_o is the status quo, we would tend to call him conservative. If the individual tends to have a "low preference" for x_o given it is the status quo we would call him a radical.

The astute reader may notice I am being rather vague at this point. What is a "high preference"? What does "tends to have" mean? What is a "low preference"? Why should there be a statistical dependence between the agenda and the vector of individuals' preferences? Taking the last question first I simply note that a *characterization* of the phenomenon is offered —not an *explanation*. Explanation presumably must follow the identification of what it is that is to be explained. In any case I offer no conjectures here.

With respect to the first three questions several more precise statements are available at first blush. For example one could examine the probability the status quo is "first ranked" relative to the probability it is "last ranked." Or one could examine the probability the status quo is in the first k ranks, etc. Or, one could look at the probability that x_i, $i = 1, \ldots, m$, is first ranked given *it* is the status quo, etc. Many measures are available so there is no need to prejudge the case here. Presumably a measure will only be important insofar as it performs (well?) the function of an explanatory variable in an empirical political model.

VI

The models mentioned above are almost microscopic from the point of view of the general model. That, however, is certainly no criticism of the results offered by the several scholars. Indeed, the model developed here can be generalized even further.

For example, the "number" of social states could be increased to the power of the continuum. Or, as mentioned above, the individual's attitude toward risk could be random. The model could also be slightly changed to allow for sequential decision making or a theory of constitutional amendments. Each social choice could be used as a statistic, by the individual, in converting his prior, $P(v, R_1, \ldots, R_n)$ to a posteriori. As he "learns" about the powers of the legislature and his social environment, his preferences for rules will change. Such changes in rules result in a constitutional amendment. The broad framework developed here can only serve as a backdrop against which problems can be formulated and results interpreted.

In defense of the framework, as it stands, the problems involved with the standard work of the field—that of Buchanan and Tullock—are brought into appropriate perspective. Furthermore, the model, in its general form, suggests a way to avoid some of the problems.

Still to be resolved, however, is the problem stated in the first sentence of this paper. "On what basis are constitutions actually adopted?" The "ethics" approach depends as much on unanimity as does the "self-interest" approach. I suggest the answer to this question will be supplied by an application of the theory of games *after* a satisfactory theory of individual preference for rules has been developed.

Part 2

COALITION FORMATION

5. A Cost/Benefit Analysis of Coalition Formation in Voting Bodies

STEVEN J. BRAMS

I. INTRODUCTION

Little attention has been paid in political science to the development of models for studying political processes that occur over time. While considerable work has been devoted to cross-sectional studies of relationships among variables at a particular point in time, the tracing of relationships that occur over time has largely been limited to correlational or other statistical analyses that point up time-dependent relationships without offering insight into the kinds of forces that produce them. A description of relationships may be useful in making certain kinds of predictions, but such a description does not provide one with an understanding of the mechanisms that "explain" why these relationships occur. For this purpose it is necessary to make assumptions from which one can derive consequences that explicate the logic of a process (Brams, 1972a).

In this article I hope to show how such a deductive form of analysis can be used to generate theoretical consequences that ultimately are amenable

I wish to thank David H. Koehler, Richard G. Niemi, G. William Sensiba, and Herbert F. Weisberg for their valuable suggestions and the National Science Foundation for its financial support under Grant GS-2798.

to empirical corroboration.[1] The substantive focus of this article will be on coalition-formation processes in voting bodies, where actors are assumed to make calculations of the costs and benefits involved in deciding whether to join or not join different coalitions. I shall draw inferences about the dynamic consequences following from different assumptions by trying to ferret out patterns and regularities emerging from these calculations, with the focus of the analysis being on the dynamic aspects of bargaining *prior* to the victory of one coalition.

In an earlier paper (Brams and Riker, 1972), Riker and I tried to show what kinds of calculations members of a voting body, considered as rational actors, might make in order to maximize their influence in the body. The influence of individual members and protocoalitions of members (coalitions not of sufficient size to be winning) was defined in terms of their ability to be the pivotal members of a winning coalition, or alternatively in terms of their ability to attract a sufficient number of members to become minimal winning or winning coalitions. Using different pivotal and probabilistic concepts of influence, we were able to derive from different assumptions about what combinatorial possibilities members and protocoalitions consider are those available from which to choose a number of consequences relating to the dynamics of coalition-formation processes in a voting body. In an illustrative application of one of the probabilistic models to voting data in multiballot national party conventions, we tried to show how the model could help us better understand, and predict the occurrence of, the "take-off" point in a convention when the so-called "bandwagon effect" sweeps the front-running candidate on to victory. In developing the models of this article, I shall allude to the findings of the previous paper for comparative purposes.

The analysis here will be restricted to the study of coalition-formation processes involving as active opponents only two protocoalitions which vie for the support of uncommitted members in a voting body in order to become winning coalitions. Unlike the previous analysis, however, the two protocoalitions will not be restricted to a strategy of achieving victory only through securing commitments of support from uncommitted members; in this analysis, defections will be permitted—that is, the switching of commitments from one protocoalition to the other. Although individual members of the two protocoalitions may defect to one another, however, the assumption that the two protocoalitions are unalterably opposed and may never coalesce will be retained, thus precluding the two protocoalitions from combining with each other, except through the defection of their members, to form a winning coalition.

---

[1] On the need for *generative explanations* in which the analyst "must demonstrate in his explanation how the behavior in question is generated," see Holt and Turner (1970, p. 3).

In allowing defections, we shall not only be interested, as before, in exploring possible calculations which leaders of the two protocoalitions might make in trying to determine how much to offer uncommitted members to join, but also how much the leaders of each protocoalition would be likely to offer members of the opposing protocoalition to defect to their respective sides. In addition, we shall suggest a way to calculate the aggregate resources which the leader of a protocoalition—relative to the other protocoalition—would need to be able to induce a number of members sufficient to win either to join or defect, as well as the portion of these aggregate resouces he should offer, at each stage in the coalition-formation process, to an uncommitted member for joining and to a committed member (of the other protocoalition) for defecting.

To illustrate this process, we shall trace our analysis through the operation of a ten-member voting body, with the decision-rule being majority rule (six out of ten). Starting with no members in each of the two protocoalitions, we shall alternately add one member to each protocoalition—either through an uncommitted member's joining or a committed member's defecting—until one protocoalition reaches minimal winning size with six members and thereby becomes always decisive, or both protocoalitions obtain commitments from five members and form two blocking coalitions which, with no uncommitted members remaining, deadlock decisions on the part of each other. As in the previous paper, it will be convenient to represent this coalition-formation process in terms of a lattice-like structure in order to draw out some implications of the concepts and assumptions which will help us to understand under what circumstances certain coalitions form rather than others.[2]

---

[2] It is important to note that the use of the lattice, as with the payoff matrix in game theory, provides a way to order and display the choices available to the members, though neither the lattice nor the payoff matrix are themselves "theories." Such ordering devices can be enormously helpful as starting points in one's analysis, nonetheless, as Thomas C. Schelling has pointed out:

Just providing a format for laying out the situation can be helpful. The idea of "double-entry" bookkeeping developed by the Venetians during the Renaissance was such a primitive accomplishment that it hardly deserves to be called a theoretical break-through, yet it has had profound consequences. The same was true of national-income accounting as developed in the late 1930's. It was only a way of recognizing and exploiting a few identities, and laying out a confining framework for the consideration of certain problems, and has to be judged separately from any empirical hypotheses or mathematical operations that could be associated with it. Yet it was profoundly important. The "equation" itself may have done much the same for mathematics . . . like double-entry bookkeeping, national income accounts, or the pay-off matrix, it offers a way of laying out a situation so that certain identities can be explored and so that one can keep track of operations and their implications . . . . Like a truth table or a conservation principle or an equation, the pay-off matrix provides a way of organizing and structuring problems so that they can be analyzed fruitfully and communicated unambiguously. (Schelling, 1966, pp. 479–80)

II. THE CONCEPT OF NET GAIN

Because the previous paper contained a detailed discussion describing the manner in which the proportion of pivots for each of the protocoalitions and the uncommitted members is calculated, it seems unnecessary to repeat it *in extenso* here. For now we need only note that in each cell of the lattice of figure 1, the weights of each of the opposing protocoalitions are given by the ordered pair (X, Y), where X is equal to the number of members in the first protocoalition and Y is equal to the number of members in the second protocoalition.

As one moves diagonally downward and to the right in the lattice, uncommitted members join the second protocoalition (Y) in each lattice cell and move the process toward an unbalanced outcome (i.e., increasing disparity in the size of the two protocoalitions); as one moves diagonally downward and to the left in the lattice, uncommitted members join the first protocoalition (X) and move the process toward a balanced outcome,[3] and as one moves horizontally to the left or the right in the lattice, members of Y and X, respectively, defect to each other.

In order to understand the decimal figures given along the diagonal

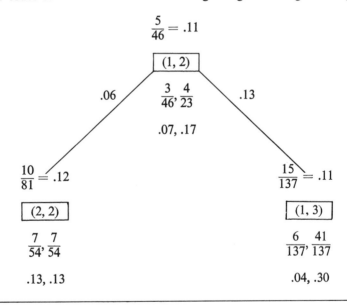

$$\frac{5}{46} = .11$$

$(1, 2)$

.06 $\dfrac{3}{46}, \dfrac{4}{23}$ .13

.07, .17

$\dfrac{10}{81} = .12$ $\dfrac{15}{137} = .11$

$(2, 2)$ $(1, 3)$

$\dfrac{7}{54}, \dfrac{7}{54}$ $\dfrac{6}{137}, \dfrac{41}{137}$

.13, .13   .04, .30

---

[3] That is, toward the tied lattice cells $(1, 1)$, $(2, 2)$, $(3, 3)$, $(4, 4)$, and $(5, 5)$; farther to the left of these tied cells X has more members than Y. Except for the inclusion of cells $(1, 0)$, $(2, 1)$, $(3, 2)$, $(4, 3)$, and $(5, 4)$, which are necessary to show the net gain of a defection (defined later) when the lead changes from X to Y or vice versa (e.g., the process moves between cells $(2, 1)$ and $(1, 2)$), possible cells farther to the left giving outcomes in which X is the larger protocoalition are omitted since they are simply a mirror reflection about the "axis of symmetry" of those already given in figure 1.

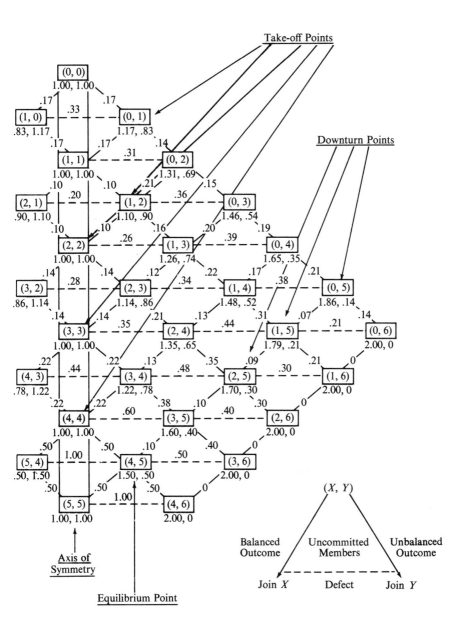

FIGURE 1. Lattice of pivotal net gains and resources needed to win using *combinations*, but excluding coalitions that contain both or neither of the protocoalitions, for ten-member body with majority rule.

and horizontal lines in figure 1, a small portion of this lattice as given in figure 1 of the earlier paper is reproduced on page 104.

Below the protocoalitions (X, Y) in each cell are given the fractional, and decimal equivalent, proportions of pivots each protocoalition has. In calculating these proportions, we assume that each protocoalition or uncommitted member is pivotal only in those winning coalitions, including either X or Y but not both, where its subtraction from that coalition would reduce the coalition to one which is blocking or losing. For cell (1,2), for example, the single-member protocoalition (X) would be pivotal in seven percent of all coalitions, and the two-member protocoalition (Y) would be pivotal in seventeen percent of all coalitions. Each uncommitted member's proportion is given above each cell; the seven uncommitted members in the present example each have eleven percent of the pivots.[4]

This percentage for an uncommitted member is greater than the percentage for the committed single-member protocoalition, X (eleven versus seven percent), because the uncommitted member is allowed to be pivotal in a coalition with X or Y and other uncommitted members, while X is not permitted to ally with Y in a winning coalition. The ideologically prepossessed X thus has fewer opportunities to act as a decisive force than a "free-wheeling" uncommitted member also with only one vote.

The decimal figures given along the diagonal lines connecting lattice cell (1, 2) to cell (2, 2), on the one hand, and to cell (1, 3), on the other, indicate the incremental proportion of pivots which an uncommitted member adds by joining either the smaller protocoalition, X (moving the process diagonally downward and to the left), or the larger protocoalition, Y (moving the process diagonally downward and to the right). Thus, the commitment of an uncommitted member to the smaller protocoalition (X) raises its pivot proportion from 0.07 at lattice cell (1, 2) to 0.13 at cell (2, 2), or by an increment of 0.06; going from cell (1, 2) to cell (1, 3), on the other hand, an uncommitted member who joins Y increases its pivot proportion by 0.13.

While this calculation, made in the earlier paper, showed up several interesting properties of the coalition-formation process in the ten-member body—for example, because an uncommitted member's pivot contribution to Y at every lattice cell is always greater than his contribution to X (as was the case in the above example), it is always to his advantage to join Y (if we assume his share in the benefits which accrue to the

---

[4] See Brams and Riker (1972) for the detailed calculations in this example. These results are based on all permissible *combinations* of the protocoalitions and uncommitted members being considered equally likely; the results when *permutations* are considered equally likely are given in figure 2 of Brams and Riker (1972).

protocoalition, should it win, is proportional to his incremental contribution)—it did not take into account the fact that an uncommitted member's joining, say, Y, simultaneously *decreases* the proportion of pivots which X, remaining unchanged, holds when the process moves to the next stage.

This is precisely the fact that we have taken into account in calculating the figures given along the diagonals in figure 1. As an uncommitted member adds $(0.30 - 0.17) = 0.13$ proportion of pivots to Y at lattice cell $(1, 2)$ when he moves the process to cell $(1, 3)$, for example, he simultaneously decreases X's pivot proportion from 0.07 to 0.04, or by a decrement of 0.03. Thus, Y's *net gain*, relative to X, when an uncommitted member joins Y and moves the process from lattice cell $(1, 2)$ to cell $(1, 3)$ is $(0.13 + 0.03) = 0.16$ proportion of pivots, which is the figure given along the diagonal connecting cell $(1, 2)$ to cell $(1, 3)$ in figure 1. Similarly, when an uncommitted member joins X and moves the process from cell $(1, 2)$ to cell $(2, 2)$, X's net gain is

$$(0.13 - 0.07) + (0.17 - 0.13) = 0.06 + 0.04 = 0.10,$$

which is the figure given along the diagonal connecting cell $(1, 2)$ to cell $(2, 2)$.

These net gain figures along the diagonals reveal that at most nontied lattice cells, where Y has more members than X, an uncommitted member can always contribute a greater net proportion of pivots if he joins Y rather than X. (The exceptions occur at lattice cells $(0, 1)$, $(0, 2)$, and $(0, 3)$—where the degenerate protocoalition X with no members receives a greater net gain with the commitment of its first member than the larger protocoalition Y receives with the commitment of an additional member[5]—and at cell $(4, 5)$, where the net gains of 0.50 to both X and Y are the same.) If the currency of voting power is reckoned in pivots, then this net proportion might well be used as an indicator of the *added value* in power that the new member can bring to the protocoalition—and what the protocoalition should be willing to expend in its resources, or commit in its expected payoffs, to entice the new member to join. If an uncommitted member acted according to those calculations, then he could maximize his power usually by following a strategy of casting his lot with the larger protocoalition.

---

[5] Thus, it pays to assert leadership to form an opposition protocoalition when an unopposed protocoalition has fewer than four members. This dynamic would tend first to push the process toward a balanced outcome, then reverse itself and push the process toward an unbalanced outcome at the next stage when the smaller protocoalition has at least one member. Such an oscillating pattern is suggestive of the often observed fluctuating growth in the size of opposed groups in politics, and in a nonpolitical context in the shifting of the lead between opponents in athletic contests.

This conclusion comports with that of the earlier paper, where we considered only the gain in pivots contributed by the uncommitted member to the protocoalition he joins and not the corresponding loss suffered by the protocoalition not favored. Because the net gain figures are larger than those based on just the increment contributed by the uncommitted member to the protocoalition he joins, however, the net gain calculation usually has the effect of moving back the *take-off points*, which are the first points at which the net proportion of pivots which an uncommitted member contributes to the larger protocoalition (Y)—as one proceeds along each diagonal from the upper left to the lower right—exceeds the proportion he would have by remaining uncommitted. At lattice cell (1, 2) in figure 1, for example, the net gain of 0.16 proportion of pivots contributed by an uncommitted member's joining Y, and moving the process from cell (1, 2) to cell (1, 3), exceeds the proportion which an uncommitted member has at cell (1, 2) by remaining uncommitted (0.11, shown in the previous example in the text but not shown in figure 1), so the process "takes off" at cell (1, 2);[6] at cell (1, 1), on the other hand, an uncommitted member's proportion of pivots (also 0.11) exceeds his net gain of 0.10 in joining Y, so at this earlier point it would not be advantageous for an uncommitted member to commit himself to either single-member protocoalition. Only at lattice cell (4, 5), which is an *equilibrium point* because the proportion of pivots the single uncommitted member has by remaining uncommitted (0.50) exactly equals what his net gain is by joining either X or Y, would an uncommitted member be indifferent between remaining uncommitted or joining either X or Y.

While lattice cell (1, 2) is also a take-off point along the (1, 1)–(1, 6) diagonal in our original calculation in the earlier paper (as well as cell (0, 1) along the (0, 1)–(0, 6) diagonal), take-off points (2, 2), (3, 3), and (4, 4) in figure 1 precede the take-off points (or coincide with the equilibrium points) in the earlier paper, suggesting that when members of voting bodies take account of both "gains" and "losses" produced by an uncommitted member's joining the larger protocoalition, Y, a bandwagon effect is likely to take hold earlier in the voting process. Yet the *downturn points* (0, 5), (1, 5), and (2, 5), prior to which the net gains along the (0, 1)–(0, 6), (1, 1)–(1, 6), and (2, 2)–(2, 6) diagonals are increasing and after which they decrease, remain the same as in the original calculations, suggesting that the new calculation has no effect on the points at which an underdog effect for the smaller protocoalition might counter

---

[6] At cell (2, 1) as well, though we have not indicated this as a take-off point in figure 1 since it is the mirror reflection of cell (1, 2). Similarly, those cells we shall label as "equilibrium" and "downturn" points in subsequent lattices will be designated only for those cells in the figures to the right of the tied lattice cells (i.e., the "axis of symmetry") and not their mirror reflections just to the left of this "axis."

a bandwagon effect for the larger protocoalition.[7] While at a take-off point it becomes for the first time advantageous to an individual to join the larger protocoalition rather than hold out to the end, an individual receives his greatest payoff for a commitment just prior to the downturn point along any diagonal.[8]

Our results so far indicate that the advantage tends to lie with the larger proportion, Y, which generally can augment its pivot proportion by a greater net amount when an uncommitted member joins than can the smaller protocoalition, X. If Y is disposed, for this reason, to offer an uncommitted member more benefits than X, we would expect that the uncommitted member would in most cases join Y and push the process toward an unbalanced outcome.[9]

III. THE EFFECT OF DEFECTIONS

How do defections affect the process? Surprisingly, there is no bias that favors one protocoalition or the other: each stands to gain (or lose) the same proportion of pivots by a defection. To illustrate this point, consider our earlier example with only the decimal values given for the pivot proportions of the protocoalitions and uncommitted members (p. 110).

Now at lattice cell $(2, 2)$, if a member from X defected to Y and moved the process to cell $(1, 3)$, he would gain $(0.30 - 0.13) = 0.17$ proportion of pivots and benefit from the loss incurred by X of $(0.13 - 0.04) = 0.09$ proportion of pivots. Thus, his net gain would be $(0.17 + 0.09) = 0.26$

---

[7] Though interesting, these consequences flowing from the different abstract calculations should probably be noted *and* forgotten until we are able to ascertain those empirical situations which most closely fit the assumptions of the different models. In the earlier paper we found empirical evidence that was at least suggestive of the operation of take-off and downturn points (i.e., bandwagon and underdog effects) in multiballot national party conventions, but it is not clear at this stage which of the different models, and sets of assumptions on which they are based, best fit particular empirical situations. It seems to me, nonetheless, that even the heuristic value of such concepts as "take-off point" and "downturn point" which emerge from, and help us summarize, the different calculations is considerable, for these theoretical concepts help us to order our knowledge and pave the way for an operationalization of process-connected empirical hypotheses that appear from the abstract models to have interesting ramifications. For an attempt to operationalize the concept of *take-off* in national party conventions as a basis for comparison with theoretical values, see Brams and Riker (1972). For an attempt to distinguish circumstances under which take-off does and does not occur in national party conventions, see Brams and Sensiba (1972).

[8] The drop in the net gain between lattice cells $(0, 1)$ and $(0, 2)$ would make cell $(0, 1)$ also a downturn point, though not in the same sense as those lower in the lattice. This early drop-off is unique among the lattices considered and indicates the relatively greater value of a first commitment to a degenerate protocoalition than a second or third commitment in the combination case.

[9] Three sets of limiting conditions on this dynamic are described in Brams (1972b).

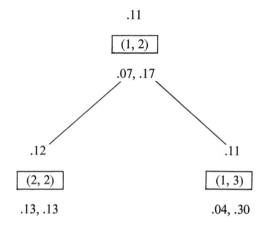

proportion of pivots (given along the horizontal dashed line connecting cell (2, 2) to cell (1, 3) in figure 1), which would be the same net gain to *X* if a member of *Y* were to defect at lattice cell (1, 3) and move the process to cell (2, 2). This is so because of the symmetry of the two cases: the "gain" to one protocoalition from a defection becomes the "benefit from the loss" to the other protocoalition when the defection is reversed, so the *sum* of the "gain" and "benefit from the loss" is the same in both cases.

But this sum, interestingly enough, is also equal to the sum of the net gains that accrue to each protocoalition at cell (1, 2) when an uncommitted member joins them. From figure 1, as we showed previously, when an uncommitted member joins *Y* at lattice cell (1, 2) and moves the process to cell (1, 3), the net gain to *Y* is 0.16 proportion of pivots; and when an uncommitted member joins *X* at cell (1, 2) and moves the process to cell (2, 2), the net gain to *X* is 0.10 proportion of pivots. The sum of these net gains is $(0.16 + 0.10) = 0.26$ proportion of pivots, which is equal to the net gain either protocoalition picks up from a defection (see figure 1) subsequent to a new commitment that brings the process to cell (2, 2) or cell (1, 3). Upon reflection, there is nothing mysterious about this identity: the leader of one protocoalition should be willing to pay the cost of *two* new commitments (one to each protocoalition) in order to be able to change by *two* votes the difference between the size of the two protocoalitions through a subsequent defection.[10]

---

[10] Except at lattice cells (1, 0) and (1, 1), however, the net gain of two new commitments to *X* or to *Y* (*not* one to each protocoalition) at a particular lattice cell, which changes the difference between the two protocoalitions by two members, will be greater than (*not* equal to) the net gain of a single defection, which also changes the difference between the two protocoalitions by two members. For example, the net gain of two new commitments to *Y* at lattice cell (1, 2) that moves the process to cell (1 ,4) is $(0.16 + 0.22) = 0.38$, which is greater than the net gain of a defection to *Y* (0.36) at

While the fact that two *prior* commitments "equal" one *subsequent* defection would seem to imply that a defection is worth twice as much as a commitment from an uncommitted member, this is not strictly true. At lattice cell (1, 2), for example, a commitment to Y is worth 60 percent more than a commitment to X (0.16 versus 0.10 in net gains); since the net gain of a defection, after a new commitment has been made and the process is at cell (2, 2) or cell (1, 3), is equal to the sum of these two figures (0.26), to Y the net gain of a defection is 63 percent ($\frac{0.26 - 0.16}{0.16}$) greater than the net gain of a prior commitment, and to X the net gain of a defection is 160 percent ($\frac{0.26 - 0.10}{0.10}$) greater than the net gain of a prior commitment. Thus, while the value of a defection will always be greater than the value of a prior commitment, the amount by which it is greater will depend on whether the comparison is with respect to X or Y. With the exception of lattice cell (4, 5) and the tied lattice cells in figure 1, where the value of a defection after a new commitment has been made is the same to both X and Y, a defection will usually be worth more to the smaller protocoalition (X), *as compared to a prior commitment*, than to the larger protocoalition (Y). Only at cells (0, 1), (0, 2), and (0, 3) is a defection worth relatively more to Y than to (the degenerate) X with no members.

Not only is the sum of the net gains from two prior commitments equal to the net gain of one subsequent defection, but the net gain produced by a defection between two lattice cells is also equal to the sum of the net gains of *subsequent* new commitments to Y of one cell and X of another cell that move the process to the same lower cell. At lattice cell (2, 2), for example, the net gain to Y when a new commitment moves the process to cell (2, 3) is 0.14; at cell (1, 3), the net gain to X when a new commitment moves the process also to cell (2, 3) is 0.12. The sum of these net gains (0.26) is equal to the net gain of a defection when the process moves between cell (2, 2) and cell (1, 3). Interpreted, this means that the smaller protocoalition (X, whose net gain from a new commitment at cell (1, 3) is 0.12 and to whom a defection is worth $\frac{0.26 - 0.12}{0.12} = 1.17$ more than a subsequent new commitment) tends to benefit more from a prior defection than the larger protocoalition (Y, whose net gain from a new commitment at cell (2, 2) is 0.14 and to whom a defection is worth $\frac{0.26 - 0.14}{0.14} = 0.86$ more than a subsequent new commitment).

---

cell (1, 2) that moves the process to cell (0, 3). Note, however, that the defection of one (committed) member costs Y 0.36 proportion of pivots while the commitment of two (uncommitted) members costs Y an average of $0.38/2 = 0.19$ proportion of pivots to each of the two (uncommitted) members, so the member defecting costs considerably more than a single new commitment. Under this alternative view of the relative worth of two new commitments and a single defection, the net gain of the two new commitments, relative to the net gain of a defection, tends to increase as the process moves to cells lower in the lattice where fewer members are uncommitted and the situation is more determined.

One way to visualize this and the previous identity is to consider the triangles formed by the horizontal dashed lines connecting adjacent cells (e. g., cells (2, 2) and (1, 3)) with the cells immediately above (i. e., (1, 2)) and immediately below (i. e., (2, 3)) the dashed lines: the sum of the net gains produced by two new commitments (along the solid diagonal sides of the triangles) equals the net gain of a defection (along the dashed horizontal side of the triangle). Or the sum of the net gains of two sides of a triangle (i. e., those produced by two new commitments) equals the net gain of the third side (i. e., that produced by a defection).

When we compare the net gain of a new commitment to X (or Y) with the net gain of a defection to X (or Y) at a particular lattice cell, the value of a defection will generally be greater than the value of a new commitment.[11] In addition, a defection to X vis-à-vis a new commitment to X is worth comparatively more than a defection to Y vis-à-vis a new commitment to Y. At lattice cell (2, 4), for example, a defection is worth 170 percent $(\frac{0.35 - 0.13}{0.13})$ more than a new commitment to X, but to Y a defection is worth only 26 percent $(\frac{0.44 - 0.35}{0.35})$ more than a new commitment.

While the above results agree with the commonsense idea that defections from the topdog to the underdog usually give the underdog a greater boost than do reverse defections help the topdog, what common sense does not provide, but what our calculations do, is a precise measure of *how great* this differential effect is. To be sure, different calculations based on different models will generate different differential effects, as we shall see later, so the problem of choosing the model most appropriate to a particular empirical situation remains. It is easier, however, to choose one from a class of models than to have nothing from which to choose as a starting point in one's analysis.

IV. THE RESOURCES NEEDED BY A PROTOCOALITION TO WIN

A quite remarkable property characterizes the net gains generated by a new commitment, or a defection, in the lattice of figure 1. To elucidate this property, we shall *assume* that at lattice cell $(0, 0)$, when the two (degenerate) protocoalitions are of equal size, the resources needed by

---

[11] The exceptions occur at lattice cells (1, 5), (2, 5), (3, 5), and (4, 5), where the net gains to Y of a new commitment are exactly equal to the net gains to Y of a defection. The reason is obvious: in the case of either a new commitment or a defection, Y becomes a minimal winning coalition with all the pivots, so its net gains are the same (e.g., 0.30 proportion of pivots going from cell (2, 5) to cell (2, 6) or cell (1, 6)) whether it becomes minimal winning through a new commitment (process terminates at cell (2, 6)) or through a defection (process terminates at cell (1, 6)).

each to win will have an arbitrary value equal to 1.00 (it could be any other value). In other words, both X and Y at lattice cell $(0, 0)$ will need resources equal to 1.00 in order to gain the support from uncommitted members, or defectors, necessary to win.

We shall now *define* the resources needed to win by the protocoalitions in all other lattice cells. For X, the *resources needed to win* at any lattice cell will be equal to

$1.00 + \sum$ (net gains along any *rightward* diagonal or horizontal path terminating at the designated lattice cell)

$- \sum$ (net gains along any *leftward* diagonal or horizontal path terminating at the designated lattice cell),

given that the origin of the path traced is lattice cell $(0, 0)$, whose values for each protocoalition we have previously assumed to be equal to 1.00. To illustrate this calculation for the lattice in figure 1, if the lattice cell in question is $(1, 1)$, the value of X traced along the paths $(0, 0)$–$(0, 1)$ –$(1, 1)$ or $(0, 0)$–$(1, 0)$–$(1, 1)$ will be equal to

$$1.00 + (0.17) - (0.17) = 1.00;$$

along the path $(0, 0)$–$(0, 1)$–$(0, 2)$–$(1, 1)$, the value of X will be equal to

$$1.00 + (0.17 + 0.14) - (0.31) = 1.00;$$

and along the path $(0, 0)$–$(0, 1)$–$(0, 2)$–$(1, 2)$–$(1, 1)$, the value of X will be equal to

$$1.00 + (0.17 + 0.14) - (0.21 + 0.10) = 1.00.$$

In fact, the value of X will be the same at cell $(1, 1)$ no matter what connecting path we choose from cell $(0, 0)$ in the lattice. It is easy to show that this result holds in general for any lattice cell (X, Y) traced from cell $(0, 0)$.

In the same manner as above, we can define for Y the resources needed to win to be equal to

$1.00 + \sum$ (net gains along any *leftward* diagonal or horizontal path terminating at the designated lattice cell)

$- \sum$ (net gains along any *rightward* diagonal or horizontal path terminating at the designated lattice cell),

given that the origin of the path traced is lattice cell $(0, 0)$, whose values for each protocoalition we have previously assumed to be equal to 1.00. As with X, it can be demonstrated that the value of Y will be the same no matter what path we trace from lattice cell $(0, 0)$ to any other cell (X, Y).

Several interesting consequences follow from this enumerative process. First, as can be seen from the figures below each lattice cell in figure 1 giving the resources needed to win for each protocoalition, the resources needed at each tied lattice cell in addition to cell $(0, 0)$—that is, at cells $(1, 1)$, $(2, 2)$, $(3, 3)$, $(4, 4)$, $(5, 5)$—are all equal to 1.00 for both protocoalitions X and Y. This means that no matter how many members X and Y have, as long as they are tied, the resources needed by each to win will be the same and equal to the constant value 1.00. Alternatively, we could have assumed, for *any* of the tied lattice cells—not necessarily cell $(0, 0)$—the resources needed to win for each of the protocoalitions are equal to 1.00—and derived as a consequence that the two protocoalitions of *all other* tied lattice cells each need resources of 1.00 to win. As justification for this consequence, it does not seem implausible that no matter how close one protocoalition is to winning, its costs will not drop—or at least will be the same as those of the other protocoalition—whenever it is in a dead-heat battle with that protocoalition.

As a second consequence of our assumption about equal resources of 1.00 needed by each protocoalition to win at any of the tied lattice cells, the resources needed by Y once it has reached minimal winning size with six members at lattice cells $(0, 6)$, $(1, 6)$, $(2, 6)$, $(3, 6)$, and $(4, 6)$—that is, has won!—plummet to zero. The corresponding resources needed by X to win at each of these cells soar to 2.00, which is the constant value of the *combined* resources needed by *both* protocoalitions to win at all lattice cells. This is simply an "accounting" convention which may be interpreted as follows: after Y has already won, X, in effect, would need the total resources available to *both* protocoalitions to win!

It is easy to see from figure 1 that *any* path chosen from any lattice cell (X, Y) to any other cell (X', Y') will result in the same cumulative gains (or losses) in pivot proportions to each protocoalition. This explains why, given the resources needed to win by X and Y at any lattice cell (not necessarily a tied cell), whatever path one traces to any other cell gives the same values for the resources needed to win at the terminal cell (which is analogous to the constant sums of "magic squares"). So in going from one point to another, you pay your money and you take your choice—the results will be the same whatever route you choose! Indeed, if you are Y and you desire to win, the results will be the same whether you win with zero or more members uncommitted (or indifferent) at cells $(0, 6)$, $(1, 6)$, $(2, 6)$, or $(3, 6)$—or all committed at cell $(4, 6)$.

This accounting scheme for pivots obviously has a bit of determinism built into it, but this does not rob it of its value for making comparisons of the relative advantages of being at different lattice cells in the voting process. For example, if one were the leader of protocoalition Y, would it be more advantageous to be at cell $(1, 3)$ or cell $(3, 4)$? While the answer to this question surely depends on how future prospects appear at each stage, which will vary from situation to situation depending on foreseeable possible future alignments of the different members, what figure 1 tells us is that, given the simplifying assumptions of the model, cell (1, 3) holds a slight advantage for the leader of Y. He would have to expend 0.74 proportion of pivots in order to reach a winning cell, whereas at cell (3, 4) the resources he would need to commit would be 0.78 proportion of pivots. Although this advantage might appear strictly academic—not to mention based on very artificial assumptions—it is not inconsistent with other simplifying assumptions made in the earlier paper that give Y at cell (1, 3) a 0.02 greater probability of winning than at cell (3, 4) when only minimal winning coalitions are considered equally likely, and a 0.06 greater probability of winning when all winning coalitions are considered equally likely.

Probably more significant than this comparison is the fact that the calculation of the resources needed to win for each protocoalition enables us to compare the relative strengths of X and Y with regard to the pivotal offers each would have to make to become winning. In the case of both cells (1, 3) and (3, 4), for example, Y has an approximately five to three advantage over X, whatever the metric used, in terms of the pivotal resources he would need to commit to win. Thus, if the leader of X at cells (1, 3) or (3, 4) were not willing to expend significantly more than the leader of Y to secure the commitments of uncommitted members or entice members of Y to defect, his chances of winning would appear to be dim.

But more than just providing us with a measure of the relative strength of X and Y at each lattice cell, the resource figures, together with the net gain figures, provide us with a prescription of how much of its resources each protocoalition should expend, at each stage, in order to win. Typically, there will be many alternative routes to victory, either through securing new commitments or engineering defections, and it is no easy task for a protocoalition leader to decide how much each new member or defector at each stage is worth. If too much is promised too early, a protocoalition might find itself on the verge of victory without the resources necessary to consummate it. On the other hand, being too niggardly in the beginning may put a protocoalition hopelessly far behind at a later stage. What the net gains connecting the lattice cells show is not only how much a new commitment is worth at each juncture but also how much more a defection is worth—and therefore whether the price asked by the potential new member is more "reasonable" than the price asked by the potential defector.

These considerations raise a host of operational questions on how empirical voting situations might be analyzed in terms of the calculations of this model. We shall return to these questions later, but for now we shall consider alternative sets of calculations based on different sets of assumptions about the coalition-formation process in voting bodies.

V. A COMPARISON WITH OTHER MODELS

The net-gain and resources-needed-to-win figures, when all permutations (instead of combinations) of uncommitted members with each of the protocoalitions are considered equally likely, are given in the lattice of figure 2.

All the take-off points, except that at lattice cell (3, 3), are one cell more advanced along each of the diagonals from the upper left to the lower right than those in figure 1, indicating that the permutation assumption tends to retard somewhat the operation of a bandwagon effect. In fact, lattice cell (1, 2), which was a take-off point in figure 1, is an equilibrium point, along with cell (4, 5), in figure 2.

The downturn points, which did not show up in this lattice in the original calculation from the earlier paper, are the same as those in figure 1, except for the addition of lattice cell (3, 5) as a downturn point in figure 2 due to the decline in the net gain to Y (from 0.42 before this point to 0.40 after this point) and the lack of a downturn point along the (0, 1) –(0, 6) diagonal (all net gains are the same and equal to 0.17). For Y, the resources needed to win at each nontied and nonwinning lattice cell tend to be somewhat less, and for X somewhat more, than in figure 1, which means that the equal-likelihood assumption for permutations slightly undercuts the advantage which the equal-likelihood assumption for combinations gives the larger protocoalition over the smaller protocoalition.

This resource advantage of the larger over the smaller protocoalition is substantially built up by the probabilistic calculations in the lattice of figure 3. Here we drop the notion of pivotalness, which was based on the proportion of all combinations (or permutations) when an actor's subtraction would reduce a winning coalition to a (losing) protocoalition, regardless of when he made his commitment, and instead assume that the members of each protocoalition are always the first to commit themselves. We then ask in what proportion of ways the uncommitted members can be added to each protocoalition, assuming all combinations[12] are equally likely, so as to make it a minimal winning coalition. These proportions for each protocoalition, which sum to 1.00 (and are not shown

---

[12] In the interest of economy, a discussion of the results based on assuming all permutations are equally likely for either this or the subsequent probabilistic model (i.e., based on any winning coalition) will not be included here.

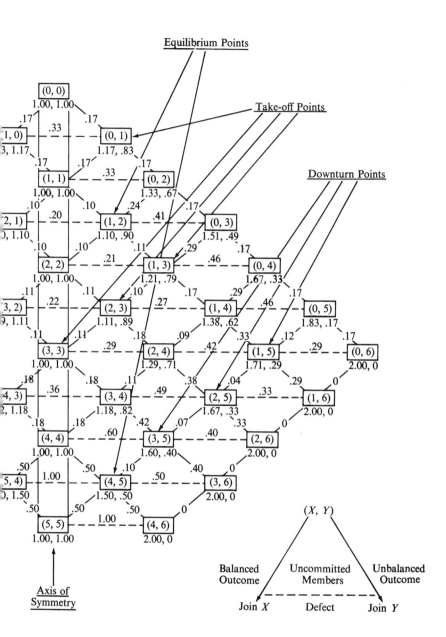

FIGURE 2. Lattice of pivotal net gains and resources needed to win using *permutations*, but excluding coalitions that contain both or neither of the protocoalitions, for ten-member body with majority rule.

in figure 3) can be interpreted as the probabilities that each of the proto-coalitions will become minimal winning.

These complementary probabilities are analogous to the pivot proportions computed for X and Y in the pivot models. As in the incremental calculations of the models, we can calculate for the probabilistic models the amount by which an uncommitted member can raise the probability of each of the protocoalition's becoming minimal winning by joining either X (moving the process diagonally downward and to the left) or Y (moving the process diagonally downward and to the right), which is precisely the computation we made in the earlier paper. But here, by also including in the calculation the amount by which this uncommitted member lowers the complementary probability, for the protocoalition he does not join, to become minimal winning, we can, as in the pivotal models, calculate the net (probabilistic) gain which an uncommitted member contributes to the protocoalition which he joins.

The net-gain figures for both new commitments and defections are given along the diagonal and horizontal lines connecting the lattice cells in figure 3. Because the probabilistic gain to one protocoalition is exactly equal to the probabilistic loss to the other (since the complementary probabilities at each lattice cell sum to one), the net gain of a new commitment to X or Y at each lattice cell is exactly twice the magnitude of just the positive probabilistic increments given in the earlier paper. Except for the cells in the lower part of the lattice where the net gain which an uncommitted member contributes to X is equal to that which he contributes to Y, the larger protocoalition (Y) is favored at all cells but cell (4, 5). At this cell, because the one uncommitted member can neutralize Y's advantage by joining X, he is worth more to X than to Y, which is already in an unbeatable position as a blocking coalition.

Since the net gains to X and Y when an uncommitted member joins are simply twice the magnitude of the positive increments based on only the gains to the favored protocoalition (and not the losses to the unfavored protocoalition), these gains bear the same relationship to each other along each diagonal as the positive increments. The downturn points, there-fore, do not change from those given in the earlier paper. Neither do the equilibrium or take-off points, which are independent of the net gains in figure 3 and based only on a comparison between an uncommitted member's "expected" probability of being in a minimal winning coali-tion and the probability that the larger protocoalition, Y, will become minimal winning.[13]

What does change, however, is the margin of superiority, in resources needed to win, which the probabilistic calculation gives the larger proto-

---

[13] For details, see Brams and Riker (1972).

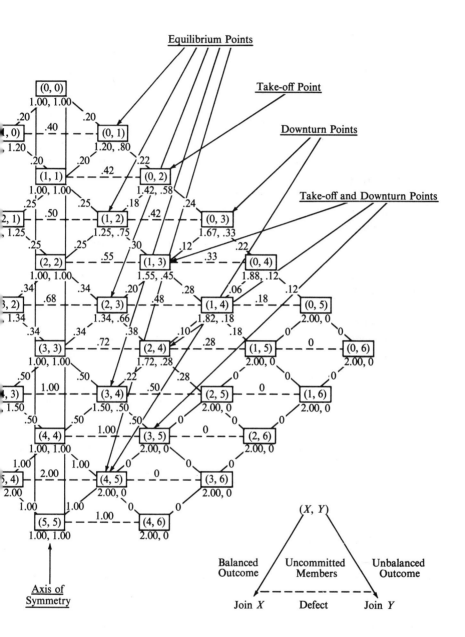

FIGURE 3. Lattice of probabilistic net gains and resources needed to win in *minimal winning coalition*, assuming all combinations of uncommitted members, with each protocoalition, are equally likely.

coalition, Y. At lattice cell $(1, 3)$ in figure 3, for example, the resources needed by X to become minimal winning are 278 percent $(\frac{1.65 - 0.45}{0.45})$ greater than those needed by Y, whereas the pivotal calculations in figure 1 for combinations give Y by comparison only a 70 percent $(\frac{1.26 - 0.74}{0.74})$ edge, and in figure 2 for permutations only a 53 percent $(\frac{1.21 - 0.79}{0.79})$ edge. The difference between the pivotal and probabilistic calculations is even more striking for the probabilistic calculation based on any winning coalitions (see figure 4), where the resources needed by X to win at cell $(1, 3)$ are 514 percent $(\frac{1.72 - 0.28}{0.28})$ greater than those needed by Y to win.

It is important to point out that since the metric for resources needed to win is based on pivot proportions in two of the cases (figures 1 and 2) and probabilistic values in the other two (figures 3 and 4), it is not meaningful to mix metrics by comparing, for example, the resources needed by X to win at a particular lattice cell in figure 1 with the equivalent value in figure 3. However, it is meaningful to compare, as we did above, the value of X with respect to Y at a particular cell in one lattice with that in another lattice, because what we are comparing is the *relationship* between two comparable values (for X and Y) in one lattice to an equivalent *relationship* between two comparable values (for X and Y) in another lattice. Since this is in effect a comparison between ratios, which are dimensionless quantities, the comparison is legitimate.

Still another comparision between lattices is revealing, this being that between the changes in resources needed to win in one lattice (again a relationship among comparable values in the same lattice) with the equivalent changes in another lattice. To illustrate this comparison, we observe the following in figure 1 as the process moves downward along the diagonal connecting lattice cell $(3, 3)$ to cell $(3, 6)$:

Resources Needed by X to Win: 1.00 ---⟶ 1.22 ---⟶ 1.60 ---⟶ 2.00

Net Gains to Y: 0.22   0.38   0.40

The same path in figure 4 gives this picture:

Resources Needed by X to Win: 1.00 ---⟶ 1.60 ---⟶ 2.00 ---⟶ 2.00

Net Gains to Y: 0.60   0.40   0

In the pivotal model (figure 1), as is evident, the resources needed by X to win rise by the greatest amount late in the process, while in the probabilistic model (figure 4) X's resource needs shoot up most rapidly early in the process. Put another way, Y parlays his greatest advantage in net gains late in the process using the pivotal calculation ("Winning

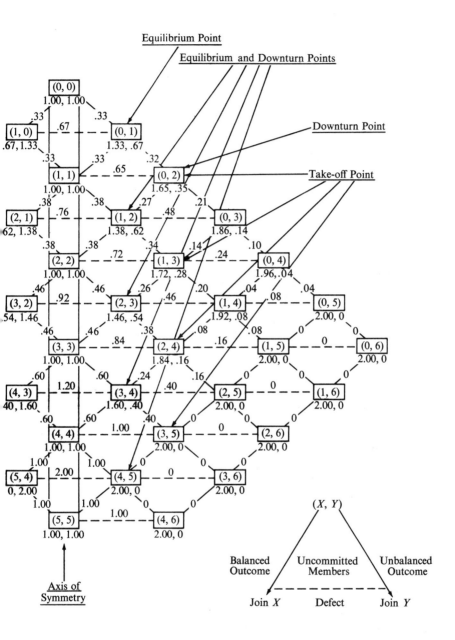

FIGURE 4. Lattice of probabilistic net gains and resources needed to win in *any winning coalition*, assuming all *combinations* of uncommitted members, with each protocoalition, are equally likely.

is everything"), early in the process using the probabilistic calculation ("It pays to take an early lead"). This conclusion tends to apply to defections (e.g., when the process moves horizontally from lattice cell $(3, 2)$ to cell $(0, 5)$) as well as to new commitments.[14]

There is another interesting difference between the net-gain values in figure 1 and figure 4 (as well as figure 3). In figure 1, the net gain of a defection to the smaller protocoalition at cells $(5, 4)$ or $(4, 5)$ is equal to 1.00, which is exactly the same as the net gain, when all members are committed, of a defection which makes a tie (process goes from cell $(4, 6)$ to cell $(5, 5)$) or breaks a tie (process goes from cell $(5, 5)$ to cell $(4, 6)$). By contrast, in figures 3 and 4 the net gain when a defection causes the lead to switch hands at cells $(5, 4)$ or $(4, 5)$ is 2.00, which is twice the net gain of 1.00 when defection makes or breaks a tie with all members committed. The latter calculations suggest that a defection which changes the lead, even when one member remains uncommitted and the defection is not decisive, is worth more than a tie-breaking or tie-making defection when all members are committed.

Empirically, it would seem, these two classes of models (pivotal and probabilistic) could be distinguished by the size of the payoffs offered prospective members of a protocoalition at different stages in the process. In the final section, we shall discuss this and other implications of the models.

VI. SUMMARY AND CONCLUSION

In this article we have introduced the concept of *net gain* to take account of the losses as well as the gains incurred by each protocoalition when an uncommitted member joins one of the two protocoalitions or a member of one protocoalition defects to the other. In showing that the net gain from a defection was exactly equal to the sum of the net gains produced by a prior commitment to each protocoalition—and the sum of net gains of subsequent new commitments to Y of one cell and X of another cell that move the process to the same lower cell—we also showed that this identity had a differential impact on each protocoalition. Specifically,

---

[14] Actually, the contrast between the pivotal and probabilistic models is not as sharp as the above example suggests. While the probabilistic models *tend* to give the greatest net gains to those who commit themselves early (to either protocoalition, not just Y), and the pivotal models to those who commit themselves late, the not-too-different downturn points in figures 1 and 2, on the one hand, and figure 3, on the other, render this statement without the qualifying "tend" erroneous. When even our simple assumptions about coalition-formation processes produce such complications as a consequent, it is not hard to imagine how complex real political processes are!

a defection is usually worth more to the smaller protocoalition, as compared to a prior or new commitment, than to the larger protocoalition, except in some cases for the commitment of the first member to a degenerate protocoalition (with no previous members). These are consequences not out of line with common sense but whose quantitative implications arising from the models at different stages in the political process remain yet to be explored in empirical situations.

The operationalization of the resources needed by a protocoalition to win, vis-à-vis other protocoalitions, would also seem to have testable consequences. Are the promises made by leaders of protocoalitions to prospective members, for example, in rough accord with the resources the models prescribe should be offered at different stages in the coalition-formation process? When this is not the case, are the protocoalitions less likely to be successful because of overspending or underspending at the wrong times?[15] Is overspending or underspending associated with pivotal (large expenditures late in the process) or probabilistic (large expenditures early in the process) kinds of calculations?

For the probabilistic models, are the resources actually spent by protocoalitions at different lattice cells related to the predicted probabilities of their becoming minimal winning? How do these predictions compare with the empirical relative frequencies of their winning? Is there a set of take-off and downturn points related to bandwagons that "peak" too soon?

These are just a few of the empirical questions suggested by the concepts and calculations of the models—and against whose answers the predictions of the models can be compared. Because of the many problems associated with operationalizing the theoretical concepts of the models, these questions will not be easy to answer. But as has been shown in applications of one of the basic models to data on voting in national party conventions (Brams and Riker, 1971; Brams, 1972b), these operational problems are not impossible to solve; they will require, however, a good deal of ingenuity and imagination, with data sources perhaps ranging from small-group experiments to campaign financial accounts.

With the computerization of the calculations of the models (Brams Heilman, 1972), the further theoretical development and refinement of the models, especially as they apply to larger voting bodies, can proceed apace empirical investigations. It seems that now that we have

---

[15] As the models show, there are many different paths to victory, and all involve a different set of calculations that most politicians probably do not take the trouble to make. (Perhaps the most successful ones do.) For one controversial view on how the Republican Party should expend its resources in order to sustain a national majority, see Phillips (1969); see also Scammon and Wattenberg (1970).

a set of models that give both very similar and very different predictions of the course of coalition-formation processes, we are in a position to try to relate both the assumptions and consequences of these models to empirical situations in order better to understand, through the simplified operation of the models, what mechanisms underlie the dynamics of different political processes.

6. The Effects of Group Size on Collective Decision Making

RICHARD G. NIEMI   HERBERT F. WEISBERG

Decision-rules and institutional arrangements exert a considerable influence on the aggregation of individual preferences into collective decisions. This has been demonstrated by a variety of studies done over the past decade. Black (1959, chap. 6), for example, has shown how voting procedures affect the outcome if certain patterns of individual preferences exist. Riker (1958) shows how the voting arrangements in the U.S. House of Representatives deal with the problem raised by Black. Buchanan and Tullock (1962) discuss the effects of institutional arrangements such as a bicameral legislature and the effects of a continuum of decision-rules expressed as the proportion of the group required to enact proposals. More recently Rae (1969) and others (chaps. 1-4 in this volume) have developed a model for selecting an "optimal" decision-rule—one that minimizes the likelihood that laws will be passed or defeated against your will.

In none of this work has there been a systematic investigation of the influence of group size on problems of collective choice.[1] Perhaps this is

---

This is a revised version of a paper presented at the Conference on Collective Decision Making held at the Fels Institute of Government, University of Pennsylvania, December 10–11, 1970. We would like to thank the participants at that conference, and especially the discussant, Amartya Sen, for their helpful comments.

[1] Group size is considered vis-à-vis particular aspects of collective choice in Schofield (chap. 3 in this volume), Niemi (1969), and Coleman (1970).

not surprising since intuitively the size of the deliberative body seems to be an irrelevant consideration in the formal procedures for aggregating preferences. Certainly group size *is* relevant if one is concerned with the power of formal leaders, interaction patterns among the membership, specialization of the members, and so on. But once the preferences of the members are established and "only" the formal problem of aggregating their preferences into a collective decision remains, the outcome would hardly seem to be affected by the size of the group.[2] Indeed, from a normative point of view one would probably not want the decision to depend on whether the group happened to be of one size rather than another.

In contrast to these intuitive thoughts and normative wishes, we intend to show that the result of aggregating individual preferences may depend heavily on the size of the voting body. Moreover, the effects on the group result of successfully influencing individual decisions may differ widely depending on the size of the body. Finally, the expected size of winning coalitions—specifically the likelihood of minimum winning coalitions— may depend on the group size. Hence, instead of being an irrelevant consideration, group size has a number of important consequences for collective decision making.

The basic components of our model are described briefly in part 1. Then in the following three sections the model is applied with increasing complexity. Implications of the analysis are discussed as they arise. As will become clear below, the importance of group size is dependent on our probabilistic formulation of voter behavior. Therefore a short appendix is devoted to a discussion of this approach.

I. COMPONENTS OF THE MODEL

Our model has three essential components—alternatives, individuals, and decision-rules. Only two alternatives are included, *A* and *B*. However, since these may be any two alternatives, such as a legislative bill and the status quo, a bill with and without an amendment, two alternate bills, candidates in an election, etc., the model is quite general in this respect. The question to be investigated is whether *A* defeats *B* or *B* defeats *A* when a vote is taken among the members of a group. In order to avoid ties we will most often assume that groups have an odd number of individuals. This is by no means a restriction, however, and some of our examples have even numbers of voters.

---

[2] An obvious exception, of course, is illustrated by the fact that majority rule in three-member groups actually means that the votes of two-thirds of the members are required in order to pass, that sixty percent of the votes are required in five-member groups, etc.

Each individual i will be characterized by the probability that he votes for A rather than B, denoted by $p_i(A > B)$. In the simplest form of the model, described in part 2, all individuals will be assumed to have the same probability. In part 3 some individuals will be assumed to vote for alternative A with a probability of 0 or 1, while the remaining individuals all have an identical probability. In part 4 the individuals will be assigned different, non-zero or one probabilities. Throughout the article all voters are assumed to act independently of one another. Though unrealistic, this asumption seems necessary in order to make the problem tractable. In later work it may be possible to relax this assumption slightly.

This probabilistic characterization of individual behavior is somewhat controversial, and a fuller discussion of it is included in the appendix. Briefly, the major distinction made there is between deterministic behavior modelled as probabilistic and behavior that is actually probabilistic. In our view this distinction is often academic since in modelling behavior we rarely know whether our assumptions about individual psyches are really correct. However, this distinction is important at one point below, since our second major conclusion (p. 134) is meaningful only if individual behavior really is probabilistic. For more details the reader is referred to the appendix.

Decision-rules in our model will be characterized by the proportion of individuals needed for A to defeat B. This proportion can vary, of course, from 0 to 100. Not all of these proportions are seriously considered as possible decision-rules, although sometimes the necessary proportion is quite extreme, as in extraordinary requirements for passage of fiscal measures or amendments to a constitution or charter. Moreover, in part 3 we shall define an effective decision-rule which can reasonably take on any value from 0 to 100.[3]

It should be noted that throughout the article we will adhere to the following interpretation, which seems consistent with most usage: majority rule will be taken to mean just over one half—$(m + 1)/2$ for odd m and $m/2 + 1$ for even m, where m is the number of individuals; other decision-rules such as two-thirds will be taken to mean that equal to or greater than this proportion of votes is required. Thus, for example, if $m = 12$, majority rule requires 7 votes to win and a two-thirds rule means that 8 votes are required.

---

[3] Rules which require the agreement of less than 50 percent of the members can cause special difficulties because more than one winning coalition can occur on the same issue—and conflicting proposals could be passed. However, as Rae (1969, p. 40) notes, there are instances in which multiple policies are no problem. (He cites *certiorari* proceedings of the Supreme Court.) Moreover, the effective decision-rule defined in part 3 can take on values less than 0.50 even if the decision-rule governing the legislative body is greater than one-half. Hence we consider the entire range of decision-rules from 0 to 100.

Finally, we should make clear that the discrete character of the voting process does not account for the findings we present. Thus, for example, because individuals are not divisible, majority rule means that a two-thirds vote is required when $m = 3$ and only a 53 percent vote (8/15) is required when $m = 15$; but this fact does not explain our findings. As a matter of fact, a casual inspection of our example would suggest that A is more likely to win in the group of 15 because a smaller proportion of votes is needed. But as the results below show, the very large majority among 3 individuals is more likely than the smaller majority among 15 individuals. This feature of the voting process does complicate our results slightly; for example, it causes the fluctuations in the rows of tables 1-9. Nevertheless it remains a minor complicating factor only.

II. THE BASIC MODEL

In this section we assume that each individual has the same probability of voting for A. While this assumption is overly simple, the problem will be clearest at this simplified level.

Let there be m individuals. Then our assumption states that $p_i(A > B)$ $= x$, for $i = 1, \ldots, m$. where $0 < x < 1$. (If $x = 0$ or $x = 1$, A obviously gets none or all of the votes, respectively; we eliminate this trivial case.) Each individual's vote can now be considered a Bernoulli trial with probability x of a "success." Hence the binomial probability distribution can be used to calculate the probability of any number of votes for A. When appropriate, the normal distribution can be used to approximate the binomial.[4]

From the law of large numbers, we know that as $m \longrightarrow \infty$ the probability approaches 1 that A receives as close to $x \cdot m$ votes as desired. Consider what this means for the choice being made by the group. For example, suppose $x = 0.45$. As $m \longrightarrow \infty$, as close to 45 percent of the votes as we desire will go to alternative A. If the decision-rule is 0.60 ($dr = 0.60$), A will lose with certainty in an infinitely large group. In general, if $x < dr$, A will certainly lose, and if $x > dr$, A will definitely win. Only if x is exactly equal to dr will there be any doubt about the outcome in infinitely large groups.

---

[4] The normal, Poisson, and beta distributions can all be used to approximate binomial probabilities. These approximations are often adequate and are highly useful in many circumstances, including some work using the model presented in this paper (see footnote 8 in Koehler, chap. 7 in this volume). However, we feel that their introduction at this point would only add another (minor) complicating factor and would contribute no new theoretical ideas. Therefore throughout this article, all probability values are taken from tables of the binomial probability distribution (*Tables . . .*, 1949, 1955).

For finite m, the situation is more complex. Consider two examples. First, suppose that $x = 0.45$, and $dr = 0.50$. By finding the appropriate values in tables of the cumulative binomial probability distribution we find the following, where $Pr(A > B)$ means the probability that A defeats B when a vote is taken among the group members:

$$m = \quad 3 \quad 5 \quad 7 \quad 9 \quad 15 \quad 25 \quad 49 \quad 100 \quad 200 \quad \infty$$
$$Pr(A > B) = .43 \ .41 \ .39 \ .38 \ .35 \ .31 \ .24 \ .13 \ .07 \ 0$$

Secondly, suppose that $x = 0.25$ and $dr = 0.60$. In this case we have the following results:

$$m = \quad 3 \quad 5 \quad 7 \quad 9 \quad 15 \quad 25 \quad \infty$$
$$Pr(A > B) = .16 \ .02 \ .01 \ .01 \ .001 \ .000+ \ 0$$

These findings illustrate the first major conclusion of this paper:

Given that $p_i(A > B) = x$ for $i = 1, \ldots, m$, $Pr(A > B)$ is a function of x, dr, and m. In other words, given the model we have described, the probability that A beats B depends on the probability with which individuals vote for A, the decision-rule, *and the size of the group.*

The truth of this proposition follows directly from the observation that values of the cumulative binomial probability distribution depend on both x and m and, that whether $A > B$ for the group depends on a comparison of the number of individuals who vote for A, and the dr. However, it is also apparent from the second example that for all practical purposes, the number of individuals is sometimes irrelevant in the determination of $Pr(A > B)$. We are led to ask, then, in what circumstances is m essentially irrelevant and when is it an important consideration?

The data in tables 1-9 help reveal these conditions.[5] They show that there are two major factors which determine whether or not the number of individuals is relevant. First of all, the smaller the difference between $p_i(A > B)$ and the dr, the greater is the impact of m on $Pr(A > B)$. This is true when $dr < p_i(A > B)$ and when $dr > p_i(A > B)$, although the $Pr(A > B)$ is not perfectly symmetric about the point $dr = p_i(A > B)$. The importance of this factor can be seen in any of the tables. For example, in table 2, in which $p_i(A > B) = 0.20$, $Pr(A > B)$ depends heavily on m if $0.15 \leq dr \leq 0.25$; whereas, if $dr \geq 0.45$, m is basically irrelevant. The lack of symmetry can easily be seen in table 4. Since $p_i(A > B) = 0.45$, $dr = 0.55$ and $dr = 0.35$ are $+0.10$ and -0.10, respectively, from dr. However, when $dr = 0.55$, and $m = 15$, $Pr(A > B) = 0.18$; when $dr =$

---

[5] These tables simply present rounded-off values taken from *Tables* . . . (1949, 1955). All of the information contained in tables 1-9 is therefore found in the more complete tabulations. We include tables 1-9 simply as a convenience to the reader.

0.35, we might expect $Pr(A > B) = 1 - 0.18 = 0.82$, but in fact $Pr(A > B) = 0.74$.

TABLES 1-9. The Probability that A Defeats B ($Pr(A > B)$) as a Function of the Number of Individuals (m), the Decision-Rule (dr), and the Individual Probability that $A > B$ ($p_i(A > B)$).

TABLE 1

$p_i(A > B) = 0.10$

Number of Individuals[a]

dr[b]	3	5	7	9	15	25	49	100	∞
.01	.27	.41	.52	.61	.79	.93	.99	1.0	1.0
.05	.27	.41	.52	.61	.79	.73	.88	.98	1.0
.15	.27	.41	.15	.23	.18	.24	.11	.07	0.0
.25	.27	.08	.15	.05	.06	.01	.00	.00	0.0
.35	.03	.08	.03	.01	.00	.00	.00	.00	0.0
.45	.03	.01	.00	.00	.00	.00	.00	.00	0.0
.50	.03	.01	.00	.00	.00	.00	.00	.00	0.0
.55	.03	.01	.00	.00	.00	.00	.00	.00	0.0
.65	.03	.00	.00	.00	.00	.00	.00	.00	0.0
.75	.00	.00	.00	.00	.00	.00	.00	.00	0.0
.85	.00	.00	.00	.00	.00	.00	.00	.00	0.0
.95	.00	.00	.00	.00	.00	.00	.00	.00	0.0
.99	.00	.00	.00	.00	.00	.00	.00	.00	0.0

[a] The dr is given in steps of 0.05 or 0.10 (except for 0.01 and 0.99). With small number of individuals, of course, many dr's are effectively the same. E.g., majority rule among three individuals is equivalent to $1/3 < dr < 2/3$. This is reflected in the number of identical entries in the columns to the left of each part of the table. Similarly, the fluctuations in many of the rows are due to the discrete character of the voting process as explained in section 1.

[b] Note that a decision-rule of 0.01 is equivalent to a decision-rule of $1/m$ (i.e., requiring only one vote) for $m \leq 100$. A decision-rule of 0.99 is equivalent to a decision-rule of m/m (unanimity) for $m \leq 99$.

TABLE 2

$p_i(A > B) = 0.20$

Number of Individuals

dr	3	5	7	9	15	25	49	100	∞
.01	.49	.67	.79	.87	.96	1.0	1.0	1.0	1.0
.05	.49	.67	.79	.87	.96	.97	1.0	1.0	1.0
.15	.49	.67	.42	.56	.60	.77	.79	.92	1.0
.25	.49	.26	.42	.26	.35	.22	.17	.13	0.0
.35	.10	.26	.15	.09	.06	.05	.00	.00	0.0
.45	.10	.06	.03	.02	.02	.00	.00	.00	0.0
.50	.10	.06	.03	.02	.00	.00	.00	.00	0.0
.55	.10	.06	.03	.02	.00	.00	.00	.00	0.0
.65	.10	.01	.00	.00	.00	.00	.00	.00	0.0
.75	.01	.01	.00	.00	.00	.00	.00	.00	0.0
.85	.01	.00	.00	.00	.00	.00	.00	.00	0.0
.95	.01	.00	.00	.00	.00	.00	.00	.00	0.0
.99	.01	.00	.00	.00	.00	.00	.00	.00	0.0

TABLE 3

$p_i(A > B) = 0.40$

| dr | Number of Individuals | | | | | | | | |
	3	5	7	9	15	25	49	100	∞
.01	.78	.92	.97	.99	1.0	1.0	1.0	1.0	1.0
.05	.78	.92	.97	.99	1.0	1.0	1.0	1.0	1.0
.15	.78	.92	.84	.93	.97	1.0	1.0	1.0	1.0
.25	.78	.66	.84	.77	.91	.93	.98	1.0	1.0
.35	.35	.66	.58	.52	.60	.73	.73	.87	1.0
.45	.35	.32	.29	.27	.39	.27	.20	.18	0.0
.50	.35	.32	.29	.27	.21	.15	.08	.02	0.0
.55	.35	.32	.29	.27	.10	.08	.02	.00	0.0
.65	.35	.09	.10	.10	.03	.00	.00	.00	0.0
.75	.06	.09	.02	.03	.00	.00	.00	.00	0.0
.85	.06	.01	.02	.00	.00	.00	.00	.00	0.0
.95	.06	.01	.00	.00	.00	.00	.00	.00	0.0
.99	.06	.01	.00	.00	.00	.00	.00	.00	0.0

TABLE 4

$p_i(A > B) = 0.45$

| dr | Number of Individuals | | | | | | | | |
	3	5	7	9	15	25	49	100	∞
.01	.83	.95	.98	1.0	1.0	1.0	1.0	1.0	1.0
.05	.83	.95	.98	1.0	1.0	1.0	1.0	1.0	1.0
.15	.83	.95	.90	.96	.99	1.0	1.0	1.0	1.0
.25	.83	.74	.90	.85	.96	.97	1.0	1.0	1.0
.35	.43	.74	.68	.64	.74	.87	.91	.98	1.0
.45	.43	.41	.39	.38	.55	.46	.45	.54	.50
.50	.43	.41	.39	.38	.35	.31	.24	.13	0.0
.55	.43	.41	.39	.38	.18	.18	.10	.03	0.0
.65	.43	.13	.15	.17	.08	.02	.00	.00	0.0
.75	.09	.13	.04	.05	.01	.00	.00	.00	0.0
.85	.09	.02	.04	.01	.00	.00	.00	.00	0.0
.95	.09	.02	.00	.00	.00	.00	.00	.00	0.0
.99	.09	.02	.00	.00	.00	.00	.00	.00	0.0

TABLE 5

$p_i(A > B) = 0.50$

| dr | Number of Individuals | | | | | | | | |
	3	5	7	9	15	25	49	100	∞
.01	.88	.97	.99	1.0	1.0	1.0	1.0	1.0	1.0
.05	.88	.97	.99	1.0	1.0	1.0	1.0	1.0	1.0
.15	.88	.97	.94	.98	1.0	1.0	1.0	1.0	1.0
.25	.88	.81	.94	.91	.98	.99	1.0	1.0	1.0
.35	.50	.81	.77	.75	.85	.95	.98	1.0	1.0
.45	.50	.50	.50	.50	.70	.65	.72	.86	1.0
.50	.50	.50	.50	.50	.50	.50	.50	.46	.50
.55	.50	.50	.50	.50	.30	.35	.28	.18	0.0
.65	.50	.19	.23	.25	.15	.05	.02	.00	0.0
.75	.12	.19	.06	.09	.02	.01	.00	.00	0.0
.85	.12	.03	.06	.02	.00	.00	.00	.00	0.0
.95	.12	.03	.01	.00	.00	.00	.00	.00	0.0
.99	.12	.03	.01	.00	.00	.00	.00	.00	0.0

TABLE 6

$p_i(A > B) = 0.55$

				Number of Individuals					
	3	5	7	9	15	25	49	100	∞
dr									
.01	.91	.98	1.0	1.0	1.0	1.0	1.0	1.0	1.0
.05	.91	.98	1.0	1.0	1.0	1.0	1.0	1.0	1.0
.15	.91	.98	.96	.99	1.0	1.0	1.0	1.0	1.0
.25	.91	.87	.96	.95	.99	1.0	1.0	1.0	1.0
.35	.57	.87	.85	.83	.92	.98	1.0	1.0	1.0
.45	.57	.59	.61	.62	.82	.82	.90	.98	1.0
.50	.57	.59	.61	.62	.65	.69	.76	.72	1.0
.55	.57	.59	.61	.62	.45	.54	.55	.54	.50
.65	.57	.26	.32	.36	.26	.13	.09	.03	0.0
.75	.17	.26	.10	.15	.04	.03	.00	.00	0.0
.85	.17	.05	.10	.04	.01	.00	.00	.00	0.0
.95	.17	.05	.02	.00	.00	.00	.00	.00	0.0
.99	.17	.05	.02	.00	.00	.00	.00	.00	0.0

TABLE 7

$p_i(A > B) = 0.60$

				Number of Individuals					
	3	5	7	9	15	25	49	100	∞
dr									
.01	.94	.99	1.0	1.0	1.0	1.0	1.0	1.0	1.0
.05	.94	.99	1.0	1.0	1.0	1.0	1.0	1.0	1.0
.15	.94	.99	.98	1.0	1.0	1.0	1.0	1.0	1.0
.25	.94	.91	.98	.97	1.0	1.0	1.0	1.0	1.0
.35	.65	.91	.90	.90	.97	1.0	1.0	1.0	1.0
.45	.65	.68	.71	.73	.90	.92	.98	1.0	1.0
.50	.65	.68	.71	.73	.79	.85	.92	.97	1.0
.55	.65	.68	.71	.73	.61	.73	.80	.87	1.0
.65	.65	.34	.42	.48	.40	.27	.27	.18	0.0
.75	.22	.34	.16	.23	.09	.07	.02	.00	0.0
.85	.22	.08	.16	.07	.03	.00	.00	.00	0.0
.95	.22	.08	.03	.01	.00	.00	.00	.00	0.0
.99	.22	.08	.03	.01	.00	.00	.00	.00	0.0

TABLE 8

$p_i(A > B) = 0.80$

				Number of Individuals					
	3	5	7	9	15	25	49	100	∞
dr									
.01	.99	1.0	1.0	1.0	1.0	1.0	1.0	1.0	1.0
.05	.99	1.0	1.0	1.0	1.0	1.0	1.0	1.0	1.0
.15	.99	1.0	1.0	1.0	1.0	1.0	1.0	1.0	1.0
.25	.99	.99	1.0	1.0	1.0	1.0	1.0	1.0	1.0
.35	.90	.99	1.0	1.0	1.0	1.0	1.0	1.0	1.0
.45	.90	.94	.97	.98	1.0	1.0	1.0	1.0	1.0
.50	.90	.94	.97	.98	1.0	1.0	1.0	1.0	1.0
.55	.90	.94	.97	.98	.98	1.0	1.0	1.0	1.0
.65	.90	.74	.85	.91	.94	.95	1.0	1.0	1.0
.75	.51	.74	.58	.74	.65	.78	.83	.91	1.0
.85	.51	.33	.58	.44	.40	.23	.21	.13	0.0
.95	.51	.33	.21	.13	.04	.03	.00	.00	0.0
.99	.51	.33	.21	.13	.04	.00	.00	.00	0.0

TABLE 9

$p_i(A > B) = 0.90$

	Number of Individuals								
	3	5	7	9	15	25	49	100	∞
dr									
.01	1.0	1.0	1.0	1.0	1.0	1.0	1.0	1.0	1.0
.05	1.0	1.0	1.0	1.0	1.0	1.0	1.0	1.0	1.0
.15	1.0	1.0	1.0	1.0	1.0	1.0	1.0	1.0	1.0
.25	1.0	1.0	1.0	1.0	1.0	1.0	1.0	1.0	1.0
.35	.97	1.0	1.0	1.0	1.0	1.0	1.0	1.0	1.0
.45	.97	.99	1.0	1.0	1.0	1.0	1.0	1.0	1.0
.50	.97	.99	1.0	1.0	1.0	1.0	1.0	1.0	1.0
.55	.97	.99	1.0	1.0	1.0	1.0	1.0	1.0	1.0
.65	.97	.92	.97	.99	1.0	1.0	1.0	1.0	1.0
.75	.73	.92	.85	.95	.94	.99	1.0	1.0	1.0
.85	.73	.59	.85	.77	.82	.76	.89	.96	1.0
.95	.73	.59	.48	.39	.21	.27	.12	.06	0.0
.99	.73	.59	.48	.39	.21	.07	.01	.00	0.0

The second factor that helps determine the importance of the number of individuals is the particular value of $p_i(A > B)$. (We could alternatively say the particular value of dr. Once the value of $p_i(A > B) - dr$ is determined, fixing either $p_i(A > B)$ or dr determines the other as well.) This can also be seen in tables 1 to 9. For example, let $p_i(A > B) - dr = -0.15$. Then if $p_i(A > B) = 0.40$ (table 3), $Pr(A > B)$ depends somewhat on m, whereas if $p_i(A > B) = 0.10$ (table 1), $Pr(A > B)$ is less dependent on the number of individuals. There is, however, no simple functional relationship which specifies this dependence on $p_i(A > B)$ (alternatively, dependence on dr). This will become clear below when we examine decision-rules in more detail.

Note that even for those combinations of $p_i(A > B)$ and dr for which m is important, once the size of the group reaches a certain point, further increases in the number of individuals can be safely ignored. What this point is, of course, depends on the values of $p_i(A > B)$ and $p_i(A > B) - dr$. However, unless $p_i(A > B)$ and dr are very close, the point is reached fairly quickly. For example, if $|p_i(A > B) - dr| \geq 0.15$, $Pr(A > B) \geq 0.90$ or ≤ 0.10 whenever m ≥ 17 (for odd m), and sometimes for even smaller m. If $p_i(A > B)$ and dr are close, on the other hand, m must be taken into account until it is quite large. Under majority rule, for example, if $p_i(A > B) = 0.45$, A has a chance of about one in four (0.24) of beating B in a group of 49 people. $Pr(A > B)$ does not drop below 0.10 until m reaches about 150.

These findings indicate that group size is especially important when the group (or the effective group to be defined below) is very small. When fewer than, say, a dozen individuals are involved, $Pr(A > B)$ depends heavily on the specific group size. In groups of this size, an alternative has a fair chance of winning even though the individuals might be characterized as basically opposed to it (i.e., $p_i(A > B) < dr$). Conversely, a proposal is not sure to win even though the group members are mainly in favor of it ($p_i(A > B) > dr$). Thus, to the extent that the model is a reasonable representation of group decision making, one can conclude that:

The decisions made by small groups less accurately reflect the preferences of the individual group members.[6]

Simply because of their size, and the results of probabilistic outcomes, proposals may be passed (defeated) in small groups that would be defeated (passed) in large groups under otherwise identical circumstances.

Now let us consider the decision-rules in more detail. Earlier we noted by way of illustration that the particular value of dr helped determine the importance of the number of individuals. A systematic examination of the relationship between dr and m reveals an interesting result. To find how the importance of m depends on dr, we have done the following. For each of the 21 values of dr listed in the left-hand column of table 10, and for a fixed m, we have found $Pr(A > B)$ for 20 of these same values of $p_i(A > B)$ (eliminating $p_i(A > B) = dr$). Now if $p_i(A > B) < dr$, the commonplace expectation is that A would lose (as indeed it would in an infinitely large group), so that $Pr(A > B) = 0$; if $p_i(A > B) > dr$, one would ordinarily expect A to win ($Pr(A > B) = 1$). Thus in the former case $Pr(A > B)$ is itself a measure of the deviation from the commonplace expectation that A will beat B. In the latter case $1 - Pr(A > B)$ is a measure of this deviation. As noted, for each dr we found $Pr(A > B)$ for 20 different values of $p_i(A > B)$. We then averaged the 20 deviations of $Pr(A > B)$ from 0 or 1.

The results of the above operations are presented in table 10 in the column labelled "Ave." The figures in these columns can be interpreted as follows. Given a fixed number of individuals and decision-rule, the "average" is the expected amount by which $Pr(A > B)$ differs from 0 or 1.[7] Thus, for example, if $dr = 0.60$ and $m = 3$, one would expect that $Pr(A > B) = 0.18$ (if $p_i(A > B) < dr$) or that $Pr(A > B) = 1 - 0.18 = 0.82$ (if $p_i(A > B) > dr$). If $m = 7$, we would expect that $Pr(A > B) = 0.11$ or 0.89 for the same dr. The larger the average deviation exhibited in table 10, the more important m is in the determination of $Pr(A > B)$.

---

[6] As noted in section 1 and the appendix, this conclusion is true only if one interprets the individual probabilities as really descriptive of human behavior. If we are only modelling it as probabilistic, then we cannot assert that the probabilities represent the individuals' preferences.

[7] We have implicitly supposed that the probability of each of the twenty values of $p_i(A > B)$ is equally likely. Hence the average deviation gives the mathematical expectation for the deviation.

TABLE 10. Average and Maximum Deviations from 0 or 1 of the Probability that A Defeats B (Pr(A > B)), for Fixed Numbers of Individuals (m) and Decision-Rules (dr).

Number of Individuals[a]

dr	3 Ave	3 Max	5 Ave	5 Max	7 Ave	7 Max	9 Ave	9 Max	15 Ave	15 Max	25 Ave	25 Max	49 Max
.01 and .99	.23	.97	.14	.95	.10	.93	.08	.91	.04	.86	.02	.78	.61
.05 " .95	.19	.86	.11	.77	.07	.70	.05	.63	.02	.54	.02	.64	.55
.10 " .90	.16	.73	.09	.59	.06	.52	.05	.61	.04	.55	.03	.54	.55
.15 " .85	.14	.61	.09	.56	.11	.72	.07	.60	.05	.60	.03	.53	.54
.20 " .80	.13	.51	.10	.67	.09	.58	.07	.56	.07	.60	.04	.58	.53
.25 " .75	.14	.58	.13	.63	.09	.56	.09	.60	.06	.54	.05	.56	.54
.30 " .70	.15	.66	.12	.53	.12	.65	.09	.54	.07	.62	.05	.51	.52
.35 " .65	.20	.72	.12	.57	.11	.53	.10	.61	.07	.56	.06	.53	.54
.40 " .60	.18	.65	.14	.66	.11	.58	.10	.52	.07	.60	.05	.58	.51
.45 " .55	.17	.57	.14	.59	.12	.61	.10	.62	.07	.55	.05	.54	.55
.50	.16	.50	.13	.50	.11	.50	.10	.50	.07	.50	.05	.50	.50

[a] The seemingly random fluctuations in each column of the table are in part due to the point noted in footnote a to table 1.

For every value of dr, of course, the deviations are largest when $m = 3$, and decrease rapidly to near zero. Note that no value of dr consistently minimizes or maximizes the expected deviation of $Pr(A > B)$ from 0 or 1. Judging by this criterion, no decision-rule is especially vulnerable to or free from the effects of varying numbers of individuals.

The second set of columns in table 10 gives the *maximum* deviation of $Pr(A > B)$ from the corresponding deterministic value of 0 or 1. Thus, for example, when $dr = 0.75$ and $m = 3$, if we have $p_i(A > B)$ just above 0.75, the commonplace expectation is that A will win ($Pr(A > B) = 1$). However, actually $Pr(A > B) = 0.42$, which is 0.58 away from 1. Note that for all dr and m, the maximum will be lowest (0.50) for majority rule and highest (1.0) for decision-rules of $1/m$ and unanimity.[8] Judging by this criterion, then, majority rule is superior to any other decision-rule.[9] Of

---

[8] Regardless of whether $p_i(A > B) < dr$ or $> dr$, the deviation of $Pr(A > B)$ from 0 or 1 increases as $|p_i(A > B) - dr|$ decreases.

If $p_{i1}(A > B) < dr$, let $Pr(A > B) = x$, and if $p_{i2}(A > B) > dr$, let $Pr(A > B) = x + \epsilon$. Then as $|p_{ij}(A > B) - dr| \longrightarrow 0$ for $j = 1, 2, \epsilon \longrightarrow 0$. Thus $Pr(A > B) = x$ as $|p_{ij}(A > B) - dr| \longrightarrow 0$ for $j = 1, 2$. But if $p_{i1}(A > B) < dr$, $Pr(A > B) = 0$ as $m \longrightarrow \infty$; and if $p_{i2}(A > B) > dr$, $Pr(A > B) = 1$ as $m \longrightarrow \infty$. Therefore as $|p_{ij}(A > B) - dr| \longrightarrow 0$ for $j = 1, 2$, the maximum deviation of $Pr(A > B)$ from 0 and 1 will be Max $(x, 1 - x)$. Obviously Max $(x, 1 - x) \geqq 0.50$ since $0 \leqq x \leqq 1$, and the maximum is smallest when $x = 1 - x = 0.50$. Now for m odd, if $dr = 0.50$, $Pr(A > B) = 0.50$ as $|p_{ij}(A > B) - dr| \longrightarrow 0$ for $j = 1, 2$. Therefore Max $(x, 1 - x)$ is smallest for $dr = 0.50$—majority rule. (Strictly speaking, the statement in the text that the maximum is 0.50 for majority rule applies only to odd m.)

Under a unanimity rule, suppose $p_i(A > B) < dr$. Then, as usual, $Pr(A > B) = 0$ as $m \longrightarrow \infty$. Let $|p_i(A > B) - dr| \longrightarrow 0$, which means that $p_i(A > B) \longrightarrow 1$. For finite m, $Pr(A > B) = 1$ as $p_i(A > B) \longrightarrow 1$. Thus as $p_i(A > B) \longrightarrow 1$, the deviation of $Pr(A > B)$ from its limit (of 0) approaches 1.

A rule of $1/m$ (only 1 vote required) can be represented as requiring $\epsilon \cdot m$ votes, where $0 < \epsilon < 1/m$. Suppose that $p_i(A > B) > \epsilon$. Then $Pr(A > B) = 1$ as $m \longrightarrow \infty$. Let $\epsilon \longrightarrow 0$ and $|p_i(A > B) - \epsilon| \longrightarrow 0$, which means that $p_i(A > B) \longrightarrow 0$. For finite m, $Pr(A > B) = 0$ as $p_i(A > B) \longrightarrow 0$. Thus as $p_i(A > B) \longrightarrow 0$, the deviation of $Pr(A > B)$ from its limit (of 1) approaches 1.

[9] For majority rule we have shown that the maximum is 0.50. To show that majority rule is superior to any other rule by this criterion, we need to show that for any $dr \neq 0.50$, there is at least one value of m such that the maximum is greater than 0.50 for any $p_i(A > B)$.

Consider $m = 3$.

a. Let $0 < dr \leqq 1/3$, so that 1 vote is needed for A to beat B. Then $Pr(A > B) = 0.50$ if and only if $p_i(A > B)$ has a certain value approximately equal to 0.205. (The exact value is not important here.) But now suppose $m = 5$; either 1 or 2 votes are required depending on where the dr falls in the specified range. But if $p_i(A > B) \approx 0.205$, then $Pr(A > B) \approx 0.68$ if 1 vote is needed and ≈ 0.27 if 2 votes are needed. In either case the maximum deviation of $Pr(A > B)$ from 0 or 1 is greater than 0.50.

b. Let $1/3 < dr \leqq 2/3$, so that 2 votes are needed. Let the dr take on a particular value x within the specified range. Then in order to maximize the deviation, let $|p_{ij}(A > B) - dr| \longrightarrow 0$ for $j = 1, 2$ where $p_{ij}(A > B)$ is defined as in footnote 8. Thus $p_{ij}(A > B) \longrightarrow x$. But $Pr(A > B) = 0.50$ as $p_{ij}(A > B) \longrightarrow x$ if and only if $x = 0.50$. Hence Max $(x, 1 - x) = 0.50$ only if $dr = 0.50$.

c. Let $2/3 < dr \leqq 3/3$ so that 3 votes are needed. An argument similar to Case (a) applies.

course, the maximum deviation occurs only under extreme conditions of $p_i(A > B)$ being very close to dr, and is obviously much greater than the expected deviations. Hence the advantages of majority rule will be realized only under unusual circumstances, though this may appeal to a group seeking to minimize the maximum deviation from the values of 0 and 1. Note also that the maximum deviations in table 10 are not dependent on the group size for majority rule, while for other decision-rules they decline steadily to the majority rule value as the group size increases.[10]

Altogether, then, these findings can be summarized by noting that (a) no decision-rule is completely free from the effects of group size; (b) on the average,[11] all decision-rules are judged to be about equally susceptible to these effects (as measured by the deviation from the expectation that A will win or lose with certainty); and (c) the maximum deviation from 0 or 1 is lowest, and is independent of group size, for majority rule. Thus while majority rule might be accepted if these were the criteria of judgment, this choice does not render the effects of group size meaningless.

III. THE EXPANDED MODEL

As promised, the basic model discussed in part 2 must be expanded to approximate reality a bit more closely. The first expansion of the model is given here. Suppose again that there are m individuals. However, suppose that we know that f individuals, where $0 \leqq f \leqq m$, are in favor of alternative A and are certain to vote for it. (Obviously this is equivalent to assuming that $p_i(A > B) = 1$ for all i in f.) Similarly, let a individuals, where $0 \leqq a \leqq m$, be against A or certain to vote for B. We must also

---

[10] Not only is the maximum deviation from the values of 0 and 1 minimal for majority rule, but that maximum deviation might be regarded as relatively benign for majority rule. The maximum deviation for any decision-rule comes when $p_i(A > B)$ is just above or just below dr. Furthermore, the individual's dissatisfaction with the vote outcome when the alternative he favored loses can be considered as being dependent on the decisiveness with which he favored that alternative. Under majority rule, the maximum deviation occurs when $p_i(A > B)$ is very nearly equal to 0.50, in which case the individuals are relatively indifferent as to the choice between A and B. Under any other decision-rule, the maximum deviation occurs when $p_i(A > B)$ is nearly equal to dr which is more extreme than 0.50, and the individuals can be regarded as more decisive as $p_i(A > B)$ departs from 0.50. Since we have assumed $p_i(A > B)$ is the same for all individuals, this means that the maximum deviation results in less dissatisfaction with the vote outcome on the part of everyone in the group for majority rule than for any other decision-rule. This analysis can be extended to a general treatment of the expected degree of dissatisfaction with the vote outcome and the minimization of that expected value as a criterion in the selection of a decision-rule, but that goes well beyond the scope of this paper.

[11] We remind the reader that in calculating the average we assumed that each of the 20 values of $p_i(A > B)$ was equally likely. Conceivably a weighted average could be constructed so that the statement in the text would no longer be true. Presently we see no way to justify any particular weighted average.

restrict f and a so that $0 \leq f + a \leq m$. Let $em = m - f - a$, so that em indicates individuals for whom our earlier probability assumptions will apply. For convenience let us call the latter group "undecided," remembering, however, that alternative interpretations may be made of the probabilities.

The situation is now as follows. The m individuals are divided into those for (f) and against (a) A, and the undecided voters (em). If $f/m > dr$, we know for certain that $A > B$. Also, if $(f + em)/m < dr$, $B > A$. But if $f/m < dr$ and $(f + em)/m > dr$, the result is not determined. Whether $A > B$ or not depends on how the undecideds vote. Let us now specify that $p_i(A > B) = x$ for all of the undecideds. The assumption is the same as that made in part 2, except that it now applies to a subset of the entire group.

With the foregoing assumptions we can make use of the basic model of part 2. There, in order to win, A needed just over $m \cdot dr$ votes. Now A needs the same number of votes but is assured of f of them; the remaining votes must come from among the em undecided voters. Hence, in the revised model A needs just over $(m \cdot dr - f)$ votes to win (in addition to the votes it is assured of). We can thus define the effective decision-rule as follows: $edr = (m \cdot dr - f)/em$.[12,13]

The analysis given in part 2 applies to this expanded model if we substitute em for m and edr for dr. As an example, let $m = 21$, $f = 7$, and $a = 5$. If $dr = 0.50$, A needs 11 votes to win. Since $em = 9$, $edr = (21 \cdot 1/2 - 7)/9 = 0.389$. Thus A needs the votes of 4 out of the 9 undecided individuals in order to win. Suppose that $p_i(A > B) = 0.40$ for the em undecided voters. Note that the situation is now completely analogous to the model in part 2 where $m = 9$, $dr = 0.389$, and $p_i(A > B) = 0.40$ for $i = 1, \ldots, 9$. Since $edr = 0.35$ also requires 4 out of 9 votes, we can use the values tabulated in table 3, from which we find that $Pr(A > B) = 0.52$.

This extension of the model is straightforward and requires no extensive analysis. It does contain some interesting features, however. First of all, the edr is determined not only by the established dr, but by the dr, m, f, and a. Since m, f, and a vary widely, the edr may reasonably be anywhere in the range $0 - 1.00$ rather than being limited to majority rule, two-thirds majorities, and other decision-rules commonly found in legislative bodies. Hence with the extended model, we will sometimes find situations with extreme edr's in which it was shown that the (effective) number of individuals is basically irrelevant unless it is extremely small.

---

[12] The formula in the text is for m odd. For m even, $edr = [(m + 1) \cdot dr - f]/em$.

[13] We could also assume here that a certain number of individuals abstain from voting. However, all this does is to change em and edr. Since no new concepts are introduced, we do not bother to bring in abstentions formally. A more formidable problem, but one of dubious value, is to assign individuals a probability of abstaining.

Secondly, it should be noted that once m, f and a are fixed, $Pr(A > B)$ depends on em (and on the difference between f and a) and not on m. But $f + a$ may be most of the individuals, even if m is very large. Thus if the votes of $f + a$ individuals are fixed and only em voters are viewed probabilistically, $Pr(A > B)$ may depend on a small number of individuals even though m is large. And when em is small, it can play an important part in determining $Pr(A > B)$. With the extended model, then, we cannot say a priori that the number of individuals is irrelevant for large groups. The number of individuals can be relevant when m or em is small (or when m or em is moderate and $p_i(A > B)$ is close to dr or edr).

A third feature of the extended model can be observed by considering the effect of influence attempts in groups of different sizes.[14] In an infinitely large effective group, note that A is defeated with certainty if $p_i(A > B) < edr$, whereas A is certain of winning if $p_i(A > B) > edr$. Now suppose that a proponent of A tries to influence the undecideds in favor of A. If $p_i(A > B) < edr$ initially, the influencer is successful in changing the probability of A winning if and only if he succeeds in making $p_i(A > B) > edr$. And if $p_i(A > B) > edr$ in the first place, he has done nothing to make it more likely that A will win. Suppose, however, that the effective group is quite small. Then if the influencer can alter $p_i(A > B)$, he may successfully increase A's chances of winning even if $p_i(A > B) < edr$ after his influence or if $p_i(A > B) > edr$ in the first place. For example, suppose that $em = 5$. Let $edr = 0.50$. If $p_i(A > B) = 0.35$ before the influence and 0.45 after the influence, $Pr(A > B)$ has changed from 0.24 to 0.41. Similarly, if $p_i(A > B) = 0.55$ before and 0.65 after the influence, the influence has successfully raised $Pr(A > B)$ from 0.59 to 0.76. What would probably be considered in most circumstances a small amount of influence (changing $p_i(A > B)$ by 0.10) has resulted in a more substantial increase in A's chances.

This leads us to a third conclusion. Given the model we have developed:

In a large group, a change in $p_i(A > B)$ is likely to have little effect on $Pr(A > B)$ unless $p_i(A > B)$ is less than edr before the change and greater than edr after it. (If these conditions *are* met, $Pr(A > B)$ is raised from near-zero to near-one.) In small groups, the same amount of change in $p_i(A > B)$ can have a substantial effect on $Pr(A > B)$ even if $p_i(A > B)$ remains less than edr after the change or was greater than edr before the change.

---

[14] Technically this feature, and the following one on coalition size, are features of the basic model also. We present them here, however, to indicate that they fit equally well into the expanded model. In addition, it probably pays to think of influence as reaching some individuals (the em individuals with non-zero or one probabilities) and not reaching others (those with zero or one probabilities).

This implies that influence attempts would be irrational in large groups unless the individual probabilities were less than *edr* initially and there was a reasonable chance of making them greater than *edr*.[15] In small groups, influence attempts would often be rational under otherwise similar circumstances.[16]

A fourth and final feature of the extended model is found in its implications for the occurrence of minimal winning coalitions. In Riker's (1962, chap. 2) game-theoretic formulation of the size-principle in which perfect information about the "player's" voting intentions is assumed, he shows that coalitions will form that are just large enough to win and no larger. This situation is analogous to a version of the present model in which $p_i(A > B)$ is only allowed to take on values of 0 and 1. In forming a coalition in support of A, individuals are presumably induced to change $p_i(A > B)$ from 0 directly to 1. As Riker shows, rational actors will always form minimal winning coalitions under these conditions.

Consider our more general case, however, in which $p_i(A > B)$ can take on values between 0 and 1. Let us retain the assumption that the probability of voting for A is known with certainty. We will show that in this situation there is sometimes a conflict between maximizing the probability of winning $(Pr(A > B))$ and the probability of a minimum winning coalition $(Pr(MWC))$. This will suggest that even with perfect information there are conditions under which rational actors will not maximize $Pr(MWC)$. The conditions have to do with the size of the group.

We noted earlier that if $p_i(A > B) = x$, very close to $x \cdot m$ individuals will vote for A in a large group. In fact, as $m \rightarrow \infty$, as close to $x \cdot m$ as desired will vote for A. This means that in an infinitely large group, we could set x just above the *dr* and be assured of winning and at the same time of forming a minimum winning coalition. The situation is not quite so simple in a large, finite body, but it is still possible to be almost assured of a relatively small winning coalition without seriously risking defeat. Suppose, for example, that $m = 394$, $f = 156$, $a = 108$, and $dr = 0.50$. Here 198 voters are needed to win, so that A must pick up at least 42 votes of the *em* of 130 individuals. If the coalition builder can influence individuals until $p_i(A > B) = 0.40$, there is a probability of 0.96 that between 50.3 percent and 56.1 percent of the votes will be cast for A. The probability of winning is thus kept at a very high level (0.97), and yet the probability of getting more than 56.1 percent of the votes is very low

---

[15] If $p_i(A > B) > edr$ initially, it would of course be rational to counter an attempt by B's proponents to make $p_i(A > B) < edr$. But it would not be rational to try to raise $p_i(A > B)$.

[16] In interpreting statements such as these one must always keep in mind the importance of the exact values of *em*, *edr*, and $p_i(A > B)$. E.g., in a very small group (*em* = 7), a change in $p_i(A > B)$ from 0.10 all the way to 0.55 changes the $Pr(A > B)$ from 0.00 to only 0.10 if *edr* happens to be ≥ 0.72.

(0.01). While strictly speaking any coalition larger than just over 50 percent is not minimal winning, the coalition builder in our example is able to sharply restrict the expected size of his coalition.[17] (For convenience, this case and the ones to follow are summarized in table 11.)

TABLE 11. Examples Showing Both the Probability that A Defeats
B and the Probability of a Minimum Winning Coalition

Case	1	2	3	3a	4	5
m	394	280	99	99	49	9
f	156	0	39	39	0	3
a	108	0	27	27	0	1
dr	.50	.50	.50	.50	.50	.50
em	130	280	33	33	49	5
$p_i(A > B)$	.40	.55	.48	.40	.61	.70
$Pr(A > B)$	.97	.95	.97	.83	.94	.97
$Pr(MWC^*)$ᵃ	.96	.57	.56	.71	.18	.13
$Pr(> MWC^*)$	.01	.38	.41	.12	.76	.84

ᵃ This is the probability that between $(50 + \epsilon)\%$ (i.e., $(m/2) + 1$ or $(m + 1)/2$) and 56% of the individuals vote for A.

Coalition managers are not always this fortunate, even in large groups. If, for example, $m = 280$ and $dr = 0.50$ (Case 2), we find that the probability of a minimum winning coalition is still moderate (0.57), although the chances are also fairly good (0.38) that a larger coalition will form. Nevertheless, even in this situation, the chances of a minimum winning coalition are much greater than in a situation that is nearly identical except for a smaller number of individuals (see Case 4).

If the manager of a group of several hundred individuals is in a somewhat less advantageous position than a leader of an infinite group, the coalition organizer in a moderate to small group is in a far worse situation. Several examples should make the point quite clear. First, let $m = 99$, $f = 39$, $a = 27$, and $dr = 0.50$ (Case 3). Here $em = 33$, and A needs to get at least 11 of these votes in order to win. This situation is virtually identical to Case 1 except that the numbers have been reduced by a factor of four. (Slight adjustments have been made in order to make use of existing tabulations of the binomial probabilities.) By raising $p_i(A > B)$ to 0.48, the probability of A winning is kept at the same level as in Case 1. But the probability of a small winning coalition is much lower than in the former case, and the likelihood of a larger coalition is correspondingly higher. To see how we might reduce the chances of a large coalition, we show Case

---

[17] Obviously the precise probabilities of minimum winning coalitions that we cite depend on the cutting point chosen. The general conclusions, however, are not so restricted (although the less restrictive the definition the smaller m must be to obtain comparable effects). We shall adhere throughout to a cutting point as close to 56 percent as possible

3a. Here we lowered $p_i(A > B)$ to 0.40, and $Pr(> MWC^*)$ declines to a fairly low level (although still higher than in Case 1). We have accomplished this at a price, however, for now there is a probability of 0.17 that A will lose. Unfortunately for the coalition-builders in Case 3, there is simply no way of duplicating the probabilities found in Case 1.[18]

Case 4 is comparable to Case 2 except that the number of individuals is substantially lower. As in all the examples, the probability of A winning can be kept very high. A direct consequence, however, is that the likelihood of a minimum winning coalition is quite small (0.18). Although we noted that coalition leaders in Case 2 are not assured of a small winning coalition, they are in a much better position than their counterparts, in Case 4.

The final case illustrates what can happen in very small groups. To see this it is necessary to compare Cases 4 and 5. On the basis of the information given in the summary table, these cases would seem to be nearly identical. Let us calculate, however, the probability of arriving at coalitions of varying proportions of the total group. The intervals for Case 4 are chosen to correspond to the precise proportions derived in Case 5. The results are as follows:

Case 4

Size of coalition	< 50%	50+ − 56%	56+ − 67%	67+ − 78%	78+ − 89%	89+ − 100%
Probability of occurrence	.06	.18	.54	.22	.00	.00

Case 5

Size of coalition	< 50%	56%	67%	78%	89%	100%
Probability of occurrence	.03	.13	.31	.36	.17	0

From these more detailed results we can observe, for example, that in Case 4 a coalition of more than 67 percent of the members will occur about one time in five (0.22). In Case 5, on the other hand, 7 of 9 (78%) or 8 of 9 (89%) members will vote for A over half of the time (0.53). This illustrates the fact that in very small groups not only are minimum winning coalitions unlikely, but large and even unanimous coalitions will occur with some regularity. In moderate sized groups such, as Case 4, grossly oversized coalitions as well as minimum winning ones are unlikely.

---

[18] There is a cost involved in raising $p_i(A > B)$ high enough to virtually assure winning, and decision makers might sometimes be willing to risk losing (as in Case 3a) rather than paying this cost (as in Case 3). This matter deserves more study, and we are currently undertaking such an investigation. Our present point, however, is that the decision maker has to make a choice—$Pr(A > B)$ and $Pr(MWC^*)$ cannot both be maximized.

These findings concerning coalition sizes can be summarized in several ways. One important conclusion is as follows:

In small groups, if rational actors maximize the probability of winning (or at least make that probability very high), they do not maximize the probability of minimum winning coalitions. Conversely, the probability of a minimum winning coalition is maximized only at the cost of reducing the probability of winning.

One can also conclude that to the extent that ours is an appropriate model of voting behavior (and we are thinking especially of the assumption of certainty):[19]

Minimum winning coalitions (or small winning coalitions) are more likely to form in large than in small groups.

The significance of these results is perhaps best observed by pointing out that they suggest that a model based on rational behavior can account for the tendency to form large coalitions in small groups. It does not seem necessary to explain this tendency solely in terms of motives such as friendship, maintenance of group solidarity (Riker, 1962, p. 51), or psychological pressure for unanimous decisions (Adrian and Press, 1968, p. 556). Instead, a single model can explain the divergent tendencies in groups of varying sizes. Finally, with regard to the general point being made in this paper, these results show another way in which the size of the group is an important element in the formal aspects of collective decision making.

IV. THE GENERAL MODEL

The model can now be made fully general by allowing individuals or groups to have different non-zero or one probabilities. We might, for example, characterize parties and/or factions by their differential probability of supporting alternative A. Since some individuals can still have $p_i(A > B)$ equal to 0 or 1, the model is fully general. With these nonrestrictive assumptions it is still theoretically possible to calculate $Pr(A > B)$ for any given set of conditions. Practically speaking, however, there may be so many different coalitions that yield a majority for A, each being represented by a different combination of individual probabilities, that it is difficult or impossible to carry out the calculations. Moreover, there are now so many parameters—since each individual could have a different

---

[19] Although we have just begun to analyze the effects of uncertainty, it appears that the following conclusion remains true when the certainty assumption is relaxed.

$p_i(A > B)$)—that it is impossible to characterize easily the variety of initial conditions. What we *can* do is to show by way of an example that the number of individuals is still an important consideration.

Our illustration is as follows. Suppose $p_i(A > B) = 0.20$ for one-fourth of the undecided individuals and that $p_i(A > B) = 0.55$ for the remaining undecideds.[20] In our first case let $m = 9$, $f = 4$, $a = 1$, and $dr = 2/3$. Here $em = 4$, and 2 of these four votes are needed for A to win. In order to obtain these 2 votes, A must get (1) the vote of the individual for whom $p_i(A > B) = 0.20$ and 1, 2 or 3 votes from the three individuals for whom $p_i(A > B) = 0.55$; *or* (2) the votes of 2 or 3 of the latter individuals. Using tables 2 and 6 we find that the probability of the first event is $0.20 \times 0.91 = 0.182$ and that the probability of the second event is $0.80 \times 0.57 = 0.456$. Thus, $Pr(A > B) = 0.182 + 0.456 = 0.638$.

Now let us triple the numbers in the above example so that $m = 27$, $f = 12$, $a = 3$, and $dr = 2/3$. Here there are 3 individuals with $p_i(A > B) = 0.20$ and 9 with $p_i(A > B) = 0.55$. But now in order for A to win, it can get (1) 3 votes from the former group and 3 or more from the latter; (2) 2 and 4 or more votes; (3) 1 and 5 or more votes; or (4) 0 and 6 or more votes. Again using tables 2 and 6, we find that $Pr(A > B) = 0.0095 + 0.0747 + 0.2418 + 0.1836 = 0.5096$.[21] The chances of A winning are still fairly good, but they are reduced well below the figure for the otherwise identical situation involving 9 individuals. Moreover, as $em \rightarrow \infty$, A will get as close as desired to the following proportion of votes: $0.20 \times 0.25 + 0.55 \times 0.75 = 0.0500 + 0.4125 = 0.4625$. Since the votes of half or more of the em individuals must be gained in order for A to win, $Pr(A > B) = 0$. With a large number of individuals, then, A has almost no chance of winning.

We can thus show that $Pr(A > B)$ is dependent on m in the general model. We think that many of the other findings for the basic and extended models also hold for the general model.[22] Proving this, however, seems

---

[20] This illustration suggests how our model can be used to represent a two party legislature. The one-fourth of the undecided individuals with $p_i(A > B) = 0.20$ may belong to one party while those with $p_i(A > B) = 0.55$ may belong to the other party.

[21] For the individuals with $p = 0.20$, the probability of exactly 3 votes for A is found in the first column of table 2; the probability of exactly two votes for A is found in the same column by subtracting 0.01 from 0.10; the probability of 1 vote is found by subtracting 0.10 from 0.49, etc. (A slight amount of rounding error results from using these figures rather than the tabulations listed in the bibliography.) For the individuals with $p = 0.55$, we can find in the fourth column of table 6 that the probability is 0.95 that 3 or more individuals will vote for A, that the probability is 0.83 that 4 or more will vote for A, etc. Then $Pr(A > B) = 0.01 \times 0.95 + 0.09 \times 0.83 + 0.39 \times 0.62 + 0.51 \times 0.36$, which is the equation given in the text.

[22] The general model also permits some additional types of analysis not encountered with the simpler versions of the model. For example, suppose one is confronted with the first example in part 4 (in which $em = 4$, $p_i(A > B) = 0.20$ for one individual and

most difficult, owing to the number of parameters involved.[23] Before such a task is undertaken, more discussion and analysis of the underlying probability model are needed.

V. CONCLUSION

There is little doubt that there are significant differences among groups of differing sizes. The differences are difficult to specify (perhaps because there is a continuum of group sizes rather than a clearcut separation into large versus small groups), but they surely exist. Most commentary on these differences tries to explain them on the basis of (1) physical concomitants of size—e.g., face-to-face communications and informal rules become difficult when the number of individuals gets large; (2) psychological factors—e.g., friendships and solidarity are said to be more important in small groups.

What we have proposed here is a formal model in which psychological and physical considerations do not come into play. We were able to proceed on this basis and still find some striking differences between groups of varying sizes. We suggest that further exploration of this or similar models may help explain previously observed features of various-sized groups as well as uncovering additional correlates of group size.

The possibility exists, moreover, that one could introduce some "sociological" characteristics of groups along with other critical factors into our model. For example, the reduced visibility of individuals (at least non-leaders) in large groups may have an analogue in a generally lowered ability to correctly estimate the $p_i(A > B)$. Intensity of issues may be reflected in larger proportions of group members with near-zero or one probabilities (although in some instances indifference may be held intensely). Similarly, alternatives, such as legislative bills and candidates, which evoke only a single issue may result in mostly zero or one probabilities while multifaceted alternatives suggest probabilities between these extremes as well as probabilities which are unstable over time. We feel that, at a minimum, these considerations suggest the value of further exploration of models using a probabilistic interpretation of individual behavior—both for studies of group size as well as other characteristics of collective decision-making institutions.

$p_i(A > B) = 0.55$ for the other three). Given a limited amount of resources, is it better to try to influence the one individual a good deal or each of the three individuals a little bit? And does the size of the group make any difference in this decision?

[23] Nonetheless, it seems like a worthwhile undertaking, since conclusions about size and probabilistic outcomes are not necessarily invariant as one moves from a single-valued probability to a distribution of probabilities.

APPENDIX : INTERPRETATION OF THE PROBABILITIES

The individuals' probabilities of voting for A, $p_i(A > B)$, are subject to two different interpretations: (a) voting is deterministic but modelled as probabilistic; (b) voting is actually probabilistic. Elaboration of each interpretation is provided here.

a. We might argue that individuals' behavior is deterministic but usefully modelled as probabilistic. Thus we would say that individuals behave *as if* they were acting randomly, even though that assumption is regarded as false. From this viewpoint our model is based on a useful though unrealistic assumption, on the grounds that the way to judge a model is by the deductions made from it rather than the assumptions on which it is based.

If we strictly adhere to this point of view, no further justification of the probabilistic assumption is necessary. Nevertheless, it may be useful to suggest some rationale for this particular assumption. One such rationale is based on the fact that we cannot perfectly predict the behavior of others, even if that behavior is completely deterministic. Thus the probabilities can be regarded as estimates of the likelihood that individuals will vote for A. Of course, individuals whose predicted behavior seems certain can be assigned a probability of zero or one. This interpretation seems to correspond roughly to the procedures employed by group leaders as well as political pundits who must estimate the chances for success of the alternatives to be voted on by making assumptions about the expected behavior of individuals. One often hears comments such as that Senator X is leaning toward the bill, that Justice Y is unlikely to vote for that type of decision, that Representative Z is not revealing his position at all, and so on. Our model differs only by specifying precisely the probability of a particular decision.

Note that in forming estimates of a person's vote one does not need to just "guess" a number. Any information relevant to the vote—past voting behavior, expressed attitudes, "hunches," etc.—can all be used in making the estimates as accurate as possible. In fact, some formal models, such as those based on probit analysis, predict individual attitudes or behavior (e.g., a vote for A) with a probability value. Other models as well, such as those by Hinich, *et al.* (1970b) and Stokes (1966), have a similar probabilistic element. Insofar as all the determinants of individual behavior are not included in these models, they cannot perfectly predict the behavior they are modelling. And our point here is that estimates such as are derived from these models could be the source of the probabilities used in the model developed in this chapter.

Another rationale for a probabilistic assumption can be made if we are concerned about future, unpredictable behavior. Thus we might assume that individuals have a certain probability of voting for A_i rather than B_i, where A_i and B_i are an unspecified pair of future proposals. This is, of course, the approach taken by Rae (1969) and in chapters 1-3 of this volume. Interestingly, in line with the ideas raised by those papers, we might think of fixing the dr and the $p_i(A > B)$, and then trying to determine what size committee individual Ego should favor in order to minimize his disappointments. Here, in constrast to the first rationale, the probability values assumed are largely gratuitous.

b. The second interpretation of the probabilities suggests that voting behavior is truly random. Not that decisions are made irresponsibly or by literally flipping a coin but psychological mechanisms controlling judgments of alternatives and preferences vary over time in a more or less random fashion.[24]

First, an individual may have difficulty discriminating between a pair of alternatives, and this would result in his not always giving the same response to that pair of alternatives. In the context of a vote, the implications or expected consequences of choosing a particular alternative are often not completely unambiguous. Thus the "meaning" of a vote for that alternative can vary from moment to moment according to the current view of an individual voter (as well as varying across individuals). To put it another way, which of a pair of alternatives seems to accomplish better the individual's goals can vary across time.

A good political example might be the question of busing to achieve racial integration in the schools. A legislator may be very clear in his goals (e.g., racial harmony, justice for all races, complete integration of blacks into American society, or whatever), but he may not be positive whether and to what degree busing of school children helps accomplish his goals. At one time he is convinced that it is a sure way to attain his ends; another time he thinks that it will probably hinder achievement of his goals; still another time he is just unsure of the effects, etc. What his behavior will be under these circumstances is unclear even to himself, and the best we can do is to state probabilities of each alternative action.

An individual's preference point (or ideal point) may also vary over time as he evaluates a pair of alternatives, and this results in his not always responding the same way to that pair of alternatives. According to this view, an individual's attitude can perhaps best be represented by a distribution of preference points, from which the individual picks one at random each time he judges the alternatives. Which alternative is preferred at a

---

[24] This point of view has a lengthy history in psychology. See, for example, chap. 5 in Coombs, *et al.* (1970).

given time depends (under some circumstances) on the precise preference point that has been drawn.[25] A political example might be legislators' judgments about what is an acceptable speed in achieving racial integration (or of controlling pollution, of curbing inflation, or whatever). One time it may seem as if we are progressing "satisfactorily," while at another time we appear to be moving at a snail's pace, and yet another time we seem to be making rapid strides. Thus how one votes on a legislative measure may depend in part on just how one feels at the time the vote is taken.

There are two major points to be derived from this discussion. First, we have suggested some basis for assuming that individual behavior is random or at least that it can profitably be modelled as such. Secondly, we have shown that the individual probabilities lend themselves to interpretations assuming either deterministic or probabilistic behavior. Only the second of our conclusions seems to depend on which interpretation is adopted. The other conclusions are not dependent on accepting one or the other point of view.

---

[25] Coombs (1964, pp. 106–18) explains this notion and gives experimental support for it with regard to judgments about shades of gray—admittedly a slightly different context from most voting situations.

7. The Legislative Process and the Minimal Winning Coalition

DAVID H. KOEHLER

I. INTRODUCTION

Professor William H. Riker, in *The Theory of Political Coalitions*, has set forth an analysis of political behavior derived from the principles of "*n*-person" games (Riker, 1962). The conclusion, which he calls the "size principle," states that rational actors, confronted by the necessity to form coalitions to effect political action, will "create coalitions just as large as they believe will ensure winning and no larger" (Riker, 1962, p. 4). Giving examples, Riker suggests that this deceptively simple norm has considerable application in the explanation of various types of political competition.

The relevance of the game-theoretic model in any particular case can be determined by establishing the quality of the fit between its assumptions and the set of empirical events under consideration. Among the diverse categories of political behavior, the legislative process, unfortunately, is

I would like to thank Steven Brams who encouraged me to pursue this line of inquiry and Richard Niemi whose patience and numerous comments and suggestions through several drafts of the paper by far exceeded the call of duty. Finally I must express my sincere gratitude to Professor William H. Riker for providing me the opportunity to spend a year on the faculty at the University of Rochester in a truly unique and always stimulating department of political science.

a sector in which the fit between the assumptions and reality is not particularly compelling. Riker himself takes note of this when he suggests that the meaning of the "payoff" to a winning legislative coalition is somewhat obscure (Riker, 1962, pp. 122-23). This problem can be traced to two of the assumptions of the model: one explicit and one implicit. First, the zero-sum condition (Riker, 1962, pp. 28-31), which is crucial to the coalition minimizing logic, is not readily identifiable as an obvious factor in the legislative process. Second, there is an implicit assumption that the game is played but once,[1] or at least not on a repetitive basis, by a given set of actors. In contrast, the legislative process in the real world involves continuous coalition formation where the game is not only repeated, but numerous different plays may actually overlap each other. This situation is likely to influence the behavior of the actors in a different fashion than if they were to confront each other but once as Riker's model implies.

Despite these reservations, we do not like to give up the "size principle" as a tool for analyzing the legislative process. The minimal winning coalition would seem to be an eminently reasonable goal for a legislative coalition manager. With the exception of the odd case in which a public show of legislative overkill is felt to be politic, coalitions are likely to be considered complete once they are large enough to serve their nominal purpose —namely, *winning* the voting contest. To resolve this dilemma, it is necessary to relax or delete the offensive assumptions and then see if it is still possible to derive a behavioral norm similar to the "size principle."

We shall show, using a tentative verbal bargaining model, that there is in fact good reason for legislators to form minimal winning coalitions. While the model makes no pretense of rigorous axiomatic proof, it does avoid the zero-sum condition and depends in part upon repeated plays of the game. We begin with the statement of a set of assumptions concerning a number of salient features of the legislative process. From these we are able to reach a conclusion which is similar to the "size principle" but which, to the extent that the assumptions accurately reflect the real world, should be readily applicable to the legislative process. The development of the model takes up the next section of the paper.

The last is devoted to a test of a legislative voting body to determine whether or not minimal winning coalitions are actually being formed. To accomplish this, a hypothesis is derived from the verbal model and is tested using a probabilistic index of voting agreement (Brams and O'Leary, 1970) and aggregate voting data from recent sessions of the U.S. House of Representatives. We will show that there is a marked tendency toward

---

[1] This is not stated directly but emerges from the "pure conflict situations" characterized by zero-sum as distinguished from cooperative games (Riker, 1962, chap. 2). The "once and for all" opportunity for the winner to gain at the expense of the loser does not reflect the norm of reciprocity so often attributed to the legislative process.

minimal coalitions and from this conclude that the model of legislative behavior outlined in this paper appears to have some value as an explanatory tool.

II. THE MODEL

This particular model of the legislative process involves the statement of seven assumptions which will serve to describe and delimit the political behavior under consideration. The rationale for minimizing legislative coalitions is then put forth, emerging as a direct consequence of the preceding assumptions.

A. Assumptions

1. *Rational Actor.* It is assumed that individual legislators exhibit economically rational behavior.[2] That is, confronted by a set of alternatives, choices (accept or reject) are based upon the desire to maximize utility which in turn is determined by individual values or preference orderings.

2. *The Decision-Rule.* The most common rule requires a simple majority of the choices, and the alternative receiving it is taken as the outcome of the group's decision. It should be noted that any such decision-rule determines the maximum size of the minimum winning coalition: the coalition size which will win regardless of the extent of voting participation or the opponent's efforts. Since it is a prevalent practice, the simple majority will be assumed to be *the* decision-rule for the rest of the paper.

This is not a restrictive assumption since the outcome of the argument would not qualitatively change if it were relaxed to include any reasonable range of decision-rules. (Rules such as "zero," or "one," or "unanimity" would destroy the reasoning, but they are uncommon in legislative voting situations and hence are outside the "reasonable range.")

3. *Differential Preference Intensity.* It is assumed that different legislators react to the set of alternatives confronting them with different relative intrapersonal intensities of preference. That is, while two legislators may each prefer A to B, one may see A as highly preferable, while the other is all but indifferent. This distinction of itself involves no interpersonal

---

[2] Rationality has been defined and redefined by political theorists. Riker (1962, pp. 15–28), Buchanan (1962, chap. 4), and Downs (1957, pp. 4–11) each devote a section of their books to a discussion of the problem and formulate an essentially economic argument for individual rationality. One of the more concise statements of the concept appears in Tullock (1965, pp. 27–29). His distinction between "instrumental" and "ultimate" motives for human actions clarifies much of this confusion which surrounds the issue. He confines the question of rationality to "instrumental actions—[those] taken for an ulterior purpose."

comparison of utility. Further, it is not a particularly difficult condition to justify since the alternative (that each actor will register the *same* relative intensity of preference over the set of motions) is clearly untenable.

4. *Interaction.* It is assumed that the legislators are found in an environment which is conducive to their interaction: they must be able to communicate and negotiate with one another and be free to form voting agreements or coalitions.

This is a restrictive assumption as it excludes from consideration a substantial sector of the legislative process where the independence of the individual members is severely curtailed. Parliamentary systems are eliminated where party discipline is rigid, or where governing coalitions remain fixed throughout a session and thereby bind the legislators' voting behavior. In these cases there may be communication among actors, but individual members are unable to make voting arrangements among themselves.

The opposite is true of the legislative systems which are admitted under the restriction. That is, the members are not only permitted to communicate with one another, but also may enter or leave voting coalitions up to the time that the decision is taken. These actions are based only upon their individual considerations of the difference in utility derived from membership as opposed to nonmembership. It is only in these circumstances that rationality and individual intensities of preference will be able to influence legislative outcomes and the voting coalitions formed to produce them.

5. *The Bargain.* The presence of (1) rational actors with (2) unequal intensities of preferences over a set of alternatives, in (3) an environment which is conducive to negotiation, suggests that a particular pattern of negotiation will emerge. It will be assumed that an actor whose relative intensity of preference for a motion is high will attempt to convince a member of the *opposite persuasion* with a *low relative intensity of preference* to change his voting intention.

This assertion should be self-evident: an actor seeking to build a legislative coalition must obviously seek recruits from among those who are not already in the coalition—that is, from among those who are either opposed or uncommitted. Seeking recruits with a low relative intensity of preference makes sense in that such individuals should be more easily persuaded to change their initial position. A bargain is said to exist when the two members reach some mutually acceptable arrangement which includes, among other things, the successful recruitment of the new member into the legislative coalition.

6. *Compensation.* Establishing the motivation to make a bargain and the resultant negotiation strategy takes into account only one side of the agreement. We must suppose that the member being encouraged to change his position took his initial stance because he valued it more highly than

the other alternatives. If he is rational, he will not change position unless one of two things occurs. First, he may be given new information which changes the utility which he had assigned to his original voting inclination. Second, he may be offered compensation such that the utility (positive or negative) which he attaches to his new voting position (on making a bargain), in combination with the utility which he attaches to the compensation, exceeds the utility attached to his original voting inclination.

The first possibility will be excluded from consideration as we expect that the legislators are generally well supplied with information and are able to rationally establish initial voting inclinations in advance of the building of formal voting coalitions. Alternatively, it is assumed that a bargain which results in the recruitment of a previously uncommitted into a voting coalition will necessarily involve a payment of compensation to the new member.

Before going on, a remark about the quantity of compensation is in order. In the real world, the value of the compensation an actor may demand is neither fixed, nor can it be determined by a simple calculation (Luce and Raiffa, 1957, pp. 114-54). There are, however, two factors which suggest that a member's demands will at least remain within reasonable limits. First, he will not be able to exercise any degree of monopoly power since other members' votes can be solicited in his place. A prospective coalition member whose vote is worth no more than that of any other nonmember, will be evaluated by the existing coalition members strictly in terms of the cost of his joining. Therefore the prospect, while desiring to maximize his compensation, must equally take care to avoid pricing his vote out of the market. The second factor tending to temper demands for compensation derives from the consideration that legislating is a continuous process. In the unlikely event that a prospective coalition member gained a degree of monopoly power, he would probably hesitate to use it on the existing coalition members since their roles could be reversed at any time. In one sense, the norm of "reciprocity," associated with the legislative process, implies that "responsible" members will avoid exorbitant demands for compensation (Lindblom, 1968, p. 94).

In examining compensation, we have tried to establish two basic points. First, the bargain whereby a new member is brought into a coalition involves remuneration in return for the actor's change in his initial voting intention. Second, while the precise amount of compensation is unclear, neither partner in the bargain is likely to be able or willing to extract an undue price from the other. This stabilizing characteristic suggests that once negotiation and exchange patterns emerge, they are likely to be self-perpetuating rather than self-destructive.

7. *Compensation Cost.* Once the existence of compensation is established, its substance or quality is of little significance provided it has one property.

It is assumed that whatever the form of compensation, it involves a transfer of value (not necessarily equal) between the actors. That is, no matter what is exchanged in return for joining a legislative coalition, it must be considered valuable by both the recruiter and the recruit.

In the case of the latter, the assumption is all but trivial: unless he valued the item to be exchanged, he would not agree to the bargain in the first place. In the case of the recruiter, however, the situation is not nearly so obvious. Rather than developing the argument at length, we will attempt to sum it up in two brief statements: (a) If compensation takes the form of side payments, it is costly unless the recruiter has an infinite supply of legislative resources. Even in the case in which the recruiter could promise the recruit a future vote on a matter which was of absolutely no concern to the former, he would necessarily incur opportunity costs. (b) If, alternatively, compensation involves an alteration in the motion under consideration, the adjustment must be Pareto optimal, or it will lower the utility of the motion for some or all of the previously committed members. The small likelihood of obvious Pareto optimal compromises, once a coalition has grown to some size, suggests that this type of compensation equally involves a transfer of value.

In sum, the importance of either of these forms of compensation converges on a single point. No matter how new members are added to a coalition, it is an unavoidably costly undertaking to some if not all the previously committed members.

8. *The Minimal Winning Coalition.* Based upon the preceding assumptions, we conclude that in constructing legislative voting coalitions, members will direct recruitment to the achievement of minimal winning size and no more. This follows from the assumption that the addition of new members is inherently costly and therefore, once the coalition is apparently large enough to meet the known minimum requirement of the decision-rule, further recruitment would have a negative marginal utility and consequently would be eschewed by rational actors.

It should be noted that while this result is similar to Riker's, it has not been necessary to assume a "zero-sum" payoff in order to achieve it. Further, the implicit assumption of single independent plays can be dropped. In fact the continuous nature of the legislative process is not only admitted, but increases the likelihood of stability in the model. This leaves us with a conclusion comparable to the "size principle," but without depending on the assumptions which have limited its applicability to the legislative process.

III. EMPIRICAL EVIDENCE

A. A Hypothesis

If the argument set forth above is in fact relevant to the formation of legislative coalitions, there should be some indication of it in the real world. To explore this possibility, a hypothesis will be drawn from the coalition model and tested using aggregate voting data from the House of Representatives. The results will demonstrate empirically that the members do tend to form minimal winning coalitions.

Before proceeding, it is necessary to define a concept of *agreement*. The term used in subsequent remarks refers to the possession in common of a given quality by two or more actors or groups. For example, *party agreement* occurs in the case when two members of a legislative body belong to the same political party. A condition of maximum party agreement refers to the situation in which *all* members of a legislative body belong to the same party. Minimum party agreement occurs when the members are equally distributed among the two or more represented parties.

In like manner, *voting agreement* exists between two members when they cast similar votes on a particular issue. The concept of maximum voting agreement refers to the situation in which all members cast similar votes on a particular issue: minimum voting agreement occurs when the members' votes are equally distributed among the voting alternatives (aye, nay, abstain, etc.). It can be seen that the formation of minimal winning coalitions would result in minimal voting agreement in a legislative process with two alternatives.

The hypothesis to be tested here involves a comparison of variations over time in party agreement among the members of the House with their corresponding voting agreement. That is, over a number of legislative sessions, party agreement (based on the size of the majority relative to the size of the minority) varies considerably. Since party plays a substantial role in legislative behavior, it would be reasonable to assume that changes from session to session in party agreement would result in directly proportional changes in voting agreement. On the other hand, if the members were primarily concerned with the formation of minimal winning coalitions, we would expect that changes in party agreement would *not* be reflected in the voting patterns. The latter consideration leads to the following hypothesis:

If the members of a legislative voting body are engaged in the formation of minimal winning coalitions, changes in party agreement will not produce changes in the corresponding voting agreement which instead will remain *fixed* and *minimal*.

B. The Index of Agreement

In determining the validity of the hypothesis, the a posteriori probabilistic index of agreement developed by Brams and O'Leary will be calculated using party alignment and voting data from the House of Representatives. The Brams-O'Leary index has been set out in detail elsewhere. Among other measures of this sort, it is unique in that it logically relates "(1) systematic characteristics of voting bodies, (2) individual characteristics of their members, and (3) relational characteristics between pairs of members in such a way as to yield operational measures that are comparative in nature" (Brams and O'Leary, 1970, p. 449). To justify its use in this application, it is sufficient to note the facility with which it provides a consistent measure of agreement over different numbers of voting alternatives and different numbers of voting members. The latter is particularly important insofar as the number of members in a body such as the House may vary between wide limits from roll call to roll call.[3]

A brief operational description of the calculations involved should be adequate to clarify this particular application of the index. "Agreement Level" is defined as follows (Brams and O'Leary, 1970, p. 459):

$$AL = \frac{E(AG) - E(AG)_{min}}{E(AG)_{max} - E(AG)_{min}} \qquad 0 \leq AL \leq 1 \qquad (1)$$

where $E(AG)$ is the expected number of voting agreements between any two members over a set of roll calls, as calculated from the votes actually cast on each roll call. $E(AG)$ corresponds to the concept of expected value from probability theory: in this application it is the sum of the probabilities of agreement $P(AG)_i$ between any two members over the set or roll calls. That is,

$$E(AG) = \sum_{i=1}^{m} P(AG)_i \qquad (2)$$

where there are m roll calls under consideration.

The probability of agreement $P(AG)_i$ may be thought of in the following way: assume that a member is chosen at random from the entire group voting and that his vote on a particular roll call i is noted. $P(AG)_i$ then is

---

[3] There have been questions raised as to why this particular index has been used in this context. It would after all be simpler to make use of straight percentages of party majorities and average sizes of voting coalitions. We have already noted the versatility of the measure in the text. Derived from the fundamental unit $P(AG)$— "probability of agreement"—it provides an excellent tool for extending this work by making comparisons with other bodies where there may be *more than two parties* or factions or *more than two voting alternatives*. For example, one could perform a similar analysis to that done in this paper using a three-way distinction between Northern Democrats, Southern Democrats, and Republicans.

the probability that another member chosen at random would have voted the same way as the first—in effect agreed with him. This probability will be greater on roll calls where a relatively larger number of members cast the same vote.

To calculate $P(AG)_i$ for a single roll call with three voting alternatives, we add the possible combinations in which two yes votes could be drawn to the possible combinations of two no votes and the possible combinations of two abstentions, and then divide by the total number of possible combinations of pairwise agreements and disagreements. This may be expressed:

$$P(AG)_i = \frac{\binom{y}{2} + \binom{n}{2} + \binom{a}{2}}{\binom{y + n + a}{2}} \tag{3}$$

where $y =$ the number of yes votes on roll call i
$n =$ the number of no votes on roll call i
$a =$ the number of abstentions on roll call i.

Returning to equation (1) which deals with the sum of the individual probabilities over the set of m roll calls, we will briefly examine the rest of the terms. $E(AG)_{max}$ is the maximum possible expected agreement, which would occur only when all of the members voted the same way on all of the roll calls. A simple calculation for $P(AG)_{i\,max}$ (i.e., for one roll call) shows that $E(AG)_{max}$ will equal one times the number of roll calls or m. Assuming, for example, that all members voted yes on a given issue, the calculations would be as follows:[4]

$$P(AG)_{i\,max} = \frac{\binom{y}{2} + \binom{n}{2} + \binom{a}{2}}{\binom{y + n + a}{2}} = \frac{\binom{y}{2} + 0 + 0}{\binom{y + 0 + 0}{2}} = \frac{\binom{y}{2}}{\binom{y}{2}} = 1. \tag{4}$$

The value of $E(AG)_{max}$ for m roll calls is:

$$E(AG)_{max} = \sum_{i=1}^{m} P(AG)_{i\,max} = \sum_{i=1}^{m} (1) = m. \tag{5}$$

$E(AG)_{min}$ refers to the opposite condition where voting agreement is at a minimum. This would occur if the voters were evenly divided three ways between yes, no and abstain (or in half if only yes and no alternatives

---

[4] $\binom{n}{2}$ means the number of possible combinations taken two at a time. Zero votes taken two at a time will be defined as equal to zero.

are considered).[5] In this case the probability of agreement $P(AG)_i$ on a single roll call would be minimal and can be calculated using the same formula (3) as above. Let the total votes $t = y + n + a$. Then where the votes are evenly distributed among the alternatives,

$$P(AG)_{i\,min} = \frac{\binom{y}{2} + \binom{n}{2} + \binom{a}{2}}{\binom{y+n+a}{2}} = \frac{\binom{t/3}{2} + \binom{t/3}{2} + \binom{t/3}{2}}{\binom{t}{2}}$$

$$= \frac{\dfrac{3(t/3)(t/3 - 1)}{2!}}{\dfrac{(t)(t - 1)}{2!}} = \frac{\dfrac{t}{3} - 1}{t - 1}.$$

$P(AG)_{i\,min}$ is a function of the total size of the body ranging from zero for a three member body and predictably approaching 0.33 for very large assemblies confronted with three alternatives. Again, to produce $E(AG)_{min}$ for the whole session, the minimal probabilities of agreement are summed over the m roll calls.

C. The Data

As has been noted, the reason for using the Brams-O'Leary index is that it is particularly well suited to the task of providing a coherent comparison between party agreement and voting agreement required to test the hypothesis. Data for the comparison were obtained from eleven sessions of the House of Representatives. The selection included all recent Congresses (83rd-90th) with the only criterion being the need to include a reasonable variation from Congress to Congress in the number of seats held by the majority party. This presented no problem as party strength ranged from a 51.3 percent majority held by the Republicans in the 83rd Congress, to the 67.8 percent majority of the Democrats in the eighty-ninth.

Once the data are selected, it is a relatively simple task to establish the index of party agreement. For a given session of the House, the number of members of each party are noted and these figures (instead of the number of yes or no votes) are used in equations (1), (2) and (3) to calculate party "Agreement Level."

The next step is to calculate the voting agreement for each session as determined by the individual sets of roll call votes. Unfortunately, the selection of roll calls from within these sets is not straightforward. In each session there are a fair number of decisions rendered by the House which

---

[5] In summarizing the model, we have assumed the existence of three alternatives, since it more effectively illustrates the potential of the device. In applying it to the House, however, only two alternatives will be used. Absence is not subject to consistent interpretation.

are not contested. The most obvious of these are indicated by outcomes of the 400-0 variety. In these cases there is obviously no coalition building taking place and questions as to whether minimal or nonminimal coalitions are being formed are not relevant.

The two common criteria for selecting roll calls are *contesting* (based on quantity of opposition) and *participation* (based upon the relative number of members who consider an issue of suffiicent import to warrant their casting a vote). Riker has gone so far as to construct an index which combines the two criteria in a single calculation for "significance level."[6] The difficulty involved with either (or both) of these methods is that arbitrary admission thresholds still must be selected. There is no logical way of determining that a particular percentage of opposition or level of participation is an adequate indication that a motion is actually being contested.

Given such uncertainty, we do not hesitate to contribute a further variation on the established theme. Working from the quantity of opposition concept, the voting data itself has been examined in the aggregate to see if a pattern in the opposition could be detected which might suggest a reasonable, or at least a somewhat less arbitrary, threshold.

A curve (figure 1) has been plotted with the "opposition distribution" (the number of votes on the losing side as a percentage of the total cast, e.g., 0 to 5 percent, 5 to 10 percent, . . . , 45 to 50 percent) on the abscissa and the total number of roll calls for all the sessions which fall into each interval on the ordinate. The most casual examination of the curve reveals a clear trend. There is a pronounced tendency for roll calls to cluster at opposite ends of the scale; at near unanimity on the right and maximum disagreement on the left.

While interpretation of such an effect cannot be undertaken with complete certainty, it would appear from the degree of polarization that there is a distinction made by the members between issues which have a chance and those which do not. Those which are contested tend to cluster around the decision-rule, while the lost causes are recognized as such and members either "get on the band-wagon" or do not bother to express their opposition. The dividing point would reasonably seem to be indicated by the minimum point on the curve (10 to 15 percent). Intuitively as well, it is difficult to picture a highly competitive situation in which the opposition was unable to produce 15 percent of the votes.

From this consideration, an admissibility threshold will be established which excludes all roll calls to the right of the minimum. Hence, to test the hypothesis, Voting Agreement Level for each session will be calculated (again using equations (1), (2), (3)) for all nominally contested decisions;

---

6 A summary of the problem is to be found in Anderson, *et al.* (1966, chap. 5), with Riker's method appearing on pp. 81–87.

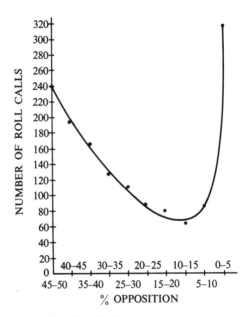

FIGURE 1. Opposition distribution

by definition, those in which at least 15 percent of the membership was willing to take the trouble to vote against the majority.

D. Results and Conclusions

The tabulated values for voting and party Agreement Level appear in table 1. For comparative purposes, several outcomes are listed using various thresholds in addition to the 15 percent requirement.

TABLE 1. Agreement Level

Session	% Party Majority	Party Agreement Level	Voting Agreement Level Minimum Opposition Requirement					
			25%	20%	15%	10%	5%	All Votes
90–1	57.0% Dem.	.020	.068	.094	.124	.158	.223	.423
89–2	67.8% Dem.	.129	.059	.093	.114	.138	.203	.446
89–1	67.8% Dem.	.129	.067	.090	.112	.150	.189	.357
88–2	59.4% Dem.	.036	.051	.078	.090	.113	.169	.316
88–1	59.4% Dem.	.036	.052	.073	.100	.154	.218	.341
87–2	60.2% Dem.	.042	.056	.081	.115	.146	.197	.377
87–1	60.2% Dem.	.042	.057	.086	.131	.144	.182	.316
86–2	64.8% Dem.	.090	.065	.092	.107	.115	.145	.292
86–1	64.8% Dem.	.090	.086	.098	.122	.150	.164	.241
85–1	53.8% Dem.	.005	.059	.066	.094	.118	.131	.204
83–1	51.2% Rep.	.001	.062	.091	.119	.119	.150	.298

These results have been used to construct a curve (figure 2) which illustrates the required comparison between voting agreement and party agreement. The 45° line from the origin is constructed to show the hypothetical case in which voting is strictly dependent upon party membership. That is, if legislators always respond to party discipline then it is clear that a party agreement level of, for example, 0.100, would produce precisely the same voting agreement. The other curve of actual voting performance is produced by a simple least squares regression. The resulting expression is $y = 0.0088x + 0.111$ with a variance, $s^2 = 0.00016$.

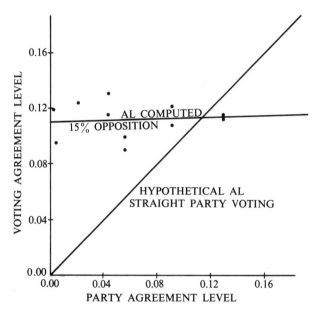

FIGURE 2.   Agreement level

To what extent does this support the contention that the actors are actually forming minimal winning coalitions? The hypothesis stated that if the practice were actually taking place, voting agreement could be expected to be fixed (or constant) and minimal. Figure 2 clearly indicates that the former condition is being met. The logic of minimal coalition formation does not change from session to session and hence the pattern in which the members cast their votes should remain reasonably constant. The data in fact demonstrate consistent voting agreement over a considerable number of sessions which cover a wide variation in party agreement. The very minor increase in voting agreement suggests, as predicted, an all but negligible relationship between the two.

The second condition, minimal coalition size, is not so obviously established. The median size of winning coalitions in contested roll calls (at least 15 percent opposition) over the eleven session is 62 percent,[7] with a between session variance $s^2 = 4.0$. This is definitely on the bulky side if one was expecting the coalitions to cluster in the immediate vicinity of the 50 percent + 1 decision-rule. It is not, however, completely clear that this is a reasonable expectation for coalitions formed under the uncertain conditions found in the real world.

A coalition manager is likely to intentionally build some margin of safety into his coalition. The legislative process is a series of "winner take all" decisions and the closer one shaves the margin of victory, the greater the probability of taking nothing. In effect, this is the same idea expressed by Riker with regard to the impossibility of perfect information (Riker, 1962, pp. 47-48). In the absence of such a condition, it makes sense to pad the coalition until one is fairly well convinced that it will win.

Still, the need for padding does not provide an explanation of our results which lends credence to the bargaining model. A rational coalition manager would pad his coalition to the extent that the number of committed members, times the probability that each of them will actually translate that committment into a vote at the appropriate moment, would produce an *expected* voting coalition of 50 percent, plus one or two percent for safety. A median voting coalition of 62 percent, as we have found, would seem to be much larger than reason would dictate.[8]

---

[7] This result does not emerge directly from the curve showing AL since the probability of agreement increases exponentially. It can easily be determined by inspection of figure 1.

[8] Commenting on an earlier draft of this paper, Herbert Weisberg constructed a probability model of coalition padding. It effectively illustrates the margin in the *voting* in excess of 50 percent + 1 which may reasonably be attributed to the attempt to build a padded coalition which has a high probability of success. The model was of considerable value in analyzing the data used in this paper and therefore I am taking the liberty of reproducing it here:

Divide the population of 435 legislators into three categories: thirty-five not voting; a second group with a probability of 0.0 voting for the bill; and a third group with a probability of, say, 0.8 voting for the bill. The question is how many of the 400 voting congressmen must belong to the third group if the bill is to have a 95 percent chance of passing. If we assume that legislators vote independently of one another, this amounts to a binomial probability situation.

Using a normal approximation we find that 95 percent of the area under the curve is above -1.65. The Z value would be the required majority (201) minus the Yates correction for continuity (0.5) minus the expected size of the majority coalition (0.8 times some number between 0 and 400 labelled Y), all divided by the standard deviation ($\sqrt{pnq} = \sqrt{[0.8 \text{ times } 0.2 \text{ times } Y]}$). Then

$$Z = \frac{(201.0 - 0.5) - 0.8\,Y}{\sqrt{[(0.8)(0.2)\,Y]}}$$

Solving for Y such that $Z = -1.65$ we find that $Y = 264$. That is, if the members of a coalition have a 0.8 probability of voting as promised, and those outside the coalition have zero probability of lending support, in order to have a 95 percent

There is, however, a related consideration which does enable us to make sense out of the data. We noted above that the "decision-rule determines the maximum size of the minimum winning coalition: the coalition size which will win regardless of the extent of voting participation or the opponents' efforts." In other words, while the decision-rule specifies that 50 percent + 1 is always required to win, the actual number of votes required in any specific case is a function of the number of votes cast. This number of course can vary from roll call to roll call, ranging from a bare quorum of 218 to the full complement of 435 members. Correspondingly the minimal winning coalition, 50 percent + 1 of those voting, will vary from 110 to 218 votes. Confronted by this unstable situation, the rational coalition manager has a choice. He may attempt to form a coalition of 218 "plus" members which would insure winning "no matter what," or he could attempt to lower the coalition cost by aiming for a smaller membership (between 218 and 110) which would still have some positive probability of winning.

In proceeding with the analysis, let us assume that the coalition manager is not only anxious to minimize cost, but the risk of failure as well. In other words, we still expect him to limit the quest for new members, but only after the coalition is all but certain to fulfill its primary function, which is winning. As we have noted, this maximum minimal winning coalition must be based on the total House membership which establishes the maximum possible opposition coalition. In this light the empirically determined 62 percent median coalition, based on votes actually cast, may be reconsidered.

Turning again to the data, we find that over the eleven sessions in question, participation on contested roll calls (at least 15 percent opposition) averaged 371 members and the median winning coalition 230 members. If this membership is then compared with the maximum, 218 member minimal winning coalition (rather than with those who on any given occasion happen to be present and voting), it turns out that the median winning coalition contains 52.8 percent of the total House membership. This result is clearly within an acceptable proximity to the decision-rule.

---

chance of passing the bill, a coalition of 264 members is required. The *expected* vote for the bill however would be 0.8 times 264 or 211.2 leaving an expected pad size of 10.2 votes out of 400, or less than 3 percent. Thus while the legislative coalition membership should number 31 percent above minimal winning value ((264–201)/201), when the typical vote is actually cast, the outcome would be padded by less than 3 percent. The view of the padding process implicit in this model is not meant as a realistic portrayal of the process, but these calculations are useful in assessing the magnitude of padding values.

It is clear from the perspective of the model that attributing the 12 percent excess coalition membership to padding is out of the question. It would require an impossibly low probability of performance on the part of the coalition members and/or an absurd demand for certainty of success on the part of the coalition manager.

It would appear then that the coalition managers are rational in the sense suggested by the model but at the same time quite conservative. With only 371 members voting on a typical roll call, it seems that coalitions could be reduced in size and therefore cost, and still have a very high probability of success. But this does not seem to be the pattern. If the data are to make sense, coalition managers must be assumed to have a dual goal: winning at minimal cost and at minimal risk. In fact they are apparently willing to trade off a degree of cost efficiency in return for decreased risk, or in effect, improved coalition performance.

From this perspective we are prepared to conclude that the data give evidence of a strong tendency toward the formation of minimal winning coalitions. The *consistent* agreement level from session to session suggests that the actors are playing their own game. The *magnitude* of the agreement level indicates that the game involves forming coalitions which are large enough to overcome adverse effects of imperfect information and inconsistent participation but without degenerating into mindless vote maximization.

In summary, we have attempted in this paper to make two points. First, it is logical, given the rational actor assumptions, to form minimal legislative coalitions. Importantly, that logic can be derived from the general propositions that legislative resources are scarce rather than assuming that legislative payoffs have a zero-sum character. Second, we have presented data which indicates that, once the concept of the minimal winning coalition is clarified, legislators show a definite tendency to act in the fashion suggested by the model. Despite what would appear to be an excessive tendency to avoid risk, there can be little question that recruitment is limited once a coalition is large enough to serve its purpose. The cost of recruitment would in turn seem to be a reasonable explanation for such behavior.

8. A Theory of the Formation of Opinion Coalitions in the U. S. Supreme Court

The attention of students of the judicial process was initially directed to coalition formation on collegial courts by the pioneering work of C. Herman Pritchett (1948). In the past decade more specific analyses of this subject have been made which explore the relative "power"[1] exercised by individuals and coalitions on the Supreme Court (Krislov, 1963; Schubert, 1964).[2]

In spite of the long and growing interest in this area, few attempts have beem made to relate group behavior on the Supreme Court to a formal theory of coalition formation. As Ulmer (1965, p. 135) has said, "The primary inquiry has been who votes together rather than why." In an initial attempt to rectify this deficiency, Ulmer analyzed Supreme Court voting data in the period 1946-61 in terms of the "size principle," formulated by William H. Riker (1962), which predicts the formation of minimum winning coalitions.[3]

I would like to thank the editors, Richard G. Niemi and Herbert F. Weisberg, and Harold J. Spaeth of Michigan State University for their helpful comments. I, of course, remain responsible for the final product.

[1] The concept of power employed in the Krislov and Schubert studies is that formulated by Shapley and Shubik (1954). The power of an individual is defined as the probability of his having been pivotal on a vote.

[2] A more extensive, but less formal, treatment of coalition formation on the Supreme Court can be found in Murphy (1964, pp. 37–90).

[3] Another attempt to formulate a theory of coalition formation is Atkinson and Newman (1969). For the problems with this approach see Rohde (1970).

Ulmer's analysis of the relevance of the size principle to coalition formation on the Supreme Court centered on the idea that

> sub-group formation in the Supreme Court may be motivated by power considerations. The competition for control of decisional outcomes has been viewed as a zero-sum game on the ground that the majority wins all and the dissenters win nothing. (1965, p. 138)

As a result of his analysis, however, Ulmer concluded that subgroup formation was not based on the operation of the size principle. Drawing a distinction between coalitions (temporary, means-oriented groups with diverse long-range goals) and cliques (a persistently cohering group with shared goals), Ulmer

> tentatively theorized that sub-group formation in the court is basically clique formation. In doing so, we have rejected power (specially defined) as a primary motivating force for Supreme Court justices. We have suggested, instead, that pursuit of common value-goals is a more weighty ingredient in sub-group processes. (1965, pp. 151–52)

One must, ask however, why this conclusion should be reached merely because "power" is rejected as the primary motivating variable for subgroup formation. Ulmer is unclear in his use of the term subgroup. If this term is not meant to refer specifically to decisional majorities (i.e., if it is meant to include nonmajority subgroups), then the size principle should not be the focus of analysis. The size principle is applicable only in regard to the formation of decisional *majorities* and the number of members they will contain. The formation of "issue cliques" (and the reasons for it) is a different question altogether.

Furthermore, if the term subgroup is meant to apply only to majority coalitions, there is no a priori reason (and Ulmer offers no evidence) to believe that shared values cannot serve as a basis for coalition formation. Ulmer rejects the "power" hypothesis because the power granted by a Supreme Court decision is so limited.

> A court decision is unlike an electoral decision in that it does not vest general authority to make or control subsequent concurrent decisions of an inconsistent nature. Like a street car ticket, the power of a coalition in the Court may be good for one case and one case only. This is not the kind of reward which motivates coalition formation, the cost of which, case after case, may be prohibitive. (1965, p. 142)

The coalition referred to in this statement is the decision majority which is formed to decide the disposition of a case, i.e., whether the decision of the court below will be affirmed or reversed. It seems, however, that the conflict which Ulmer sees between the size principle and the pursuit of value-goals may be disposed of if we do not make the decision coalition the focus of analysis.

If it is the pursuit of value-goals which is an important motivation for the Justices, then we should consider coalition formation from the point of view of the coalition that can turn those value goals into authoritative policy. That is, instead of studying the decision coalition as Ulmer did, we should analyze the formation of the coalition which creates the majority opinion. It is in the majority opinion, rather than in the decision coalition, that the Supreme Court makes policy.

In constructing this theory of majority opinion coalitions, we will consider two types of situations in which we will assume that the motivations of the Justices are different. First, we will consider the normal policy-making situation which will be governed by the individual Justices pursuing their personal policy preferences. In these cases, Riker's prediction of minimum winning coalitions will be applicable if, as we argued, opinion coalitions rather than decision coalitions are considered. The second situation, however, will include those types of cases which contain issues that may involve a threat to the Court, in which case it will be argued that at least some of the Justices will be motivated by a desire to protect the Court. In this instance, Riker's theory will be inapplicable.

I. THE MOTIVATION OF THE JUSTICES AND THE OPINION COALITION

In the formation of the decision coalition, what the Justices must decide is whether the lower court which made the decision under review should be affirmed or reversed. Here the decision is between two clearly specified alternatives. However, in making his decision on this issue each Justice may perceive entirely different factors to be relevant than those which are the basis of the decisions of his colleagues. In other words, two Justices may reach the same decision to reverse or affirm but for entirely different reasons.

For example, in the case of *Smith* v. *California*,[4] petitioner was convicted under a Los Angeles city ordinance which made unlawful the posession of obscene books in a place where books were sold. The ordinance did not require that the person in whose possession the books were found know that they were obscene in order to be found guilty. When the Supreme Court reviewed the conviction, a majority of the Court, speaking through Justice Brennan, voted to reverse. They held that the statute,

---

[4] 361 U.S. 147 (1959).

because it did not require knowledge of the obscene nature of the books, had such a tendency to inhibit constitutionally protected expression that it could not stand.

In the same case Justice Black also voted to reverse the conviction, yet he did not agree on the grounds given. He contended that the ordinance was unconstitutional because he believes any attempt at censorship is forbidden by the First Amendment, and he expressed this position in a concurring opinion. In addition to the five Justice who agreed in the majority and Black, the other three Justices also voted to reverse, and each of them wrote a concurring opinion to express his views.

The importance of this lies in the fact that the major role of the Supreme Court in the American political system is not merely to guard against errors by lower courts, but to articulate general constitutional and legal principles. Thus, in any specific case, the important thing is not simply whether the decision of the lower court is affirmed or reversed, but the holding of the majority (if a majority holding can be attained) on why the decision was made. It is this majority opinion which contains the general principle, upon which the decision is based, that is binding upon lower courts in all similar cases. In *Smith* v. *California*, it was established that a person cannot be convicted of possession of obscene material unless it is shown that he knew the material was obscene. Lower courts, in making their decisions, are therefore bound to find a similar law, which does not include this requirement, unconstitutional.

The selection, by members of the decision majority, of the principles which will be held to govern the disposition of a particular case is related to, but distinct from, the formation of the decision coalition. The primary responsibility for formulating these principles rests with the Justice to whom the majority opinion is assigned. He is not, however, a free agent. If there is to be a majority holding, he must fashion his opinion so that it will gain the agreement of at least four of his colleagues (if all nine members participate in the case). While the process of writing opinions takes place in secret, we know from the private papers of Justices that a good deal of bargaining and modification of the majority opinion may take place in order to obtain the necessary agreement.[5]

It is probable, then, that since it is not whether the lower court is affirmed or reversed that is of prime importance, but the holding of the Court contained in the majority opinion, it is the desire to control the content of the majority opinion which is the major motivation of a Justice in the decision-making process. It is the making of this decision (which may be termed the formation of the opinion coalition), rather than the decision coalition formation that Ulmer considered, which will be the focus of analysis for this study.

---

[5] For a detailed description of this bargaining process, see Murphy (1964, pp. 56–73).

It was noted above that Ulmer rejected his power-motivation hypothesis for the alternative that the pursuit of value-goals is a more important element to the Justices in forming their decision. In fact, a great many studies of the judicial process in the past decade have been devoted to examining this value-motivation hypothesis, and the evidence to support it seems strong.[6] These findings suggest that it is a Justice's values regarding policy issues, rather than technical legal questions, which govern his decision in certain classes of cases.

Thus the theory of judicial decision making which is presented here will have as one of its core assumptions that a Justice is primarily motivated in his decision in *specified types of cases* by a desire to have the opinion of the Court approximate his own position on the issue in question. That is, the amount of utility a Justice derives from a Court decision will be determined by how close that decision is to his preferred position. When a decision is made, a Justice has three alternatives: he can dissent (with or without an opinion), he can concur (also with or without an opinion), or he can join in the majority opinion. Which of these alternatives is chosen will be determined by the concurrent decisions of his colleagues and the groupings (i.e., coalitions) which they form. Since each Justice wishes his position on an issue (or an acceptable approximation thereof) to become the majority ruling of the Court, a great effort will be made to join in coalition to achieve this purpose. The decision to be made by each Justice is whether or not to join in forming a majority opinion coalition.

As was noted above, the assumption that the Justices are motivated by the pursuit of value goals in making their decisions will be assumed to hold for most policy-making situations. However, there is, it will be argued, a special type of policy-making situation in which the Court is involved that necessitates making a different motivational assumption.

The second assumption is that in cases which produce a threat to the Court's authority or power, the Justices will not be primarily concerned with the content of the majority opinion *per se*, but with protecting the Court itself. While this assumption may be open to some question, it seems to be reasonable. When such a threat exists, the nature of the game changes. It is no longer primarily an intra-Court game, but a game between the Court and another part of the political system or society. Glendon Schubert (1959, pp. 192-210), in analyzing such a threat situation (the "Court-packing" fight of 1937), has shown how the threat brought about a change in the behavior of certain members of the Court and thus in the substantive output of the Court as a whole. It seems probable that when a threat to the Court exists, at least some of the members will become more concerned with protecting the Court than with having the Court espouse

---

[6] See, *inter alia*, Schmidhauser (1961), Schubert (1962, 1965), Danelski (1966), Spaeth (1962), Tanenhaus (1960).

their own value position. Thus the impetus would be away from minimum winning coalitions and toward more unanimity in opinion coalitions.

The major difficulty with this assumption lies not in justifying it, but in operationalizing it. It does not seem possible, short of asking the Justices themselves, to derive an objective, dependable indicator of such threat situations. It seems, therefore, that we are left with the necessity of making some kind of subjective judgment. To minimize the changes for error from this judgment, the existence of threat situations will be defined as narrowly as possible. Threats to the Court's power will be defined as serious pending attempts by Congress to limit the Court's jurisdiction in an issue area (as in the removal of the Reconstruction Acts from the Court's jurisdiction in the late 1860s, and in the attempt to do the same in regard to some criminal procedures issues in the Omnibus Crime Bill of 1968), or to change the Court's personnel (as in the Court-packing attempt or by impeachment). Threats to the Court's authority also will be defined to exist in issue areas in which it is probable that there may be serious resistance or disobedience to the Court's mandate by those to whom it will apply (as in the school desegregation cases of 1954-55). Obviously such a "soft" indicator is undesirable in that it entails a good deal of subjective interpretation. However the disadvantages from employing this operationalization would seem to be fewer than those which would result if this necessary assumption were discarded.

II. THE THEORY OF POLITICAL COALITIONS

If we are to employ Riker's theory of political coalitions as a model of coalition formation on the Supreme Court, the first question we must deal with is whether the requirements of the theory are met in the empirical situation. There are five requirements for the size principle to hold: the game must be n-person, it must be zero-sum, the members of the winning coalition must be able to control additional entries into their coalition, side payments must be permissible within the game, and the worst a player can do (in terms of payoffs) is to enter a coalition of himself alone. If these five conditions are met, then the theory specifies that the size principle should govern the formation of winning coalitions.

1. n-person: The game is n-person with n specified (nine, if all Justices participate).

2. zero-sum: This condition demands that the gains of the winners exactly equal in absolute amounts the losses of the losers (i.e., that the gains and losses sum to zero). This condition places a further restriction on the payoffs in that a coalition of the whole has no value. This is necessary because if the winning coalition includes all players, the members win nothing since there are no losers.

The situation in which opinion coalitions are formed cannot be said to meet this condition. It was postulated above that the payoff to the Justices is the ability to control the content of the majority opinion. While it may be accurate to say that the gains of the winners do equal the losses of the losers (i.e., that the members of a majority coalition gain the power to control the opinion of the Court and those who are outside the majority lose this power), it is probably not correct to assume that a coalition of the whole is worthless. This problem, however, is easily met. If the payoff to the majority coalition is the ability to control the ruling of the majority opinion, then the payoff is the same regardless of the size of the majority. The majority coalition, if one forms, controls the content of the opinion, whether than coalition contains five or nine members. A game in which the total payoffs of the winners are the same, regardless of the number of winners, is called a constant-sum game. It has been shown in game theory that a constant-sum game is mathematically equivalent to a zero-sum game.[7] The constant-sum condition does not, however, entail the additional requirement that the coalition of the whole be worthless.

3. *Control over entrance to the coalition*: Due to the zero-sum situation, this condition was necessary since, if the winners "have no such control, all losers could invariably join the winners and thereby produce a valueless coalition of the whole and nullify the winners' victory" (Riker, 1962, p. 39). While under the constant-sum conditions the coalition of the whole is no longer valueless, the control over entrance to the coalition is still necessary because losers could still join the winners and thereby reduce the amount of payoff to each of the members of the winning coalition.

It can be seen, however, that what the condition really requires is not that the members of the winning coalition be able to prevent losing players from nominally joining the coalition, but that the winners be able to control access to the *benefits* of the winning coalition. If, after a winning coalition is formed, one or more of the losers chooses to join the winners, the "control over access" condition is essentially met so long as the losers who are joining cannot thereby demand and receive a share of the payoff for doing so.

When defined in this manner, the condition is met in the case of the Supreme Court. It was stated above that the members of an opinion coalition which has not yet attained the agreement of a majority may induce other players to join them and form a majority coalition by an offer to modify the content of the proposed majority opinion. Equivalently, a player who is not a member of the forming majority coalition may approach the Justice to whom the writing of the opinion has been assigned and offer to join the coalition, if his demands for revision of the opinion are met.

---

[7] See Luce and Raiffa (1957, pp. 158–59).

If a majority opinion coalition has already formed (i.e., if at least five Justices have already consented to the content of the opinion), a losing player may still offer to join the majority if his policy demands are met, but there is no longer any necessity for the members of the majority to modify the opinion to suit any other player. They have achieved a majority and have thereby won. While there is nothing in the rules of the Court to prevent the losing Justice from voting with the majority, he gains none of the benefits of winning, in the policy sense, from doing so. Thus the "control over entrance" condition can be said to be satisfied.

4. *Side payments:* Side payments refer to private agreements about the division of the payoffs. This condition means that the amount of payoff to each of the winners is not predetermined by the rules of the game. In the rules governing the "Supreme Court game," there are obviously no stipulations concerning how much control over the content of the majority opinion may be exerted by one member of the majority coalition relative to the other members. It is probable that the last player to join the majority coalition (in this case the fifth) will be able to demand and receive a larger payoff than the players who joined earlier, since five members are necessary to a majority and the other four members of the prospective coalition may be willing to concede a disproportionate amount to ensure a majority. Furthermore, if two players with different preferences offer to join the majority as its fifth member, it will be the player who demands the smallest side payment who will be admitted, *ceteris paribus*.

5. *The worst a player can do is to enter a coalition of himself alone:* the reason for this requirement is that if the members of a coalition tried to force a player to lose more than he would lose if he were not part of that coalition, he can always "resign" from it and form a coalition of himself alone. As regards the Court, this condition means that if player *A* were a member of an opinion coalition and the other members, in order to attract an additional player (or players), were to modify the content of the opinion so that it became unacceptable to player *A*, he could always withdraw his consent from the opinion and file a solo concurrence or dissent. Such an action is permissible up to the time the opinions in a case are announced in open court.

III. THE HYPOTHESES OF THE THEORY

The theory of coalition formation of the Supreme Court presented above leads us to two testable hypotheses concerning the formation of opinion coalitions:

H_1: **In issue areas in which there is no external threat to the Court, the opinion coalitions formed will be minimum winning (i.e., will contain five members).**

H_2: In issue areas in which there is an external threat to the Court, the opinion coalitions will tend to be larger than minimum winning.

Concerning the first hypothesis, it should be noted that defining the minimum winning coalition to be only those which contain five members may tend to underestimate in one sense the actual number of minimum winning coalitions. If the policy demands of a prospective member of the majority are met and he is induced to join the coalition, this may mean the "automatic" inclusion of one or more other Justices whose policy preferences are the same as those of the last new member. Thus the majority coalition will in principle be minimum winning, despite the fact that it is numerically somewhat larger. There does not, unfortunately, seem to be any satisfactory way to take this phenomenon into account in the testing of the hypotheses. The definition of a minimum winning coalition will, therefore, be restricted to opinion coalitions of five members.

The set of data which will be used to test the hypotheses is all First Amendment cases decided by the Supreme Court, in the 1953 through 1967 terms, in which a majority opinion was reached. First Amendment cases were chosen for two reasons. First, they were clearly identifiable. If the Court stated that a First Amendment issue was raised, the case was chosen for analysis. (Furthermore, the cases were also easily classified as to sub-issues. As can be seen from the table below, the cases conveniently broke down into six issue areas, and sixty-six of the seventy-six cases were covered by those six issues.) Second, they were chosen for their importance. These cases, collectively and individually, involve many of the most controversial policy questions to face the Warren Court. If the Justices are motivated by personal policy preferences, it seemed reasonable to choose for analysis a set of cases all of which were concerned with broad policy issues. [8]

The set yielded a total N of seventy-six cases. Of these cases, eighteen were construed as involving an issue which offered a threat to the Court's power or authority. Seventeen of the cases were divided between two issue areas: freedom of association and freedom of religion. One case involved the issue of internal security. (These cases were eliminated for the purposes of testing hypothesis 1, but served as the basis for testing hypothesis 2.) [9]

---

[8] Obviously future development of the theory should be concerned with broader policy areas. Perhaps the next step would be to consider all civil liberties cases. For this initial test, however, First Amendment cases were thought to be particularly appropriate, since the theory should be more applicable the more salient and policy relevant the issues involved.

[9] In classifying the cases according to size of opinion coalitions, only those cases decided by full opinion were considered (i.e., *per curiam* cases were ignored). In deciding whether a Justice was included in the majority opinion, a Justice who joined in the majority opinion *and* wrote a concurring opinion was counted in the majority

The freedom of association cases primarily involved statutory attempts by southern states to restrict or terminate the operation of the National Association for the Advancement of Colored People within their jurisdictions. Such laws were part of what has been called the "southern counterattack" in the years following *Brown* v. *Board of Education.*[10] The danger of massive resistance and disobedience to all attempts by the Supreme Court to end legal discrimination and protect the rights of Negroes in the South was well known both to members of the Court and all other observers of the situation. Furthermore, the Court had to rely on southern federal district and appeals courts and state supreme courts for the enforcement of their rulings in similar cases which would obviously continue to arise. The Justices of the Supreme Court had ample experience with the resistance of southern judges in such matters. In the face of such attitudes, it is probable that only the clearest, most united mandate of the Court would have real effect. Thus, it seems, a threat situation could fairly be said to exist in relation to the freedom of association cases.[11]

A situation that was analogous to that of freedom of association existed in regard to the freedom of religion cases, except the threat of disobedience and resistance was much more widespread, encompassing not merely the South, but the whole nation. Decisions by the Court regarding religion in the late 1940s and early 1950s had met with a great deal of controversy. There was a great deal of hostility to a number of these earlier rulings, and in some areas open defiance was the order of the day. These tendencies reached their culmination with the "school prayer" decisions (Engel and Abington) in 1962 and 1963. Disobedience to these decisions was widespread, with local school boards deliberately continuing with school sponsored prayers which they publicly recognized were in violation of the Supreme Court's rulings.[12] Such a situation precisely fits the operational definition of a threat to the Court's authority within the theory.

The final threat situation involved not a threat of disobedience to the Court's orders by large segments of the populace but a threat from the Congress of the United States. In reaction to certain "liberal" decisions by the Court in the area of internal security, bills were introduced into both Houses of Congress to reverse or modify certain Court decisions. A moderate bill was passed on August 30, 1957, but a much more fundamental challenge to the Court was offered in the Jenner-Butler bill early in 1958. The bill was an attempt to remove from the Supreme Court's

---

opinion, while a Justice who wrote a concurring opinion but did not join with the majority opinion was classified as outside the majority opinion.

[10] 347 U.S. 483 (1954), 349 U.S. 294 (1955).

[11] For an extended discussion of the freedom of association cases see Kalvern (1965, pp. 65–122).

[12] Two very interesting recent studies of the impact of, and response to, the school prayer decisions are Muir (1967) and Johnson (1967).

appellate jurisdiction five types of internal security cases. The controversy over the bill raged in Congress throughout 1958 until the bill was finally defeated in late August, and the threat to the Court was ended.[13] The Court reached a majority opinion in one case[14] during the October 1957 term, and that case has been included with the other "threat" cases.

In operationalizing and testing the hypotheses deduced from the theory, a number of alternatives present themselves. Since there are five possible sizes of majority opinion coalitions (5, 6, 7, 8, or 9 members), it might initially seem logical to accept a uniform distribution among these sizes of coalitions as the null model, and to conclude that the first hypothesis will be "verified" if there is a significantly larger proportion of minimum winning coalitions than any other in issue areas lacking an external threat. On closer analysis, however, such a test proves unacceptable. Particularly given the subjectivity involved in the definition of a threat, a more stringent test of the hypotheses is desirable. Moreover, it seems that instead of assuming for the purposes of the null model an equiprobability of occurrence of each size coalition, a more reasonable assumption would be that the probability of any Justice joining a majority opinion coalition is equal to the probability that he will not join (i.e., pr (joining) = pr (not joining) = 1/2). If this assumption of equiprobability of joining or not joining is made, then there is not an equal probability of each of the possible coalitions occuring. The proper means of calculating the expected proportion of a given coalition size, assuming random voting between the two alternatives, is the combinatorial probability formula

$$\binom{n}{r}\left(\frac{1}{2}\right)^n = \frac{n!}{r!(n-r)!}\left(\frac{1}{2}\right)^n$$

where n is number of voters and r is a specific coalition size. Employing this formula, we calculate the probability of various majority coalitions occurring in a nine member body. These probabilities are listed in table 1.[15] It can be seen from this table that there is far from equal probability distribution among the various size coalitions. If voting were random on the Supreme Court, one would expect a significantly higher proportion of minimum winning coalitions than any other. To accept the first hypothesis, therefore, we would need not only a larger proportion of minimum winning coalitions than other coalitions, but also a significantly larger proportion than would have been expected by random voting.[16]

---

[13] For an extended treatment of this controversy see Murphy (1962).

[14] Speiser v. Randall 357 U.S. 513 (1958).

[15] The values of the formula are doubled in the table because, for example, 9-0 and 0-9 coalitions are equivalent.

[16] The author would like to thank Richard McKelvey, of the University of Rochester, for suggesting this means of testing the hypothesis.

TABLE 1. Probability of Majority Coalition Sizes in a Nine Member Body (assuming equiprobable voting)

Coalition Size	Probability
5	.492
6	.328
7	.141
8	.035
9	.004

This fact leads to the following formulation of Hypothesis 1:

H_1: **In issue areas in which there is no external threat to the Court, the proportion of minimum winning coalitions formed will be significantly larger than 49.2 percent.**

Similarly the operationalization of Hypothesis 2 will be:

H_2: **In issue areas in which there is an external threat to the Court, the proportion of minimum winning coalitions formed will be significantly smaller than 49.2 percent.**

IV. TESTING THE HYPOTHESES

Table 2 presents the distribution of various size coalitions by issue area in cases where no external threat to the Court exists, and table 3 does the same for cases which involve a threat situation.

TABLE 2. Distribution of Opinion Coalition Sizes in Nonthreat Issue Areas

Issue Area	Coalition Size				
	5	6	7	8	9
Internal Security	16	2	2	0	1
Censorship	9	2	2	0	0
Assembly	5	0	1	1	0
Libel	2	4	0	1	0
Miscellaneous	5	1	1	2	1
Total ($n = 58$)	37	9	6	4	2
	(.64)	(.16)	(.10)	(.07)	(.03)

The proportion of minimum winning opinion coalitions in the issue areas listed in table 2 is sixty-four percent. The null hypothesis corresponding to Hypothesis 1 would be:

$$H_{01}: \pi \leq .492$$

where π is the proportion of minimum winning coalitions. The probability that H_{01} is true, given the proportion of minimum winning coalitions in the sample is 0.01.[17] Since this probability is less than the traditionally accepted 0.05 significance level, we may reject the null hypothesis and conclude that there is a significant difference between the actual proportion of minimum winning coalitions and the proportion which would be expected if voting were random.[18]

In the cases which involve a threat issue, the proportion of minimum winning coalitions is twenty-eight percent. Thus there is a substantial difference (twenty-one percent) between the expected and actual proportions of minimum winning coalitions. The null hypothesis corresponding to Hypothesis 2 is:

$$H_{02}: \pi \geq .492$$

When H_{02} is tested, the probability that it is true is 0.04. We are, therefore, justified in rejecting the null hypothesis and concluding that there is a statistically significant difference between the expected and actual proportions of minimum winning opinion coalitions in threat issue areas.

TABLE 3. Distribution of Opinion Coalition Sizes in Threat Issue Areas

Issue Area	Coalition Size				
	5	6	7	8	9
Religion	2	3	1	2	0
Association	3	1	2	0	3
Internal Security (1957)	0	1	0	0	0
Total ($n = 18$)	5	5	3	2	3
	(.28)	(.28)	(.17)	(.11)	(.17)

More important than the statistical significance is the substantive significance of the finding. If the definition of a threat to the Court is accepted,

[17] The test used here is a simple one-tailed Z test, $Z = (p_s - p_u)/\sqrt{(p_u q_u/n)}$ (here p_s is the sample proportion, p_u is the population proportion, and $q_u = (1 - p_u)$. For a further explanation see Blalock (1960).

[18] Furthermore, it will be noted from table 2 that there is a monotonic decrease in the proportion of minimum winning opinion coalitions from five to nine. This is the pattern which would be expected if some Justices were "automatically" included in the winning coalition (as was discussed above) since it is more likely that one Justice would be "automatically" included than two, two is more likely than three, etc.

there seems to be a clear difference in the behavior of the Court in the two types of areas. The difference between the expected and actual proportions of minimum winning coalitions (fifteen percent in nonthreat areas, twenty-one percent in threat areas) seems to be substantial, especially in light of the rather stringent nature of the test. (Moreover, it should be noted that the combined deviations from the expected proportion produce a difference of thirty-six percent in the proportion of minimum winning coalitions between the two samples. Certainly this is a significant difference by any criterion). Therefore it seems fair to conclude that the size principle is important for understanding and explaining the process of coalition formation in the Supreme Court, at least in issue areas of the type considered in this study.

In closing, it seems appropriate to make some general comments about the application of the size principle to particular political situations. It is probable that in applying the size principle to any specific decision-making body, the zero-sum condition will not always be met. There will usually be unimportant decisions in which minimum winning coalitions will not occur. Furthermore, there may be some situations (as in the threat cases in this study) where we might expect a tendency away from minimum winning coalitions. Thus, if we lump all decisions of a particular body or group together and attempt to test the size principle, not only is it improbable that we would obtain significant results, but the test itself seems inappropriate. It would seem much more reasonable to attempt to determine in each decision-making body those types of decisions to which we may have particular reasons to believe the size principle may apply, and make our test on those decisions. This would seem to be the most appropriate research strategy, for there is no reason to believe that a theory will apply to a particular decision situation unless the assumptions of the theory are met (at least to a significant degree) in that situation. We have shown in this paper that the theory on minimum winning coalitions applies, in the Supreme Court, only to particular types of issues. The same may be true of other decision-making bodies as well.

Part 3

THE PARADOX OF VOTING

9. Toward an Estimate of the Frequency of Occurrence of the Paradox of Voting in U.S. Senate Roll Call Votes

BRUCE D. BOWEN

The paradox of voting has been a fascination for political scientists since Duncan Black reintroduced it to modern scholars in his *Theory of Committees and Elections* (1958). However, the principal focus of the vast majority of the work has not been empirical, that is, it has not concentrated on discovering how often the paradox actually occurs. Either the work centered on the paradox as a theoretical problem, or it attempted to estimate the theoretical frequency of occurrence of the paradox. Although there have been notable exceptions, the majority of the literature that does exist can be described as above.

It seems that the reason for neglecting the search for the frequency of concurrence of the paradox is at least related to the structure of our voting system. The system is so constructed that under normal circumstances there is insufficient evidence to say whether the paradox occurred. Normally there are at most one fewer votes taken than there are alternatives from which the body was choosing. This fact not only prevents political scientists from discovering occurrences of the paradox, but it also makes it

Much of the work reported here was begun by this author as a Ph.D. dissertation at the University of Kentucky. This work is a major revision and addition to a section of the work reported in that dissertation (Bowen, 1969). Thanks are certainly due my dissertation advisor, S. Sidney Ulmer, many of whose criticisms have been included; needless to say the final responsibility for the work is my own.

impossible for the political actors themselves to be aware that a majority of the body in question may not support the final outcome of the voting process.

The ideal data from the standpoint of the political scientist would be either the results of all possible pairwise votes on all the alternatives or a complete ordering of all alternatives by all individuals. The former would in fact yield the latter if each individual's preferences, which were reflected in his pairwise voting, were transitive. Obviously there are very few circumstances where this type of data is available, and when it is available, it is often not from the type of institution or decision-making body which has a great deal of impact on the political system.

If one were to examine the major decision-making bodies which publicly choose from among alternatives in the American system, he would find that the vast majority use some system of proposing motions, amending the motions or other amendments, and then voting on these parliamentary constructions in approximately the inverse order in which they were proposed. It is this type of voting system which normally leads to the situation described above where there is at least one less vote taken than alternatives considered. For example, take one of the simplest cases which occurs frequently in any decision-making body where there is an original motion (C) and an amendment is offered to that motion (B). There are actually three alternatives from which the body can choose: (1) the original motion or bill (C); (2) the amended version of the motion (B); or (3) status quo, i.e., no motion at all (A). However, this three alternative situation normally results in two votes: one on whether to amend the motion and one on whether to adopt the motion (amended or not).

Under the assumption that it is important to discover the frequency of occurrence of the paradox of voting in the basic decision-making bodies of the political system, a modified probability model was developed to bridge the gap between the type of data needed to make statements about the frequency of occurrence and that type of data (roll call votes on motions and amendments) that is normally available in those bodies. This model and an application of it to the roll call votes taken in five different years in the United States Senate follow.

I. THE MODEL

Because of the limitations in the data described above, it is not generally possible to state with certainty whether the paradox has occurred in a given situation; however, with the aid of this model and its accompanying assumptions, it will be possible in a limited set of circumstances to attach a probability to whether the paradox has occurred. For clarity, the model is explained below in terms of a series of examples.

Suppose there were a set of two roll call votes on a bill to allow the President to send wheat to underdeveloped nations. The first vote taken on the measure was on an amendment which would require such shipments to be made only in ships registered in the United States, and the second vote was on passage of the final version of the bill. Clearly there are three alternatives before the legislators: (1) the original proposal alone (C), (2) the original proposal with the amendment regarding shipping (B), and (3) no bill at all (A).

Since there are more alternatives than there are votes taken, this case is one in which there could be a hidden occurrence of the paradox.

The number of possible preference orders for legislators in this example is the number of alternatives factorial [$a!$] or six. The six preference orderings are as follows:

(1) *CBA*	(2) *CAB*	(3) *BCA*
(4) *BAC*	(5) *ABC*	(6) *ACB*

The first preference ordering, "*CBA*," is read as $C > B > A$, where the symbol "$>$" should be read as "is preferred to." Also, there are 2^n voting patterns where n is the number of votes taken. Four is the number in this case: yes-yes, yes-no, no-yes, and no-no.

If we know the outcome of the first vote and which voting pattern each legislator has exhibited, information which is usually readily available, we can make some judgments about which rank order of alternatives each legislator is likely to hold.

For example, if the amendment were adopted, then a person who voted yes-yes would have to hold rank order (3) $B > C > A$ or rank order (4) $B > A > C$; however, without additional information we could not determine which of the two rank orders he had.[1] The first yes vote was in effect a choice between B, the bill amended, and C, the bill without any amendment, and our hypothetical legislator chose the bill as amended, B. The second vote, given the amendment passed, was a choice between B, the bill as amended, and A, no bill at all. Again, he chose the amended bill. However, we are still in doubt as to whether he would rather have seen the original bill passed or no bill at all passed if the amendment had failed. Hence, the two possible rank orderings which differ only with respect to the positions of C and A.

In this situation the hypothetical legislator who votes yes-no is easier to categorize. Assuming the amendment has passed, he must have the following rank order: $A > B > C$. His first vote indicates the same information as our first hypothetical legislator, that he would rather have the

---

[1] It should be noted that throughout this paper the terms "preference order" and "rank order" are used interchangeably.

bill in its amended form, B, than in the original form, C. His second vote indicates, however, that his first choice is no bill at all, A. Hence, his rank ordering is complete.

Like our second hypothetical legislator, the preference ordering for the third legislator (with the third voting pattern) who voted no-yes is complete. His first vote indicated preference of the original bill, C, over the amended form, B, and his second vote indicated that although his first choice, C, was not possible, he still preferred the amended bill, B, to no bill at all, A. Hence, the single preference (or rank) ordering: $C > B > A$.

The final legislator with the voting pattern no-no has two possible preference orderings consistent with that vote: $A > C > B$ and $C > A > B$. His first vote shows a preference of C over B, and the second vote shows the preference of A over B; however, his preference between C and A is unknown.

On the other hand, if the amendment were not to pass, then a different set of rank orderings would correspond to each voting pattern. This is true because the alternative which is paired against no bill at all (A) in the final vote is determined by the outcome of the first vote.

Using the fact that on the first vote the amendment lost, then the voting pattern yes-yes would be sufficient to determine a unique preference ordering: $B > C > A$. The first vote indicated the preference of B over C; however, in the second vote A was paired against C, since the amendment lost in this example.

The preference orderings consistent with each of the voting patterns when the amendment loses are as follows:

yes-yes	*BCA*	
yes-no	*BAC*	or
	ABC	
no-yes	*CBA*	or
	CAB	
no-no	*ACB*	

Note that all six of the possible preference orderings are accounted for by the four voting patterns. They are arranged differently, however, for different outcomes on the first vote.

In order to determine the probability that the paradox occurred on a given set of roll call votes, it is necessary to determine exactly how many individuals hold each of the possible preference orderings. The first step in that process is to determine how many voters have each of the possible voting patterns. This is easily determined from the record for any roll call type vote.

Using this last example, assume one hundred voters were distributed as follows:

yes-yes	21
yes-no	25
no-yes	30
no-no	24

Obviously, the first vote indicates defeat for the amendment 46-54. Hence, we could expect the following distribution of persons on the possible rank orders.

21	(yes-yes)	BCA	
25	(yes-no)	BAC	or
		ABC	
30	(no-yes)	CAB	or
		CBA	
24	(no-no)	ACB	

The twenty-five people who voted yes-no are distributed in some un-known way between the two possible rank orders, $B > A > C$ and $A > B > C$, while the twenty-five persons who voted no-yes are also dis-tributed in some unknown manner between the rank orders $C > A > B$ and $C > B > A$. There is no question of distribution for those who voted yes-yes or no-no.

If we are willing to make an assumption, which is similar to but not exactly the same as that made by Niemi and Weisberg (1968) who devel-oped the general equations for the probability of the paradox, we can proceed to make an estimate of the chances that the paradox occurred in this case. The assumption is that where a person could possibly have had more than one rank order associated with his voting pattern that all such possible rank orders are equally likely for each individual. This can be called the modified "equally likely" assumption.

Although this modified "equally likely" assumption is similar in form to the one used by Niemi-Weisberg and others, it has a quite different effect. Using the assumption provided by Niemi and Weisberg, each of the six rank orders would be equally likely for each of the one hundred voters; however, with the assumption in the modified form as it is used in this model, only each of the two rank orders compatible with the voting pattern yes-no are equally likely for those who voted yes-no and the two rank orders compatible with the voting pattern no-yes are equally likely for each of those voting no-yes. This reduction in the range of choice is possible because we have added information, i.e., the number of persons with each voting pattern and the rank orders which correspond to each voting pattern.

The next step in determining the likelihood of the paradox is to randomly distribute our n persons over the r, equally likely rank orders possible with the voting pattern ascribed to the n persons. There are r^n possible ways the n persons could be distributed on r equally likely rank orders. We can randomly assign each individual to one of the equally likely rank orders which can be considered as analogous to randomly drawing one distribution from our population of r^n distributions. In the example, this is twenty-five persons over two orderings for yes-no and thirty persons over two orderings for no-yes.

After a complete random distribution is obtained for the rank orders for which the exact number of persons was unknown, we can then determine whether or not the paradox would have occurred if the actual distribution were the same as our one sample. This is accomplished by conducting all of the hypothetical pairwise votes, and determining whether there is one alternative which defeats all of the others.[2] For example, assume that the random process and our actual figures yielded the following distributions of persons on rank orders:

21 *BCA* 10 *BAC* 15 *ABC*
12 *CAB* 18 *CBA* 24 *ACB*

The results of the hypothetical pairwise votes would be as follows:

B vs. *C* 46-54
B vs. *A* 49-51
C vs. *A* 51-49

Note that *C* defeats all other alternatives; hence, the paradox could not have occurred if the voters were distributed on the rank orders as in the example. The paradox occurs when there is a cyclical majority, i.e., where no single alternative can defeat all other alternatives in the pairwise elections.

---

[2] This is the procedure used throughout the paper to determine whether the paradox has occurred. Klahr (1966) has referred to a paradox in these circumstances as a Type II intransitivity. Obviously Type I intransitivities which allow a majority winner but have an intransitivity among some subset of the remaining alternatives are not possible with only three alternatives; however, in the more complex case the model deals with only the Type II situation. The Type I intransitivity does not seem particularly offensive in this type of decision-making situation where only the final result is implemented.

In order to calculate the probability of the paradox in a given situation, we randomly assign individuals to one of their possible rank orders and evaluate the pairwise votes to determine whether the paradox would have occurred with that distribution. Then the process is repeated up to a given number of times which is equivalent to a sample of the r^n distributions possible for each voting pattern. The proportion of times the paradox occurs in this quasisample is the probability of the paradox.

Normally one would draw a sample from a complete listing of all possible arrangements with each element of the population having equal probability of being placed in the sample. This is called a simple random sample with replacement. However, although it would be possible to actually enumerate the population in these cases, it is highly impractical. Instead we use a random number generator which produces random numbers uniformly distributed between zero and one which are used to assign each individual to one of the equally likely rank orders consistent with his vote. This should yield the same result as a simple random sample with replacement since the important factor of equal probability of all elements in the population being selected is present in both cases.

Given the assumption that we are actually taking a random sample from all possible distributions we can calculate confidence intervals for our estimate of the probability from the following formula where p is the probability, q equals one minus p, f is the sampling fraction, n is the sample size, and t is the area under the normal curve associated with the degree of confidence desired (Cochran, 1963, pp. 56–59).

$$p \pm \left(t\sqrt{1-f} \cdot \sqrt{\frac{pq}{n-1}} + \frac{1}{2n} \right)$$

These preceding inferences from voting patterns to preference orderings are based upon the following assumptions:

1. For all individuals and alternatives: either alternative A_i is preferred to alternative A_j or A_j is preferred to alternative A_i. Indifference is not permitted.

2. All individuals' rank orders are transitive.

3. Each person's vote is consistent with his rank order, that is if A_i is preferred to A_j in his rank order, he will vote for A_i over A_j.

The first assumption, that of strong ordering, is reasonable in that any indifference can be considered as just an extremely weak preference one way or the other. The second assumption is probably a true empirical statement except for some evidence of intransitivity found by Edwards

(1953) and others, and even some of that evidence has been challenged (Rose, 1957). The third assumption is probably slightly weaker than the other two. However, this assumption greatly simplifies the analysis.[3]

Now that the outlines of the model are clear, it would be useful to examine how it would work when expanded to five alternatives, the normal situation of a bill with two amendments in the legislative context. With five alternatives there are 5! or 120 possible preference orderings. The three alternative case was relatively simple because there were only six alternatives to be arranged on four voting patterns; the five alternative case is obviously more complex.

Before looking at this legislative example in more detail, a few terms and symbols should be defined. There are five alternatives: (1) the bill with just the first amendment, B_1; (2) the bill with just the second amendment, B_2; (3) the bill with both amendments, B_{12}; (4) the bill with no amendments, C; and (5) no bill at all, A (the status quo). In most legislatures there would be three votes taken: (1) on the acceptance of the first amendment, B_1; (2) on the acceptance of the second amendment, B_2; and (3) on the final version of the bill—passage.[4] We shall call these the legislative votes to distinguish them from the hypothetical pairwise votes which we shall conduct based upon the inferred rank orders.[5]

In order to determine which rank orders correspond to which voting

---

[3] The third assumption might appear to raise some questions regarding the paradox where it is said to be contrived, that is, that some legislative strategists have altered the way they would normally vote in order to cause the paradox and, hence, prevent some undesirable (to them) alternative from being adopted. This technique is much more successful in preventing action than in aiding a particular proposal in passage. Some might say that these persons are not voting their true preferences and are violating assumption (3). The fact that they may or may not be voting some abstract or "true" preferences is really irrelevant. We are attempting to make inferences about a preference ordering for each individual so that we can say how he would have voted in the pairwise elections if they were held. Therefore, we need to know something about their voting behavior, and we look for it in their previous behavior.

[4] Normally the notation "B_2" refers to the bill with only the second amendment added. However, occasionally "B_2" is used to refer to the second amendment itself. Context should make it clear whether the bill or the amendment is being referenced. Possible confusion may arise when referring to the vote on the adoption of amendment B_2 when amendment B_1 has already been adopted. In one sense the vote is whether to adopt B_2, but it can also be construed as a choice between alternatives B_1 and B_{12}. These two perspectives should be kept in mind.

[5] This analysis differs in several important areas from that of Weisberg and Niemi in their paper in this volume (chap. 10). As long as the first and second amendments are not mutually exclusive, the five alternative model as proposed here is preferred to the four alternative model examined by Weisberg and Niemi. Although, the fifth alternative in this analysis is one which is never voted upon, it is certainly present. One could certainly argue that in most roll call situations in major decision-making bodies there are very few surprise amendments, and that given the fact that the voter knows he is to face two amendments which are not mutually exclusive, he must rank order five alternative outcomes.

patterns, it is necessary to know the results of the first two legislative votes because these results affect the voters' strategy on votes two and three.

In the following section of this paper we shall follow through the example where the first two votes carry and each amendment is accepted in turn. The same basic process is used for each of the other three possible outcomes (B_1 wins and B_2 loses, B_2 wins and B_1 loses, both B_1 and B_2 lose). Each possible voting pattern is examined below.

It is necessary to examine this process in steps. The first question that must be asked is what does a yes mean on the first legislative vote? It could mean (1) $B_1 > C$, or (2) that the first preference *for amendments* is the combination of both, B_{12}. Note that the actual first preference among all alternatives might still be A, and/or either or both of (1) and (2) above, and that B_2 is not ranked first, or second to A. A vote of yes on the second vote should indicate that $B_{12} > B_1$, since B_1 has already been adopted. Finally a yes on the last vote shows $B_{12} > A$. Unfortunately all of these inequalities when combined do not give us very much information about the rank orders that are consistent with the above votes (yes-yes-yes). It tells us that B_{12} is preferred to all other alternatives but gives us no other definite information; hence, all twenty-four rank orders which rank B_{12} first are possible. (They are not listed.)

The case of the voting pattern yes-yes-no is much simpler. As in the first case, the first yes implies $B_1 > C$, or that B_{12} is ranked above all other alternatives with the possible exception of A, or both, and that B_2 is not first or second to A. The second yes vote also implies the same as it did before $B_{12} > B_1$. The no on the final vote signifies $A > B_{12}$. Combining these we find that the first and second alternatives in the rank order must be A and B_{12} respectively and the remaining alternatives may be in any order. Hence, the six possible rank orders are:

$$AB_{12}B_1B_2C \quad AB_{12}B_1CB_2 \quad AB_{12}B_2B_1C$$
$$AB_{12}B_2CB_1 \quad AB_{12}CB_1B_2 \quad AB_{12}CB_2B_1$$

With the pattern yes-no-yes we have $B_1 > C$ or B_{12} ranking above all alternatives with the possible exception of A, or both; and B_2 is not first or second to A. From the second vote we have $B_1 > B_{12}$, and from the final vote $B_{12} > A$. All this tells us is that B_1 must be his first choice and that among the other alternatives B_{12} must be ranked above A. This leaves twelve possible rank orders:

$$B_1B_{12}ACB_2 \quad B_1CB_{12}AB_2 \quad B_1B_2B_{12}AC$$
$$B_1B_{12}CAB_2 \quad B_1CB_2B_{12}A \quad B_1B_2CB_{12}A$$
$$B_1B_{12}B_2CA \quad B_1CB_{12}B_2A \quad B_1B_{12}AB_2C$$
$$B_1B_{12}CB_2A \quad B_1B_2B_{12}CA \quad B_1B_{12}B_2AC$$

For the vote yes-no-no we have $B_1 > C$, or B_{12} ranked above all other alternatives with the possible exception of A; and B_2 not ranked first or second to A. The second vote gives $B_1 > B_{12}$, and the third vote gives $A > B_{12}$. This leaves A and B_1 as the possible first choices; A must be ranked above B_{12}, and B_1 is second if A is first. There are eighteen such rank orders.

$$AB_1CB_2B_{12} \quad AB_1CB_{12}B_2 \quad AB_1B_2CB_{12}$$
$$AB_1B_2B_{12}C \quad AB_1B_{12}B_2C \quad AB_1B_{12}CB_2$$
$$B_1ACB_2B_{12} \quad B_1ACB_{12}B_2 \quad B_1AB_2CB_{12}$$
$$B_1AB_2B_{12}C \quad B_1AB_{12}B_2C \quad B_1AB_{12}CB_2$$
$$B_1CAB_2B_{12} \quad B_1CB_2AB_{12} \quad B_1CAB_{12}B_2$$
$$B_1B_2CAB_{12} \quad B_1B_2ACB_{12} \quad B_1B_2AB_{12}C$$

The next voting pattern no-yes-yes introduces the implications of a no on the first vote: $C > B_1$, or B_2 is ranked above all other alternatives with the possible exception of A, or both; and B_{12} is not ranked first or second to A. The second vote implies $B_{12} > B_1$, and the third implies $B_{12} > A$. The combined result is that either C or B_2 is first and B_{12} is ranked above A and B_1. Sixteen rank orders meet these criteria.

$$CB_{12}AB_1B_2 \quad CB_{12}AB_2B_1 \quad CB_{12}B_1AB_2$$
$$CB_{12}B_1B_2A \quad CB_{12}B_2B_1A \quad CB_{12}B_2AB_1$$
$$CB_2B_{12}AB_1 \quad CB_2B_{12}B_1A \quad B_2CB_{12}B_1A$$
$$B_2CB_{12}AB_1 \quad B_2B_{12}B_1CA \quad B_2B_{12}B_1AC$$
$$B_2B_{12}CAB_1 \quad B_2B_{12}CB_1A \quad B_2B_{12}ACB_1$$
$$B_2B_{12}AB_1C$$

The sixth voting pattern no-yes-no has slightly fewer possible rank orders associated with it, fourteen. The criteria here are $C > B_1$ or B_2 ranked above all with the possible exception of A, or both; and B_{12} is not first or second to A. We also have $B_{12} > B_1$ and $A > B_{12}$ which all taken together yield $A > B_{12} > B_1$ and $C > B_1$ with no restrictions on B_2. There are three possible first place choices B_2, C, and A, and if B_2 is first then the condition $C > B_1$ can be dropped. The possible rank orders are:

$$B_2ACB_{12}B_1 \quad B_2CAB_{12}B_1 \quad B_2AB_{12}CB_1$$
$$B_2AB_{12}B_1C \quad AB_2CB_{12}B_1 \quad ACB_2B_{12}B_1$$
$$ACB_{12}B_2B_1 \quad ACB_{12}B_1B_2 \quad AB_2B_{12}CB_1$$
$$AB_2B_{12}B_1C \quad CAB_{12}B_1B_2 \quad CAB_{12}B_2B_1$$
$$CAB_2B_{12}B_1 \quad CB_2AB_{12}B_1$$

For the voting pattern no-no-yes, the number of possible rank orders is again low at eight. The limits imposed by the legislative votes are $C > B_1$

or B_2 ranked above all but possibly A, and B_{12} not ranked first. Also $B_1 > B_{12}$ and $B_{12} > A$, with B_2 placed anywhere in the order; however, if B_2 is first then the condition that $C > B_1$ is dropped. The following are the allowable rank orders:

$$CB_2B_1B_{12}A \quad CB_1B_2B_{12}A \quad CB_1B_{12}B_2A$$
$$CB_1B_{12}AB_2 \quad B_2CB_1B_{12}A \quad B_2B_1CB_{12}A$$
$$B_2B_1B_{12}CA \quad B_2B_1B_{12}AC$$

The final voting pattern no-no-no has twenty-two consistent rank orders conforming to the following conditions: $C > B_1$ or B_2 ranked first with the possible exception of A or both, and B_{12} is not first and $B_1 > B_{12}$ and $A > B_{12}$. Either A, C, or B_2 can be first and B_{12} is always ranked below A and B_1.

$$AB_2CB_1B_{12} \quad ACB_2B_1B_{12} \quad ACB_1B_2B_{12}$$
$$ACB_1B_{12}B_2 \quad AB_2B_1B_{12}C \quad AB_2B_1CB_{12}$$
$$B_2ACB_1B_{12} \quad B_2CAB_1B_{12} \quad B_2CB_1AB_{12}$$
$$B_2AB_1CB_{12} \quad B_2AB_1B_{12}C \quad B_2B_1AB_{12}C$$
$$B_2B_1ACB_{12} \quad B_2B_1CAB_{12} \quad CAB_2B_1B_{12}$$
$$CB_2AB_1B_{12} \quad CB_2B_1AB_{12} \quad CAB_1B_2B_{12}$$
$$CB_1AB_2B_{12} \quad CB_1B_2AB_{12} \quad CAB_1B_{12}B_2$$
$$CB_1AB_{12}B_2$$

Exactly the same process is used for determining the rank orders consistent with each voting pattern with the other three outcomes for the first two votes. Obviously, the conditions placed upon possible rank orders by a yes to the second vote when the first amendment has failed are different from those imposed when the amendment has passed. For example, when amendment B_1 passes, a yes on the second legislative vote implies $B_{12} > B_1$; however, if the first amendment fails, a yes vote on the second roll call would imply $B_2 > C$. In the first case the question is whether to also add B_2 as an amendment (B_1 having already been added), while in the second case it is whether to adopt B_2 as the only amendment (B_1 having failed).

In order to further demonstrate the differences associated with the results of the first two legislative votes, table 1 shows the number of rank orders which are consistent with each of the voting patterns for each of the four possible outcomes with respect to the amendments.

The next step in the model is completely analogous to that in the three alternative model except that it is more complex. To illustrate, assume we are operating under conditions where A and B both win; the model would randomly assign each of the n_1 persons who voted YYY to one of the twenty-four possible rank orders. The same would be true for the n_2 per-

TABLE 1. Number of Orderings Consistent with the Four Possible Outcomes

Voting Pattern	B_1 Wins B_2 Wins	B_1 Wins B_2 Loses	B_1 Loses B_2 Wins	B_1 Loses B_2 Loses
YYY	24	12	16	8
YYN	6	18	14	22
YNY	12	24	8	16
YNN	18	6	22	14
NYY	16	8	24	12
NYN	14	22	6	18
NNY	8	16	12	24
NNN	22	14	18	6
Total	120	120	120	120

sons voting *YYN*. They would be distributed among the six possible rank orders in that case. Note that $\sum_{i=1}^{8} n_i = N$, that is, the sum of all the separate n's for the individual voting patterns should equal the total number of persons voting. Likewise the sum of all the possible rank orders for each voting pattern should equal 120, the total number of possible rank orders for five alternatives.

After a set of random assignments has been made, the hypothetical pairwise votes are conducted to determine whether there exists a majority winner under that distribution, i.e., whether the paradox occurs. The number of trials of sets of random assignments depends upon how large of a sample one wishes to take.[6]

As with the three alternative case the probability of the paradox is the ratio of the number of times random assignments yield the paradox to the total number of trials.

Ideally, one would want to test every possible distribution rather than use the Monte Carlo or quasisampling technique described above just as in most sampling situations one would rather have the entire population. However, as soon as a rough estimate is made of the number of possible distributions, it becomes very clear why it is not practical to enumerate the population.

If there were no constraints at all except the equal probability of all 120 rank orders, then the total number of ways in which 100 voters could be arranged among the rank orders is 120^{100} or 8.28×10^{207}. However, by stipulating that an individual can only be assigned to a rank order consistent with his voting pattern, the total number of possible distributions

---

. [6] The question of tie votes may be raised at this point. Given the definition of a Type II intransitivity or the paradox of voting, if no alternative can defeat (without a single tie) all other alternatives, then the paradox is said to occur. Hence, ties among alternatives competing for the second, third, etc., rankings are not relevant; however, there is no majority winner unless it can actually win, not tie, all pairwise contests.

is the product of the number of possible distributions for each voting pattern. That product is approximately 1.3×10^{112}.

Hence, regardless of whether one is testing all possible distributions or only the restricted set used here, it is not practical to test even 1.3×10^{112} distributions. Given a computer capable of a billion operations per second (none are yet that fast), the total amount of computer time required would exceed 10^{95} years. Hence, some method has to be used to reduce the number of operations required. The Monte Carlo technique described above is one such method and yet still maintains the equal probability of each element of the population being selected.

II. Senate Roll Call Analysis

The first question to arise in the testing or use of this model is what voting body should be used as the data source. Three basic criteria were established for a data source: (1) It should be an important decision-making body in the political system. (2) The voting body should be reasonably large so as to avoid any of a number of types of problems that might arise with a small number of voters. (3) The data should be readily available.

Obviously, the United States Senate meets all three of the established criteria. Clearly the Senate is an important decision-making body; it has one hundred members; and the results of its votes, i.e., the roll call votes are available in machine readable form (computer tape) from the Inter-University Consortium for Political Research.[7] The Senate is certainly not the only body meeting all three of these criteria; however, no other institution which met the criteria stood out as especially more interesting. Hence, the Senate was selected somewhat by default.[8]

Since the model is capable of handling only those situations where there are either one or two amendments to a bill and a final vote on passage (a maximum of five alternatives), the data had to be transformed slightly before it could be fed into the model. The first problem was to include

---

[7] The Congressional roll call data utilized in this study were made available by the Inter-University Consortium for Political Research. The data were supplied in partially proofed form and the Consortium bears no responsibility for either the analyses or interpretations presented herein.

[8] The time periods for the study were selected with two objectives in mind. The first was to cover a somewhat wide portion of the more recent past. The second was that three particular years, 1958, 1960, and 1962, were to be included so that some relationships might be examined between this analysis and some earlier unpublished work by this author. (That examination is not reported here but was partially responsible for the years selected for analysis.) The fourth year reported here, 1966, was selected representing the later end of the time period for which machine readable data was available. The last year to be selected, 1965, was chosen at random from the remaining years which were available on tape. Limitations imposed by the cost of computer time and other resources are responsible for the fact that only five years of roll calls were analyzed.

only those bills in the analysis which had one to two amendments offered. However, this greatly reduced the set of possible bills available for study for each year. By considering the bill with all of the amendments accepted up until the second to the last amendment functionally equivalent to what is called the original bill, C, in the five alternative model, we can expand the possible number of bills we can analyze.

The above procedure works as follows. Suppose we have a bill with four amendments and a vote on final passage. Also assume that the first amendment passed and the second failed. So, as we approach the vote on the third amendment, the bill has already been amended once. For purposes of analysis, the model calls the bill at this stage the original bill and begins the analysis at that point. It should be noted that it is entirely possible that the paradox could be occurring earlier in the voting process than the point at which the analysis begins and no probability will be attached to the likelihood of that event. In general, if the paradox occurs on a subset of all alternatives it occurs for the entire set; however, if the paradox does not occur for any subset that is not sufficient to say that the paradox does not occur for the entire set. The results will be presented with those limitations in mind.

In actually operationalizing the model in terms of Senate roll call votes, it was necessary to make some modifications and clarifications of the roll call used. Because of the nature of the model, it was necessary to exclude those senators from the analysis who did not vote on all three of the roll calls. In order to reduce the error generated by this exclusion, those senators who were declared paired on a missed roll call were not excluded.[9] The master roll call computer tapes from the Inter-University Consortium for Political Research place each senator into one of the following categories for each roll call: (1) voting yes, (2) voting no, (3) paired for, (4) paired against, (5) announced or answering Congressional Quarterly Poll for, (6) announced or answering the Congressional Quarterly Poll against, and (7) voting present, or absent and position undetermined. This coding was taken as authoritative and not further verified. Hence, a person coded 1 or 3 was treated as voting for the bill and those coded 2 or 4 were treated as having voted against. The basic purpose of this was to avoid reduction or distortion of the votes used because of a senator's being present for one vote and not the other.[10]

---

[9] All senators recorded as paired were treated as voting. In a few cases this means that a small number of senators may have entered the analysis who were paired on all the roll calls and did not vote on any. This does not appear to be a very serious problem, however, because the preferences are probably nearly as clear from a pairing on a roll call as on the actual vote.

[10] An independent test was made on each computer run to determine how much the vote used as input to the computer model (which had those not voting and not paired on all votes dropped) differed from the actual vote reported by *Congressional*

As was stated earlier, the votes on the last two amendments and the vote on passage are used as input to the model. However, occasionally it is more meaningful to use the vote on a motion to table, a motion to reconsider, or the reconsideration itself. This is necessary when what we might call the primary vote on an amendment or passage was a voice vote and, therefore, not available to us. For example, suppose there were a roll call vote on a motion to table an amendment and the tabling motion lost. The next vote might well be a voice on passage of the amendment; in which case the motion to table with the votes reversed could be used as an indicator of the actual vote on the amendment. In fact, one of the primary reasons that no roll call vote may be asked for on the amendment is that both proponents and opponents of the amendment feel that the roll call on the motion to table represents a fairly accurate picture of the actual vote on the amendment.

Approximately the same argument can be made for a motion to recommit a bill to committee in place of the vote on passage. On the other hand, an actual vote taken after a motion to reconsider has been passed is reconsideration or in effect a second vote on the original proposition whether it be an amendment or the final version of a bill. Reconsideration votes (not votes to reconsider) are always used as substitutes for the original vote in this analysis.

However, as in the case of the motion to table, the motion to reconsider can be used as a substitute for the actual vote if it is not available because of a voice vote. As with the motion to table, the votes must be reversed in order to make the action analogous to a passage vote. These are used primarily where the motions fail because when they pass, a reconsideration vote as described above is taken, and it would be used in the analysis.

Before the final data runs were made on the computerized version of the model, one final check was made on the accuracy of the computer program. With only the most minor changes, the model could be asked to calculate the probability of the paradox given 99 senators and the fact that all of the 120 possible rank orders from 5 alternatives were equally likely. According to Niemi and Weisberg, as the number of voters (senators in this case) approaches infinity (in fact, merely gets very large) the probability of the paradox with equally likely rank orders approaches the

---

Quarterly Almanac for that year. If there were more than a few votes difference, or the outcome was reversed, the roll call would have been dropped. This independent test also provided an excellent opportunity to verify that the computer was correctly programmed to remove the correct votes from the tape for each analysis run. If the voting splits on each roll call did not correspond with those provided by *Congressional Quarterly* it would indicate the possibility of a format error in the computer program. Hence, this technique further insured the absence of a particular type of error which can often be present in computer analyses of data and is often very difficult to detect.

limit 0.2513 (Niemi and Weisberg, 1968). The result of this model using a quasi-sample size of 281 was 0.253, which has range of 0.202 to 0.304 at the 95 percent confidence level if we assume our quasisample to be really a simple random sample.[11] The accurate value of this probability as calculated by Niemi and Weisberg is well within the range of the value generated by the model.

Table 2 is a summary of the results obtained from the runs made on the Senate roll call data from the five years under analysis. The table separates the bills according to the number of amendments because, as was noted earlier, the model yields the probability of the paradox for the entire consideration only in the cases of two or less amendments. Where there are three or more amendments, the probability listed in table 2 (or later in table 3) is the probability of the paradox occurring during the consideration of the last two amendments with no implications for what the prob-

TABLE 2. Number of Bills with Probability of the Paradox Greater than Zero by Year and Number of Amendments

Year	No. of Amendments	No. of Bills with $p = 0.0$*	No. of Bills with $p > 0.0$
1958	1	5	0
	2	4	0
	3 or more	6	0
	Total	15	0
1960	1	5	0
	2	1	0
	3 or more	6	4
	Total	12	4
1962	1	4	0
	2	3	1
	3 or more	11	1
	Total	18	2
1965	1	10	0
	2	6	0
	3 or more	12	2
	Total	28	2
1966	1	11	0
	2	4	0
	3 or more	10	5
	Total	25	5
Five Year Totals		98	13

* 95 percent confidence interval for $p = 0.0$ is $+0.0025$. Confidence intervals for $p > 0$ are reported in table 3. The quasisample size for these runs is 200.

[11] The quasisample size of 281 is the result of letting the computer try as many times as it could in 5 minutes. Since this test consumed so much time, it was considered better to limit the time rather than the number of tries.

ability may be for the paradox on the entire consideration of the bill. For example, one of the bills adopted by the Senate in 1958 was the Labor-Management Reporting and Disclosure Act of 1958; this particular bill had twenty-two amendments proposed to it. Although the model reports a probability of zero, this probability is only for the last two of the twenty-two amendments.

Of the fifteen bills analyzed in 1958 none was found to have a probability of the paradox greater than zero. Table 2 indicates that the figures for the other four years were also quite small. The largest number of bills with nonzero probabilities occurring in 1966 with five. The five year total is only thirteen.

Table 3 includes all bills which had a probability of the paradox greater than zero. However, some of the bills reported there do not have particularly high probabilities either. Of the four bills listed for 1960, only one, the Wheat Act of 1960 with a probability of the paradox of 0.940 can be said to involve the paradox with any certainty. Table 3 also indicates about an even chance (0.460) that the paradox occurred on the Housing Act of 1960 and a slight chance that the paradox occurred on the amendments to the Social Security Act, although the probability is quite low (0.045) on this bill.

It should also be noted that there is considerable variation in the size of the confidence intervals reported in table 3. This results from the fact that the calculation depends upon the size of the probability (p) as well

TABLE 3.   Bills with Probability of the Paradox Greater than Zero

Bill	Year	Number of Amendments	Probability of the Paradox	95% Confidence Interval*
Constitutional Amendment re:				
House Vacancies	1960	3	.020	±.0220
Wheat Act of 1960	1960	3	.940	±.0355
Housing Act	1960	3	.460	±.0717
Social Security Amendment	1960	3	.045	±.0313
Food and Agriculture Act (S3225)	1962	9	.965	±.0280
Foreign Assistance Appropriations	1962	2	.150	±.0521
Inter-American Development Bank	1965	6	.085	±.0412
Economic Opportunity				
Amendments	1965	16	.630	±.0696
Tax Adjustment Act	1966	7	.050	±.0328
Alternate Crops (Farm)	1966	5	.390	±.0703
Appropriation for Independent				
Offices & HUD	1966	10	.030	±.0262
Foreign Investors Tax Act	1966	6	.025	±.0242
Suspension of Investment Tax				
Credit & Accelerated				
Development	1966	3	.220	±.0601

* The 95 percent confidence interval is $p\pm$ error, which is reported in this column. This is calculated as though our quasisample were a simple random sample with replacement.

as on the sample size. From the formula given by Cochran (1963) it can be seen quickly that the width of the interval depends upon the size of the sample, the sampling fraction, and the probability.

$$p \pm \left(t\sqrt{1-f}\cdot\sqrt{\frac{pq}{n-1}} + \frac{1}{2n} \right)$$

However, only the term $\frac{pq}{n-1}$ depends upon the size of p, and the interval will be largest when this term is at its maximum. Since we are holding the sample size constant and the operation "square root" does not alter the relationship, the confidence interval is at its maximum when pq is at the maximum. Since $q = 1 - p$, $pq = p(1 - p) = p - p^2$, the maximum for $p - p^2$ occurs when its first derivative is zero; hence, $1 - 2p = 0$ or $p = 0.50$. Therefore, the chance of error increases as the split or probability approaches 0.50. The smallest error is for $p = 0.0$ or $p = 1.00$.

In table 3 the results for 1962 resemble the results for 1960 more closely that those for 1958. Again there is at least one instance where the model indicates that the paradox quite probably occurred. The analysis here indicates a very high probability that the paradox occurred ($p = 0.965$) on the Food and Agriculture Act (S3225). This is really a classic type of case for the paradox. Much of the previous literature cited indicated that the paradox was more likely to occur where unidimensionality was not present, i.e., where two or more dimensions are present. The Food and Agriculture Bill illustrates this point quite well. There are eight rather straightforward amendments offered to the bill which would have made changes in ways in which grain farmers (particularly wheat farmers) would be treated under the price support program. However, the next to the last amendment would require all public lands under Title I of the act to be free from discrimination. Hence, an entirely new dimension enters the situation and the result is a high probability of the paradox.

It seems unusual that the other highly likely occurrence of the paradox occurred while the Senate was considering a bill dealing with wheat price supports. The cause in this case is not quite as obvious. However, the additional dimension may have arisen as a result of the fact that some amendments dealt with the support price of wheat (as a percentage of parity) while another amendment dealt with payment-in-kind for acreage taken out of production. It is possible that this additional feature of the second amendment added the second dimension and introduced the possibility of the paradox.

In analyzing the second 1962 Food and Agriculture Bill (HR 12391), responses to the Congressional Quarterly Poll were considered as votes on the bill in order to maintain sufficient votes so that the outcome would not be altered by the dropping of those senators whose preferences were not known on all the amendments and passage.

Although foreign aid bills are usually likely candidates for multidimensionality, in this case the probability is only 0.150 for the Foreign Assistance Appropriations Act. One would expect that an appropriations bill would have a lower probability of the paradox than other types of bills as long as the principal element in the appropriations bill is financial with the other problems and questions regarding the program handled in the authorization bill. However, the Foreign Assistance Act which preceded this appropriations bill in 1962 had a probability of the paradox of 0.0.

In the data for 1965 there is only one case where the probability of the paradox is substantially greater than zero. However, the number of bills considered has increased by fifty percent from twenty to thirty. One would expect the number of bills involved to be subject to some fluctuation; however, a fifty percent increase does appear to be substantial.

The only candidate for a possible occurrence of the paradox in 1965 is the Economic Opportunity Act Amendments of 1965 (HR 8283), and the model indicates that the probability of the paradox is only 0.630. The two amendments proposed to this bill do not give one a very solid clue that the paradox may be occurring. The first amendment considered by the model was one which provided for continuation of the voluntary assistance program for children without requiring a report. The amendment passed. However, the second amendment was a straightforward reduction in the dollar authorization for the poverty program. At least on the surface there does not appear to be anything about the content of these two amendments that would suggest that the paradox could be occurring such as the content of the amendments to the Food and Agriculture Act suggested.

The probability of the paradox having occurred on the Inter-American Development Bank Bill is probably so low (0.085) that it requires no more than a mention.

In table 2, reporting the results from 1966, the number of bills analyzed is the same as for 1965, thirty bills, which indicates that the increase in 1965 over the number of 1962 was not just a minor fluctuation and that there is an increase over time in the number of bills on which roll calls on amendments are taken. However table 3 reports a generally low probability of the paradox for all bills included in the 1966 analysis.

The highest probability of the paradox is 0.390 recorded for the Alternate Crops Bill which determined the circumstances under which farmers should be allowed to plant alternate crops. The two amendments considered were (1) whether payments under the program should exceed

10,000 dollars for any one individual and (2) whether the legislation should be for one or two years. The payment limitation probably represents a slightly different dimension than the remainder of the bill and may be responsible for its moderate probability of the paradox.

The other bill worth mentioning is the one to suspend the investment tax credit and accelerated depreciation allowances. However, the amendments considered on this bill are so similar that one would not suspect the paradox at all. The first amendment provided for exceptions to the provisions of the act for the trucking industry. This amendment passed, while the second amendment, which would have exempted airlines with regard to aircraft purchased before the bill was passed, failed.

Another point about the 1966 data should be noted. Two bills which qualified in all respects for inclusion in the analysis were not included because when those who did not vote or express some preference on all of the roll call votes used in the analysis were dropped, the outcome of one or more of the votes was changed. This results from the fact that some senators voted on one amendment and not the other. Unfortunately this may be a systematic bias in that the votes were rather close on the amendments on both of these bills, and the data so far seems to indicate that the probability of the paradox is high when there are relatively close votes.

It is possible to further refine our analysis by moving slightly beyond the model. From the description of the model above, we know that the following rank orders correspond to the given voting patterns or one amendment and that amendment winning. These rank orders are just those which are consistent with each voting pattern. Each rank order is also numbered for convenience in referring to it.

YY	(1)	BCA
	(2)	BAC
YN	(3)	ABC
NY	(4)	CBA
NN	(5)	CAB
	(6)	ACB

If we were to conduct the pairwise votes, we could tell how each group (those persons who have a particular rank order) would vote. The assumption is that if a person ranks B over A in his preference ordering then he would vote for B over A in a pairwise vote. Consider the following pairwise votes, where "$B(BvC)$" indicates the number of people voting for B in the pairwise election between B and C where (3) stands for the number of people who hold the rank order $A > B > C$ which is associated with (3) above.

$$B(BvC) = (1) + (2) + (3) = YY + YN$$
$$C(BvC) = (4) + (5) + (6) = NY + NN$$

$$A(AvB) = (3) + (5) + (6) = YN + NN$$
$$B(AvB) = (1) + (2) + (4) = YY + NY$$

$$C(CvA) = (1) + (4) + (5)$$
$$A(CvA) = (2) + (3) + (6)$$

In the first vote between B and C those persons with orders (1), (2), and (3) have ranked $B > C$; therefore, we count them as voting for B over C in the pairwise vote. The same process is used in each of the other votes. Note that no votes are associated with the contest between C and A because a unique classification of votes similar to the other pairwise comparisons is not possible. For example, those voting YY could prefer A to C or C to A.

Since we assume that B wins, that is, it defeats C, then $YY + YN > NY + NN$. If the paradox is to occur, no alternative must be able to defeat all other alternatives; hence, B must be beaten by A if the paradox occurs. If $A > B$ then, $YN + NN > YY + NY$. Combining $YY + YN > NY + NN$ with $YN + NN > YY + NY$ yields $YN > NY$. In summary then, we have established three necessary conditions (which yield a fourth) that must be met for the paradox to occur in the three alternative case when the amendment passes:

1. The final bill must fail[12]
2. $YY + YN > NY + NN$
3. $YN + NN > YY + NY$
4. Combining (2) and (3) $YN > NY$

The same analysis can be repeated in slightly different form for B being defeated, that is $C > B$. For that assumption the rank orders are as follows:

YY	(1)	$B > C > A$
YN	(2)	$B > A > C$
	(3)	$A > B > C$
NY	(4)	$C > B > A$
	(5)	$C > A > B$
NN	(6)	$A > C > B$

---

[12] The condition that the final version of the bill must fail was originally proven in this author's doctoral dissertation (Bowen, 1969, pp. 119–21).

The results of the pairwise votes are as follows:

$$C(BvC) = (4) + (5) + (6) = NY + NN$$
$$B(BvC) = (1) + (2) + (3) = YY + YN$$

$$A(AvC) = (2) + (3) + (6) = YN + NN$$
$$C(AvC) = (1) + (4) + (5) = YY + NY$$

$$B(BvA) = (1) + (2) + (4)$$
$$A(BvA) = (3) + (5) + (6)$$

Since we assume $C > B$, then $NY + NN > YY + YN$. As before, if the paradox is to occur C must be beaten, and the only alternative left to defeat it is A. If $A > C$, then $YN + NN > YY + NY$. Combining these two inequalities, the expression $NN > YY$ results. As in the case of the amendment winning there are three necessary conditions (which yield a fourth) for the paradox to occur:

1. The final bill must fail
2. $NY + NN > YY + YN$
3. $YN + NN > YY + NY$
4. Combining (2) and (3) $NN > YY$

Regardless of the outcome of the first vote, if the paradox is to occur, conditions (1) and (3) must be met. (Note that these conditions are the same for both preconditions.)

Of the 111 bills considered in this analysis, 35 involved only one amendment and in none of those cases did the final version of the bill fail to pass; hence, the paradox could not have occurred on any of those bills. The simulation model also had indicated the probability of the paradox was zero for all cases where there was only one amendment. This later analysis allows us to state definitely that it did not occur on any of the one amendment bills.

In summary, of 111 bills studied, the probability of the paradox is very high in only two bills. In 4 other bills the probability is between 0.20 and 0.70. Assuming for a moment that the paradox occurred on the 2 bills with high probability estimates and on 2 of the 4 with moderate estimates, that would indicate that the paradox occurred 4 times out of 76 cases where there were 5 or more alternatives (2 amendments) or about 5.3 percent of the time. Using Niemi and Weisberg's calculation of the theoretical probability of the paradox with 5 alternatives (the only restraint being equally likely rank orders) one would expect the paradox to occur about 25 percent of the time (Niemi and Weisberg, 1968).

The probable explanation for the difference between the expected and calculated percentages is that this model has shown that the paradox does not occur as frequently as one would expect mathematically from the fact that five alternatives are present. It is also worth noting that not one case of the paradox was possible in any of the thirty-five instances where there were only three alternatives present.

Ideally one should proceed with a model which treated the multitude of cases where more than 5 alternatives (2 amendments) were present. Unfortunately the present model is not well suited to that task because of the extremely large number of rank orders associated with the more complex case. For example, in the situation with 5 roll call votes (or 4 amendments) there are 32 voting patterns, 17 alternatives, and approximately 3.56 $\times 10^{14}$ possible rank orders.

The limitations of this analysis, then, are somewhat obvious. No statement can really be made about the case where more than five alternatives are present, and in the five alternative case only the likelihood of the paradox is actually known.

The principal substantive conclusion is that in the relatively uncomplex case of two or fewer amendments, the United States Senate very seldom has a problem with the paradox of voting. The suspicion is that the paradox is not very important in the more complex situations either. However, the only data on this last point is that the paradox occurs very infrequently on the last amendments of a more complex bill.

10. Probability Calculations for Cyclical Majorities in Congressional Voting

HERBERT F. WEISBERG   **RICHARD G. NIEMI**

A very considerable amount of theoretical work has been devoted to the search for conditions under which the paradox of voting cannot occur—that is, for circumstances in which one alternative could defeat each of the other alternatives in pairwise voting (or in some cases, where the entire social ordering of alternatives is transitive).[1] By comparison, almost no work has been done to uncover actual instances of the paradox in real-world voting or to suggest ways of conducting a search for such occurrences. In this chapter we shall examine the possibility of calculating the probability of the paradox of voting for congressional and other legislative and committee votes. A calculation procedure will be presented and will be illustrated through the examination of several cases. Though the cases considered are hypothetical, frequent reference is made to actual characteristics and procedures of congresssional voting.

I. DEVELOPMENT OF THE PROBLEM

Empirical studies of the paradox have been impeded by the fact that in most situations it is impossible to tell whether the paradox has actually

---

[1] A definition, examples, and a brief history of scholarly work on the paradox can be found in Riker (1961).

occurred. As has often been pointed out, legislative voting generally does not provide complete information about the choices available. For example, when a legislature votes to adopt an amendment to a bill and then the amended bill is defeated, the legislature does not go back to determine whether the unamended bill could have passed. The result of the vote which was not taken has been inferred in a few historical instances (Riker, 1958, 1965), but rarely is there sufficient information to reconstruct that vote with confidence. Newspaper accounts occasionally suggest that there was intense maneuvering on a bill which would make the paradox particularly likely, as when the opponents of a bill join in adding an amendment making it even stronger with the hope that it will cause the bill to lose support. But it is difficult to judge even in these circumstances exactly what support existed for each of the alternatives. Interviewing might possibly be used to determine individual preference orders (from which it can be determined whether the paradox occurred), although this method could not be used more than occasionally.[2] Rarely, then, can we determine whether the paradox has actually occurred in legislative voting. In light of this, estimation procedures are of considerable utility.

In the past, estimates of the probability of the paradox have been made on the basis of gratuitous assumptions about the probability of various individual preference orders (Campbell and Tullock, 1965; DeMeyer and Plott, 1970; Garman and Kamien, 1968; Klahr, 1966; Niemi and Weisberg, 1968; Pomeranz and Weil, 1970; Weisberg and Niemi, 1971). Exact solutions are sometimes possible using these procedures, although the complexity of the calculations sometimes requires approximation through simulation (sampling from the possible distributions of preference orders) or the investigation of limiting cases (as in finding the probability of the paradox in a legislature of infinite size as an approximation to the probability for actual legislatures).

Solutions of this form have the defect that they are very dependent on the initial probability assumptions about the individual preference orders. For example, the limiting probability of the paradox can be made to range all the way from zero to one by varying the initial probability assumptions. Typically, of course, it has been assumed that all possible preference orders are equally likely, but that assumption is difficult to justify. We would not expect all legislators to be indifferent to the alternatives nor would we expect a uniform distribution of legislators across all possible preference orders, two conditions leading to the "equally likely" assumption. We can

---

[2] This procedure might be far more efficient than it seems. As we indicate below, it is sometimes possible to infer most individuals' preference orders from the votes that are taken, leaving only a few legislators to be interviewed. One could also interview a sample of the legislators and employ conventional statistical procedures to estimate the likelihood of the paradox.

perhaps interpret the "equally likely" assumption as referring to our lack of knowledge about the actual distribution of the legislators' preference orders, but we are then modelling *our uncertainty* more than the behavior of the legislators.

This extreme dependence on the initial probability assumptions, along with the difficulty in justifying any specific set of assumptions, suggests two appropriate strategies. First, we should not be concerned with any single probability calculation. Instead we should emphasize general classes of probability assumptions leading to similar results and general conditions which make the paradox more or less likely. This is in fact the motivation behind Bjurulf's study (chap. 11 in this volume) and those of Niemi (1969) and Weisberg and Niemi (1971). Here we shall pay particular attention to conditions affecting the likelihood of the paradox in congressional voting. Secondly, we should utilize all available information as fully as possible so as to minimize the dependence on the initial probability assumptions. The legislative voting case is of particular interest in this regard because of its ubiquitousness and because the votes which are taken yield some information about the votes which were not taken.

Viewed from this vantage point, a major consideration here is to determine just how the information from actual votes can be used to make inferences about individual preference orders. When that information takes us as far as we can go, we then incorporate probability assumptions in order to be able to estimate the expected occurrence of the paradox of voting. That neither of these tasks is obvious or trivial is indicated by the differing approaches used by Bowen (chap. 9 in this volume) and by us. It turns out that a crucial factor in the legislative setting is the number of amendments on bills. We therefore treat the case of a single amendment first and then turn to the more complicated two amendment case.

Before turning to the estimation procedures, we will mention a few preliminary considerations which affect our estimates of the likelihood of the paradox in legislative voting. Our estimates will be based solely on the legislators' voting. We cannot take into account the possibility that the legislators' votes do not reflect their actual preferences, as when they vote for an amendment only to make the bill objectionable to some of its supporters. We shall examine the likelihood of the paradox on specific bills, though we recognize that logrolling across bills may vitiate the paradox (Coleman, 1966; Wilson, 1969). Furthermore, we are limited to estimating the probability of the paradox for alternatives which are brought to a roll call vote. We cannot determine whether the paradox could have occurred on proposals which were not brought to a roll call vote, which especially reduces the probability of the paradox when legislative rules make recorded votes on amendments difficult to obtain.

As an indication of just what this restriction to roll call votes means, table 1 shows the number of roll calls taken on bills during 1968 for the Senate and House. We can obtain probability estimates for the paradox only when there was more than one vote on the bill—a condition met on 50 percent of the bills on which the Senate voted but on only 27 percent of the bills on which the House voted. This initial fact may limit the possible occurrence of the paradox in the House, though the paradox would be more likely if preferences on proposals not voted upon could be taken into account. Indeed these considerations suggest that the paradox may be more likely in committee voting than in voting on the floor of Congress.

TABLE 1. Number of Votes Taken on Bills during 1968[a]

Number of Votes		Number of Bills	
		Senate	House
1	(unanimous)	17	18
1	(non-unanimous)	23	101
2		13	31
3		10	8
4		—	4
5		2	1
6		2	—
7		3	1
8		3	—
9		2	—
10		1	—
11		1	—
20		1	—
29		1	—
30		1	—
Total number of bills		80	164
Total number of votes		281	233

[a] Votes on original passage of a bill are considered separately from votes on passage of the conference report on the same bill.

II. THE SINGLE AMENDMENT CASE

When a legislature votes on a bill on which only a single amendment has been proposed, it chooses among three alternatives—the unamended bill (which we shall label C), the amended bill (B), and the status quo (A). Two votes will be taken—one on adopting the amendment (B against C) and one on passing the possibly amended bill (A against the winner of the first vote).[3] The third possible vote (A against the loser of the first

---

[3] We assume that the bill is not significantly altered by unrecorded vote or unanimous agreement between these two votes, so the second vote pits the winner of the first vote against the status quo.

vote) is not taken. The occurrence of the paradox is dependent only on the outcome of that vote which is not taken (along with the known results). Estimation of the probability of the paradox thus amounts to estimation of the outcome of that unknown vote.[4]

The analysis by Bowen (chap. 9 in this volume) indicates that the paradox is possible only when the motion is defeated (assuming only that abstention is not permitted). For example, the passage of an amended bill means that the amended bill was preferred to both the unamended bill and the status quo. Similarly, the passage of an unamended bill means that it was preferred to both the prospect of the amended bill and the status quo. So the single amendment case requires us to consider only defeated bills. This is noted schematically in figure 1 which outlines the possible outcomes in the one amendment case.

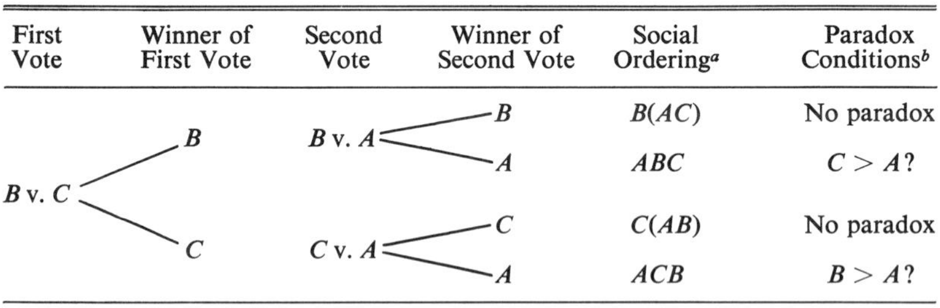

First Vote	Winner of First Vote	Second Vote	Winner of Second Vote	Social Ordering[a]	Paradox Conditions[b]
			B	$B(AC)$	No paradox
	B	B v. A	A	ABC	$C > A$?
B v. C					
	C	C v. A	C	$C(AB)$	No paradox
			A	ACB	$B > A$?

[a] The parentheses mean that any ordering of the alternatives inside them is possible.
[b] The notation $C > A$ means that C is preferred to A.

FIGURE 1.   Tree Diagram of Possible Outcomes in One Amendment Case

The fact that the paradox can occur only on defeated bills when there is a single amendment sharply decreases the likelihood of the paradox in congressional roll call voting. Few bills are actually defeated in floor voting in the American Congress. As an example, of the 244 bills con-

---

[4] There may be some difficulty in stating the alternatives under consideration, particularly when the first vote is on a negative motion (such as an amendment to delete a provision of the bill or a recommittal motion). For example, the sponsors of an amendment to delete a provision of a bill may plan to submit an amendment to take the place of that provision if their first amendment is passed, so that voting on the adoption of their first amendment actually involves taking into account preferences on additional alternatives which are never considered explicitly by the legislature if that first amendment is defeated. In fact, just this sort of difficulty creates problems in an analysis by Blydenburgh (1971). Also, bills frequently reach the House floor under rules permitting only a recommittal motion. In some instances the vote on recommittal is actually a vote on killing the bill while in other cases recommittal implies instructions for the committee to report a substitute bill. Even a procedural vote on the rule under which a bill is to be considered on the floor may involve preferences on amending the bill, as those advocating changes in the bill would vote to have the bill considered under rules allowing them to propose their amendments. We disregard these complications here, but interpreting the alternatives can be a very difficult task in an analysis of actual votes.

sidered by either the Senate or the House in 1968, only a single bill was rejected by a majority vote. In that case only a single vote was taken on the bill so that the paradox could not have occurred. A few more bills lost when a two-thirds vote was required (passage under suspension of rules in the House or cloture votes in the Senate), but again only a single vote was taken in these instances. There was not a single case in which there was exactly one amendment considered and the bill was defeated.

Nevertheless, it is useful to begin our analysis with this simple case. For one thing, defeated bills may be more likely in some particular circumstances, such as when the presidency and Congress are controlled by different parties or in periods of history during which congressional committees were less powerful. Moreover, the examination of committee voting might be revealing since bills are more likely to be killed in committee than to be defeated on the floor. Similarly, defeated motions may be more frequent in other legislative bodies such as city councils. Finally, whatever the empirical frequency of bills with one (attempted) amendment which are subsequently defeated, this analysis is useful because more complicated cases build onto it.

Probability Solution

As we indicated above, a probability model of legislative voting should take advantage of all available information about the legislators' preference orderings. Specifically, the votes which are taken can be used to make inferences for some individuals as to how they would have acted on the vote which was not taken. Consider the case in which the amendment is adopted, so that it is B v. C in the first vote and B v. A in the second vote. If we assume that all individuals have transitive preference orders, then legislators who vote for the adoption of the amendment (prefer B to C) and for the status quo over the amended bill (prefer A to B) would prefer the status quo over the unamended bill (prefer A to C). Similarly, members who vote against the adoption of the amendment (prefer C to B) and for passage of the amended bill (prefer B to A) would prefer the unamended bill to the status quo (prefer C to A). Exact inferences cannot be derived for the other legislators. For example, members voting for the adoption of the amendment (prefer B to C) and for the passage of the amended bill (prefer B to A) might prefer the unamended bill over the status quo (preference order BCA) or vice versa (preference order BAC). We cannot tell how such legislators would have voted had the third vote been taken, but we will assume they were equally likely to have the two consistent preference orders. We are still making an "equally likely" assumption as in previous work (Niemi and Weisberg, 1968), but we are doing so only for the legislators for whom the transitivity assumption does not provide exact inferences.[5] Figure 2 shows the preference orders which correspond to the various voting patterns when the amendment is adopted. A very similar figure applies to the case in which the amendment is defeated.

Actual Votes		Corresponding Preference Orders	Proportion of Corresponding Preference Orders in which $C > A$
(1) $B > C$	(2) $B > A$		
Yes	Yes	BAC, BCA	1/2
Yes	No	ABC	0/1
No	Yes	CBA	1/1
No	No	CAB, ACB	1/2

FIGURE 2.   Data for Single Amendment Case in Which Amendment Is Adopted

The probability of the paradox can now be derived either by simulation or analytically. The simulation approach is illustrated by Bowen (chap. 9 in this volume). We shall instead concentrate on the analytic solution. We assume as in figure 2 that the amendment was adopted, so we are interested in estimating the vote between A and C. Denote the total number of members of the group as m, the number who can be inferred to favor the unamended bill over the status quo as f, and the number who can be inferred to be against the passage of the unamended bill as a.[6] The number of members with unknown preferences as to the passage of the unamended bill will be denoted by $em = m - f - a$ and we shall call these members "undecided" or "uncommitted." We shall assume majority rule in the legislature and we shall assume a probability of one-half that each uncommitted member would favor passage of the unamended bill. Note from figure 2 that for each voting pattern our assumptions about the vote between C and A corresponds to the proportion of preference orders in which $C > A$. Additionally we assume that the votes of the uncommitted members are independent of one another.

---

[5] Obviously any information about legislators' preferences (derived from debates, interviews, past voting behavior, etc.) could be used to assign some of these legislators to a specific preference ordering or to modify the equally likely assumption. To the extent that such information was reliable, it would improve the estimate of the probability of the paradox.

[6] In the case in which the amendment is rejected, f would be the number of members who can be inferred to favor the amended bill over the status quo and a would be the number who can be inferred to be against the passage of the amended bill. With this definition the results of this section hold equivalently when the amendment is rejected.

This formulation of the problem places it directly into the framework of section 3 of the paper on group size (chap. 6 in this volume). An effective decision-rule must be calculated to indicate the proportion of the uncommitted members who must vote for the unamended bill if it is to pass, its value being $edr = (m/2 - f)/em$.[7] The probability that enough of the uncommitted members vote for the unamended bill to pass it can be evaluated either as a binomial probability or through a normal approximation to that binomial. This is the probability of the paradox for the case in which the amendment is adopted (and the amended bill defeated). A parallel procedure can be used to obtain the probability of the paradox when the amendment is rejected.

As an example of the calculation procedure, say that 99 senators vote on a bill. Assume that the bill has already been amended (i.e., $B > C$), and that the amended bill was then defeated ($A > B$). Say that 40 can be inferred to prefer the status quo to the unamended bill ($a = 40$) and that 34 can be inferred to favor the original bill over the status quo ($f = 34$). The number of members for whom no inference can be made is then 25 ($em = 25$). Passage of the unamended bill would require 50 votes, 16 more than the bill is known to be able to command. Thus the unamended bill would hypothetically pass (and the paradox occur) if and only if at least 16 of the 25 uncommitted members voted for it. If we assume that each uncommitted member has a probability of 1/2 of voting for the bill, the probability of its passage is $\sum_{i=16}^{25} \binom{25}{i}(\frac{1}{2})^i(\frac{1}{2})^{25-i} = \sum_{i=16}^{25} \binom{25}{i}(\frac{1}{2})^{25}$. An exact binomial evaluation is possible, but a normal approximation is usually simpler.[8] According to the normal approximation, the probability of the unamended bill winning equals the probability of a Z score above $[16 - 1/2 - (1/2)25]/\sqrt{[(1/2)(1/2)25]}$, where the subtraction of 1/2 is a correction for the approximation of the discrete binomial by the continuous normal, the $(1/2)25$ is the expected value of the binomial, and $\sqrt{[(1/2)(1/2)25]}$ is the standard deviation of the binomial. This simplifies to the probability of a Z score above 1.2, which equals 0.115. Thus the probability of the unamended bill winning, which is the probability of the paradox of voting, is 0.115.

The exact probability of the paradox under this procedure depends on the specific values of the parameters involved, but its maximum value can be derived. We assume the amendment was adopted so a majority of the body prefers B to C, and we assume the amended bill was defeated so a majority prefers A to B. We shall denote the number of legislators with

---

[7] We assume throughout that m is odd. For even m there are slight modifications (including necessary changes in the definition of the paradox due to ties).

[8] For a large number of values of em, especially $em < 100$, tables of the cumulative binomial probability distribution exist. See *Tables . . .* (1949; 1955).

a specific rank order by that rank order. Then we have $BAC + BCA + ABC > CBA + ACB + CAB$ $(B > C)$ and $ABC + ACB + CAB > BAC + BCA + CBA$ $(A > B)$, so that $(ABC - CBA) > (BAC + BCA) - (ACB + CAB) > (CBA - ABC)$. But if $ABC - CBA > CBA - ABC$, then $ABC > CBA$. Thus more individuals will be inferred to favor A over C than vice versa, or $a > f$. Now if $a = f$ and the probability of an uncommitted member voting for the unamended bill is one-half, the probability of the unamended bill passing and the paradox occurring would be one-half. But we have shown that the number of individuals who can be inferred to oppose the passage of the unamended bill will always be greater than the number who can be inferred to favor its passage, so the probability of the unamended bill passing and the paradox occurring will always be below one-half.

This upper limit of one-half for the probability of the paradox in the single amendment case is a major feature of the probability procedure we have presented. A natural question is whether it is an artifact which calls the validity of the procedure into doubt. This upper limit is real enough, but only as a function of the initial probability assumptions. If the equally likely assumption were not made for the uncommitted legislators, different assumptions could lead to different upper limits. If the analyst has reason to believe a different set of initial probability assumptions would be more appropriate, he should employ them, and may obtain a paradox probability greater than one-half. We shall continue to employ the equally likely assumption, but the bias of this assumption against the paradox should be understood.

Conditions Affecting the Probability of the Paradox

Further consideration of the parameters of the probability model leads to various conditions under which the paradox is more or less likely. These conditions are of particular interest, indeed possibly of more interest than the probability solution itself.

First, the likelihood of the paradox depends directly on the degree of disparity between the number of individuals inferred to favor the bill (whether amended or unamended) and the number inferred to support the status quo. The paradox has a probability approaching one-half as the sizes of these two groups become more equal. As the number inferred to oppose the bill becomes much larger than the number inferred to favor it, the probability of the paradox drops to zero.

Second, the likelihood of the paradox can be shown to depend directly on the number of uncommitted members. The number of uncommitted voters who must be attracted to pass the bill equals $(m + 1)/2 - f$ when there is an odd number of voters. Using the normal approximation as above, this would give the probability of the paradox as the probability of a Z score above $[(m + 1)/2 - f - 1/2 - (1/2)(m - f - a)]/\sqrt{[(1/2)(1/2)}$ $(m - f - a)] = (a/2 - f/2)/(1/2)\sqrt{[m - f - a]} = (a - f)/\sqrt{em}$. The larger the value of this Z score, the smaller the probability of the paradox. Thus the probability of the paradox is smaller when a and f are more imbalanced. Also the smaller the denominator, the larger the fraction; so the smaller the number of uncommitted members, the larger the Z score and the smaller the probability of the paradox. The paradox is more likely with more uncommitted members.

The joint effects of these two conditions can be systematically observed. For example, we can state the circumstances under which there is 99 percent certainty that the paradox has not occurred (i.e., only a 0.01 probability that the paradox *has* occurred). The normal approximation for the likelihood of the paradox is the probability of a Z score above $(a - f)/\sqrt{em}$ $= (a - (m - em - a))/\sqrt{em} = (2a - m + em)/\sqrt{em}$. The 99 percent certainty level corresponds to a Z score of at least 2.33, or $(2a - m + em)$ $> 2.33\sqrt{em}$ or $a > (0.5)(m - em + 2.33\sqrt{em})$. This function can be evaluated for different values of m and em, yielding the number of committed members who would have to oppose the bill for us to be 99 percent certain that the paradox would not occur. Figure 3 plots this function for groups of various sizes in which different proportions of the members are uncommitted. For example, in a group of 25 members, 40 percent (10) of whom are uncommitted, 80 percent (12) of the 15 committed members must oppose the bill for us to be 99 percent certain that the paradox has not occurred. In general, the smaller the proportion of members for whom inferences can be made (that is, moving to the right in figure 3), the greater the proportion of those committed who oppose the bill would have to be for us to be 99 percent certain that the paradox would not occur.[9] Similar graphs could be prepared for other degrees of certainty. The corresponding curves for the 95 percent level, for example, would be lower than those shown in figure 3.

The first condition—that the probability of the paradox depends on the imbalance between the numbers of individuals inferred to favor and oppose the bill—can be further simplified. We shall consider only the case in which the amendment is adopted and the amended bill is defeated, though the argument generalizes. Once again we denote the number of individuals with a given preference order by that preference order. For the amendment to have been adopted, $ABC + BAC + BCA = CBA + CAB + ACB + d$ where d is a positive constant. For the bill to be defeated, $ABC + CAB + ACB = CBA + BAC + BCA + e$ where e is another positive constant. The constants d and e refer to the winning margins on

---

[9] Also, holding constant the proportion of uncommitted members, the fraction of committed members having to oppose the bill for us to be 99 percent certain that the paradox does not occur approaches one-half as the size of the group increases.

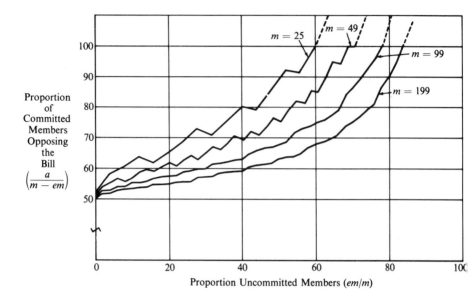

FIGURE 3. Proportion of Committed Members Having to Oppose the Bill for 99 Percent Certainty the Paradox Has Not Occurred, by Proportions of Uncommitted Members for Groups of Size 25, 49, 99, and 199*

* This figure plots the smallest integer greater than or equal to $0.5(m - em + 2.33\sqrt{em})$, divided by $(m - em)$ for $em = 0, 1, \ldots, m$. The curves are not smooth because of the peculiarities of the smallest integer function. The curve for $m = 99$ plots the values only for even em and that for $m = 199$ plots values only for em in multiples of four, the full curves being less smooth than those shown. Note that 99 percent certainty that the paradox has not occurred cannot be attained for large proportions of uncommitted members.

the votes. For example, if the amendment was adopted by a 55-45 vote, d would be 10. If we switch the expressions on the two sides of the second equation and then subtract the second from the first, we obtain $ABC - CBA - e = CBA - ABC + d$. Simplifying, we obtain $2ABC - 2CBA = d + e$ or $ABC - CBA = (d + e)/2$. But in this case $ABC - CBA$ is the same as the imbalance between the numbers of individuals inferred to favor and oppose the bill, $a - f$. Thus the imbalance is minimal when the two votes are decided by minimal majorities. Or in other words, the probability of the paradox is greatest when the imbalance is slight, as when both votes are decided by but a single vote. In general, the closer the votes, the greater the probability of the paradox.

It is possible to establish limits on how close the votes must be for there to be any realistic chance of the paradox occurring. We have shown that we can be 99 percent certain that there was no paradox if $(a - f)/\sqrt{em} > 2.33$. The preceding paragraph showed that $a - f = (d + e)/2$, where d and e are the winning margins on the two votes. Putting these results together, we obtain a 99 percent certainty of no paradox if $(d + e)/(2\sqrt{em})$ < 2.33 or $d + e > 4.66\sqrt{em}$. As a conservative estimate, we can be at least 99 percent certain that there was no paradox if $d + e > 4.66\sqrt{m}$.[10] In a legislature with 99 members, $4.66\sqrt{m} = 46.4$, so we can be 99 percent sure that the paradox of voting has not occurred if either vote was at least 73-26 ($d + e \geq 48$ since the winning margin on the other vote must be at least one) or if the two votes were at least 62-37 and 61-38 ($d + e = 48$). (Obviously, the same holds true for any other combination of votes such that $d + e > 46$). In a legislature with 399 members, $4.66\sqrt{m} = 93.1$, so we can be 99 percent sure of no paradox if either vote was at least 246-153 ($d + e \geq 94$) or if both votes were at least 223-176 ($d + e = 94$).

Expressing $d + e$ (the sum of the winning margins on the two votes) as a proportion of the legislature's size, in figure 4 we have plotted the size of the legislature against that proportion which would be needed for various levels of certainty of there being no paradox. It is apparent from this figure that in large legislatures relatively small vote margins are sufficient to rule out the paradox with a given degree of confidence. In smaller bodies the votes must be more one-sided in order to rule out the paradox. In any event figure 4 is a rough, conservative guide to whether it is worth investigating the bill more closely to determine whether or not the paradox occurred.

We can now summarize the conditions under which the paradox is likely when only a single amendment is involved. The paradox is possible only when the bill is defeated, a fact which severely constrains the possibility of the paradox in congressional roll call voting. It is then most likely when the votes on adoption of the amendment and on passage of the bill are both very close, a condition, incidentally, that would seem to characterize the most controversial aspects of legislation. The paradox is also more likely when exact inferences based on the assumption of individual transitivity are possible for few members. In any case if we assume that each uncommitted individual is equally likely to vote yes or no on the vote which is not taken, the upper-limit on the probability of the paradox is one-half.[11]

---

[10] This is a conservative estimate because m is used instead of em, and $m > em$. Since we use the square root of m or em, the effect of this change is not as great as it might seem. But obviously, the smaller the proportion of uncommitted members (i.e., the smaller em/m is) the more conservative the estimate becomes.

[11] There is a relationship between the size of the group and the upper limit for the probability of the paradox. The probability of the paradox is greatest if $a - f = (d + e)/2$ is minimized. As the chart below shows, regardless of whether em is even or odd, the probability of the paradox cannot be greater than the probability of a Z score above $1/\sqrt{m}$. If m is 9, for example, the probability of the paradox cannot exceed 0.37. Similarly for $m = 25$ the limit is 0.42, for $m = 99$ the paradox probability cannot

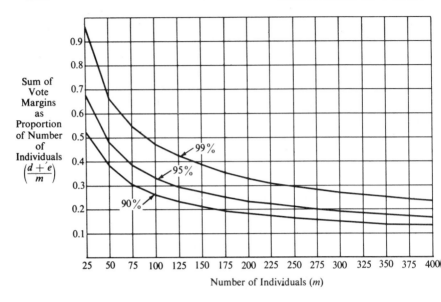

FIGURE 4. Necessary Size of Vote Margins for Various Degrees of Certainty That the Paradox Has Not Occurred, by the Group Size*

* This figure plots the smallest integer greater than or equal to $4.66\sqrt{m}$, $3.29\sqrt{m}$, and $2.56\sqrt{m}$, each divided by m, for $m = 25, 50, \ldots, 400$. The curves are neither smooth nor monotonic when incrementing m in units of 1.

III. THE TWO AMENDMENT CASE

We shall now turn to the case in which the legislature considers two amendments to a bill. Three votes are taken in this case—one on adopting each amendment and one on final passage of the bill. As before, the voting procedure does not provide enough information to determine whether the paradox occurred. In addition, the question of the occurrence of the

---

exceed 0.46, and for $m = 399$, the paradox probability cannot be greater than 0.48.

m	$a-f=$ $(d+e)/2$	$a+f=$ $(a-f)+2f$	$em=$ $m-(a+f)$	min $a-f$	Upper limit for probability of no majority winner
odd	odd	odd	even	1	$Pr(Z > 1/\sqrt{em}) < Pr(Z > 1/\sqrt{m})$
odd	even	even	odd	2	$Pr(Z > 2/\sqrt{em}) < Pr(Z > 2/\sqrt{m})$ $< Pr(Z > 1/\sqrt{m})$

The calculations in this section have relied heavily on the normal approximation to the binomial distribution. When the equally likely assumption is made, the p value is 0.5. Hays (1963, p. 229) points out that "the normal distribution gives a respectable approximation to binomial probabilities for $p = 0.5$" even when the number of individuals is as small as 5. When p is not always equal to 0.5, as in the next section, "the normal approximation may ordinarily be used safely if the *smaller* of Np, the number of successes expected, or Nq, the expected number of failures, is 10 or more" (Hays, 1963, p. 230).

paradox is complicated in this case by definitional problems as to what are the alternatives and as to what forms of the paradox are of interest.

With two amendments there are five possible outcomes of the legislative voting. The unamended bill can be passed (to be denoted again as C). A bill with only the first amendment added can be passed (to be denoted B_1). A bill with only the second amendment added can be passed (B_2). A bill with both amendments added can be passed (B_{12}). Or no bill might pass, the status quo (A) prevailing. The first vote taken is on the first amendment, between B_1 and C. If that amendment passes, the second vote is between B_1 and B_{12}. If the second amendment also passes, the third vote is between B_{12} and A; otherwise the third vote is between B_1 and A. If the first amendment fails, the second vote is between B_2 and C. If the second amendment passes, the third vote is between B_2 and A; otherwise the third vote is between C and A. There are ten possible paired comparisons among the five outcomes listed above, but the legislature votes on only three of them. Inferences can be made from the known votes to the corresponding preference orders of the five alternatives. Proceeding in this fashion, Bowen (chap. 9) employs an equally likely assumption in a simulation procedure, finding the paradox to occur with virtual certainty on two bills and with a moderate probability (0.2-0.7) on four bills of seventy-six bills with two amendments which he investigated in five recent Senate sessions.

We shall adopt a different formulation of the problem. The legislature only considers four alternatives when choosing between two amendments. If the first amendment passes, the three votes involve alternatives C, B_1, B_{12}, and A, the legislature never explicitly considering the possibility of adopting only the second amendment. If the first amendment fails, the three votes involve alternatives C, B_1, B_2, and A, the legislature never having an opportunity to vote on the passage of the two amendments as a package. There are six possible paired comparisons among the four alternatives which the legislature does consider, on which it takes three votes. Inferences can be made from the known votes to the corresponding preference orders of the four alternatives. This permits us to make estimates of the probability of the paradox among the four alternatives explicitly considered by the legislature.

We shall not claim that either of these formulations is totally superior to the other. There is a sense in which the legislator voting on only four alternatives may indeed take into account his preference for the other possible outcome. For example, he may vote for the first amendment because his preference order is $AB_{12}CB_1B_2$; he actually prefers the unamended bill to the bill with only the first amendment but finds that he must vote for the first amendment in order to have both amendments adopted, a combination which he prefers to the unamended bill and to the bill with only a single amendment. Bowen's formulation admits of this possibility whereas ours does not.

On the other hand the legislature never considers all five alternatives in a voting sequence, so that allowance for the fifth alternative requires extra inferences. Moreover, in some situations the amendments are mutually exclusive. If the amendments have to do with the amount of a single appropriation, for example, the adoption of one amendment negates the other. If C provides an appropriation of ten billion dollars for a project, B_1 is an amendment cutting the appropriation to eight billion, B_2 is an amendment cutting the appropriation to seven billion, and A denotes the rejection of the complete appropriation bill, the legislature can only consider four possible alternatives and there are only four possible outcomes of the legislative voting. Our formulation is particularly appropriate in this case. Our formulation also seems particularly appropriate when the second amendment is drafted only after the outcome of the first amendment is known. In that case the legislators could not take their preference on the second amendment into account when voting on the first amendment. A third situation in which our formulation seems useful is when the two amendments involve totally different parts of the bill so that they are not cumulative in any sense. If the first amendment involves a substantive change to the bill, for example, while the second amendment is a totally unrelated rider, legislators would have opinions on the separate amendments but no opinion on their combination per se. The votes on one amendment would not be at all affected by their attitudes on the second amendment, so that there are really only four relevant alternatives. In the end, the real questions are whether the two formulations yield different estimates of the probability of the paradox and, if so, exactly why the differences arise. These are questions better considered after completing our analysis of the two amendment case.

With two amendments possible, two basic types of intransitivities can occur. One alternative may be able to defeat all the others while there is an intransitivity among the defeated alternatives, a case which Klahr (1966) has labelled a Type I intransitivity. It is also possible that no single alternative will be able to command a majority against all other alternatives, Klahr's Type II intransitivity. On substantive grounds, there is no problem so long as the alternative which is passed can defeat all the other alternatives. Therefore we will only be concerned with the case in which the alternative which is passed could be defeated by some other alternative which was voted upon, the Type II intransitivity. This restriction of our focus will necessarily diminish the obtained likelihood of the paradox.[12]

---

[12] Bowen's formulation admits another unusual possibility. The alternative never explicitly considered in the voting might be preferred to all the alternatives which are considered even though there is no intransitivity in the social ordering. This is relevant

Probability Solutions

When there are two amendments, there are three votes taken and $2^3 = 8$ possible sequences of voting outcomes. These sequences are shown in figure 5, with case numbers assigned to correspond to the order in which we will consider the various possibilities.

The paradox cannot occur if the alternative winning on the first vote is eventually adopted (case i). Thus, the unamended bill (C) can be passed only if it defeats all the other alternatives ($C > B_1$, $C > B_2$, $C > A$). Similarly, in order for the bill to pass with only the first amendment (B_1) added, the first amendment must be added to the bill ($B_1 > C$), the second amendment must be defeated ($B_1 > B_{12}$), and the amended bill must defeat the status quo ($B_1 > A$). In both of these situations, there is a majority winner and a Type II intransitivity is precluded.

The paradox can occur if the bill is passed with the second amendment added (case ii), in contrast to the single amendment case in which the paradox can occur only when the bill is defeated. If both amendments are adopted ($B_1 > C$, $B_{12} > B_1$) and the bill is passed ($B_{12} > A$), a majority might prefer the unamended bill to the doubly amended bill ($C > B_{12}$). If only the second amendment is adopted ($C > B_1$, $B_2 > C$) and the bill is passed ($B_2 > A$), a majority might prefer the bill with only the first amendment to the bill with only the second ($B_1 > B_2$). In both of these instances, the paradox would occur if the alternative which lost on the first vote (C or B_1) could defeat the bill with the second amendment added (B_{12} or B_2).

The probability of the paradox can be estimated in this case (case ii) using evidence from the votes which were taken to make inferences about the votes not taken. We shall follow through the situation in which only the second amendment is adopted, though a very similar set of considerations would underlie the situation in which both amendments are adopted. Now we know that $C > B_1$, $B_2 > C$, and $B_2 > A$, and we wish to estimate the probability that $B_1 > B_2$. The first two known votes involve pairings of B_1 and B_2 with C, so we could obtain an estimate of the probability of B_1 defeating B_2 by employing the procedure used in the single amendment case by basing inferences only on these two votes.

A better estimate of the probability of the paradox in this case can be obtained by taking advantage of the information provided by the third vote, that between B_2 and A. In figure 6 we list the preference orders corresponding to each possible voting sequence along with the proportion of these preference orders in which B_1 is preferred to B_2. Note that if one

---

because in the legislative case the focus should be on the probability of the winning alternative not being the majority winner regardless of whether or not there is an intransitivity.

First Vote	Winner of First Vote	Second Vote	Winner of Second Vote	Third Vote	Winner of Third Vote	Social ordering[a]	Paradox Conditions	Case
B_1 v. C	B_1	B_1 v. B_{12}	B_1	B_1 v. A	B_1	$B_1(AB_2C)$	No paradox	(i)
					A	$AB_1(B_{12}C)$	$C > A$? $B_{12} > A$?	(iii)
			B_{12}	B_{12} v. A	B_{12}	$B_{12}(AB_1), B_1 > C$	$C > B_{12}$?	(ii)
					A	$AB_{12}B_1C$	$C > A$? $B_1 > A$?	(iii)
	C	C v. B_2	C	C v. A	C	$C(AB_1B_2)$	No paradox	(i)
					A	$AC(B_1B_2)$	$B_1 > A$? $B_2 > A$?	(iii)
			B_2	B_2 v. A	B_2	$B_2(AC), C > B_1$	$B_1 > B_2$?	(ii)
					A	AB_2CB_1	$B_1 > A$? $C > A$?	(iii)

[a] The parentheses mean that any ordering of the alternatives inside them is possible.

FIGURE 5. Tree Diagram of Possible Outcomes in Two Amendment Case

Actual Votes				Proportion of Corresponding Preference Orders in which $B_1 > B_2$
(1) $B_1 > C$	(2) $B_2 > C$	(3) $B_2 > A$	Corresponding Preference Orders	
Yes	Yes	Yes	$B_2AB_1C, B_2B_1AC, B_1B_2CA,$ B_1B_2AC, B_2B_1CA	2/5
Yes	Yes	No	$AB_2B_1C, AB_1B_2C, B_1AB_2C$	2/3
Yes	No	Yes	B_1CB_2A	1/1
Yes	No	No	$B_1CAB_2, B_1ACB_2, AB_1CB_2$	3/3
No	Yes	Yes	$B_2CAB_1, B_2CB_1A, B_2ACB_1$	0/3
No	Yes	No	AB_2CB_1	0/1
No	No	Yes	$CB_2AB_1, CB_2B_1A, CB_1B_2A$	1/3
No	No	No	$CB_1AB_2, CAB_1B_2, ACB_2B_1,$ CAB_2B_1, ACB_1B_2	3/5

FIGURE 6. Data for Case in Which Only the Second of Two Amendments Is Added

were to combine the first two rows (i.e., ignore the third vote), B_1 is ranked above B_2 in exactly half of the preference orders. The separation of these two rows, and the diverging proportions of preference orders in which $B_1 > B_2$, is what is added by including the third vote. A parallel phenomenon can be observed for the last two rows of the figure. In making our estimates of the probability of the paradox, we shall again employ an "equally likely" assumption such that the probability of a voter favoring B_1 over B_2 equals the proportion of preference orders consistent with his voting pattern on which $B_1 > B_2$. Now, however, not all the probabilities are one-half.

As an illustration of the calculation procedure, table 2 gives a set of hypothetical frequencies for the voting patterns and indicates how the expected proportion favoring B_1 over B_2 would be calculated. In the example, about 35 percent of the legislators would be expected to favor B_1 over B_2, suggesting that the paradox is not very likely. This is confirmed by calculating the probability that B_1 would beat B_2, as is done at the bottom

TABLE 2. Hypothetical Frequency Distribution of Voting Patterns

VOTING PATTERN				Expected number	
$B_1 > C$	$B_2 > C$	$B_2 > A$	Frequency	for whom $B_1 > B_2$	Variance
Yes	Yes	Yes	6	12/5	$(12/5)(3/5) = 36/25$
No	Yes	Yes	3	0	0
No	No	Yes	3	3/3	$(3/3)(2/3) = 6/9$
No	No	No	3	9/5	$(9/5)(2/5) = 18/25$
Total					
6–9	9–6	12–3	15	5.2	2.83

$Pr(B_1 > B_2) = Pr(Z > (7.5 - 5.2)/\sqrt{2.83}) = Pr(Z > 2.3/1.68) =$
$Pr(Z > 1.37) = 0.085$

of the table. Although the number of cases in table 2 is small, we have illustrated a normal approximation. The result is that in this example the paradox has a probability of 0.085, there being only a small chance of the paradox occurring.

It may be noted that the votes in table 2 follow a Guttman scale pattern. A well-known result is that the paradox is impossible when all the individual preference orders are unidimensional (Arrow, 1963, pp. 74-80; Black, 1958, chapter 4; Coombs, 1964, chapter 18). However, unidimensional individual preference orders are not equivalent to a Guttman scale.[13] In the present example, the votes fit a perfect Guttman scale but there is a possibility of the paradox occurring. More generally, the fact that the votes fit a Guttman scale does not preclude the possibility of the paradox.

The probability of the paradox in the case we are examining (case *ii* in figure 5) cannot exceed one-half. While we shall not prove this claim here, the situation is actually quite similar to the single amendment case in that the occurrence of a Type II intransitivity depends solely on the outcome of a single vote which is not available, and the transitivity assumption will necessarily lead to a prediction that a minority of the committed members will vote in such a way as to cause an intransitive social ordering.

In the remaining case to be considered (case *iii* in figure 5), the bill is defeated. The paradox would occur if any form of the bill which was rejected in the earlier balloting could defeat the status quo. The status quo was only paired in the actual voting with the final form of the bill, so it is necessary to see whether the loser of the first vote or the loser of the second vote could defeat the status quo. The probability of each of those two events can be estimated separately using the procedure employed above (case *ii*). The probability of the paradox is the probability that the first losing alternative or the second losing alternative *or both* could defeat the status quo. We shall present the procedure for calculating this probability by means of an example.

We shall examine the situation in which only the first amendment is added to the bill before the bill is defeated. On the first vote $B_1 > C$, on the second vote $B_1 > B_{12}$, on the third vote $A > B_1$. The status quo is not the majority winner if either $C > A$ or $B_{12} > A$ or both. In figure 7 we list the preference orders which correspond to the possible voting pat-

---

[13] Table 2 and figure 6 can be used to demonstrate this claim. Sixteen preference orders are consistent with the four voting patterns in table 2. These rank orders have as their last choice A, C, B_1, and B_2. By contrast, when preference orders are unidimensional, all must end with either of only two alternatives (Coombs, 1964, pp. 85-86), so these preference orders are not unidimensional. On the other hand, if the content of the alternatives definitely can be ordered along a single dimension—for example if the alternatives in table 2 can be ordered A, C, B_2, B_1 with B_1 being the hardest of the alternatives to accept—then only the preference orders consistent with the dimension should be employed, in which case the paradox would be precluded.

Actual Votes (1) $B_1 > C$	(2) $B_{12} > B_1$	(3) $B_1 > A$	Corresponding Preference Orders	Proportion of Corresponding Preference Orders in which $C > A$	$B_{12} > A$	$C \& B_{12} > A$
Yes	Yes	Yes	$B_{12}B_1AC$, $B_{12}B_1CA$	1/2	2/2	1/2
Yes	Yes	No	$AB_{12}B_1C$, $B_{12}AB_1C$	0/2	1/2	0/2
Yes	No	Yes	$B_1AB_{12}C$, B_1ACB_{12}, $B_1B_{12}AC$, $B_1B_{12}CA$, $B_1CB_{12}A$, B_1CAB_{12}	3/6	3/6	2/6
Yes	No	No	$AB_1B_{12}C$, AB_1CB_{12}	0/2	0/2	0/2
No	Yes	Yes	$B_{12}CB_1A$, $CB_{12}B_1A$	2/2	2/2	2/2
No	Yes	No	$B_{12}ACB_1$, $AB_{12}CB_1$, $ACB_{12}B_1$, $CAB_{12}B_1$, $B_{12}CAB_1$, $CB_{12}AB_1$	3/6	3/6	2/6
No	No	Yes	CB_1AB_{12}, $CB_1B_{12}A$	2/2	1/2	1/2
No	No	No	ACB_1B_{12}, CAB_1B_{12}	1/2	0/2	0/2

FIGURE 7. Data for Case in Which only the First of Two Amendments Is Added

terns. Also indicated for each voting pattern is the proportion of preference orders consistent with $C > A$, with $B_{12} > A$, and with both C and $B_{12} > A$.

Table 3 provides a hypothetical distribution for the frequencies of the various voting patterns. C is certain to gain 100 of the 401 votes which it needs to defeat A and it is expected to gain an additional 100. The probability of C defeating A is 0.47, as shown by the calculations below table 3. Similarly B_{12} is certain to gain 100 votes over A, is expected to gain an additional 100, and has a probability of 0.47 of defeating A. Thus the probability of A being defeated by either C or B_{12} or both is at least 0.47 and at most 0.94.

According to set theory, the probability that either C defeats A or B_{12} defeats A or both is equal to the probability that C defeats A plus the probability that B_{12} defeats A minus the probability that both C and B_{12} defeat A. The probability that C and B_{12} both defeat A can be obtained by using the same calculation procedure employed by Niemi and Weisberg (1968) for the probability of one alternative defeating both of two alternatives. A multivariate normal distribution can be used as an approximation to the exact multinomial distribution which would be tedious to evaluate. The multivariate normal requires the calculation of a correlation term which in turn requires the calculation of the expected number of individuals preferring both C and B_{12} to A. The data in the last columns of figure 7 and table 3 show the calculation of that expected value. The number of individuals expected to favor both C and B_{12} over A is 100 out of the total of 401. Together with the expectation that 200 will favor C over A and 200 will favor B_{12} over A, this yields a correlation of 0.0025 between the vote between C and A and the vote between B_{12} and A. The lower limits on the integrals of the bivariate normal are the proportion required for a given alternative to defeat A expressed in standardized form—$(200.5 - 200)/\sqrt{50} = 0.07$. The tabulated bivariate normal distribution (*Tables ...*, 1959) gives an approximate probability of 0.23 of both C and B_{12} defeating A. The probability of A being defeated by either C or B_{12} or both is thus $0.47 + 0.47 - 0.23 = 0.71$, which is the probability of no majority winner given the voting sequence and frequency distribution of table 3.

The probability of the paradox can thus exceed one-half in the two amendment case when the bill is defeated (case *iii* of figure 5). This is the first instance we have seen in which the paradox's probability has exceeded one-half. The maximum value can be derived for this case. As m becomes infinitely large, the maximum probability of C defeating A approaches one-half as does the maximum probability of B_2 defeating A. The minimum correlation between the two votes (C against A and B_2 against A) will approach zero while the lower limits of the integrals also approach

TABLE 3. Hypothetical Frequency Distribution of Voting Patterns

$B_1 > C$	VOTING PATTERN $B_{12} > B_1$	$B_1 > A$	Frequency	Expected number for whom $C > A$	Variance $C > A$	Expected number for whom $B_{12} > A$	Variance $B_{12} > A$	Expected number for whom $C \& B_{12} > A$
Yes	Yes	Yes	100	50	25	100	0	50
Yes	Yes	No	100	0	0	50	25	0
Yes	No	No	1	0	0	0	0	0
No	No	Yes	100	100	0	50	25	50
No	No	No	100	50	25	0	0	0
Total 201–200	200–201	200–201	401	200	50	200	50	100

$Pr(C > A) = Pr(B_{12} > A) = Pr(Z > (200.5 - 200)/\sqrt{50}) = Pr(Z > 0.5/7.07) = Pr(Z > 0.07) = 0.47$

zero, so the minimum probability of C and B_2 both defeating A approaches one-quarter. The maximum probability of the paradox for the two amendment case is then 0.75.[14]

Conditions Affecting the Probability of the Paradox

As in the single amendment case, the probability of the paradox depends on the vote margins. For example, if we consider the case when the bill is defeated (case *iii* of figure 5), the probability of the paradox cannot be greater than the sum of the probabilities of two alternatives defeating the status quo. The paradox is therefore unlikely if both of these latter probabilities are small. This will be true if all the votes are one-sided. (Conversely, the probability of the paradox will be greatest when all the votes are very close.) In addition, it is also true that the paradox is unlikely when the final passage vote is one-sided.

These results severely limit the likelihood of the paradox in congressional roll call voting because of a pronounced bandwagon tendency on final passage votes. As an example, in the Senate voting on final passage of fifty-four bills in 1968, there were twenty or fewer dissenting votes on forty-seven bills; only five bills were passed by less than a two-to-one margin. This would again suggest that the paradox occurs more frequently in committee voting than in the entire House or Senate.

We can now summarize our results for the two amendment case. The paradox cannot occur when either the original version of the bill is passed or when the bill is passed with only the first amendment added. The probability of the paradox cannot exceed one-half when the bill is passed and cannot exceed three-quarters when the bill is defeated. The paradox is most likely when the votes are close and is unlikely if the final passage vote is one-sided.

Comparison with Bowen's Results

Bowen (chap. 9) has found some cases with two amendments in which the probability of the paradox was near one. The direct conflict of this result with the 0.75 maximum found here requires explanation.

We have interpreted the voting on two amendments to involve four alternatives whereas Bowen's interpretation involves five alternatives.

---

[14] Actually when the second amendment is adopted but the bill is defeated (data not shown), the minimum correlation between the votes which would cause a paradox (C against A and B_1 against A) will approach 0.20, so the maximum probability of the paradox in that situation approaches 0.72. The 0.75 maximum probability cited in the text refers specifically to the instance in which the second amendment and the bill are both defeated. However, the basic results remain valid—the probability of the paradox can exceed 0.50 only when the bill is defeated and the maximum probability of the paradox for the two amendment case is 0.75.

The direct and indirect implications of this difference lead to sizable disparities in the estimate of the probability of no majority winner. First, the use of an additional alternative is bound to increase the likelihood of the paradox, since that extra alternative could defeat the winning alternative. Second, the use of the additional alternative alters the implications derived from the first vote. We have assumed that a yes vote on the first amendment means that the individual prefers B_1 to C. Bowen admits that interpretation (so long as the individual does not prefer B_2 to C, B_1, and B_{12}) as well as the possibility that the individual prefers B_{12} to C, B_1, and B_2.[15]

The precise differences between these approaches can best be seen by considering an instance in which very different probability estimates are obtained. Bowen reports a probability of 0.940 (± 0.0355) for the paradox in Senate voting on the Wheat Act of 1960. Following his rules for handling paired votes and missing data, we obtain the frequency distribution for the voting patterns shown in the lefthand column of table 4. Price supports on wheat were at 75 percent of parity when the bill was considered (and they remained at 75 percent when the House eventually defeated its version of this bill). The Senate agriculture committee reported a bill providing for 80 percent, a figure opposed by the Eisenhower administration. The first amendment (an Ellender amendment to set price supports at 75 percent in 1961, 70 percent in 1962, and 65 percent in 1963 and cut acreage 20 percent) was rejected (this being on a reconsideration vote). The second amendment (an Ellender amendment to continue existing price supports at 75 percent of parity for crop years 1961-63, to cut total acreage by 20 percent, and to authorize payments-in-kind equal to 50 percent of potential production on land retired under the acreage cut) was passed. The bill with the second amendment added was passed by the Senate.

Since B_2 passed, we would treat the only possible paradox as the case of $B_1 > B_2$, which is seen to have a probability of 0.198. Bowen's interpretation of the voting patterns yields a probability of 0.829 that $B_1 > B_2$. This substantial difference in the estimates of the likelihood that $B_1 > B_2$ is almost wholly due to the different interpretations of the preferences of those who voted yes on both amendments and on final passage—and we view them as basically preferring B_2 to B_1 while Bowen views them as

---

[15] To facilitate comparisons, we list here the preference orders we would consider consistent with the case that Bowen details in which both amendments are passed: Yes-Yes-Yes $B_{12}AB_1C$, $B_{12}B_1AC$, $B_{12}B_1CA$; Yes-Yes-No $AB_{12}B_1C$; Yes-No-Yes $B_1B_{12}AC$, $B_1B_{12}CA$, $B_1CB_{12}A$; Yes-No-No $AB_1B_{12}C$, $B_1AB_{12}C$, AB_1CB_{12}, B_1ACB_{12}, B_1CAB_{12}; No-Yes-Yes $CB_{12}B_1A$, $CB_{12}AB_1$, $B_{12}CB_1A$, $B_{12}CAB_1$, $B_{12}ACB_1$; No-Yes-No $CAB_{12}B_1$, $ACB_{12}B_1$, $AB_{12}CB_1$; No-No-Yes $CB_1B_{12}A$; No-No-No CB_1AB_{12}, CAB_1B_{12}, ACB_1B_{12}.

TABLE 4. Voting on the Wheat Act of 1960

Voting Pattern				WEISBERG-NIEMI FORMULATION			BOWEN FORMULATION		
				Proportion of Corresponding Preference Orders in which $B_1 > B_2$	Expected number for whom $B_1 > B_2$	Variance $B_1 > B_2$	Proportion of Corresponding Preference Orders in which		
$B_1 > C$	$B_2 > C$	$B_2 > A$	Frequency				$B_1 > B_2$	$B_{12} > B_2$	$B_1 \& B_{12} > B_2$
Yes	Yes	Yes	30	2/5	12	7.20	10/16	10/16	4/16
Yes	Yes	No	12	2/3	8	2.67	10/14	10/14	6/14
No	Yes	Yes	7	0	0	0	0	0	0
No	Yes	No	1	0	0	0	0	0	0
No	No	Yes	8	1/3	2.67	1.78	1/3	1/3	1/3
No	No	No	27	3/5	16.2	6.48	11/18	11/18	8/18
Total 42–43	50–35	45–40	85		38.87	18.13			

BOWEN FORMULATION (Cont'd.)

Expected number for whom $B_1 > B_2$	Variance $B_1 > B_2$	Expected number for whom $B_{12} > B_2$	Variance $B_{12} > B_2$	Expected number for whom $B_1 \& B_{12} > B_2$
18.75	7.03	18.75	7.03	7.50
8.57	2.45	8.57	2.45	5.14
0	0	0	0	0
0	0	0	0	0
2.67	1.78	2.67	1.78	2.67
16.50	6.42	16.50	6.42	12.00
46.49	17.68	46.49	17.68	27.31

Weisberg-Niemi formulation: $Pr(B_1 > B_2) = Pr(Z > (42.5 - 38.87)/\sqrt{18.13}) = Pr(Z > 0.85) = 0.198$

Bowen formulation: $Pr(B_1 > B_2) = Pr(B_{12} > B_2) = Pr(Z > (42.5 - 46.49)/\sqrt{17.68}) = Pr(Z > -0.95) = 0.829$
$Pr(B_1 \& B_{12} > B_2) =$ bivariate normal with lower limits of -0.95 on the integrals and correlation of $0.0884 = 0.693$
$Pr(B_1 \&/or B_{12} > B_2) = 0.829 + 0.829 - 0.693 = 0.965$

basically preferring B_1 to B_2 (which may indeed be most appropriate given the substance of the two amendments).[16] Additionally, Bowen's interpretation adds the possibility that $B_{12} > B_2$ which also has a probability of 0.829 (though the substance of the two amendments would seem to preclude both being adopted). Altogether, Bowen's formulation yields a probability of 0.965 that B_1 and/or B_{12} would defeat B_2.[17]

Neither formulation seems totally superior for the general case. Our formulation seems necessary when the amendments are viewed as a sequential process, when the amendments are mutually exclusive, and/or when the amendments are noncumulative. When the alternative amendments are known prior to the voting, are not mutually exclusive, *and* involve related parts of the bill, Bowen's formulation may be preferable.

Bowen's formulation can lead to higher estimates of the probability of no majority winner. A choice between the two formulations will be necessary when non-zero probabilities of the paradox are found. We leave it to the reader to determine which formulation he finds more congenial.

IV. CONCLUSIONS

We shall draw upon the preceding results to form some conclusions about the likelihood of the paradox in legislative voting.

First, the probability of the paradox can be larger when there are more amendments. This probability has a maximum value of zero with no amendments, one-half with a single amendment, and three-quarters with two amendments. With more than two amendments, the maximum probability would be larger yet. This has direct substantive implications. The number of amendments considered in roll call voting by the House of Representatives is generally small because of restrictive rules, so the prob-

---

[16] In the interpretation of the Yes-Yes-Yes voting pattern on this bill, the mechanical application of our procedure is somewhat misleading and the interpretation of this voting pattern should be more contextual and subjective. This illustrates the general point made in footnote 5.

[17] In line with footnote 12, we have solved here for the probability that the winning alternative could be defeated by another alternative. Bowen instead solves for the probability that there is no majority winner. This slight difference in the definition of the problem means that we may be overestimating the quantity sought by Bowen— the 0.829 probability that B_1 defeats B_2 certainly involves the paradox but the 0.136 probability that B_{12} defeats B_2 while B_1 does not defeat B_2 includes the possibility that B_{12} is a majority winner. We have not attempted to solve the complex multivariate normal approximation for the probability that B_{12} is a majority winner. However we have determined that the probability that B_{12} defeats both A and C is only 0.057, so the probability that B_{12} is a majority winner can be no more than 0.057. If we count this entire probability against the 0.145 probability that B_2 is defeated by B_{12} but not by B_1, we get a conservative estimate of the probability that Bowen seeks of 0.908 against the liberal estimate of 0.965 shown below table 4. This range fits well with Bowen's simulation results.

ability of the paradox is kept small. By contrast there are instances of dozens of amendments to a bill being voted upon in the Senate, making the paradox more likely. Similarly, in other legislative bodies where numerous contested amendments are permitted, we would expect the paradox to occur more regularly.

Second, the paradox's probability is larger when the bill is defeated. Relatively few bills are defeated in floor voting in Congress, making the paradox less likely on roll call votes. The paradox may be more likely in Congresses when different parties control the presidency and Congress so that administration bills are defeated with some frequency. Even then, however, the tendency for legislative in-fighting to be concluded before the vote on final passage reduces the likelihood of the paradox at this stage of the legislative voting.

Third, the probability of the paradox is larger when the votes are close. The tendency toward going along with the majority on final passage votes is therefore bound to decrease the likelihood of the paradox. Another way of looking at this, however, is that the paradox may be more likely on controversial issues on which bandwagon effects are minimized. Thus while the paradox may occur infrequently, it is likely to surface precisely when the issues are most contentious.

These considerations also suggest that the paradox may be less likely in recorded floor votes in Congress than at other stages of the legislative process. Committee voting is marked by freer rules governing the submission of amendments, and committee defeat of a bill seems more common than defeat on the floor. Also amendments are freer and the votes are closer during the Committee of the Whole House consideration of a bill than during subsequent House action. Votes taken in committee and in Committee of the Whole House will be more available to scholars starting in 1971, after which these possibilities may be systematically explored.

We have seen that there can be a sizable likelihood of the paradox under certain voting distributions. We do not regard these particular distributions themselves as very likely, a fact which diminishes the seriousness of the paradox. We should point out that even if the probability of the paradox is much below one on any given bill, a considerable expected frequency of the paradox can accumulate if it has a moderate probability for each of a large number of bills. Thus to consistently report small probabilities of the paradox is not totally benign when those probabilities are non-zero. Yet on balance our analysis confirms the less systematic hunches of most political scientists that the paradox of voting is by far the exception and not the rule in legislative voting.

Finally, we would suggest that highlighting the conditions making the paradox likely would be valuable as a future direction for research. For example, the effect of different parties controlling the presidency and Congress deserves systematic empirical attention. Also, a comparison of floor voting with earlier stages of the legislative process would be worthwhile. Future work may well be usefully devoted to systematically analyzing a variety of collective decision-making settings to determine whether there are settings and institutional arrangements which facilitate the occurrence of the paradox.[18] Hopefully we have provided the framework for such examination of the conditions making the paradox likely.

---

[18] A good example is the theoretical analysis by Bjurulf (chap. 11 in this volume), which suggests that multiparty systems sometimes lead to higher probabilities of the paradox.

11. A Probabilistic Analysis of Voting Blocs and the Occurrence of the Paradox of Voting

BO H. BJURULF

The objectives of this paper are first, to make a classification and probabilistic analysis of systems of voting blocs, and secondly, to simulate the effects of these voting blocs and other factors on the occurrence of the paradox of voting.

General probabilities of the paradox have been extensively tabulated using both exact and approximate calculations (DeMeyer and Plott, 1970; Garman and Kamien, 1968; Gleser, 1969; Niemi and Weisberg, 1968) as well as computer simulation methods (Campbell and Tullock, 1965; Klahr, 1966; Pomeranz and Weil, 1970). Usually these calculations are based on the assumption that all individual rank orders are equally likely (except for some calculations in Garman and Kamien). While it is easy to criticize this assumption as unrealistic, it is difficult to justify any other particular assumption(s). One possible way out of this dilemma is to place less emphasis on the exact numbers that come out of the probabilistic analyses and to put greater stress on the identification of factors (other than the probability assumptions) that increase or decrease the

I would like to thank Richard Niemi who not only transformed my paper into readable English but whose valuable comments·and criticism added rigor to the paper. I also wish to thank Rune Dahlgren for technical help. The University of Lund Computing Center provided computer time and the Swedish Council for Social Science Research provided me most generously with money.

likelihood of the paradox. One obvious result of previous work is that paradox seems more likely to occur as the number of alternatives rises. More recently Niemi (1969) has shown that the proportion of individuals with single-peaked preferences is directly related to the frequency of occurrence of the paradox.

It was with these considerations in mind that the present investigation was undertaken. What our work adds to previous findings is a consideration of the effects of voting blocs and several other features of the voting situation (tied ranks in the individual preferences, the presence of two dimensions, and a measure of the degree of conflict present) on the likelihood of the occurrence of the paradox. What is stressed is not the particular probabilities which result for they are highly dependent on our use of the "equally likely" assumption. Rather, what is important is the extent to which voting blocs and other factors seem to inhibit or facilitate the occurrence of cyclical majorities.

The paper is divided into five sections. The first two are devoted to a classification of systems of voting blocs and to a probabilistic analysis of the frequency of the resulting categories. It is hoped that this analysis by itself will be a small though significant contribution to the formal study of voting in assemblies where multiple blocs are present for example, in multiparty legislatures. Here the classification is considered specifically as it is related to the probability of the paradox.

In the third section of the paper we introduce the notion of two dimensions and establish six cases determined by the amount of overlap between these dimensions. A fourth section explains our assumptions about the degree of conflict in the decision situation and about tied ranks. Finally, we describe our simulation procedures and present the results of our analysis.

I. A CLASSIFICATION OF SYSTEMS OF VOTING BLOCS

In this section we present an exhaustive and mutually exclusive classification of systems of voting blocs, where each bloc consists of voters who have agreed to rank the alternatives in the same way. The classification will be carried out for assemblies with up to five voting blocs. Throughout the analysis blocs will be considered cohesive. Since our interest lies primarily in situations governed by majority rule, the classification is based on the ability of the blocs to form majority coalitions. A motivating assumption is that, *ceteris paribus*, it is easier to form a two-bloc coalition than a three-bloc coalition, a three-bloc coalition than four-bloc one, and so on.

A simple example helps clarify our approach. Listed below are four different systems each consisting of four or five blocs.

Example: I. $A = 0.4$ $B = 0.3$ $C = 0.25$ $D = 0.05$
         II. $A = 0.3$ $B = 0.3$ $C = 0.3$ $D = 0.1$
       III. $A = 0.4$ $B = 0.2$ $C = 0.2$ $D = 0.2$
      IV. $A = 0.4$ $B = 0.2$ $C = 0.2$ $D = 0.15$ $E = 0.05$

The weight attached to each bloc is simply the proportion of assembly members who belong to that bloc. In each system, of course, the weights sum to one.

Note that these systems differ in the ability of various blocs to form majority coalitions. In the first system blocs A, B and C can form two-bloc majority coalitions freely among themselves. Bloc D, on the other hand, is unable to transform any coalition into a winning one. That is, no coalition rises from a minority to a majority position when D enters. The second system is exactly the same as the first with regard to the ability of the blocs to form majority coalitions. In the third system bloc A has a uniquely advantageous position in that it can form two-bloc majority coalitions with any of the other blocs in the system. The other blocs can form two-bloc majority coalitions only with A. The fourth system is the same as the third except that the fifth bloc (E) is unable to create any majority coalition.[1]

The following classification is thus based on the ability of the blocs to form majorities alone or in coalition with one or more of the other blocs in the system. The proof of the exhaustive and mutually exclusive nature of the classification is included only for the systems with five blocs.

1. *Two blocs* in the voting process.
Except when both blocs have equal weights, one bloc will hold a clear majority with a weight > 0.5. Cases in which both blocs (or coalition of blocs) have a weight of 0.5 will be regarded as a special case here and below. Since tie-breaking mechanisms are usually available, these cases will not be treated further.

2. *Three blocs* in the voting process.
    a. One bloc has a clear majority. (Ex. $A = 0.6$, $B = 0.3$, and $C = 0.1$)
    b. All two-bloc coalitions have a clear majority. (We will call this the three-bloc case.) (Ex. $A = 0.4$, $B = 0.4$, and $C = 0.2$)

---

[1] Duverger (1965) pointed out that "three kinds of party can be distinguished on the basis of strength; parties with a majority bent, major parties and minor parties" (p. 283). I have tried to indicate with these examples that Duverger's classification can be expanded and stated more precisely.

3. *Four blocs* in the voting process.
   a. One bloc has a clear majority. (Ex. $A = 0.6$, $B = 0.2$, $C = 0.1$, and $D = 0.1$)
   b. The "three-bloc case": All two-bloc coalitions among the three largest blocs have a clear majority. The fourth bloc cannot contribute to a majority coalition (i.e., by changing a minority coalition to a majority one.) (Ex. $A = 0.4$, $B = 0.28$, $C = 0.28$, and $D = 0.04$)
   c. The largest bloc is the only one which can create a two-bloc majority. (Ex. $A = 0.4$, $B = 0.2$, $C = 0.2$, and $D = 0.2$)

4. *Five blocs* in the voting process.
   a. One bloc has a clear majority. (Ex, $A = 0.60$, $B = 0.15$, $C = 0.10$, $D = 0.10$, and $E = 0.05$)
   b. The "three-bloc case." All two-bloc coalitions among the three largest blocs have a clear majority. Blocs D and E cannot contribute to a majority coalition. That is, no three-bloc majority can be created in which two of the three blocs do not belong to the three largest, and thus already have a clear majority position. (Ex. $A = 0.30$, $B = 0.30$, $C = 0.30$, $D = 0.05$, and $E = 0.05$)
   c. All two-bloc coalitions which include A have a clear majority. No three-bloc coalition without A has a clear majority position because a two-bloc coalition containing A can always form in opposition to this. (Ex. $A = 0.45$, $B = 0.15$, $C = 0.15$, $D = 0.15$, and $E = 0.10$)
   d. The smallest bloc cannot contribute to a majority coalition. Otherwise, all two-bloc coalitions which include A have a clear majority. (Ex. $A = 0.40$, $B = 0.20$, $C = 0.20$, $D = 0.15$, and $E = 0.05$)
   e. A is necessary for the formation of a two-bloc majority. This can, however, only be done with B or C. Either A or $(B + C)$ is thus necessary and sufficient for the existence of a three-bloc majority. (Ex. $A = 0.40$, $B = 0.24$, $C = 0.24$, $D = 0.07$, $E = 0.05$)
   f. A and B are necessary for the formation of a two-bloc majority. All three-bloc coalitions containing A or B form a majority. (Ex. $A = 0.40$, $B = 0.40$, $C = 0.08$, $D = 0.07$, and $E = 0.05$)
   g. No two-bloc majority can be created. All three-bloc coalitions form a majority. (Ex. $A = 0.21$, $B = 0.20$, $C = 0.20$, $D = 0.20$, and $E = 0.19$) A special case in this category occurs when all blocs have equal weights. This is equivalent to the case of five individuals considered by previous investigators.

For convenience of nomenclature and to facilitate the proof, A will always be considered as large as or larger than B, B will always be as large as or larger than C, etc. In other words, $A \geq B \geq C \geq D \geq E$. Systems in which two coalitions have a weight of 0.5 belong to a special relatively trivial category. Its existence will not always be pointed out in this proof.

Proof: (Five bloc case) Every system in which $A > 0.5$ is said to belong to category *a*. For the systems in which $A < 0.5$ the proof will be based on an analysis of the following mutually exclusive and exhaustive situations:

1. $A, B, C \geq 0.25$; $D, E < 0.25$ ($A, B, C,$ and $D \geq 0.25$ does not exist in the five-bloc situation.)
2. $A, B \geq 0.25$; $C, D, E < 0.25$
3. $A \geq 0.25$; $B, C, D, E < 0.25$
4. $A, B, C, D, E < 0.25$

Each of these cases can now be examined in detail:

1. $A, B, C \geq 0.25$; $D, E < 0.25$

All two bloc coalitions among A, B, and C have a majority. D and E cannot help create a majority coalition because no three-bloc majority can be formed in which two of the three blocs do not belong to the three largest and thus already have a clear majority position. (The largest of the other possible coalitions, viz., $A + D + E \leq 0.5$ because by definition $B + C \geq 0.5$.) Hence this case falls into category *b* of our classification.

2. $A, B \geq 0.25$; $C, D, E < 0.25$

I. If $A + E \geq 0.5$, all two-bloc coalitions which include A have a majority (since $B \geq C \geq D \geq E$). No other two-bloc coalition has a majority because it can always be opposed by a coalition involving A. We thus have category C.

II. If $A + E < 0.5$ and $A + D \geq 0.5$, then we have case *d* because A can form two-bloc majority coalitions with all but E (since $B \geq C \geq D$). E cannot help create majority coalitions for the following reasons: (1) No two-bloc coalition including E has a majority (since $A + E < 0.5$); (2) Suppose that a three-bloc coalition $X + Y + E$ has a majority and that $X + Y < 0.5$. Then neither X nor Y can be bloc A since all two-bloc coalitions including A and B, C, or D have a majority. But then the remaining two blocs, Z and W, must have a majority because one of them is bloc A. This contradicts the assumption that $X + Y + E$ has a majority. Hence E cannot turn a minority coalition into a majority one. Furthermore, E is unimportant in a four-bloc majority. This is trivial if A is in the four-bloc coalition. If not, then $B + C + D$ already has a majority (since $A + E < 0.5$), and E has not helped create the majority.

III. If $A + E$, $A + D < 0.5$ and $A + C \geq 0.5$, then either $B + C \geq 0.5$ which implies case *b* or $B + C < 0.5$ which implies that $A + B$ and $A + C$ are the only two-bloc majority coalitions. In the latter case, A or $(B + C)$ is necessary and sufficient for the existence of a three-bloc majority. This can be seen by observing first that $A + D + E$, which is the smallest three-bloc coalition including A, has a majority (since

$B + C < 0.5$). Hence all three-bloc coalitions including A have a majority. Similarly $B + C + E$ is the smallest three-bloc coalition including $(B + C)$, and it has a majority because $A + D < 0.5$. Furthermore, the only three-bloc coalition which does not include A or B, viz., $C + D + E < 0.5$ (since $A + B \geq 0.5$.) Hence, we have category e.

IV. If $A + E$, $A + D$, $A + C < 0.5$, and $A + B \geq 0.5$, then A *and* B are necessary for the existence of a two-bloc majority. Furthermore, all three-bloc coalitions including A or B have a majority because the smallest three-bloc coalition including B—$B + D + E$—has a majority (since $A + C < 0.5$). This constitutes category f.

3. $A \geq 0.25$; $B, C, D, E < 0.25$

 I. If $A + E \geq 0.5$, then category c. See 2.I.

 II. If $A + E < 0.5$, and $A + D \geq 0.5$, then category d. See 2.II.

 III. If $A + E$, $A + D < 0.5$ and $A + C \geq 0.5$, then category b if $B + C \geq 0.5$ and category e if $B + C < 0.5$. See 2.III.

 IV. If $A + E$, $A + D$, $A + C < 0.5$ and $A + B \geq 0.5$, then category f. See 2.IV.

 V. If $A + E$, $A + D$, $A + C$, and $A + B < 0.5$, then no two-bloc majority can be created. It that follows that all three-bloc coalitions have a majority. This defines category g.

4. $A, B, C, D, E < 0.25$

In this situation no two-bloc majority can be created and all three-bloc coalitions have a majority. This is again category g. We have now shown that our set of categories for the five-bloc case is exhaustive. The mutually exclusive character of the set can be deduced from the fact that each of our cases or subcases belongs to one and only one category.[2] A direct analysis of our categories also makes this conclusion apparent.

Before concluding this section let us return for a moment to the categories for systems with two, three, four, or five blocs in the voting process. Note the great similarity between categories 1, 2a, 3a and 4a; in each case the largest bloc has a clear majority. Similarly, consider categories 2b, 3b and 4b; the three largest blocs can form two-bloc majority coalitions freely among themselves, while the other blocs, if present, are unimportant from the point of view of creating majorities. Finally, compare 3c and 4c; all two-bloc coalitions in which A is a part have a clear majority position. Hence, the five-bloc case includes all possibilities for the cases with smaller numbers of blocs, and the analysis can to a large extent be confined to the seven cases of five blocs in the voting process (though of course cases with more than five blocs may involve additional possibilities).

---

[2] We do not include a formal proof of this here since it is trivial but rather tedious.

II. THE PROBABILITY OF OCCURRENCE OF THE CATEGORIES IN THE CLASSIFICATION

Our next analytic step is to estimate the probability of occurrence of the different categories assuming that the occurrence can be treated as a random phenomenon. That is, we can create a large number of systems at random and see how they are distributed among the different categories.

The fact that in most assemblies the total number of voters is constant suggests the following method for estimating the desired probabilities. In the situation with five blocs, generate four different random numbers between 1 and n-1 inclusive, where n represents the total number of voters in the assembly. Arrange the numbers according to size. An example is given below, in which n was assumed to be 351.

Example:

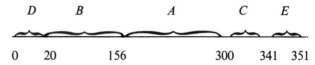

D	B		A	C	E
0	20	156		300	341 351

In this case the four random numbers turned out to be 20, 156, 300, and 341. Assign to bloc A the weight that corresponds to the largest distance between the numbers, to bloc B the weight that corresponds to the next largest distance, etc. In the example, the largest distance is between 156 and 300. Therefore A's weight should be $(300-156)/351$ or 0.41. B's weight should be $(156-20)/351$ or 0.39 and so on. Then compare the obtained system with the classification given earlier in order to find out to which category the system belongs. Repeating this process many times gives us an estimate of the random likelihood of each of the categories.

Using a computer program to perform the calculations, we have reiterated this process 1000 times for each of the following values of n: 101, 200, 233, 351, 601, 751, 901. The resulting distributions are given in table 1. As expected, the results are invariant, except for "sampling" error, across the different n's.[3] Note, however, that the probabilities of the various systems differ widely, from only 0.01 for system g to about 0.30 for a. Significantly, even with as many as five blocs, the system most

---

[3] This was expected (except for very small n's of course) since the exact probabilities can be calculated for each case. The calculations are, however, fairly complicated except for the a-case where the probability can be calculated as follows: the probability of this case equals the probability that one of our distances is > 0.5. Any distance has the same probability. We will here calculate the probability for the distance to the extreme left. The probability that this distance is > 0.5 equals the probability that all of our four random numbers turn out to be larger than $n/2$. This probability is $(1/2)(1/2)(1/2)(1/2)$. Hence the probability that one of our distances is greater than 0.5 is $5(1/2)^4 = 5/16 = 0.3125$.

likely to occur by chance is one in which a single bloc has a clear majority.

These estimates of the random probability of the different categories of voting systems will be used below in our analysis of the effects of voting blocs on the expected probability of cyclical majorities. Hopefully they will also provide a stimulus for other probabilistic work on the interaction of multiple blocs of voters.

TABLE 1. Probability of Occurrence of the Categories of Systems of Voting Blocs, for Assemblies of Different Sizes

Sizes of the assembly	Categories of systems of voting blocs							
	a	*b*	*c*	*d*	*e*	*f*	*g*	Total[a]
101	29%	14	13	16	22	4	0	98%
200	31%	15	10	21	16	6	1	100%
233	31%	14	10	19	19	5	1	99%
351	30%	16	12	20	17	5	1	101%
601	29%	16	12	19	18	5	1	100%
751	28%	17	11	19	17	5	1	98%
901	30%	15	11	22	17	5	1	101%
Total	30%	15	11	19	18	5	1	99%

[a] Totals do not always add to 100 because of rounding and because of a few cases in which two coalitions have exactly the same weight.

III. THE DIMENSIONALITY OF THE PREFERENCE ORDERINGS

A group of preference orderings can always be characterized by a set of dimensions on which individuals and alternatives are placed. Occasionally all of the preference orderings will "fit" a single dimension. This case is important, of course, because of Black's (1958, chap. 4) well-known finding that the voting paradox cannot occur when preference orderings are single-peaked (which is equivalent to unidimensionality).[4] Most often, however, two or more dimensions are needed to fully characterize the preference orderings. While it is notoriously difficult to work with more than one dimension, some aspects of the multidimensional situation have succumbed to the analysis of Davis, Hinich, and Ordeshook (1970). In probabilistic analyses, however, little attention has thus far been paid to the dimensionality of the preference orderings. One exception to this is Niemi (1969), who worked with the proportion of individuals having

---

[4] A set of preference orderings is single-peaked if there is an ordering of the alternatives on the abscissa such that when utility or degree of preference is indicated by the ordinate, each preference ordering can be represented by a curve which changes its direction at most once, from up to down (i.e., has at most one peak). A dimension is said to exist in a set of alternatives if a set of voters has a complete agreement on a standard of judgment in such a way that their preference orderings will be single-peaked.

single-peaked preference functions. Here we utilize a different approach which we hope will be useful both in this and other applications.

Let us assume that in a decision situation there are two primary dimensions. Now for each preference ordering, it can be determined whether it is single-peaked with regard to neither, one, or both of these primary dimensions.[5] A set of preference orderings can obviously then be characterized by the proportion that satisfy 0, 1, or 2 of these dimensions. It is this feature of the preference orderings that will be used in the analysis below.

Such an approach is complicated, however, by the fact that many pairs of dimensions could be chosen with five alternatives. The single dimensions might be *ABCDE* and *DACBE*. In this case two and only two preference orderings—*BCADE* and *CBADE*—are single-peaked with respect to both dimensions. On the other hand, if the dimensions are *ABCDE* and *DACEB*, no preference orderings are single-peaked with respect to both dimensions. The number of preference orderings that will be single-peaked on 0, 1, or 2 dimensions thus depends on just which dimensions are chosen. At one extreme, illustrated by the second example, no preference orderings will be single-peaked on more than one dimension. At the other extreme—the degenerate case in which the dimensions are mirror images of each other—all preference orderings that are single-peaked on one dimension will also be on the other dimension.

To obtain some idea of the "overlap" among dimensions, we wrote a computer program to generate all possible pairs of single-dimensions— $\binom{10}{2} = 7140$ in all. For each pair of dimensions the program considered all $5! = 120$ preference orderings that are possible with five alternatives. This determined the frequency of each degree of overlap among the two dimensions. The results are given in table 2.

The results show that there are six degrees of overlap in the case of five alternatives and two single dimensions. In Case 1 there is no overlap among the sixteen preference orderings that are single-peaked with respect to each dimension. At the other extreme, as indicated above, there is a complete overlapping.

The frequency distribution among the six cases can be interpreted as the probability that a randomly chosen pair of dimensions will belong to a specific case. Hence the probability is over two-fifths that two dimensions are completely nonoverlapping, while the probability is only about one in a hundred that they are mirror images of one another. This probabilistic interpretation is useful for giving us an idea of the likelihood of each of the six cases. However, our purpose in the analysis below is to

---

[5] Theoretically the analysis could be extended to more dimensions, although the amount of work involved increases very rapidly.

TABLE 2. Distribution of Pairs of Single Dimensions Among Six Cases

The number of preference orderings which are single-peaked with respect to:	Case 1	Case 2	Case 3	Case 4	Case 5	Case 6
Neither dimension	88	90	92	94	96	104
Dimension 1	16	14	12	10	8	0
Dimension 2	16	14	12	10	8	0
Both dimensions	0	2	4	6	8	16
Total	120	120	120	120	120	120
Distribution of the 7140 pairs of single dimensions among the six cases.	3,120 44%	2,160 30%	1,200 17%	240 3%	360 5%	60 1%

determine the effects of each case on the expected probability of the paradox of voting. Thus in one version of our simulation, preference orderings will be drawn randomly from each of the six cases, and the likelihood of the paradox for each case will be established.

As an additional variant we will alter the "dominance" of each dimension. It seems likely that very often one of the two single dimensions will be shared by more voters than share the alternate dimension. Accordingly in choosing preference orderings from the sets satisfying each dimension, we will sometimes choose from each set with equal probability, sometimes from one set three times as often as the other set, and sometimes from one set five times as often as the other.[6] The question is just how this variation in the relative dominance of one dimension affects the likelihood of the paradox.

IV. ASSUMPTIONS ABOUT CONFLICT AND TIED RANKS

In addition to the systems of voting blocs and the dimensional character of the preference orderings, two other factors will be varied in the simulation. First, we will make several assumptions about the possibility that two or more blocs have the same first choice. Theories of decision making are most concerned with situations of conflict. Hence cases in

---

[6] When the dimensions were used in the ratio three to one, this procedure was carried out as follows. Since there are five voting blocs, three of the five preference orderings were randomly selected from the sixteen preference orderings that are single-peaked with respect to dimension 1; one was randomly selected from the sixteen that are single-peaked with regard to dimension 2; the fifth preference ordering was selected from the first set three times out of four and from the second set one time out of four. A similar procedure was used when the dimensions were used in the ratio five to one.

which two large blocs (especially the two largest) have the same first preference are of somewhat less interest. In parts of the simulation, therefore, we will require that some or all of the voting blocs have different first choices.

Secondly, for a part of the simulation we wish to introduce the possibility of ties in the preference orderings. We will do this in a limited way here by assuming either that preferences below the first choice may be tied or that preferences other than the first and last choices may be tied. These assumptions strike us as a somewhat realistic initial way of bringing in tied ranks, since we presume that best and worst alternatives are among the easiest to discriminate. The probability of different types of ties under these assumptions is given in appendix 1.

V. A COMPUTER SIMULATION OF THE PARADOX OF VOTING

The probability of the paradox of voting can be closely approximated by a simulation in which sets of individual (or in this case, bloc) preference orderings are chosen at random and then tested to see whether or not cyclical preferences occur when they are combined into a social ordering. An excellent description of the detailed procedure is given by Klahr (1966). As in other probabilistic analyses, we assume throughout that all individual (bloc) preference orderings are transitive and that in voting on a pair of alternatives each bloc votes for the alternative which is higher in its preference ordering. We also assume that all preference orderings are equally likely—subject to the constraints discussed in the last two sections.

Our first results[7] are derived from simulations based on the same assumptions as made in previous studies, except for the addition of systems of voting blocs. That is, in this first step there are no dimensional assumptions made, no guarantee that different blocs have conflicting first choices, and no tied ranks permitted. The results for each system of voting blocs are given in table 3.[8]

Note, first of all, that our results for the "five-individual case" (g_2) are virtually identical to the exact probabilities given by Garman and Kamien (1968). This should be true, of course, and is one validation of our simulation procedure. Conveniently, then this system can be used as a standard of comparison for the probabilities generated in the other

---

[7] A sample size of 10,000 implies a 0.95 confidence level that our estimated probability is within 0.01 of the true probability (see Dixon and Massey, 1957, pp. 84–85). In all simulations that follow we have sampled 10,000 sets of preference orderings.

[8] Any weighting system within each category of the classification will give the same result (except for sampling errors). The specific systems we used are listed in appendix 2.

TABLE 3. The Probability of the Paradox of Voting Within Systems of Five Voting Blocs, for Three, Four and Five Alternatives[a]

Systems of voting blocs[b]	Five alternatives	Four alternatives	Three alternatives
b_1	.16	.10	.06
c_1	.11	.08	.04
d_1	.16	.11	.06
e_1	.19	.13	.07
f_1	.20	.13	.07
g_1	.20	.14	.07
g_2	.20	.14	.07

[a] In each simulation we have sampled 10,000 sets of preference orderings.

[b] System a is not shown since the probability of the paradox is zero when one bloc has a weight of >0.5.

systems. Three of the cases in table 3 (b, c and d) show a consistent decrease in the frequency of the paradox when compared with the system of five equal blocs. Among these the sharp decreasing effect of a c-system should be noted. This is no doubt attributable to the dominant position of bloc A in this system. Note also that these three cases, plus the a-case, have a random probability of occurrence of more than 0.75. Thus frequently occurring (on a random basis) systems of voting blocs have a decreasing effect on the frequency of the paradox when compared with a system of equally weighted blocs or individuals. However, it should also be emphasized that none of the differences in probabilities is too large. Even when one bloc has a uniquely advantageous position, as in system c, the paradox occurs with an annoying frequency. Finally, the effect of the number of alternatives is clear: an increase in the frequency of the paradox with increasing numbers of alternatives is always found, regardless of the system of voting blocs.

Turning for an instant to the real world and viewing political parties as voting blocs, these results indicate that the bloc sizes would make a cycle slightly more probable, for example, in the Belgian Senate (an e-case after the 1968 elections) than in any Scandinavian parliament in the sixties (a, c, or d cases). From an empirical point of view, then our analysis of voting blocs helps suggest assemblies in which the paradox is more or less likely to occur.

The first change in the parameters of our voting system is to permit indifference between alternatives—i.e., ties are allowed in the bloc's preference orderings. This adds two complicating factors. First, we cannot eliminate tied ranks in the social ordering simply by seeing that no pairs of blocs have weights that sum to exactly 0.50. This is most easily seen in the case of equal weights, in which each bloc in the five bloc system has a weight of 0.20. With no indifference permitted, a unique majority alternative always exists. With ties, however, we may have a weight of of 0.40 for one alternative, 0.40 for another, and 0.20 indifferent. We will see, however, that this problem usually does not change our results very much. A second complication is that our classification of systems of voting blocs would have to be considerably expanded to take care of all the "subcases" which can arise when ties are permitted. For example, the following two examples are both e-systems:

$$e_1: \quad A = 0.31, \quad B = 0.24, \quad C = 0.23, \quad D = 0.12, \quad \text{and} \quad E = 0.10$$
$$e_2: \quad A = 0.46, \quad B = 0.30, \quad C = 0.19, \quad D = 0.03, \quad \text{and} \quad E = 0.02$$

However, if bloc A is indifferent between alternative 1 and alternative 2, D and E can contribute to a majority coalition in e_1 but not in e_2. Rather than creating an elaborate classification, we have used two or more subcases for each of our previously defined cases. The exact systems used are given in appendix 2.

The results of the simulation with ties permitted are given in table 4. In the first column we repeat the probability results when no ties were permitted. The figures show a small but consistent decrease in the expected frequency of the paradox when ties are allowed. Interestingly, if ties are not permitted on either the first or last choices, the likelihood of cyclical results seems to be greater than with more limited indifference. The sharpest decrease, occurring in the c_2-system, is due to the extremely large weight of A, even larger than in the other c-systems.

Overall, our first two simulations have shown that neither blocs nor ties normally have a great effect on the expected probability of the para-

TABLE 4. The Probability of the Paradox in Subcases of Systems of Voting Blocs, with Two Assumptions about Ties

Systems of voting blocs	Five alternatives, no ties in bloc preference orderings	Five alternatives, no ties for first choice	Five alternatives, no ties for first and last choices
b_1	.16	.15	.15
b_2		.14	
b_3		.15	
c_1	.11	.10	.11
c_2		.06	
c_3		.11	
d_1	.16	.12	.13
d_2		.12	
d_3		.14	
e_1	.19	.15	.15
e_2		.15(.03)[a]	
e_3		.16	
f_1	.20	.17	.18
f_2		.16	
f_3		.16	
g_1	.20	.16	.18
g_2	.20	.06(.30)	

[a] The figures in parentheses are the percentage of ties in the social ordering. See appendix 2.

dox. However, both of these factors consistently reduce that probability by a small amount, and under certain circumstances by a large measure. In real world voting, the frequent presence of these two factors no doubt helps keep the paradox from appearing more often than it does.

Our third simulation is intended to show the effects of intense conflict. Here we required that as many blocs as possible have different first choices. The effects of this constraint are clearly seen in table 5. In every case the probability of the paradox increased considerably ove · the figures generated in the original simulation (table 3). Even with only three alternatives the paradox is likely to occur more than ten percent of the time, and with some systems of voting blocs, twenty percent or more of the time. Moreover, it appears that in conflict situations the specific bloc system is of considerable importance. For example, in the original simulation an e-system was no more likely than others to yield cyclical majorities; but in the conflict situation this same system gave the highest or second highest probabilities of the paradox. Nearly the opposite is true of the g_2-system.

TABLE 5.   The Probability of the Paradox in Systems of Five Voting Blocs, with Several Assumptions about the Degree of Conflict

System of voting blocs	Five alternatives, all blocs have different first choices	Four alternatives, four largest blocs have different first choices	Three alternatives, three largest blocs have different first choices
b_1	.34	.30	.25
c_1	.25	.18	.10
d_1	.33	.29	.16
e_1	.38	.31	.22
f_1	.39	.30	.18
g_1	.35	.25	.12
g_2	.35	.24	.13

In variation of this conflict situation, ties were permitted below the first choice and a number of subcases with five alternatives were analyzed. As before, the effect of ties was to reduce the likelihood of the paradox, while by no means eliminating it. Compared to the figures in the first column of table 5, the average reduction in the probabilities was 0.06.

Our last simulation incorporated the dimensional character of the preference orderings as outlined above. Using a method of transformations which reduced the 7140 pairs of preference orderings to only 32 distinct pairs, we estimated the probability of the paradox for all of these distinct sets.[9] Since the pairs are distributed over Cases 1-5 (and the result for

---

[9] The 7140 possible pairs of dimensions are reduced to 32 distinct pairs by the following transformations:

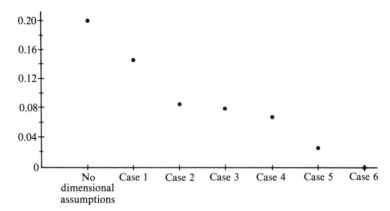

FIGURE 1.   Probability of the Paradox in the Six Cases of Two Single Dimensions.[a]

[a] All estimates are based on five blocs with equal weight (g_2-system), five alternatives, and when neither dimension is dominant.

Case 6 is known analytically) we have an estimate for each of the cases defined above (table 2).

We limited our analysis to the system of five equally weighted decision-makers (g_2-system) and five alternatives. The results for this situation are given in figure 1.[10] For comparison we have added the simulation results when no dimensional assumptions were made. The results show a clear decrease in the expected frequency of the paradox as one moves from no dimensional assumptions to two single but nonoverlapping dimensions, and a further decrease as the two single dimensions overlap more and more. Case 6, of course, is the familiar situation in which all the preference

a. One member of any pair can always be transformed into the dimension $A_1A_2A_3A_4A_5$ by simply relabelling the alternatives. This reduces the 7140 pairs into the 120 in which the first member is $A_1A_2A_3A_4A_5$.

b. Since we have single-peaked preference orderings, second dimensions which are mirror images of each other generate the same preference orderings and hence need not be distinguished. E.g., $A_1A_4A_3A_2A_5$ is not distinct from $A_5A_2A_3A_4A_1$. This reduces the number of pairs to 60.

c. Since the first dimension can be transformed into its mirror image by relabelling the variables as follows: $A_1 = A_5$, $A_2 = A_4$, $A_3 = A_3$, $A_4 = A_2$, $A_5 = A_1$, we can perform this same transformation on the second dimension, and the transformed dimension need not be distinguished from the original. E.g., $A_4A_1A_5A_3A_2$ is not distinct from $A_2A_5A_1A_3A_4$.

These transformations reduce the number of distinct pairs to 32. These 32 pairs are distributed among our six cases as follows: Case 1—14, Case 2—9, Case 3—5, Case 4—1, Case 5—2, and Case 6—1. The odd number in some of the cases is due to the fact that a few dimensions transform into the same dimension by steps b and c. E.g., $A_4A_5A_3A_1A_2$ is changed into $A_2A_1A_3A_5A_4$ by both transformations.

[10] The actual estimates behind the averages given in figure 1 and table 6 are presented in appendix 3.

orderings are single-peaked on one dimension, and the paradox cannot occur.

The outcome of this simulation is strikingly similar to that found by Niemi (1969). In that analysis, limited to three alternatives and one dimension, the larger the proportion of preference orderings that were single-peaked, the lower the likelihood of the paradox (for a fixed number of individuals). Here we have more alternatives and two single dimensions, but the general conclusion is the same: as one moves from an unstructured situation to one in which common dimensions (and not just a single dimension) are perceived, the likelihood of the paradox drops; and as the perceived dimensions are increasingly overlapping, the probability of the paradox drops even further.

The variant of this simulation involving the relative dominance of one dimension further strengthens this conclusion. We performed the simulation two additional times, once choosing preference orderings from those satisfying dimension 1 three times as often as those satisfying dimension 2, and once choosing these preference orderings in the ratio five to one. As shown in table 6, this had the expected result of lowering the probability of the paradox still further than the original dimensional assumptions. Thus the expected frequency of the paradox is dependent not only on the overlapping of perceived dimensions, but on the proportion of individuals or blocs who share each dimension. The greater the dominance of a single dimension, the less often cyclical majorities will occur.

TABLE 6.   The Probability of the Paradox with Variations in the Dominance of One Dimension

Ratio of preference orderings chosen from dimension 1 to those from dimension 2	Case 1	Case 2	Case 3	Case 4	Case 5
1:1	.145	.084	.078	.067	.024
1:3	.082	.056	.052	.053	.017
1:5	.051	.039	.040	.037	.013

VI. CONCLUSION

The results of our simulation can be summarized in terms of the effect of each factor we introduced on the expected probability of the paradox. First, voting systems in which blocs had unequal weights usually had the effect of lowering (or at least not raising) the likelihood of cyclical results. Significantly, however, in cases of considerable conflict the effects of the bloc system were mixed. When the largest blocs were assumed to have conflicting first choices, systems of larger and smaller blocs sometimes raised the expected frequency of the paradox. This means that the existence of a multiparty system, in which the voters are cast as if by a small number of weighted blocs or teams, will not uniformly reduce the occurrence of circular preferences. In fact, there appear to be conditions under which a multiparty system will make the paradox more likely than with a comparable number of individuals (or equally weighted blocs).

In contrast, the effect of conflict was uniform and strong, resulting in a substantial increase in the likelihood of the paradox. Tied ranks had just the opposite effect, always reducing the expected probability of the paradox. The existence of shared single dimensions had the same effect as ties; it was especially noteworthy when the dimensions were overlapping or when one dimension was shared by a larger proportion of the decision makers.

In general, then, our results indicate several factors that encourage or inhibit the occurrence of the paradox at least in the theoretical model used. Hopefully these results will encourage empirical investigations by suggesting the type of situations in which the paradox is most likely to be found. Such work would no doubt give greater political meaning to the voting paradox and would also give added support for theoretical investigations of the type carried out here.

Finally, we hope that our efforts will stimulate other more general work utilizing the factors we have explored here with regard to the paradox of voting. We feel that the classification and probabilistic analysis of bloc systems in particular might be useful for researchers interested in coalition formation in mulitiparty legislatures, committees, and electorates. By narrowing down the number of unique cases and showing the similarity of system of different numbers of blocs, this approach might expand the types of voting systems which can be analyzed with some degree of theoretical rigor.

APPENDIX I

A preference ordering with ties can be created as follows. First, if there are to be no ties for the first choice, choose a number 1-5 (for the five alternative case) randomly. Suppose it is 2. Then alternative 2 is said to be the first preference. Then randomly select four numbers with replacement from the numbers 2-5 inclusive. Suppose the numbers are 4, 3, 3, 2. We then assign alternative 1 to the fourth preference, alternatives 3 and 4 to the third preference and alternative 5 to the second preference.

The resulting preference order is thus

Alternative 2

Alternative 5

Alternative 3, 4

Alternative 1.

A similar method is used when ties are not allowed for the first or last choices.

With this procedure for creating ties, we have the following probabilities:

No ties for first choice

$$Pr \text{ (no ties)} \quad = \quad 1\binom{4}{1\,1\,1\,1}/4^4 = \; 24/256$$

$$Pr \text{ (two tied)} \quad = \; 12\binom{4}{2\,1\,1\,0}/4^4 = 144/256$$

$$Pr \text{ (2 tied pairs)} = \quad 6\binom{4}{2\,2\,0\,0}/4^4 = \; 36/256$$

$$Pr \text{ (three tied)} \; = \; 12\binom{4}{3\,1\,0\,0}/4^4 = \; 48/256$$

$$Pr \text{ (four tied)} \quad = \quad 4\binom{4}{4\,0\,0\,0}/4^4 = \quad 4/256$$

No ties for first or last choice

$$Pr \text{ (no ties)} \quad = \quad 1\binom{3}{1\,1\,1}/3^3 \quad = \quad 6/27$$

$$Pr \text{ (two tied)} \quad = \quad 6\binom{3}{2\,1\,0}/3^3 \quad = \; 18/27$$

$$Pr \text{ (three tied)} \; = \quad 3\binom{3}{3\,0\,0}/3^3 \quad = \quad 3/27$$

In these fractions, the multinomial coefficient represents a way of distributing scores to three or four alternatives. The preceding coefficient is the number of ways of obtaining this distribution. For example in Pr (four tied), $\binom{4}{4\,0\,0\,0}$ means that the same random number was drawn each time and the preceeding coefficient denotes the fact that this number could be any one of 4 numbers—2, 3, 4, or 5.

APPENDIX II

The specific systems used are as follows:

Case		Voting bloc			
b_1	$A = .47$	$B = .46$	$C = .045$	$D = .014$	$E = .011$
c_1	.41	.20	.15	.14	.10
d_1	.40	.22	.17	.14	.07
e_1	.41	.24	.22	.07	.06
f_1	.40	.39	.09	.07	.05
g_1	.24	.23	.21	.18	.14
b_2	.40	.31	.25	.03	.01
c_2	.47	.21	.15	.10	.07
d_2	.46	.30	.15	.07	.02
e_2	.46	.30	.19	.03	.02
f_2	.40	.36	.09	.08	.07
g_2	.20	.20	.20	.20	.20
b_3	.29	.27	.25	.10	.09
c_3	.37	.18	.16	.15	.14
d_3	.31	.23	.21	.20	.05
e_3	.31	.24	.23	.12	.10
f_3	.31	.20	.18	.16	.15

In systems e_2, f_3, and g_2, ties in the social ordering can occur. In case g_2 this possibility is greatest, and the random chance of a tie in the social ordering is 0.30.

APPENDIX III

Case 1

Pair	Ratio of preference orderings chosen from dimension 1 to those from dimension 2		
	1:1	1:3	1:5
$A_1A_2A_3A_4A_5$ and $A_3A_1A_5A_2A_4$	.23	.12	.07
" $A_2A_5A_1A_4A_3$	.22	.11	.06
" $A_2A_4A_5A_1A_3$	.21	.11	.06
" $A_3A_4A_5A_1A_2$	.18	.10	.06
" $A_1A_4A_5A_2A_3$	.15	.10	.07
" $A_2A_3A_5A_1A_4$	.15	.07	.04
" $A_2A_1A_4A_5A_3$	.15	.08	.06
" $A_4A_3A_5A_1A_2$	.14	.07	.04
" $A_2A_5A_4A_1A_3$	.14	.09	.06
" $A_1A_3A_5A_2A_4$	.13	.07	.04
" $A_3A_5A_2A_4A_1$	.13	.10	.07
" $A_2A_1A_4A_3A_5$	.09	.06	.04
" $A_2A_5A_3A_1A_4$	.06	.04	.03
" $A_4A_5A_3A_1A_2$	.05	.03	.02

Case 2

Pair	1:1	1:3	1:5
$A_1A_2A_3A_4A_5$ and $A_1A_3A_5A_4A_2$	.12	.05	.03
" $A_1A_5A_2A_4A_3$	.12	.11	.08
" $A_1A_2A_4A_5A_3$	.10	.08	.06
" $A_1A_2A_5A_3A_4$	.10	.05	.03
" $A_1A_4A_5A_3A_2$	.10	.04	.02
" $A_1A_5A_4A_2A_3$	.09	.09	.07
" $A_5A_2A_3A_1A_4$	.05	.03	.02
" $A_1A_5A_3A_2A_4$	.05	.04	.03
" $A_2A_1A_3A_4A_5$	.03	.02	.01

Case 3

Pair	1:1	1:3	1:5
$A_1A_2A_3A_4A_5$ and $A_3A_2A_1A_4A_5$	.14	.08	.07
" $A_1A_4A_2A_3A_5$	.07	.06	.05
" $A_1A_3A_4A_5A_2$	.07	.04	.03
" $A_1A_5A_2A_3A_4$	.06	.04	.02
" $A_4A_2A_3A_1A_5$	.05	.04	.03

Case 4

Pair	1:1	1:3	1:5
$A_1A_2A_3A_4A_5$ and $A_1A_2A_4A_3A_5$	.067	.053	.037

Case 5

Pair	1:1	1:3	1:5
$A_1A_2A_3A_4A_5$ and $A_5A_2A_3A_4A_1$	.019	.016	.012
" $A_1A_5A_4A_3A_2$	.028	.018	.014

12. The Paradox of Voting and Uncertainty

KENNETH A. SHEPSLE

The paradox of voting is a paradox in one sense of the word only. It may be "a tenet contrary to received opinion," as Webster defines it, but it is not "a statement actually self-contradictory or false." Its paradoxical nature is resolved by logical scrutiny of group decision making. Put simply, the paradox of voting asserts that, when there are three or more alternatives to be voted upon by a collection of three or more decision makers, neither (1) a consistency rule for individual preferences, nor (2) a reasonable rule of preference aggregation, is sufficient to guarantee consistent aggregate preferences. That is, "group preferences" may be inconsistent even if individual preferences are not.

Observations and commentary on the voting paradox and its logical consequences date back to the eighteenth century and the Marquis de Condorcet. However, only in recent years have scholars taken note of its possibly harmful effect on traditional democratic procedures (Black, 1958, pp. 46-51, 156-214; Arrow, 1963, passim; Riker, 1961). In this paper we introduce the notion of voting in uncertain contingencies and trace

I would like to thank the editors, Richard Niemi and Herbert Weisberg, for reading and commenting on various drafts of this paper. I am responsible for the finished product, however.

the logical implications of uncertainty on the voting paradox. We conclude the paper with an examination of some interesting political implications of the analysis. In particular, we argue that uncertainty provides rational actors with an additional strategic dimension, and that its inclusion in formal models permits a logical explanation of frequently observed empirical regularities.

I. THE PARADOX OF VOTING

We begin with a set of voters $V = \{v_1, v_2, \ldots, v_m\}$ and a set of outcomes (alternatives) $0 = \{o_1, o_2, \ldots, o_n\}$, one of which is selected by the collectivity V by majority vote. We suppose that each $v_i \in V$ has a preference ordering over the $o_j \in 0$ satisfying the following assumptions:

A.1 For any two alternatives $o_r, o_s \in 0$, either $o_r \underset{i}{\geq} o_s$ or $o_s \underset{i}{\geq} o_r$, where $\underset{i}{\geq}$ is the weak preference relation for v_i.

A.2 For all triples of alternatives $o_r, o_s, o_t \in 0$, $o_r \underset{i}{\geq} o_s$ and $o_s \underset{i}{\geq} o_t$ imply $o_r \underset{i}{\geq} o_t$, for all i.

The first assumption—connectivity—asserts that each voter is able to make a preference comparison for each dyad of alternatives. The second assumption—transitivity—suggests that a voter's preferences exhibit a certain modicum of consistency. Throughout this analysis we assume a *strong* preference ordering for each voter.

The *collective preference relation* $\underset{c}{\geq}$ may be defined as follows:

For any two alternatives $o_r, o_s \in 0$, o_r is said to be *collectively preferred* to o_s—$o_r \underset{c}{\geq} o_s$—if at least a simple majority of the $v_i \in V$ prefer o_r to o_s.

With this definition, then, we specify an interpretation of "collective preference" which avoids the problems of false personification. Collective preferences are defined by a rule of individual preference aggregation—in this case majority rule—rather than by some metaphysical group preference.

The paradox of voting is an observation about the logical implications of this voting arrangement. It asserts that when there are at least three alternatives and three voters, assumptions A.1 and A.2 as applied to the individual preference relation $\underset{i}{\geq}$ do not necessarily hold for the collective preference relation $\geq_c$.[1] The result is a cycling of collectively preferred alternatives. That is, the collective preference ordering is intransitive.[2]

The following well-known example is instructive. To establish the problem we imagine a collectivity of three voters: $V = \{v_1, v_2, v_3\}$. The voters are assigned the task of choosing a most preferred alternative, by majority rule, from among a set of three alternatives $0 = \{o_1, o_2, o_3\}$. The voters' preferences over 0 are represented as follows:

v_1	v_2	v_3
o_1	o_2	o_3
o_2	o_3	o_1
o_3	o_1	o_2

FIGURE 1. Preference Orderings

We say that an alternative is *collectively most-preferred* if it is collectively preferrred (see above definition) to *all* other alternatives. We now ask whether it is possible for the group to accomplish its task. That is, does a collectively most-preferred alternative exist? The results appear in table 1. As the table indicates, the collectivity prefers o_1 to o_2, o_2 to o_3, but o_3 to o_1. Majority rule cannot resolve the incompatibility of preferences in the collectivity. The collective intransitivity is a direct result of the changing make-up of the winning coalition.

TABLE 1. An Example of a Cyclical Majority

Dyad	Vote Outcome	Vote	Winning Majority
(o_1, o_2)	$o_1 \underset{c}{>} o_2$	2–1	$\{v_1, v_3\}$
(o_2, o_3)	$o_2 \underset{c}{>} o_3$	2–1	$\{v_1, v_2\}$
(o_1, o_3)	$o_3 \underset{c}{>} o_1$	2–1	$\{v_2, v_3\}$

---

[1] This statement is a special case of the more general Possibility Theorem proved by Arrow (1963, pp. 51–60). The theorem states that for any aggregation principle (voting rule) satisfying certain reasonable conditions, the collective preference relation may violate A.2.

[2] It is useful to distinguish two different types of cycles. In the first case a collectively-preferred alternative emerges unchallenged, but intransitivities occur among some of the less-preferred alternatives. Klahr calls this a Type I intransitivity. In the second case the most-preferred alternative(s) is involved in the intransitivity. That is, no alternative emerges as the unchallenged collective preference. Klahr calls this a Type II intransitivity (Klahr, 1966). Since most political bodies are concerned with selecting a most-preferred alternative, rather than an entire collective preference ordering, we concentrate on the latter type of intransitivity.

Although the logical properties of this example are of some interest, the political implications which follow as logical consequences have fascinated a number of students of voting. In particular, this example raises a number of questions about the strategic misrepresentation of preferences, the timing of dyadic votes, the existence of alternatives which generate cyclical majorities, and, in general, legislative machinations (Black, 1958; Farquharson, 1969; Riker, 1965).

The other side of this coin involves the matter of whether and how a collectivity can avoid the consequences of cyclical majorities. Investigations of this kind may be classified into three categories depending upon whether (1) restrictions on preferences, (2) alternative criteria for aggregation, or (3) probabilistic considerations are recommended.

The preference restriction receiving the greatest attention is that of *single-peakedness* of individual orderings. For Black, who first proposed it, a set of preference functions is single-peaked if an ordering of the alternatives along a horizontal axis exists such that each preference function "changes its direction at most once, from up to down" (Black, 1958, pp. 7, 14-15). Black shows that the single-peakedness restriction on individual preferences is sufficient to guarantee a collectively most-preferred alternative. Indeed, the restriction guarantees complete transitivity of collective preferences. Generalizations of the single-peakedness restriction have been provided by Arrow (1963, pp. 74-81), Dummett and Farquharson (1961), Inada (1955; 1964), Plott (1967a; 1967b), Sen (1966; 1969), Vickrey (1960), and Ward (1961; 1965). In sum, these studies have shown that if admissible preference orderings are restricted in certain, rather general ways, then the cyclical majority problem is a logical impossibility.[3]

Arrow's conditions for preference aggregation have served as something of a focal point for scholars interested in collective decision making and its welfare implications. As the preceding paragraph has indicated, one set of investigations has focused on Arrow's first condition. In a second class of investigations, conducted primarily by welfare economists, Arrow's conditions have been roundly criticized and alternative criteria proposed.

Hildreth's work is representative of this approach (Hildreth, 1953). His argument, which stands on the shaky ground of interpersonal utility comparisons, is beyond the scope of this essay.[4] Suffice it to say that Hildreth questions the reasonableness of one of the Arrow conditions (Independence from Irrelevant Alternatives) and suggests a particular weakening of that condition which results in the elimination of the cyclical majority problem.

---

[3] That is, a specific relaxation of Arrow's first condition, known as the Universal Admissibility of Individual Orderings, eliminates the possibility of a voting paradox.

[4] For a good review of the controversy, see Rothenberg (1961, pp. 17-61, 127-45) and the citations therein.

In his later writings Black has argued against the Arrow conditions for rules of preference aggregation on the grounds that the procedures they imply are unsuitable in other respects. Although he is specifically interested in restrictions on admissible preferences, and hence belongs in the first category above on this score, his arguments might equally apply to other of Arrow's conditions. He argues that, with appropriate modifications, the voting rule of complete unanimity satisfies Arrow's conditions, but that it is inherently unsuitable as a collective decision-rule, especially in large voting bodies. Yet Arrow's conditions deem this rule "suitable" and deem more practicable rules "unsuitable." If this is accepted, then ". . . the Arrow requirements must be inappropriate to the task assigned to them, namely to discriminate between more suitable and less suitable procedures" (Black, 1969, pp. 227-28). The lesson to be learned here is that the cyclical majority problem may be eliminated for a price, viz, the violation either of one of Arrow's conditions or of some ethical norm.

Finally, there are a number of scholars who implicitly suggest that we defer evaluating the potential harm the cyclical majority problem may inflict on a group decision process until first determining the likelihood that the problem will arise. Using a variety of techniques, they have sought to generate the a priori probability of a voting paradox for different numbers of voters and alternatives. The reader is referred to the work of Bjurulf (chap 11 in this volume), Campbell and Tullock (1965), DeMeyer and Plott (1970), Garman and Kamien (1968), Gleser (1969), Klahr (1966), Niemi (1969), Niemi and Weisberg (1968), Pomeranz and Weil (1970), Riker (1961), Weisberg and Niemi (1971), and Williamson and Sargent (1967). The general conclusion of these investigations is that majority rule is extremely susceptible to the cyclical majority problem, especially when the number of alternatives and/or the number of voters is large.

The question may now be put: why have examples of the cyclical majority problem not regularly been observed in voting bodies? The first and most obvious reason is the rather excessive data requirements. In order to examine a voting situation for the existence of a voting paradox, the entire preference ordering of each voter is required. Since most real-world voting bodies neither require members to submit preference orderings nor consider all pairs of alternatives in a vote, it is often impossible to generate the necessary data.[5]

Although this explanation for the general failure to observe instances of the paradox of voting is important, we argue below that two institutional features of most voting arrangements serve to reduce the likelihood

[5] But see Niemi (1970a).

of the paradox. First, there are restrictions on the kinds of alternatives permitted into the collective decision-making arena. That is, there are *rules of entry* or *constraints* which govern the composition of the choice set facing the collectivity. Whether by law or by custom, there are many examples of systematic exclusion of certain classes of alternatives.[6] Consider the following three instances:

1. Until a 1968 court order permitted George Wallace's name to appear on the Ohio ballot, it was extremely difficult for third party candidates to compete effectively in that state.

2. In national party conventions, a relatively large number of signatories is required in order to add a minority plank to the convention agenda.

3. Many legislative bodies permit the chairman to rule on the relevance or germaneness of amendments.

The first example suggests the importance of an electoral system which, by custom and law, inhibits competition by more than two parties. With fewer than three alternatives the cyclical majority problem can never arise. The second example reinforces this point. When the number of alternatives remains small, the paradox of voting is unlikely; when that number is smaller than three, the paradox is impossible.

The third example applies Black's important insight concerning single-peaked curves. The germaneness rule permits many decisions to be decided on the basis of preferences along a single dimension. The chairman is empowered to declare alternative which raise new dimensions nongermane. Since it seems reasonable that a collectively most-preferred alternative is more likely when the number of decision dimensions is limited, the rule of germaneness goes a long way toward eliminating the paradox in legislative bodies.

The second institutional feature of most voting arrangemens is the existence of uncertainty. Only rarely and trivially are the outcomes of a decision problem well-specified.[7] Hence, the typical decision context is one of uncertainty. Downs, in fact, argues that uncertainty "is a basic force affecting all human activity. . . . Coping with uncertainty is a major function of nearly every significant institution in society; therefore it shapes the nature of each" (Downs, 1957, p. 13). We argue in the remainder of the paper that the concepts of *constraint* and *uncertainty* account for a counter-intuitive regularity—the infrequent occurrence of cyclical majorities despite high, a priori probabilities—and thus provide some insight into the functioning of majority rule decision systems.

---

[6] Admirable defenses of this proposition may be found in Schattschneider (1960) and Bachrach and Baratz (1962).

[7] On this subject, see Churchman (1961, pp. 174–250).

II. THE IMPORTANCE OF UNCERTAINTY AND ITS USE IN THE ANALYSIS

It is customary in decision theory to distinguish among the choice contingencies of certainty, risk, and uncertainty:

> We shall say that we are in the realm of decision making under:
> (a) *Certainty* if each action is known to lead invariably to a specific outcome . . . .
> (b) *Risk* if each action leads to one of a set of possible specific outcomes, each outcome occurring with a known probability . . . .
> (c) *Uncertainty* if [each action] has as its consequence a set of possible specific outcomes, but where the probabilities of these outcomes are completely unknown . . . . (Luce and Raiffa, 1957, p. 13)

Elsewhere (Shepsle, 1970a, chap. 1) we have argued that this distinction is irrelevant in many respects—that all decision problems involve risk so long as a rather broad and subjective definition of probability is employed. We assert that despite the fact that individual voters have preferences over basic outcomes, the alternatives on which they vote are rarely identical to those basic outcomes. Decision makers collectively choose *actions* which have an uncertain[8] relationship to basic outcomes.

The ambiguous nature of the relationship of actions to outcomes is captured by the notion of a *lottery*. That is, voters choose not from the set of basic outcomes 0, but rather from a set of actions $A = \{a_1, a_2, \ldots, a_r\}$, where each $a_i \in A$ is a lottery over basic outcomes:

$$a_i \equiv [p_1^{(i)} o_1, p_2^{(i)} o_2, \ldots, p_n^{(i)} o_n].$$

A suggestive example is found in the field of electoral behavior. Voters may have preferences over the set of governmental activities in different issue areas, but only rarely do they ever vote on these activities. Rather, they cast votes for *candidates* who take "stands" on these issue dimensions. However, as is frequently observed, the positions taken by candidates are usually vague and ambiguous.[9] The lottery concept provides a useful device for modelling a candidate's position vis-à-vis the basic outcomes.

In general, then, a collective choice problem may be viewed as a choice among lotteries over basic social alternatives. In terms of the cyclical majority problem, we may imagine a set of outcomes which cycle (see

---

[8] We use the terms "uncertainty" and "risk" interchangeably. Unless otherwise specified we mean *risk* as defined above. "Uncertainty" is simply a more convenient term.

[9] This argument originally appeared in Shepsle (1970a, chap. 3) and is reported in chap. 13 in this volume.

figure 1), and a choice set A which is a superset of the basic set 0:

$$A = \{(p_1^{(i)}o_1, p_2^{(i)}o_2, \ldots, p_n^{(i)}o_n) \mid \sum_{j=1}^{n} p_j^{(i)} = 1 \text{ for all } i\}.[10]$$

Assume that all voters are able to rank-order the elements of A in accord with A.1 and A.2, thus, they possess von Neumann-Morgenstern utility functions and are expected-utility maximizers. For the three-voter case, utility functions are presented in table 2.

TABLE 2. Utility Functions for the Three-Voter Case

	v_1	v_2	v_3
o_1	1	0	n
o_2	k	1	0
o_3	0	m	1

where $0 < k < 1$
$0 < m < 1$
$0 < n < 1$

Having outlined the way in which we shall employ the uncertainly concept, we now consider a special case of the cyclical majority problem. In order to facilitate the discussion we suppose that we are dealing with a specific kind of collective choice—the election of a public official. This particular example is only illustrative and need not disconcert those who find it too restrictive. At the same time we introduce, via the back door, the constraint concept, i.e., rules of entry, we discussed earlier. The cyclical majority problem provides a vehicle for a more careful specification of this concept.

III. PARADOX LOST: A SPECIAL CASE[11]

Let the set $V = \{v_1, v_2, v_3\}$ be an electorate to which two candidates, X and Y appeal for votes. Suppose the election hinges on one issue, 0, for which there are three possible positions: $0 = \{o_1, o_2, o_3\}$. Let table 2 represent the utility function of each v_i. Each voter votes for that candidate, Mr. X or Mr, Y, who advocates the position more preferred by him. From table 1 it is clear that no alternative is collectively most-preferred. Given this situation, how should a rational candidate campaign?

In order to answer this question, we distinguish the candidates according to the roles they play. Mr. X, we suppose, is an incumbent candidate

---

[10] To see that 0 is a subset of A, simply observe that each $o_i \in 0$ is a degenerate lottery and is thus an $a_j \in A$.

[11] This example is drawn from Shepsle (1970b).

campaigning for reelection, whereas Mr. Y is the challenger. The incumbent, because he has occupied the political limelight during his tenure in office, and because he can manipulate the resources of the state in order to demonstrate commitment, is perceived as a sure prospect by the electorate. That is, whatever policy position in 0 he espouses is believed by the electorate. However, he may change his commitment to some other o_j by a dramatic act, e.g., a halt in the bombing of North Viet Nam. The challenger, on the other hand, is perceived by the electorate as inherently risky. The challenger, however, need not be perceived as an extreme risk. He may have a history of pronouncements on the issue 0 and thus be perceived as leaning in one direction or another. To summarize, the incumbent, Mr. X, is perceived as a certain alternative, and thus is *restricted to the class of degenerate lotteries* on 0, viz. $\{o_1, o_2, o_3\}$. The challenger, Mr. Y, is perceived as inherently risky and is restricted to the class of nondegenerate lotteries on 0, viz. $A = \{(p_1^{(i)} o_1, \ldots, p_n^{(i)} o_n) \mid \sum_{j=1}^{n} p_j^{(i)} = 1; 0 \leq p_j^{(i)} < 1$, for all i and $j\}$. We now determine the conditions in which an alternative in one of the candidate's strategy sets can secure a majority against *all* of the alternatives in the other's strategy set, even though the basic outcomes cycle. If such an alternative exists, then the paradox, at least as it manifests itself empirically, disappears. It is important to note that the elimination of the paradox is ultimately dependent upon the constraints on candidate positions we have postulated, a fact we prove in the next section.

Consider a typical lottery from Mr. Y's set of alternatives: $(p_1 o_1, p_2 o_2, p_3 o_3)$. Employing the expected-utility hypothesis, each voter evaluates the lottery as follows:[12]

$$v_1: \quad p_1 u(o_1) + p_2 u(o_2) + (1 - p_1 - p_2) u(o_3)$$
$$= p_1(1) + p_2 k + (1 - p_1 - p_2)(0)$$
$$= p_1 + p_2 k$$

$$v_2: \quad p_1 u(o_1) + p_2 u(o_2) + (1 - p_1 - p_2) u(o_3)$$
$$= p_1(0) + p_2(1) + (1 - p_1 - p_2) m$$
$$= p_2 + (1 - p_1 - p_2) m$$

$$v_3: \quad p_1 u(o_1) + p_2 u(o_2) + (1 - p_1 - p_2) u(o_3)$$
$$= p_1 n + p_2(0) + (1 - p_1 - p_2)(1)$$
$$= p_1 n + (1 - p_1 - p_2).$$

---

[12] The utility values are taken from table 2. In these expressions we use the fact that the probability numbers sum to unity. Thus, $p_3 = 1 - p_1 - p_2$.

We say that (p_1o_1, p_2o_2, p_3o_3) is a *majority lottery* if it can secure a majority of the votes when paired against any of the certain prospects. With this definition we prove

THEOREM 1.   Every Pair of Voters—Second-Ranked Alternative Theorem: A lottery (p_1o_1, p_2o_2, p_3o_3) is a majority lottery if and only if the expected utility it provides exceeds the utility of the second-ranked alternative of each voter.

PROOF:

a. *Necessity*

Suppose the contrary. Then, either

(1) $p_1 + p_2k < k,$

(2) $p_2 + (1 - p_1 - p_2)m < m,$

or   (3) $(1 - p_1 - p_2) + p_1n < n$ (see table 2).

For (1), Mr. X may select o_2 and secure the majority $\{v_1, v_2\}$. For (2), X may select o_3 and secure the majority $\{v_2, v_3\}$. For (3), X may select o_1 and secure the majority $\{v_1, v_3\}$. Thus, any lottery not satisfying the hypothesis of the theorem is not a majority lottery. Necessity is established.

b. *Sufficiency*

By observation, if the hypothesis of the theorem holds, and if Mr. X chooses o_1, then the lottery is preferred by the majority $\{v_2, v_3\}$. If X chooses o_2, the lottery is preferred by the majority $\{v_1, v_3\}$. Finally, if X chooses o_3, the lottery is preferred by the majority $\{v_1, v_2\}$. Thus, any lottery satisfying the hypothesis of the theorem is a majority lottery. Sufficiency is established.

Q.E.D.

Theorem 1 is a contingent statement. It asserts that (p_1o_1, p_2o_2, p_3o_3) is a majority lottery *if and only if*:

$$p_1 + p_2k > k \tag{1}$$

$$p_2 + (1 - p_1 - p_2)m > m \tag{2}$$

$$(1 - p_1 - p_2) + p_1n > n \tag{3}$$

We are now interested in proving an existential statement that gives the conditions on voter utility functions which imply the existence of a (not necessarity unique) lottery consistent with (1)–(3). Without burdening the reader with the proof (Shepsle, 1970a, chap. 5), we state

THEOREM 2.   If $kmn \leq (1 - k)(1 - m)(1 - n)$, then a lottery $(p_1o_1,$

$p_2 o_2, p_3 o_3$), consistent with (1)–(3), exists. If $kmn = (1 - k)(1 - m)(1 - n)$, the lottery is unique.[13]

Upper limits for k, as m and n vary over their entire range, are given in table 3. The table and the result of theorem 2 permit several points to be made. First, from the inequality of theorem 2, it may be seen that the result is symmetric with respect to the v_i. This follows from the fact that the preference aggregation rule confers equal status on the voters: one man–one vote. Thus, tables analogous (in fact, identical) to table 3 can be constructed, relating upper limits on m and n to values of the dyads (k, n) and (k, m), respectively.

TABLE 3. Upper Limits on k for Values of m and n

m \ n	.1	.2	.3	.4	.5	.6	.7	.8	.9
.1	.988	.974	.954	.931	.900	.858	.794	.693	.500
.2		.941	.904	.858	.800	.727	.632	.500	.307
.3			.845	.778	.700	.609	.500	.368	.206
.4				.693	.600	.500	.391	.273	.142
.5					.500	.400	.300	.200	.100
.6						.307	.222	.142	.069
.7							.155	.096	.046
.8								.059	.026
.9									.012

A second point follows from the cell entries of table 3 which have been generated from the above inequality. It is seen that at least one of the elements in the triple (k, m, n) never exceeds 0.5. This may be interpreted to mean that at least one of the voters *intensely* prefers his first-ranked alternative. Elsewhere we argue that this property completely characterizes the concept of intensity. That is, for a triple of alternatives (o_1, o_2, o_3), a decision maker intensely prefers his first-ranked alternative if and only if he prefers the lottery giving equal probabilities of obtaining his first- and last-ranked alternatives to the certainty of obtaining his middle-ranked

[13] In order to allay any fears, we note that this result is invariant under positive, linear utility transformations. That is, the result is not dependent upon the choice of any particular normalization of individual utllity functions. Thus, no interpersonal comparisons of utility are implied. In addition, we note that the result is compatible with the axioms of probability.

alternative (Rabushka and Shepsle, 1972, chap. 2). The risky candidate, then, thrives in an environment of intense preference. The implication here is that on the so-called critical issues in an election (which are "critical" precisely because many people have intense feelings on them), we might expect politicians to be vague and ambiguous. Considered in this light, Richard Nixon's vague rhetoric on the Viet Nam issue in the 1968 presidential campaign, e.g., "I have a plan," is explicable.[14]

To summarize, if the inequality of theorem 2 holds for a collective decision-making contingency in which no collectively most-preferred pure alternative exists, and if the constraints on dyadic comparisons apply, then the cyclical majority problem is avoided. This result, we emphasize, follows from the rather restrictive constraint we imposed on dyadic comparisons, namely comparisons in which a degenerate lottery (pure alternative) is paired against a strictly nondegenerate lottery. In the next two sections more general contingencies are entertained.

IV. PARADOX REGAINED: THE UNCONSTRAINED CASE

A caveat is appropriate at this point. We have not shown that Arrow's famous Possibility Theorem (Arrow, 1963, chap, 5) is wrong. Rather we have indicated that under the conditions specified in theorem 2, a relaxation of the connectivity axiom, i.e., the imposition of constraints, implies the existence of a collectively-preferred alternative. The importance of constraints is demonstrated in a result stated shortly (theorem 4). In order to introduce this result, suppose now that the respective constraints on Mr. X and Mr. Y are removed. Each candidate is free to advocate any alternative, risky or certain. This situation may be regarded either as an election in which the incumbent does not seek reelection or as a nonpartisan contest.

If a lottery $(p_1 o_1, p_2 o_2, p_3 o_3)$ is collectively most-preferred, then it can obtain a majority against any other lottery $(p_1^* o_1, p_2^* o_2, p_3^* o_3)$. In terms of our three-voter electorate, this statement implies that one of the following conditions holds:

1. v_1 and v_2 prefer $(p_1 o_1, p_2 o_2, p_3 o_3)$; v_3 prefers $(p_1^* o_1, p_2^* o_2, p_3^* o_3)$ or is indifferent between the two.
2. v_2 and v_3 prefer $(p_1 o_1, p_2 o_2, p_3 o_3)$; v_1 prefers $(p_1^* o_1, p_2^* o_2, p_3^* o_3)$ or is indifferent between the two.

---

[14] Although we do not show it here, the relationship between intensity of preference and dominance of risky strategies holds for electorates with single-peaked curves as well.

3. v_1 and v_3 prefer (p_1o_1, p_2o_2, p_3o_3); v_2 prefers $(p_1^*o_1, p_2^*o_2, p_3^*o_3)$ or is indifferent between the two.
4. v_1, v_2, and v_3 prefer (p_1o_1, p_2o_2, p_3o_3).[15]

From table 2 and the expected-utility hypothesis, conditions 1—4 may be represented by the following sets of inequalities:

condition 1
$$p_1 + p_2k > p_1^* + p_2^*k$$
$$p_2 + p_3m > p_2^* + p_3^*m$$
$$p_3 + p_1n \leq p_3^* + p_1^*n \tag{4}$$

condition 2
$$p_2 + p_3m > p_2^* + p_3^*m$$
$$p_3 + p_1n > p_3^* + p_1^*n$$
$$p_1 + p_2k \leq p_1^* + p_2^*k \tag{5}$$

condition 3
$$p_1 + p_2k > p_1^* + p_2^*k$$
$$p_3 + p_1n > p_3^* + p_1^*n$$
$$p_2 + p_3m \leq p_2^* + p_3^*m \tag{6}$$

condition 4
$$p_1 + p_2k > p_1^* + p_2^*k$$
$$p_2 + p_3m > p_2^* + p_3^*m$$
$$p_3 + p_1n > p_3^* + p_1^*n \tag{7}$$

We define an *objection*[16] to (p_1o_1, p_2o_2, p_3o_3) as a feasible lottery $(p_1^*o_1, p_2^*o_2, p_3^*o_3)$ for which none of the sets of inequalities (4)–(7) is satisfied. From this definition and the definition of "collectively most-preferred," a simple lemma follows directly:

LEMMA 1. A lottery to which an objection exists is not collectively most-preferred.

An Impossibility Theorem is now stated. The proof is deferred to an appendix.

THEOREM 3. Impossibility Theorem—There exists, for every (p_1o_1, p_2o_2, p_3o_3), at least one objection.

In words, theorem 3 states that in the absence of constraints, no alternative, whether a lottery or a sure prospect, is collectively most-preferred.

---

[15] We exclude from consideration the possibility that one of the voters prefers the alleged collectively most-preferred lottery and the other two voters are indifferent. However, the theorem we prove is still valid if this possibility is included.

[16] This term is adopted from Aumann and Maschler (1964).

The unconstrained case is directly comparable to Arrow's general contingency. As in the Arrow case, our general unconstrained case produces a cyclical majority problem in which an infinity of lotteries cycle.

The juxtaposition of special case (section 3) and general unconstrained case is instructive. It suggests that constraints may eliminate the devastating effects of the cyclical majority problem by admitting alternatives (which may include lotteries) in one candidate's constrained set that defeat *all* alternatives in the other candidate's set. In the real political world a candidate is constrained by the historical record of his party, by the preferences of important supporters, e.g., financial contributors, and by his personal history.[17] Thus, it is of some interest to examine the role played by constraints in a more general context. We begin this task in the next section.

V. SYSTEMATIC CONSTRAINTS

We have examined a number of general constraints elsewhere (Shepsle, 1970a, pp. 258-72). Here we examine what are called *continuity constraints*. We suppose that each candidate belongs to a political party which, by tradition, is perceived by the voters as the "probable representative" of a particular policy outlook.[18] As a result, Mr. X and Mr. Y are probabilistically constrained to one of the sure prospects in 0. The effect of this kind of constraint is to assign to each candidate a *subset* of A from which he selects an alternative. That is, the continuity constraints restrict each candidate to a specific class of lotteries and systematically exclude many alternatives.

In order to proceed in a general fashion, we now define the set of voters as

$$V = \{r, s, t\}$$

and the set of certain outcomes as

$$0 = \{o_r, o_s, o_t\},$$

where the subscripts distinguish outcomes and denote the voter for whom a particular outcome is most-preferred, e.g., voter r prefers o_r to all other

---

[17] The important point here is that the constraints limit voters' potential perceptions. For example, whether Humphrey was a dove or not in 1968, his participation in the incumbent administration influenced and restricted voters' perceptions of him.

[18] Examples of this abound in the folklore of American politics. The Democracy is the "party of the little man" and the "party of war"; the GOP is the "party of big business" and the "party of depression." For some empirical details, see Campbell, *et al.* (1960).

outcomes. The constraints are specified in the following assumptions:

$$\text{C.1 } p_x(r) \geq 1/2 + \epsilon \qquad \epsilon > 0$$

$$\text{C.2 } p_y(s) \geq 1/2 + \delta \qquad \delta > 0.$$

The first constraint states that Mr. X can choose any lottery over the elements of 0 so long as the probability number associated with o_r is greater than 1/2. An analogous interpretation applies to C.2.

We call voter t a *free voter* since no candidate is constrained to his most-preferred outcome. The particular form of the paradox of voting depends upon the preferences of t, namely whether he preferes o_r to o_s or o_s to o_r in the dyad (o_r, o_s). Once the free voter's preferences are known the precise form of the paradox is determined. These appear in table 4.

TABLE 4. Alternative Voting Paradoxes as a Function of the Free Voter's Preferences

| | | \multicolumn{3}{c}{Voter} | | |
		r	s	t
Outcome	o_r	1	0	$u_t(o_r)$
	o_s	$u_r(o_s)$	1	0
	o_t	0	$u_s(o_t)$	1

(a) Free Voter Prefers o_r to o_s

| | | \multicolumn{3}{c}{Voter} | | |
		r	s	t
Outcome	o_r	1	$u_s(o_r)$	0
	o_s	0	1	$u_t(o_s)$
	o_t	$u_r(o_t)$	0	1

(b) Free Voter Prefers o_s to o_r

For each case we present the conditions which insure Mr. Y a collectively most-preferred alternative. Analogous conditions, of course, exist for Mr. X. Since the constraints insure that each candidate receives the vote of the voter to whose preferred outcome he is probabilistically constrained, the free voter is the key to obtaining a winning coalition. For each of the cases of the paradox, then, we say that Mr. Y possesses a winning strategy if:

$$u_s(Y) > \max u_s(X) \tag{8}$$

and

$$u_t(Y) > \max u_t(X). \tag{9}$$

For case (a) a condition sufficient to insure a winning strategy for Mr. Y is, after some algebraic manipulation,

$$\delta < [1 - u_t(o_r)]\epsilon - (1/2)u_t(o_r) \tag{10}$$

where ϵ and δ are the constraint parameters of C.1 and C.2. Two implications follow from (10). First, if Mr. X's constraint is less binding than Mr. Y's, i.e., $\epsilon < \delta$, then Mr. Y does not possess a winning strategy. Second, upon rearranging (10), we may write the condition as

$$u_t(o_r) < \frac{\epsilon - \delta}{\epsilon + 1/2}. \tag{11}$$

The maximum value of the right-hand side of (11) is $1/2$ for $\epsilon = 1/2$ and $\delta = 0$. However, even in this situation (where the constraint parameters are more favorable to Mr. Y), if the free voter is "relatively satisfied" with o_r, i.e., $u_t(o_r) > 1/2$, then Mr. Y has no winning strategy.

For case (b), after some tedious algebraic manipulations, a general sufficient condition for Mr. Y, independent of ϵ and δ, is derived:

$$u_t(o_s) > \frac{u_s(o_r)}{1 + u_s(o_r)} \tag{12}$$

Inequality (12) holds for the most unfavorable configuration of constraint parameter values for Mr. Y. Thus, we say that it is independent of the parameter values. Of course, for more favorable values, the condition for a winning strategy weakens. However, in its present form ([12]), we can draw one interesting conclusion. Since the right-hand side of (12) has a maximum of $1/2$, it follows that if the free voter does not intensely prefer o_r, i.e., $u_t(o_s) > 1/2$, Mr. Y possesses a collectively most-preferred alternative in his constrained set.

VI. CONCLUDING REMARKS

In this essay we examined the three voter-three alternative cyclical majority problem under uncertainty. We introduced uncertainty via the lottery concept in order to examine the problem in a more general context (certainty is a special case of uncertainty) and to account for the paucity of observed paradoxes in real decision-making bodies. We found that once constraints are introduced, the paradox disappears. One might question whether our conclusions depend on the specific constraints we examined. However, other kinds of constraints, e.g., information-theoretic constraints, not presented here, support the conclusions reported above.

In addition to the introduction of uncertainty, our essay has emphasized two elements in the decision-making process not ordinarily treated by economists. Since the elements are inherently political in nature, they correct to some extent the economic bias in the field of political economy. The first element falls under the rubric "rules of entry." The traditional welfare economics treatment of collective choice takes the set of alternatives as given. Arrow, for example, speaks of the opportunity set, S, from which a collective choice is made (Arrow, 1963, p. 12). No mention is made, however, of how S came to be the appropriate set. Economists, it seems, are less concerned with so-called rules of entry than with concepts of efficiency and welfare. Steiner captures the flavor of this point in his discussion of the public interest:

> [I]t is . . . [economists] who are the primitives in the sophisticated world of public decision making. It is the [economists] who know *how* to choose between two public housing proposals but not *whether* public housing is right and proper; while the bureaucrats and Senators have less difficulty deciding when public housing is required than in choosing between alternative schemes of public housing. (Steiner, 1969, p. 14)

We are suggesting, then, that political scientists ought to be concerned with rules of entry as well as with rules of aggregation (voting procedures).

The second point we have made concerns the existence of constraints which operate on the mechanisms of group choice. In the cyclical majority problem, we found that certain kinds of constraints permit consistent collective choice. Although consistency is purchased at the cost of connectivity, it seems to us that the price is not exorbitant if constraints are in fact operative in real decision systems.

As to future research, generalization of the results reported here is a first-order priority. However, generalization or not, the points above provide some justification for political scientists to begin retracing the footsteps of the welfare economist in an effort to uncover some of the inherently political aspects of collective choice.

APPENDIX: PROOF OF THEOREM 3.

To prove this theorem it must be shown that no lottery satisfies (4)–(7) when paired against all other feasible lotteries. Our proof is constructive. It demonstrates that a simple "reallocation" of probability of an alleged collectively most-preferred lottery produces a lottery which can defeat it. Relabel the voters so that, after standardizing utility schedules, the voter receiving the highest expected utility is called I, the one receiving the second highest II, and the remaining one III. Since we draw no further implications directly related to the ranking technique, no interpersonal utility comparisons are made. Relabel the utility of I's second-ranked alternative a (instead of k, m, or n). Similarly, relabel the second-ranked alternatives of II and III as b and c, respectively. Finally, relabel the probability components of the alleged, collectively most-preferred lottery so that p is associated with I's most preferred outcome, p' with his second-ranked outcome, and p'' with the remaining outcome.

We prove the theorem for one particular arrangement of labels. By symmetry the result holds for the five other arrangements. Suppose $p_1 + p_2 k \geq p_2 + p_3 m \geq p_3 + p_1 n$. Then v_1, v_2, v_3 are relabeled I, II, and III, respectively. The utilities of the second-ranked alternatives k, m, and n, becomes a, b, and c, respectively. Finally, the probability numbers p_1, p_2, p_3 become p, p' p'', respectively.

Choose an ϵ and δ such that $\epsilon > 0$, $\delta > 0$, and $\epsilon + \delta \leq p$. Add ϵ to p', δ to p'', and subtract $\epsilon + \delta$ from p. We compare the lottery (p, p', p'') to the "reallocated" lottery $[p - (\epsilon + \delta), p' + \epsilon, p'' + \delta]$ and show that the latter can defeat the former by majority vote. The comparison is made in table 5.

TABLE 5. Lottery Comparison

Newly Numbered Voter	Utility Provided by	
	(p, p', p'')	$[p - (\epsilon + \delta), p' + \epsilon, p'' + \delta]$
I	$p + p'a$	$[p - (\epsilon + \delta)] + (p' + \epsilon)a$
II	$p' + p''b$	$(p' + \epsilon) + (p'' + \delta)b$
III	$p'' + pc$	$(p'' + \delta) + [p - (\epsilon + \delta)]c$

Voter I:

$\epsilon > \epsilon a$ since $a < 1$ by assumption of strong preference
$\epsilon + \delta > \epsilon a$ since $\delta > 0$ by construction
$0 > \epsilon a - (\epsilon + \delta)$ by subtraction
$p + p'a > p + p'a + [\epsilon a - (\epsilon + \delta)]$ by adding $p + p'a$ to both sides of the inequality
$$p + p'a > [p - (\epsilon + \delta)] + (p' + \epsilon)a.$$
From table 5, we have the relevant comparison. Voter I prefers (p, p', p'').

Voter II:

$p' + \epsilon > p'$ since $\epsilon > 0$ by construction
$p'' + \delta > p''$ since $\delta > 0$ by construction

$(p'' + \delta)b > p''b$ since $b > 0$ by assumption of strong preference
$(p' + \epsilon) + (p'' + \delta)b > p' + p''b$ by addition of first and third inequalities.
This gives us the required comparison. Voter II prefers $[p - (\epsilon + \delta),$
$p' + \epsilon, p'' + \delta]$.

Voter III:

Choose ϵ sufficiently small so that

$$\delta > \epsilon \frac{c}{1 - c}$$

$\delta(1 - c) > \epsilon c$ since $1 - c > 0$ by assumption of strong preference
$\delta > (\epsilon + \delta)c$ by addition of δc to both sides of the inequality
$(p'' + \delta) - p'' > (\epsilon + \delta)c$
$(p'' + \delta) - p'' > pc - [p - (\epsilon + \delta)]c$
$(p'' + \delta) + [p - (\epsilon + \delta)]c > p'' + pc$ by addition of $p'' + [p -$
$(\epsilon + \delta)]c$ to both sides of the inequality.
From table 5, then, voter III prefers $[p - (\epsilon + \delta), p' + \epsilon, p'' + \delta]$. Thus,
an objection exists. From lemma 1, it follows that (p, p', p'') is not collectively most-preferred. Since (p, p', p'') is an arbitrary lottery, it follows
that no lottery is collectively most-preferred.

Q.E.D.

Part 4

SPATIAL MODELLING OF COMPETITION

13. Parties, Voters, and the Risk Environment: A Mathematical Treatment of Electoral Competition Under Uncertainty

KENNETH A. SHEPSLE

In the last two decades, political science has witnessed a staggering growth of interest in electoral phenomena. The field has been inundated with studies, large and small. The terrain has been mapped with a surprising sophistication, both in concepts and techniques. This activity has resulted in the identification of a large number of empirical regularities.

More recently, deductive models of the electoral process have attracted attention, primarily because of the unquestionable need to bring some order to an overwhelming number of hypotheses and counter-hypotheses. The seminal piece in this more recent trend is Downs's classic, *An Economic Theory of Democracy* (Downs, 1957). Downs attempts to trace the implications of economic rationality for party campaigning and voter decision making. In this paper we take Downs's work as a starting point in order to examine the effects of risk and uncertainty on Downsian decision makers. In this effort we begin the task of integrating mathematical theories of decision making with rational theories of politics in order to provide explanations for a growing number of observed behavioral regularities.

This paper was prepared for delivery at the Sixty-sixth Annual Meeting of the American Political Science Association, Los Angeles, September, 1970. Mssrs. Richard Niemi, Peter Ordeshook, William Riker, and Herbert Weisberg read various drafts of this research paper and contributed by way of critical comment. The author remains responsible for errors, but is most willing to share any credits.

The first section is devoted to a cursory review of Downs's spatial model of party competition. We then propose a mathematical device which permits the introduction of uncertainty. In the third and fourth sections we trace the implications of uncertainty for voters and party strategists. Finally, we examine the effects of uncertainty on majority rule.

I. ANTHONY DOWNS, THE VOTER, AND THE POLITICAL PARTY

In the Downsian political world, there are two types of actors—citizens and candidates for office. Each actor is assumed to behave rationally. That is, each has a set of well-defined goals exhibiting a certain modicum of consistency, and each acts in accordance with his goals. Analytically, an actor is represented by a connected, transitive preference ordering over alternative outcomes. In order to complete a description of the actors, it is necessary to make some substantive statements about individual goals.

The Downsian citizen qua political actor is a utility maximizer. He is cognizant of the effects of governmental decisions on his well-being and thus has preferences for some collective choices rather than others. His "choice" of political behavior, then, is governed by his preference schedule over the set of possible collective decisions, the likelihood that his behavior will affect the collective decision, and the costs (benefits) of manifesting that behavior.[1] The most important resource at his disposal is the vote. Although other resources have productive uses, e.g., time, skills, money, access, "the vote merits attention because it is one of the most widely distributed of all political resources, because all decisions in a democratic form of government rest ultimately on votes, and because it is perhaps the major mechanism for translating popular preferences into governmental decisions" (Keech, 1968, p. 3). For our purposes, then, the citizen is a utility maximizer who employs a single resource—the vote—in order to influence the streams of utility he derives from governmental decisions.

The typical candidate of Downs's polity is an office-seeker. His behavior is determined solely by the effect it is likely to have on his quest for office. "Politicians in our model are motivated by the desire for power, prestige, and income. . . . Their primary objective is to be elected" (Downs, 1957, p. 30).[2] A candidate may have policy preferences, but they are of

---

[1] This point is carefully examined in Riker and Ordeshook (1968).

[2] Downs does not consider individual candidates in his model. Rather he chooses the political party as his unit of analysis. In order to avoid some thorny philosophical problems, he assumes that candidates of a political party are team-like in their behavior. In this way, Downs may consider the party as a unified entity (Downs, pp. 24–30).

marginal importance compared to his election goal. "Politicians . . . never seek office as a means of carrying out particular policies; their only goal is to reap the rewards of holding office, *per se*" (Downs, 1957, p. 28).[3]

Having described the actors we now turn to Downs's notion of spatial competition. Stokes characterizes it well:

> The root idea of Down's model is that the alternatives of government action on which political controversy is focused can be located in a one-dimensional space, along a left-right scale. At least for illustration, Downs interprets this dimension as the degree of government intervention in the economy. . . . Each voter can be located on the scale according to how much government control he wants and each party according to how much government control it advocates. (Stokes, 1963, p. 368)

For the purposes of this essay, we may assume that the voter possesses a von Neumann-Morgenstern utility function defined on a policy dimension. He perceives candidates as points on this dimension and assigns utility values to them, depending upon their positions. After assigning a utility value to each candidate, the voter, a utility maximizer, votes for the one which provides more utility.

The candidate's task is that of choosing a point on the dimension as his policy position. Assuming that he is an office-seeker, and assuming, with Downs, that he prefers more votes to less,[4] it follows that his policy choice is a function of the distribution of voter preferences. Downs shows that if voters have symmetric,[5] single-peaked preference functions, and if everyone votes, then candidates will converge in their policy selection to the median of the distribution of voter preferred points.[6] If abstention is permitted then the candidate decision-rule is altered. Candidate choice is based on a criterion of plurality maximization rather than vote maximization (at least for two-party systems). Convergence, in this case, does not necessarily occur. Nonetheless, the candidate posi-

---

[3] Downs is incorrect in assuming that this statement follows from the axiom of goal-seeking behavior. As a citizen of the polity, the politician is affected by governmental decisions as well. That is, the assumption of the primacy of office-holding does not preclude the existence of nonoffice-holding influences on utility schedules. Rather, it suggests a lexicographic ordering of preferences. Politicians with lexicographic utility functions are examined by Rothenberg (1961, pp. 231–34; 1965, pp. 1–38).

[4] Riker has argued that Downs's assumptions do not imply vote-maximizing behavior by candidates. Rather, they imply that strategy choice is based on the maximization of the probability of winning. See Riker (1962, chap. 4). Elsewhere we have commented on Downs's assertion and Riker's criticism (Shepsle, 1970a, chap. 6).

[5] Downs assumes only that distance (from one's preferred policy) is a measure of preference. However, given a policy continuum and single-peaked preference functions, this assumption is equivalent to symmetry.

[6] It may be shown that the median of the distribution of preferred points is a minimax strategy. See Shepsle (1970a, chap. 4).

tions are dependent on the shape of the voter distribution in this case as well.

In essence, then, Downs's model of spatial competition involves a unidimensional issue space, a set of voters with preferences defined on the space, and candidates represented by points in the space. Candidates choose their spatial locations (when there is no abstention) in order to maximize votes, and citizens vote for the candidate whose position they prefer.

We do the reader a disservice if we leave the impression that anything like a complete description of the Downsian model has been presented. Like any other complex theoretical argument, it should be read in the original. However, inasmuch as Downs's model has been something of a focal point for contemporary research, we suggest below some of its weak points.

Perhaps the weakest link in Downs's analysis is the assumption of a unidimensional issue space (Stokes, 1963, pp. 370-71). The political world is typically more complex, and a number of important strategic elements, e.g., coalition of minorities strategies, are lost if multidimensionality is not admitted.[7] Second, turnout may be as important a variable as vote direction (Kramer, 1966, pp. 137-60). The absence of its formal treatment by Downs has created a void which, judging from the sheer quantity of papers on the topic, a number of scholars abhor.[8] A third point of dispute involves Downs's party decision-rule. Riker (1962) has defended a probability maximization decision-rule on the basis of his "size principle." Hinich and Ordeshook (1970) examine two decision-rules—vote maximization and plurality maximization—in the context of variable participation. Downs's concept of rationality has been questioned in several different ways. Riker and Ordeshook (1968, pp. 25-43) find the concept too restrictive. Choices, they argue, do not depend exclusively on consequences. Actions, independent of outcomes, have implications for utility streams. In addition, one might question the information demands Downs makes of his actors and their implications for rational behavior. Finally, "the assumption of a commonly perceived space of party competition that allows the model to serve at once as a theory of voter motivation and of party positioning" (Stokes, 1963, p. 374) imposes a severe restriction on the applicability of the model. However, as Stokes recognizes, the complexity which accompanies the introduction of subjective features would overwhelm the theoretical structure.

Although the criticisms are important, the Downsian model has survived

---

[7] See Davis and Hinich (1966; 1967; 1968); Davis, Hinich, and Ordeshook (1970), and Chapman (1967; 1968).

[8] See Garvey (1966), Ordeshook (1969; 1970) and Hinich and Ordeshook (1969; 1970; 1971),

a decade as a basis for the formal treatment of electoral competition. The research we have cited represents attempts to build upon Downs's basic scheme by removing some of its weaknesses. Our essay follows this pattern.[9] We examine a structural feature of the environment and its implications for voter and candidate decision making. The structural feature is called the *risk environment*. We contend that the voting decision is analagous to the decision to purchase an insurance policy or a lottery ticket. It is a decision involving *probable* outcomes. Thus, a decision calculus for contingencies of risk and uncertainty is especially appropriate. In addition, as we see below, the uncertain nature of voter decision making has strategic importance for candidates—importance that does not go unnoticed. In the next section we specify the concept of uncertainty more carefully and present an analytical device, the lottery ticket, which permits us to incorporate uncertainty in the spatial model.

II. UNCERTAINTY AND ELECTORAL COMPETITION

Why introduce uncertainty into an already complex analysis? We believe there are several reasons why a consideration of uncertainty serves as a natural extension and generalization of Downs's work, on the one hand, and as a corrective on the other. First, we can accept, with Downs, the assumption that politicians do not lie—that false information does not enter the communication system—while still recognizing that it may be advantageous for politicians to speak "half truths" and that they may vary their appeals with variations in audience and political climate. That is, incentives to equivocate are present in electoral contingencies.

A second justification of the examination of uncertainty follows from the nonteamlike behavior of parties (see note 2). Downs chooses to treat the competition for office as a contest between teams of activists. Since the internal workings of each team involve complete cooperation among members, the team (party) may be treated as a unified entity and the analysis is accordingly simplified. The simplification effected, however, ignores the deviant behavior of the candidate whose official career depends on an electorate different from those of his colleagues. This observation "underscores the limits to the empirical usefulness of models that assume that party leaders always act in common. . . . An awareness that party leaders (i.e., politicians) act for private motives ought to prompt an extension of models of rational behavior . . ." (Schoenberger, 1969, pp. 520-21). The concept of uncertainty permits us to retain the team notion by tempering its unique, unambiguous identity.

---

[9] However, it should be pointed out that we make some of the same simplifying assumptions in order to facilitate our own analysis.

This point, along with a third—namely, that voters possess neither perfect nor complete information about candidates—further underscores the need to introduce uncertainty formally. "[U]ncertainty and the lack of information prevent even the most intelligent and well-informed voter from behaving in precisely the fashion [Downs has] described" (Downs, 1957, pp. 45-46). The voter can, at best, determine only an *expected party position* in the policy space.

We are now prepared to specify our meaning of uncertainty. In the mathematical decision theory literature, one finds decision contingencies partitioned into those of certainty, risk, and uncertainty. Specifically,

> We shall say that we are in the realm of decision making under:
> (a) *Certainty* if each action is known to lead invariably to a specific outcome. . . .
> (b) *Risk* if each action leads to one of a set of possible specific outcomes, each outcome occurring with a known probability. The probabilities are assumed to be known to the decision maker. . . .
> (c) *Uncertainty* if [any of the actions] has as its consequence a set of possible specific outcomes, but where the probabilities of these outcomes are completely unknown or are not even meaningful. (Luce and Raiffa, 1957, p. 13)

Elsewhere we have shown that these three categories are not logically distinct—that *all* decision problems may be treated, subjectively at least, as risky choice (Shepsle, 1970a, chap. 1). Briefly, we argued, on the one hand, that certainty is clearly a degenerate case of risk—a known probability distribution collapsed on a single point. Uncertainty, on the other hand, seems to describe a contingency in which the *process* by which outcomes are generated is unknown. This does not imply, however, that probabilities of outcomes are unknown or that actors are unable to act as if they possess knowledge about probabilities. "A moment's reflection will make it clear that there are some logical difficulties involved in giving meaning to the statement that the probabilities are unknown. If we insist that we are *completely ignorant* as to which of the events [outcomes] . . . will occur, it is hard to escape the conclusion that all the events [outcomes] are equally probable. This . . . implies that the probabilities become known. . ." (Borch, 1968, p. 78). If we are only *partially ignorant*, then there are several decision-rules, e.g., minimax, minimax regret, we might employ which exploit the available information, and which, in effect, imply an expected utility calculation. In either case we have a contingency of risk. Thus, the philosophical distinction ordinarily made for decision contingencies does not prove to be fruitful for our purposes; instead, we assume that all decision contingencies may be placed under the rubric of risk.

We now may replace the Downsian candidate of the certain world—a point on the policy continuum—with the risky candidate. Analytically, the risky candidate is represented by a probability distribution or a *lottery ticket* defined on the policy continuum. With parties represented by lottery tickets, the *risk environment* is identified by three characteristics. These characteristics describe the parameters necessary to determine a priori expectations about competition between risky alternatives.

First, the nature of risky competition is related to the *shape* of voter utility functions. A voter's evaluation of a risky alternative—via the expected utility calculation—depends on the functional form of his utility schedule.[10] This feature is demonstrated in figure 1, where the utility functions of three voters, each of whom has an identical preference ordering over the alternatives, are graphed. Note that the shapes of the utility functions are different. Suppose the issue in dispute involves a budgetary dimension. The voters are to choose between two budget policies. One policy involves a great deal of uncertainty about future expenditures, e.g., the possibility of cost-overruns. To keep things simple, suppose this policy may be represented by the lottery $L = (\frac{1}{2}x, \frac{1}{2}z)$—prob (budget $= \$x) = \frac{1}{2} =$ prob (budget $= \$z$). Suppose its expected dollar value, $\frac{1}{2}x + \frac{1}{2}z$, is y. The second budget policy involves an expenditure of y dollars with certainty. As the graphs indicate, a simple expected utility calculation shows that the first voter prefers the first policy (L), the second voter prefers the second policy (y), and the third voter is indifferent, *despite the fact that their preference orderings are identical.* Stated in terms of gambles, for a fair gamble, i.e., one for which the net expected value is zero, a decision maker with a convex utility schedule (figure 1a) prefers the gamble to the certainty of the expected value, one with a concave schedule (figure 1b) prefers the certainty of the expected value, and one with a linear schedule (figure 1c) is indifferent between the two. These decision makers are said to be risk-acceptant, risk-averse, and risk-neutral, respectively (Friedman and Savage, 1948).[11]

A second parameter defining the risk environment is the *range* of the risk. The range determines which policy alternatives have positive proba-

---

[10] The fact that Downs employed distributions of voter *most-preferred points,* and did not worry about the functional form of utility schedules, suggests why he might not have observed the strategic possibilities that uncertainty permits.

[11] That is, if $p(x)$ is the lottery, and $\bar{p}$ its expected value along the x-dimension, then if decision maker i has a concave, twice differentiable, utility function, $u_i(x)$, i.e., $u_i''(x) < 0$, then

$$\sum_x p(x)u_i(x) < u_i(\bar{p}).$$

If $u_i(x)$ is convex, i.e., $u_i''(x) \geq 0$, then

$$\sum_x p(x)u_i(x) \geq u_i(\bar{p}).$$

For the continuous case, replace the summation sign with the Riemann integral. See Shepsle (1970a, chap. 2) and Pratt (1964, pp. 122–36) for additional clarification.

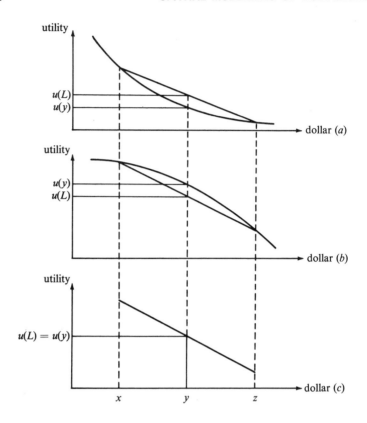

FIGURE 1

bility weight and in which portion of an individual's utility function the risk is located.

Finally, there is the *density* of the risk which provides the weights, i.e., probability numbers, for policy alternatives.

Given these three parameters and the assumption that voters are (expected) utility maximizers, we can analyze party competition and voter decision making with somewhat weaker information demands for the actors than in Downs's model. Voters simply choose among the ambiguous alternatives so as to maximize expected utility. *Parties, on the other hand, may manipulate the risk environment to their electoral advantage.*

III. VOTER CHOICE AND THE RISK ENVIRONMENT

As we noted above, there are two categories of actors in the model: voters and candidates (parties). Voters cast ballots for candidates under conditions of "one man, one vote" and mandatory voting in order to influence "the streams of utility derived from government activity" (Downs, 1957, p. 36). Whereas policy is treated as an end by the voter, it is a resource for the candidate. Candidates "formulate policies in order to win elections, rather than win elections in order to formulate policies" (Downs, 1957, p. 28).

We assume that voter preferences are well-defined in the policy space which, along with Downs, we suppose is unidimensional. Specifically, we assume that each voter possesses a von Neumann-Morgenstern utility function which is symmetric and single-peaked.

Finally, we distinguish between incumbent and challenging candidates. The former is, and has been, the prime political mover and is treated in a distinctive fashion by the communications media. Not only is his visibility enhanced by the communications media, which transmit his messages (intended and otherwise) to the voter; but also he is in a position to communicate directly to voters through his control of government activities which alter their utility streams. The challenger, on the other hand, is an advocate. Voters are informed of his policy stands only through his pronouncements, and even these are given less attention than the incumbent's.

The thesis we propose is that of voting as risky choice.[12] The voter is faced with two alternatives (assuming a two-party political system), neither of which are clear and unambiguous. On the one hand, the variety of competing, often conflicting, points-of-view the voter employs to inform himself of candidate intentions fails to provide clear cues about these intentions. On the other hand, uncertainty may be of strategic benefit to the candidates. If so, the self-interest axiom implies that uncertainty may be generated purposely.

This last statement clarifies our reasons for distinguishing between incumbent and challenger. The position of the incumbent in the structure of government and in the communications network provides the voter with more information about this candidate than about the challenger. This suggests that the incumbent is always perceived as a less uncertain entity. In fact, we suppose that all voters

1. perceive the incumbent's position with *certainty*,
2. perceive the challenger as inherently risky, and
3. agree about their perceptions, although they will, in general, differ on preferences.

That is, information is received and interpreted by all voters identically. There is agreement on the incumbent's position, the range of possible positions for the challenger, and the probability distribution over that

---

[12] We use the terms "risk" and "uncertainty" interchangeably. Unless otherwise specified, we intend these terms to convey the same meaning as the technical definition of risk given earlier—namely, a known probability distributions over outcomes.

range (an *information consensus*). This assumption,[13] though obviously a distortion of reality, facilitates the analysis and leads, we believe, to several nonobvious insights.

As a baseline we suppose that the incumbent, a rational competitor, behaves as though he were in a certain world, even though he knows his opponent will be perceived as inherently uncertain. As a number of scholars have shown (Downs, 1957, chap. 8; Black, 1958, pp. 16-18; Garvey, 1966; Davis and Hinich, 1966, 1967, 1968; Tullock, 1967, pp. 59-61; Ordeshook, 1969; Hinich and Ordeshook, 1970), the self-interest axiom and full participation imply the following:

THEOREM 1. For an electorate composed of N voters (assume N odd), each of which has a single-peaked utility curve arrayed along the issue dimension from most extreme in one direction to most extreme in the other, the policy positions represented by the median "most-preferred" point, a_{med}, receives at least a simple majority against every other point, and it is the only point that can do so.

Thus, we suppose that the rational incumbent moves to the median, and that the entire electorate perceives this to be his position. The question may now be put: In an uncertain world can a_{med} be characterized as the majority preferred position? In other words, does the availability of risky strategies to the challenger invalidate the theorem presented above?

In order to examine these questions, we postulate reasonable utility and risk functions, and then trace the logic of risky choice for an individual voter. This amounts to comparing the utility he derives from the certain position of the incumbent to the expected utility derived from the risky challenger. We focus on the single voter's choice in this section, taking up the more complex problem of party strategy selection shortly.

We suppose that a voter's utility function may be characterized by a normally distributed random variable. This representation, though certainly not general, will suffice to make our point. The ith voter's utility for policy position x is:

$$u_i(x) = \frac{g_i \cdot \exp\left[-(x - a_i)^2/2s_i^2\right]}{s_i\sqrt{[2\pi]}} \tag{1}$$

---

[13] The reader may wish to refer, from time to time, to the last few paragraphs, for they contain a number of assumptions which underpin the analysis that follows. The assumptions may be partitioned into:
1. those defining voter preferences (symmetry, single-peakedness);
2. those defining voter decision-rules (mandatory voting, expected utility maximization);
3. those describing the status of voter information (information consensus);
4. those distinguishing the candidates and their permissible strategies; and
5. those relating to party decision-rules.
Other assumptions are discussed as they arise.

where g_i is a positive constant, a_i is i's most-preferred point, and s_i is the standard deviation.[14] We assume that $s_i = s$ (finite) for all i, so that all voters are characterized by identically shaped utility functions, differing only in most-preferred points. Equation (1) identifies the first element of the risk environment: the shape of voter utility functions.[15]

In order to specify the second and third elements of the risk environment, we invoke the information consensus assumption. All voters isolate a common interval within which the challenger's policy intention lies. However, voters possess neither knowledge of the precise point in the interval nor additional information which might serve to narrow the range further. Having no justification to employ a "partial ignorance" decision-rule (Borch, 1968, pp. 77-87; Shepsle, 1970a, chap. 1), the voter applies Laplace's Law of Insufficient Reason:

> In the absence of any information concerning the likelihood of alternative events, treat the events as equiprobable.

In probability terms, the challenging candidate's strategy is perceived as a uniform probability distribution over the finite interval $[a, b]$:

$$r(x) = \frac{1}{b - a} \text{ for } a \leq x \leq b$$
$$= 0 \text{ elsewhere.} \qquad (2)$$

Equation (2) defines the *risk function*, specifying its density and its domain. In the next section we investigate how the challenger may manipulate voter perceptions by altering the domain of $r(x)$. We further assume that $[a, b]$ is an interval of fixed length with a_{med} as its midpoint. That is, the expectation of $r(x)$ is a_{med}: $\int_a^b x r(x)\, dx = a_{\mathrm{med}}$.

The expected utility of the risky alternative is represented by the convolution integral:

$$\int_a^b r(x)u(x)\, dx.$$

---

[14] Since g_i affects the height of the utility function, which will be of no consequence in the analysis, we set it to unity for all i. For notational convenience we drop the subscript i. Unless otherwise specified, the analysis focuses on a randomly selected voter.

[15] Our choice of the normal utility function is motivated by three considerations:
1. it satisfies the single-peakedness assumption;
2. it is symmetric; and
3. it is characterized by both concave and convex regions.

We emphasize that the general implication of this section does not depend on the particular choice of function made. Although much of the mathematical development of this section may be taken as example, the general implication holds nonetheless.

The ith voter prefers the challenging candidate if

$$\int_a^b r(x)u(x)\, dx > u(a_{\text{med}}) \tag{3}$$

where $u(a_{\text{med}})$ is the utility derived from the incumbent's position. From (2), and some algebraic manipulation, the challenger is preferred if

$$\int_a^b \left(\frac{1}{b-a}\right) u(x)\, dx > u(a_{\text{med}})$$

$$\int_a^b u(x)\, dx > (b-a)\cdot u(a_{\text{med}})$$

$$U(b) - U(a) > (b-a)\cdot u(a_{\text{med}}), \tag{4}$$

where $U(x)$ is the cumulative normal density.

At this point we introduce the well-known Mean Value Theorem:

Let $y = f(x)$ be continuous for $a \le x \le b$ and possess a derivative at each x for $a < x < b$. Then there is at least one number c between ab such that

$$f(b) - f(a) = f'(c)\cdot(b-a). \tag{5}$$

If we let $f(a) = U(a)$ and $f(b) = U(b)$, then the theorem implies that there is a point(s) $c \in [a, b]$ which serves as a certainty equivalent for the risk $r(x)$. Given the special kind of monotonicity associated with single-peaked functions, it follows that, for a particular c, there are points in $[a, b]$ less preferred to it by the ith voter, as well as points more preferred to it. That is, the point(s) c partitions $[a, b]$ into preference subintervals vis-à-vis $r(x)$. We would like to determine the conditions which would place a_{med} in a subinterval less preferred than c (and hence $r(x)$). If those conditions are satisfied, then $r(x)$ is preferred to (provides greater expected utility than) a_{med}, and the ith voter supports the challenger.

In order to locate the point(s) c, we first exploit the assumption that places a_{med} at the midpoint of the interval $[a, b]$. Symbolically, for some $k > 0$, the assumption asserts relationship (6):

$$a = a_{\text{med}} - ks$$

$$b = a_{\text{med}} + ks. \tag{6}$$

That is, a and b are equidistant (in standard deviation units) from a_{med}. From (2), (5), and (6), the equation of indifference follows:

$$\int_{a_{\text{med}}-ks}^{a_{\text{med}}+ks} u(x)\, dx = 2ks\cdot u(c). \tag{7}$$

for some $c \in [a, b]$. In figure 2 we present a graphic representation of the equation of indifference. The left-hand side of (7) is the area under $u(x)$ in $[a, b]$, while the right-hand side is the area of the rectangle of height $u(c)$ and width $2ks = b - a$. Of course, the two areas are equal.

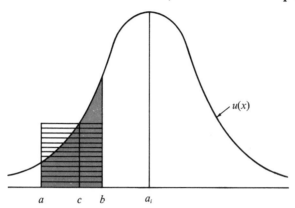

FIGURE 2

Although a_{med} is not shown in figure 2, its location has a bearing on the analysis that follows. We know, from (6), that a_{med} is the midpoint of $[a, b]$. Now, we relate it to the ith voter and his utility schedule:

$$a_{\text{med}} = a_i + w_i s, \qquad (8)$$

where w_i is a real number. Substituting (8) into (6),

$$a = a_{\text{med}} - ks = (a_i + w_i s) - ks = a_i + (w_i - k)s$$
$$b = a_{\text{med}} + ks = (a_i + w_i s) + ks = a_i + (w_i + k)s. \qquad (9)$$

Substituting (9) into (7) we may solve directly for c:

$$U[a_i + (w_i + k)s] - U[a_i + (w_i - k)s] = 2ks \cdot u(c)$$
$$= \frac{2ks}{\sqrt{2\pi} s} \exp\left[-\frac{(c - a_i)^2}{2s^2}\right]$$
$$c = a_i \pm \left[-2 \log_e \frac{U[a_i + (w_i + k)s] - U[a_i + (w_i - k)s]}{\sqrt{2k^2/\pi}}\right]^{1/2}. \qquad (10)$$

In (10) two points are mathematically possible (due to the fact that the inverse utility function is not single-valued). However, in many cases only one of them falls in $[a, b]$. In particular, for $w_i \geq k$ the positive sign applies, for $w_i \leq -k$ the negative sign holds, and for $-k < w_i < k$ either may hold.

From (10) the conditions which imply preference for the challenger can be derived. For the case in which $w_i \geq k$, i's most-preferred point is to the left of the entire interval $[a, b]$.[16] Thus, $c \in [a, b]$ is to the right of a_i, i.e., $c > a_i$. Since $u(x)$ is monotonically decreasing to the right of a_i, it follows that any point to the right of c is less-preferred than c. Therefore, if $a_{\text{med}} = a_i + w_i s > c$, then the challenger is preferred. From (10), we obtain the following condition:

$$w_i > \left[-2 \log_e \frac{U[a_i + (w_i + k)s] - U[a_i + (w_i - k)s]}{\sqrt{2k^2/\pi}} \right]^{1/2}. \quad (11)$$

For the case in which $w_i \leq -k$, (11) with inequality sign reversed is the condition obtained. Finally, for $-k < w_i < k$, either of the two inequalities applies. We summarize these results in

THEOREM 2. If either of the forms of (11) is satisfied, then the ith voter prefers the challenging candidate, whose expected position is a_{med}, to an optimizing incumbent candidate.

Stating a sufficient condition is not the same as establishing existence. Without bothering with the "espilontics," however, it easily may be shown, via simulation, that values of a_i, w_i, and k exist for which one of the variants of (11) is satisfied. At the very least, this theorem establishes the *partisan* nature of the risk environment. That the risk environment may be exploited for partisan reasons is a consequence of the following.

THEOREM 3. Consider an electorate composed of N voters. Let

$$d = \begin{array}{ll} (N + 1)/2 & \text{if } N \text{ is odd} \\ (N/2) + 1 & \text{if } N \text{ is even.} \end{array}$$

Select the set D, comprising d voters, such that $|a_i - a_{\text{med}}|$ is smaller for any $i \in D$ than for any $i \notin D$. For a given risk, $r(x)$, if (11) or its variant holds for any $i \in D$, then the incumbent is defeated.

To establish this theorem, note that D is the set of voters, a bare majority in number, whose most-preferred points $\{a_i; i \in D\}$ are closest to a_{med}. If one of the $i \in D$—say, the one for which $|a_i - a_{\text{med}}|$ is maximum—satisfies (11), then (11) holds for all voters more distant from a_{med}. Since D is a bare majority, $D - \{i\}$ is a minority. Its complement, i.e., those voters satisfying (11), then, is a majority. The theorem is established.

---

[16] The interval $[a, b]$ extends a distance ks in either direction from a_{med}. If $w_i \geq k$, then, from (8), a_i is to the left of a_{med} (since $k > 0$) and is entirely outside $[a, b]$:

In the next section we systematically examine some of the strategic possibilities that flow from the results here. For now, suffice it to say that risky strategies bear electoral fruit in some elections. Voters may prefer an equivocal stand by a candidate, one that admits the possibility of a highly preferred policy position if the candidate is elected, to the certainty of a more moderate (yet only marginally preferred) position. That is, in some contingencies an unequivocal stand is an antagonistic stand for some voters, and the antagonized voters may consititute a majority. This result provides an explanation (a sufficient condition) for a frequently observed event: a candidate's "addiction to equivocation and ambiguity" (Key, 1958, p. 241).

IV. PARTY STRATEGY SELECTION AND THE RISK ENVIRONMENT

Frequently, professional political observers note, with despair, the ambiguous role played by the major political parties in American electoral processes. "Why," asks Pendleton Herring,

> cannot there be more direction and less confusion in our political life? Surveying the history of our parties, we find discord among their members and frequent evasion in their platforms. Our parties have generally side-stepped the issues that have divided the nation most deeply. (Herring, 1965, p. 188)

On the critical issues, upon which parties are expected to enunciate policy statements, politicians opt for vagueness and ambiguity. In this section we argue that uncertainty, i.e. "vagueness and ambiguity," has implications for electoral outcomes, that politicians are aware of its implications, and hence that politicians manipulate uncertainty to their advantage.

Some assumptions are needed to facilitate the analysis.[17] We assume that all voters, $\bar{V} = \{v_i\}$, possess symmetric, single-peaked utility functions, u_i, with most-preferred point a_i. The u_i are defined on the real line which also contitutes the strategy sets of the candidates. The density of voter preferred points, i.e., the Downsian voter distribution, is represented by $f(\cdot)$, and its integral by the distribution function $F(\cdot)$. Citizens, all of whom vote, are expected utility maximizers, and parties are vote maximizers. Finally, we assume there exists a finite interval $[C, D]$, on the real line, containing the preferred point of every voter. By construction, the midpoint of $[C, D]$ is a_{med}.

In most of this section we restrict attention to a special class of risky strategies. Specifically, the risky candidate is represented by a proba-

---

[17] A detailed discussion of these assumptions is found in Shepsle (1970a, chap. 3).

bility function $r(x)$, defined on the real line, where $r(x)$ is a member of the family of uniform risks, R, i.e.,

$$R = \left\{ r(x) \mid r(x) = \frac{1}{\theta}, \, 0 \le \theta \le |D - C| \right\}.$$

Each $r(x) \in R$ must be finite in length (less than $|D - C|$) and consistent with the axioms of probability. Whenever possible, we generalize to *any* probability distribution, $p(x)$.

Our task, now, is to examine electoral contingencies in order to identify those that favor risky strategies and those that favor certain strategies. Initially, we assume that the challenger is restricted to nondegenerate risks, while the incumbent is restricted to degenerate risks (certain positions).

Without proof we state

LEMMA. For every $r \in R$ not restricted to $[C, D]$, there exists an $r^* \in R$, restricted to $[C, D]$, that obtains a majority when paired against it.[18]

This lemma permits us to restrict risk functions to $[C, D]$. With an appropriate construction of $[C, D]$, one can show that for some $r(x)$ in $[C, D]$, risk functions not so restricted are unable to defeat it.

Recalling that a voter is *risk averse* if he prefers the certain alternative to a risk with the same expected position, the following result is easily proved:

THEOREM 4. If every voter is risk averse in the interval $[C, D]$, then a_{med} defeats any $r \in R$.[19]

PROOF. Three cases exhaust all possibilities:

1. $r \in R$, r distributed over $[C, a_{\text{med}})$,
2. $r \in R$, r distributed over $(a_{\text{med}}, D]$, and
3. $r \in R$, r distributed over $[E, F] \subseteq [C, D]$, $a_{\text{med}} \in [E, F]$.

We show that the theorem is true in case (1). The other cases follow in a similar manner.

For all i for which $a_i \ge a_{\text{med}}$, any point $p \in [C, a_{\text{med}}]$ is less preferred than a_{med}: $u_i(p) \le u_i(a_{\text{med}})$, where the strict inequality holds for some p. This follows from the single-peakedness of u_i. Therefore, the convolution integral (continuous weighted average) over the domain of the risk is less than $u_i(a_{\text{med}})$:

$$\int_C^{a_{\text{med}}} r(x)u_i(x) \, dx < u_i(a_{\text{med}}).$$

---

[18] The proof of this lemma is found in Shepsle (1970a, pp. 141–44).
[19] The electorates considered by Davis and Hinich are composed of voters all of whom are risk averse. In particular, they have quadratic loss functions. See Davis and Hinich (1966; 1967; 1968).

The ith voter, then, prefers a_{med}. But $a_i \in [a_{med}, D]$ and $\int_{a_{med}}^{D} f(x)\, dx = 0.5$. Therefore, at least a simple majority prefers a_{med}.

Similar proofs may be constructed for the remaining cases

Q.E.D.

The theorem can be generalized to the entire class of risky strategies. We state, without proof, the generalized version as

THEOREM 5. If all voters have strictly concave utility functions in $[C, D]$, then a_{med} defeats *any* nondegenerate risk.

Several substantive implications follow from these theorems. First, the theorems provide a nonobvious explanation for the electoral dominance of incumbent officials. In a political climate often regarded as consensual and low-keyed, the incumbent's ability to commit himself with certainty is a marked advantage. Combine this observation with theorem 1, above, and it is seen that the median preferred point is strategically desirable. Thus, it is likely that the incumbent candidate will move to the median, *ceteris paribus*, and will be more successful than the challenger in committing himself to that policy.

A second implication concerns a potential campaign tactic. For the class of low-keyed issues (those for which voters are risk averse), it is not necessary for a candidate to discredit his opponent's position in order to win. He need only discredit the certainty with which his opponent advocates his policy positions. That is, vagueness is as much a sin as nonoptimal policy selection in consensus politics. Commitment, then, is an important feature of campaign strategy (Schelling, 1960, *passim*). Of course the challenger often finds it difficult to discredit the certainty of the incumbent's policy position.

Before examining the effects of uncertainty in so-called high intensity political environments, we can relax the distinction between incumbent and challenger somewhat. In order to do this, several new terms are defined. First, we say that of two risk functions, r and r^*, in R, one is *less risky* than the other if its domain has smaller length than the other. In figure 3

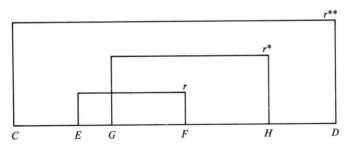

FIGURE 3

r is less risky than r^* which, in turn, is less risky than r^{**}, i.e., $|E - F| < |G - H| < |C - D|$. Second we say that a candidate's strategy is *winning* if it is feasible (i.e., in the candidate's strategy set), and if it can defeat (secure a majority against) any strategy in his opponent's strategy set. Three properties of this definition should be noted:

1. It is impossible for both candidates to possess winning strategies.
2. Winning strategies need not be unique.
3. Winning strategies need not exist at all.

Finally, we distinguish between incumbent and challenger by assuming that the former is less risky than the latter.

With the new concepts and the additional assumption, we prove

THEOREM 6. If a *majority* of voters is risk averse in the interval $[C, D]$, then the challenger has no winning strategy.

PROOF. We show that for any $r^*(x) \in R$ offered by the challenger, there exists an $r(x) \in R$, nested in the interval associated with $r^*(x)$, which defeats it. Let $r^*(x)$ be distributed over $[E, F] \subseteq [C, D]$ and let $r(x)$ be distributed over $[G, H] \subset [E, F]$. In addition, suppose that $[G, H]$ is a symmetrically nested subinterval of $[E, F]$, i.e., $|E - G| = |F - H|$. Thus $\int_G^H xr(x)\, dx = \int_E^F xr^*(x)\, dx$. In figure 4 the utility function, $u_i(x)$, of a risk-averse voter is graphed.

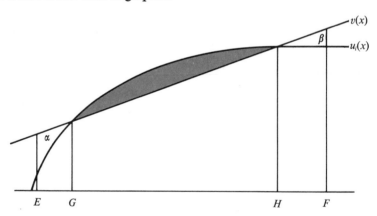

FIGURE 4

Consider the linear function $v(x)$, where

$$v(G) = u_i(G)$$
$$v(H) = u_i(H).$$

That is, $v(x)$ intersects $u_i(x)$ at $x = G$ and $x = H$. We write $u(r)$ and $u(r^*)$ to represent the utility to the ith voter of $r(x)$, and r^*x, respectively.

$$u(r) = \int_G^H r(x)u(x)\, dx = \frac{\int_G^H u(x)\, dx}{H - G}$$

$$= \frac{\int_G^H [u(x) + v(x) - v(x)]\, dx}{H - G}$$

$$= \frac{\int_G^H v(x)\, dx}{H - G} + \frac{\int_G^H [u(x) - v(x)]\, dx}{H - G},$$

where the latter integral is the shaded area in figure 4. But, $\int_G^H v(x)\, dx/(H - G) = \int_E^F v(x)\, dx/(F - E)$, since $v(x)$ is linear and $[G, H]$ is symmetrically nested in $[E, F]$.
Thus,

$$u(r) = \frac{\int_E^F v(x)\, dx}{F - E} + \frac{\int_G^H [u(x) - v(x)]\, dx}{H - G}$$

$$> \frac{\int_E^F v(x)\, dx}{F - E} + \frac{\int_G^H [u(x) - v(x)]\, dx}{F - E}$$

since $|F - E| > |H - G|$. From figure 4, the integrals above (neglecting the denominators for the moment) may be seen to represent the area under $u(x)$ in $[E, F]$ plus the two areas, α and β. The above inequality may be rewritten:

$$u(r) > \frac{\alpha + \beta + \int_E^F u(x)\, dx}{F - E}$$

Since α and β are positive, it follows, a fortiori, that

$$u(r) > \frac{\int_E^F u(x)\, dx}{F - E} = \int_E^F r^*(x)u(x)\, dx = u(r^*).$$

By transitivity, then, $u(r) > u(r^*)$. Since this result is obtained for any concave utility function, and since a majority of the voters is risk averse, a nested risk can defeat any strategy proposed by the challenger.

Q.E.D.

Theorem 6 demonstrates the strategic problem confronting the riskier candidate (the challenger) in a risk-averse world. For every strategy he selects, his opponent has a strategy which defeats it. Nothing is said, however, about the existence of a *winning strategy* for the incumbent. In order to isolate winning strategies (if they exist), one must specify:

1. the precise number (percentage) of risk-averse voters, and
2. the distribution of risk-averse voters.

The premise of theorem 6—the existence of a majority of risk-averse voters—is not precise enough to satisfy the specifications above.

We do not propose to deal with the existence question in a systematic fashion at this time. Rather, we demonstrate the existence of winning strategies for electorates composed entirely of risk-averse voters (the Davis-Hinich electorate). This procedure satisfies condition (1) above, and eliminates the need for condition (2). The simplification permits us to state

THEOREM 7. If all voters are risk-averse, then the less risky candidate's minimal risk, symmetric about a_{med}, is winning.

PROOF. Let the incumbent's minimal risk, $r(x)$, be distributed symmetrically about a_{med} in the interval $[a_{med} - \delta, a_{med} + \delta]$. Suppose the challenger's risk, $r^*(x)$, with length $\theta > 2\delta$, has expectation $\bar{r}^* < a_{med}$. Choose a v_i for whom $a_i \geq a_{med}$. By concavity and the inequality $\theta > 2\delta$, the certainty equivalent of $r^*(x)$ is to the left of the certainty equivalent of $r(x)$. Therefore, $u_i(r^*) < u_i(r)$ by virtue of the monotonicity associated with single-peaked functions. For the case in which $\bar{r}^* > a_{med}$, it may be shown by a similar argument that any voter for whom $a_i < a_{med}$ prefers $r(x)$ to $r^*(x)$. In either case, the class of voters that prefer $r(x)$ total at least a simple majority. For the case in which $\bar{r}^* = a_{med}$, $\theta > 2\delta$ and concavity imply that *all* voters prefer $r(x)$ to $r^*(x)$.

Q.E.D.

Theorems 4, 5, 6, and 7 provide additional support for the assertions of Black, Downs, and Davis and Hinich. The median and its immediate neighborhood are strategically compelling. Moreover, we have seen that another strategic feature is important in spatial competition, namely *commitment*. The optimal strategy in a risk-averse polity involves committing oneself irrevocably to the median, as well as discrediting the credibility of one's opponent. The conclusion one must draw at this point, then, is that the major effect of the risk environment is negative—it undoes commitment. However, once one removes the restriction of risk averseness, this conclusion no longer obtains. We now turn to an examination of electorates composed partially (entirely) of risk-acceptant voters.

Recall that a voter is said to be risk acceptant if he prefers a lottery (probability distribution) to its fair equivalent. That is, he prefers a lottery to a certain alternative equal to the expected position of the lottery. In addition, if a voter is risk acceptant, then his utility function is convex, i.e., $u''(x) > 0$, in some regions. First we consider the competition between a challenger constrained to uncertain prospects and an incumbent constrained to sure prospects.

THEOREM 8. If a *majority* of voters is risk acceptant in some interval containing a_{med}, then *any* risk with an expectation at a_{med} defeats the median most-preferred point.

PROOF. Let $p(x)$ be a risk over an interval B such that

$$(1)\ a_{\text{med}} \in B$$

$$(2)\ \int_B xp(x)\, dx = a_{\text{med}}$$

$p(x)$ satisfies the premises of the theorem. Choose a voter i who is risk acceptant. For i,

$$\int_B u(x)p(x)\, dx > u\left[\int_B xp(x)\, dx\right]$$

since $u''(x) > 0$, $x \in B$. But, $\int_B xp(x)\, dx = a_{\text{med}}$, by construction. Therefore,

$$\int_B u(x)p(x)\, dx > u(a_{\text{med}}).$$

Since this inequality holds for any risk-acceptant voter, and since a majority of the voters is risk acceptant, $p(x)$ can secure a majority over a_{med}.

Q.E.D.

An immediate corollary of theorem 8 follows: if a majority of voters is risk acceptant, then any uniform risk $r \in R$, symmetric about a_{med}, defeats a_{med}.

Theorem 8 is significant. It should disabuse the reader of the universal superiority of the median, even in elections with full participation. Its substantive import deserves some comment. If a voter is risk acceptant, and yet still possesses a single-peaked utility curve, it is likely that the convex portion of that curve appears at the extremes of its domain. For example, if a voter has a normally distributed utility schedule, it is convex for all points at least one standard deviation distant from the most preferred point, i.e., $u''(x) > 0$ for $|a_i - x| > s$. Thus, an electorate, many of the members of which are risk acceptant in the neighborhood of the median, is likely to be highly polarized. It is depicted by a so-called U-shaped or bimodal voter distribution. In addition, the convexity property suggests *intense preference*, i.e., a voter would prefer some probability of obtaining his most-preferred alternative, even if it meant tolerating a rather high probability associated with less-preferred alternatives, as opposed to the certainty of obtaining a middle-ranked alternative. In substance, then, theorem 8 suggests that an incumbent candidate finds his electoral position tenuous on those issues which polarize the electorate into groups who feel there is much riding on the election. Furthermore, one suspects that it is precisely this kind of "critical issue" that encourages *deliberate* ambiguity by the challenger, e.g., Richard Nixon's "I have a plan" statement on the Viet Nam issue in the 1968 presidential campaign.

Theorem 8 demonstrates only that a_{med} is not winning. We have not determined whether sure prospects other than the median are more successful in a risk-acceptant electorate. Stated differently, we have not demonstrated that a strategy in the challenger's strategy set can defeat *all* certain strategies. Below we offer two conjectures on this problem. Although a "proof" is presented for the first conjecture, it contains some unjustified leaps of logic which suggest either that the conjecture is incorrect or that it is not well-specified. In fact, the latter is the case.

CONJECTURE. If "almost all" voters are risk acceptant in some interval B containing a_{med}, *any* nondegenerate risk over that interval with an expectation at a_{med} defeats any certain strategy.

Our reasoning is as follows:

Let $p(x)$ be the proposed risk, where

$$\int_B xp(x)\,dx = a_{\mathrm{med}}.$$

By definition, for "almost all" i,

$$\int_B p(x)u(x)\,dx > u(a_{\mathrm{med}}).$$

Suppose that the riskless party chooses a point $y > a_{\mathrm{med}}$.
For any i for which $a_i < a_{\mathrm{med}}$, $u(y) < u(a_{\mathrm{med}})$.
This follows from the single-peakedness of individual utility functions.
Thus for "almost all" i for which $a_i < a_{\mathrm{med}}$,

$$\int_B p(x)u(x)\,dx > u(y).$$

Thus, a "near majority" prefers the risk to y. If we assume either
a. that some i, for which $a_i \gg y$, prefer the risk to y,[20] or
b. that those voters for which $|a_i - a_{\text{med}}| < \epsilon$—those that have con-
cave utility functions in B—prefer $p(x)$ to y, though they prefer
a_{med} to $p(x)$,

then $p(x)$ receives a majority over y. A similar argument holds for
$y < a_{\text{med}}$.

The problem of course, follows from the use of the imprecise "almost
all." First, it is not possible for all voters to be risk acceptant in any interval B without producing a violation of either the assumption of single-
peakedness or the assumption of a continuous voter distribution $f(x)$.
Second, in order to make a more precise assumption about the number of
risk-acceptant voters, one must, in addition specify their distribution.
To transform this conjecture into a theorem, then, a more careful specification is required.

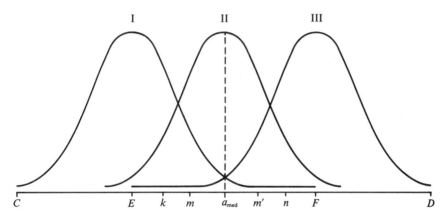

FIGURE 5

Although we plan to report on this problem elsewhere, an example
illustrates the approach we take. Consider an electorate of twenty-one
voters which is partitioned into three groups. Ten voters are in group
I, one in group II, and ten in group III (figure 5). Let $p(x)$ be a risk over
$[E, F]$ with an expectation at a_{med}. The points k and n are the certainty
equivalents of $p(x)$ for voters in groups I and III, respectively. The points
m and m' are certainty equivalents for the single voter of group II. If the
incumbent candidate, who is restricted to sure prospects, chooses a_{med},
$p(x)$ wins by a vote of 20-1, i.e., $u_i[p(x)] = u_i(k) > u_i(a_{\text{med}})$, for $i \in I$;
$u_j[p(x)] = u_j(n) > u_j(a_{\text{med}})$, $j \in III$. In order to appeal to group I voters,

---

[20] This is clearly possible if $y \in B$.

the incumbent must choose a point $x < k$, i.e., if $x < k$ then $u_i(x) > u_i(k)$, $i \in I$. However, for an $x < k$, the incumbent loses 11-10: $u_{II}[p(x)] = u_{II}(m) > u_{II}(x)$; $u_{III}[p(x)] = u_{III}(n) > u_{III}(x)$. Similarly, he would lose if he appealed to group III voters, since he must then choose a point $y > n$. In general, if $[m, m'] \subseteq [k, n]$, then a risky strategy exists which defeats any certain alternative.

We state, without discussion or proof, one final

CONJECTURE. If "almost all" voters are risk acceptant in some interval $[E, F]$, symmetric about a_{med}, and if the incumbent is *less risky* than the challenger, then there exists an $r(x) \epsilon R$ for the challenger that defeats any of the incumbent's admissible strategies.

V. MAJORITY RULE AND UNCERTAINTY: SOME CONCLUDING COMMENTS AND CAVEATS

From the classic analysis of Anthony Downs, it has been argued that (1) since "ambiguity . . . increases the number of voters to whom a party may appeal," (2) since "this fact encourages parties to be as equivocal as possible about their stands on each controversial issue," and (3) since "this makes it more difficult for each citizen to vote rationally," it follows that "rational behavior by political parties tends to discourage rational behavior by voters" (Downs, 1957, p. 136). Our analysis discredits the premises of this argument. Thus the conclusion does not follow.

Consider the first premise. Theorems 4, 5, 6, and 7, indicate that ambiguity *decreases* the appeal of a candidate under certain circumstances. Theorem 8 and the two conjectures render the first premise correct *if certain conditions are met*. As a result, doubt is cast on the second premise as well.

The third premise—what Downs calls the "fundamental tension" between party rationality and candidate rationality (Downs, 1957, pp. 137-39)—is simply a misunderstanding of the rationality concept. It implies, perhaps inadvertently, that rational decision making can occur only in a world of certainty. As the analysis of the third section of this paper shows, however, the expected-utility-maximization definition permits voter rationality, even if candidates "becloud their policies in a fog of ambiguity" (Downs, 1957, p. 136).

We summarize the results of this paper by drawing attention to two variables that affect the success of strategic uncertainty in electoral competition:

1. the dispersion of individual utility functions, $u_i(x)$, and
2. the dispersion of the distribution of most-preferred points, $F(x)$.

The fourfold table below clarifies this importance:

Dispersion of Utility Function $u(x)$

		small	large
Dispersion of Voter	small	Depends	Favors less risky strategy
Distribution $F(x)$	large	Favors risky strategy	Depends

When the voter distribution is widely dispersed and voter utility functions are "spiked," then we may expect many voters to have convex preferences in the neighborhood of the median.[21] As a result many voters are likely to be risk-acceptant in the neighborhood of the median, and the implications of theorem 8, and the two conjectures apply.

Alternatively, when the voter distribution has small variance and voter utility functions large variance, then most voters will be risk averse in the neighborhood of the median. The implications of theorems 4, 5, 6, and 7 apply in this case.

The two remaining cases do not admit of such sweeping generalizations. Precise parameter specification is needed for these cases. We suspect that such an analysis would quickly become intractable.

---

[21] Recall, from previous discussion, that voter preferences are convex at some specified distance from his most-preferrred point.

14. Spatial Strategies for Sequential Elections

PETER H. ARANSON   PETER C. ORDESHOOK

I. INTRODUCTION

Though the spatial theory of candidate competition is a recently developed
approach to the study of collective decision making in general and to the
analysis of electoral choice in particular, today this theory explains a
large number of situations and events that constitute real elections.[1] Spatial
analysis is limited, however, to the examination of the strategies a candidate
for office might use *in a single election* in which a *unique preference distribution* describes the electorate's wishes. This limitation is stringent not only
because most candidates must win more than one contest to gain office,
but also because only infrequently do the wishes of the different groups of
people who decide each contest's outcome concur.

Often the candidate must win a caucus struggle, a convention nomination, a party endorsement, or a primary election victory before he can
enter the general election contest. The American presidential aspirant,
for example, must be victorious in his party's nominating convention
before he can enter the presidential election campaign with his party's

---

[1] This literature includes: Downs, 1957; Davis and Hinich, 1966; Garvey, 1966;
Chapman, 1967; Davis, Hinich, and Ordeshook, 1970; Hinich, Ledyard, and Ordeshook, 1971.

label. The would-be senator, congressman, and governor, often must survive a primary election to run in the general election. The potential mayor or city councilman frequently must vie for a political machine's endorsement as its official candidate before challenging an opposing nominee.

There are other examples of intermediate contests the candidate must win to gain access to the office he most desires. Election to a governorship or to the Senate are traditional routes to the American presidency. Professional politicians—especially influential party leaders—watch these elections carefully to find attractive and capable men for higher offices. They evaluate these men on their appeal to the electorate, on their ability to salvage maneuverability on salient issues for which taking a strong and clear position would disqualify them in the minds of the larger electorate, and finally, on other indications of their political shrewdness and finesse.[2]

Spatial analysis isolates dominant strategies a candidate should use for a single constituency during a single election campaign. We seek here to extend the spatial theory's applicability by finding optimal strategies a candidate can use for two sequential elections in which the preferences of the first electorate differ from those of the second.

We could advise the candidate to consider the two elections (e.g., the primary and general elections) separately. Consider each electorate as independent of the other, taking those positions on the issues that maximize the chance of election in each contest. But there are a number of constraints present in any modern election that inhibit the candidate's spatial mobility—his maneuvering room on the issues.

First, a candidate depends usually upon a limited group of people for his support. Financial contributors, party workers, endorsing group leaders, and other donors of aid, may be particular about the candidate's positions on the issues. Those who offer such support, moreover, often are those who are responsible for his nomination. The candidate may desert these people for a more favorable position in the general election, but if their memories of this defection linger until the next election, the candidate may find renomination difficult.

Second, the candidate whose promises please nearly everyone may find his electoral coalition so unwieldy that it has no permanence. Even should sophisticated supporters ignore the candidate's duplicity for the sake of winning, the demands they are liable to place on his resources he may not be able to satisfy. A small coalition is likely to be coherent and loyal,

---

[2] Parts of our analysis might impinge, additionally, upon the problem the candidate faces for political systems with formalized run-off elections, as in the Fifth French Republic. But our study is not directed specifically to these problems.

its demands limited; a large group is likely to be factious and of questionable loyalty, its demands unreasonable.[3]

Third, though many elected officials (e.g., legislators) shield themselves from raw public inspection, different stands on a single issue for the sake of two voting bodies can bring forward charges of lying, crass politicking, and irresponsibility. Careful media today expose much duplicity, making an issue of credibility itself.

These three constraints operate, largely, because of the *public nature* of political issues and decisions. Politicians cannot manufacture products like automobiles in many styles, colors, and sizes; their products are unique, quantum decisions that all citizens must consume, whether they approve of them or not.[4]

We assume in this study that the candidate must adopt a single position on the issues that stands as his issue strategy in the nominating contest and in the general election.[5] The candidate's task, then, is to find a position on the issues that maximizes the joint probability of nomination and election. This problem is not new; writing for a different age, Machiavelli advised, "Well-ordered states and wise princes have studied diligently not to drive the nobles to desperation, and to satisfy the populace and keep it contented, for this is one of the most important matters that a prince has to deal with" (Machiavelli, 1950, p. 69).

If we assume that the prince is like the modern candidate, that the nobles are like the party activists or convention delegates (i.e., those who nominate), and that the populace is like the mass electorate (i.e., those who elect), then Machiavelli's *verstehen* outlines the problem, but offers no solutions. Though the "princely" candidates have no personal policy preferences save getting elected, pleasing the activist or delegate "nobles" while pleasing simultaneously the mass electorate "populace" is exceedingly difficult if the preferences of the former do not coincide with those of the latter.

We cannot deduce candidate strategies unless we know something about the candidate's environment. Specifically, the candidate seeks a position on the issues that prompts enough citizens to vote for him to insure victory. But there may be ambiguities in decision-rules that candidates,

---

[3] Riker's (1962) work on coalitions is relevant here. Specifically, payoff functions for *n*-person zero-sum games indicate that coalitions of the whole or other "over-weighted" coalitions are worthless to their members. See also Meltz (1970) on the relationship between coalition size and coalition stability.

[4] We refer here to the concept of public goods. Although some political goods do not exhibit jointness of consumption, enough of them do to suggest that elections produce unique decisions, if only in the choice of the elected official.

[5] There are no apparent reasons to relax this assumption, even though candidates enjoy *some* spatial mobility. The assumption's credentials, however, both in terms of empirical reality and mathematical simplicity, convince us that it is not far-fetched.

activists, and citizens employ. Hence, we discuss candidate, citizen, and activist choice in section 2, inferring from this analysis appropriate decision-rules for each. We conclude from this examination that the crucial distinction is the activist decision-rule. We construct, in section 3, the mathematical analogue for the sequential election problem, and deduce optimal strategies for situations in which activists (those who control the nomination stage) choose a nominee strictly on the issues—without considering the would-be nominee's viability in the general election. We enlarge upon this analysis in section 4, considering the effects of his nomination and general election opponents' likely issue positions (and the candidate's information about these positions) on the candidate's strategy choice. In section 5, we consider the candidate's strategy choice problem if activists choose a nominee on the basis of mixed motives; they consider not only the ideological satisfaction they receive from a potential nominee, but also the aspirant's likely viability in the general election. Finally, in section 6, we review our findings and discuss their importance for spatial theory and election studies.

II. PARTICIPANT DECISION-RULES

The axiomatic assumption that candidates and citizens (those who are able to vote) are rational decision makers underlies most deductions in spatial model literature. This assumption states that if a person has a set of alternative actions he can take, he acts *as if* he calculates the expected utility from each action and chooses that action which promises the greatest reward (expected utility).

To give the rationality assumption substantive political meaning beyond a purely mathematical and procedural exercise, however, we must know not only what goals (outcomes) people seek to achieve, but also the way in which they value these goals and the instrumental strategies they use to attain them. Whether candidates maximize votes or plurality, for instance, may depend upon constitutional circumstances (Downs, 1957). Spatial models rely, furthermore, on the citizen's choice being the outcome of a two-step sequential decision process: first, the citizen ascertains the direction and the strength of his preference between the candidates; second, he decides to vote or to abstain, depending on whether or not the rewards from voting exceed the cost of voting (Riker and Ordeshook, 1968; Rosenthal and Sen, 1970; McKelvey and Ordeshook, 1972; Aranson, forthcoming). It is not clear, though, whether we should regard abstention from indifference (i.e., the positions of the candidates are equally attractive or unattractive) or abstention from alienation (i.e., the citizen's preferred candidate is too unattractive) as more important in the citizen's voting decision. The search for dominant strategies must progress, therefore, considering indifference and alienation motives separately (Davis, Hinich, and Ordeshook, 1970; Hinich and Ordeshook, 1971), or postulating formulations of a citizen's calculus that admit both alienation and indifference simultaneously (Hinich, Ledyard, and Ordeshook, 1971; Garvey, 1966). Finally, spatial analysis does not consider the mixed motive case of the activist who supports an aspiring nominee not only because he minimizes spatial loss, but also because he can win the general election.

Because of the ambiguities in the candidate and citizen cases, and the lack of formulation in the activist case, we review existing hypothetical decision-rules for citizens and candidates and suggest three possible decision-rules for activists.

A. Citizens

Downs (1957, pp. 36-50) argues that the citizen (the enfranchised person) calculates an expected utility from each party and votes, if he votes at all, for the party that promises the greater expected benefit. The range of party competition is a single ideological dimension. A number of elaborations added to Downs's hypothetical citizen decision-rule portray the citizen's choice as a more complex and realistic one. First, we can specify *candidate* competition rather than *party* competition, to eliminate much of the ambiguity that accompanies differences of issue proposals within a single party. Second, Davis and Hinich (1966; 1967) extend the range of competition to n-dimensions, to correct for Downs's single "ideology dimension." Third, Ordeshook (1969; 1970) and Hinich and Ordeshook (1969; 1970) not only analyze different motives for abstention, but also generalize Downs's "benefit" function to a loss function, which can be convex or quasi-convex. Finally, Hinich, Ledyard, and Ordeshook (1971) formulate a general multidimensional model that admits of indifference, alienation, partisan bias (e.g., nonspatial considerations), and multidimensional non-symmetric preference densities simultaneously. It is clear that these developments add scope, generality, and rigor to the initial spatial conception of electoral competition and collective decision making. We note in table 1 the spatial model's present state of development with respect to symmetric preference densities.

Though table 1 does not exhaust the spatial theory literature, it does provide a convenient base from which we can deduce strategies for candidates who seek to please two constituencies with dissimilar preferences. Whether people abstain from indifference, from alienation, or from both, whether the citizen's loss function is convex or quasi-convex, and whether abstentions occur or all citizens vote, for symmetric unimodal distributions of citizen or activist preference, taken singly, the mean of the distribu-

TABLE 1. Deductions from Spatial Model (Assuming Plurality Maximization)

ABSTENTION FROM ALIENATION		
Loss Function	*Convex*	*Quasi-convex*
Distribution:		
Symmetric Unimodal	Mean*	Mean*
Symmetric Bimodal	No general solution**	No general solution**

ABSTENTION FROM INDIFFERENCE		
Loss Function	*Convex*	*Quasi-convex*
Distribution:		
Symmetric Unimodal	Mean***	Mean***
Symmetric Bimodal	Mean**	Not yet researched

ABSTENTION FROM ALIENATION AND INDIFFERENCE		
Loss Function	*Convex*	*Quasi-convex*
Distribution:		
Symmetric Unimodal	Mean****	Mean**** (Conjecture)
Symmetric Bimodal	Mean****	No general solution**** (Conjecture)

* Hinich and Ordeshook (1969)
** Ordeshook (1969)
*** Ordeshook (1970)
**** Hinich, Ledyard, and Ordeshook (1971)

tion is always the dominant strategy. Hence, though there are certain problems in the basic spatial model which compel the explicit statement of assumptions—convexity or quasiconvexity of loss functions and abstention from alienation or indifference—these problems need not concern us if we limit our discussion to symmetric unimodal densities of activist and citizen preference: the mean always dominates any other strategy; the candidate whose position is closer to the mean wins the election.

B. Candidates

This assumption that citizen and activist preference functions are symmetric and unimodal limits the problem of defining the citizen's decision-rule. Virtually any monotone increasing loss function (or no abstention) yields a mean strategy as dominant. But there can be some question about whether candidates maximize votes or maximize plurality.[6] Hinich and

___

[6] The point is not trivial, as both Downs (1957) and Garvey (1966) use plurality maximization and vote maximization as interchangeable, analytically equivalent, concepts.

Ordeshook (1970) find that if the electorate preference density is distributed unimodally, and if indifference induces abstention, a vote maximizing candidate chooses a strategy off the mean and, though he maximizes votes, he loses the election to another candidate at the mean.[7]

Although it is conjecture at this time, there is some indication that the candidate in a single-member district constituency maximizes plurality —the difference between the number of votes he receives and the number of votes his opponent receives—while the candidate in a proportional representation, multicandidate system maximizes votes.

The important consideration for this study is that if the distribution of citizen preferences is symmetric and unimodal, and if the election is in a two-candidate single-member district system, then the candidate's winning strategy is the mean of the citizen preference distribution—a strategy produced by maximizing plurality. The distinctions among candidate decision-rules, therefore, offer no difficulty if we assume: (1) candidates maximize plurality; (2) there are only two candidates in each of the contests (e.g., primary and general elections); and (3) each election or contest has but one winner, as it has the properties of the single-member district system.

C. Activists

We mean by activists those people who are responsible for nominating the party's general election candidate, whether by primary election, by nominating convention, or by other devices. Present spatial analysis, though, does not attempt to analyze activist choice. There are certain problems, moreover, that arise from such an attempt, since activists may have decision-rules that differ from those that candidates and citizens employ.

1. Activists with Candidate Decision-Rules. First, it might be natural to assume that activists and candidates have the same hypothetical motives: they both seek to win the general election. In this instance, any solution to the candidate's problem of pleasing both activists and citizens is trivial. Activists would prefer to nominate a candidate who can win the general election; such a candidate adopts the mean of the citizen preference density. If the density of citizen preferences is symmetric and unimodal, the nomination process is simply an appendage to the political

---

[7] If, for example, two candidates adopt the mean of a symmetric unimodal density of citizen preferences, they tie in the vote. But if one candidate begins to move off the mean, his number of votes increases up to a certain point (the point of vote maximization) after which his number of votes declines. Throughout this divergence, however, if the opponent remains at the mean, he picks up votes at a faster rate than the diverging candidate.

process that reinforces the power and importance of the mean citizen preference.

2. Activists with Citizen Decision-Rules. A second, and more interesting, case occurs if activists have decision-rules like citizens. These activists, apparently, do not consider the candidate's viability in the general election. They judge a candidate simply on his avowed position's closeness to their own. The candidate has two important strategy considerations if activists share the citizen decision-rule. First, it might be the case that the means of the citizen and activist preference distributions coincide. If both distributions are symmetric and unimodal, then the candidate adopts the coinciding mean strategy. Second, the means of the citizen and activist preference densities may not coincide. There is much evidence that activists and citizens do not agree on most policy matters (McClosky, *et al.*, 1960; Eldersveld, 1964, chap. 8). If activists consider only ideological satisfaction, then, the candidate might be betwixt and between in trying to satisfy two groups of people (activists and citizens) whose mean preferences differ.

3. Activists with Mixed Motives. Finally, activists may share motives in common with those imputed both to candidates and to citizens. The activist may seek not only to support a viable candidate—one who can win the general election—but also a satisfying candidate—one who most nearly shares certain policy preferences. This case is far more complex than the first (activists like candidates) and the second (activists like citizens). It portrays the activist as a person with complex motives that he must weigh and measure before making a decision.

These three views of the activist accord with many existing conceptions of his choices and characteristics. Wilson (1966), for example, divides activists into two categories or pure types, whose edges, admittedly, are blurred. The first type, the "professional," corresponds to our conception of the activist with candidate motivations.

> The professional . . . is preoccupied with maintaining his position in party and elective offices. Winning is essential, although sometimes electoral victory must be subordinated to maintaining the party organization. Candidates will be selected on the basis of their electoral appeal . . . . Issues will be avoided except in the most general terms or if the party is confident that a majority supports its position. Should a contrary position on the same issue seem best suited for winning a majority at the next election, the party will try to change or at least to mute its position. (Wilson, 1966, pp. 17–18)

Wilson's second type, the "amateur," corresponds most closely to our conceptualization of the activist as citizen.

The amateur politician . . . would in the ideal situation prefer to recruit candidates on the basis of their commitment to a set of policies. Voters would be mobilized by appeals to some set of principles or goals. The party would be held together and linked to the voter by a shared conception of the public interest . . . . Private interests, which for the professional are the motive force of politics, the amateur would consider irrelevant, irrational, or immoral . . . . Amateur politicians thus seek to alter fundamentally the way in which the functions of parties are carried out. Instead of serving as neutral agents which mobilize majorities for whatever candidates and programs seem best suited to capturing public fancy, the parties would become the sources of programs and agents of social change. (Wilson, 1966, pp. 18–19)

A combination of the two types yields Polsby and Wildavsky's characterization of the American national nominating convention delegate who seeks, "to gain power, to nominate a man who can win the election, to unify the party, to obtain some claim on the nominee, to protect. . . [his] central core of policy preferences, and to strengthen. . . [his] state party organization" (Polsby and Wildavsky, 1968, p. 74). This delegate mixes together the motives of both citizens and candidates.

III. SEQUENTIAL STRATEGY PROBLEM: ACTIVISTS JUDGE BY ISSUE STRATEGY

The major assumptions of this analysis, from earlier spatial theory and the preceeding section, are:

1. The density of citizen preferences is symmetric, unimodal, and continuously differentiable.
2. The densities of activist preferences are symmetric, unimodal, and continuously differentiable.
3. Candidates seek to maximize the probability of winning each contest (nomination and election).
4. In each contest there are at most two candidates; the candidate with the greater number of votes wins.
5. Citizens evaluate candidates solely on ideological distance; indifference or alienation may induce abstention; citizen loss functions may be convex or quasi-convex.
6. Activists may seek nominees who (a) can win the general election, (b) are closest ideologically, or (c) combine the qualities of (a) and (b).

We picture the major problem that the candidate encounters in figure 1.
We assume without loss of generality, that $E(x) = 0$, $E_1(x) = a$, and $E_2(x) = b$ and that $E_1(x) \leq E(x) \leq E_2(x)$ (or $a \leq 0 \leq b$).

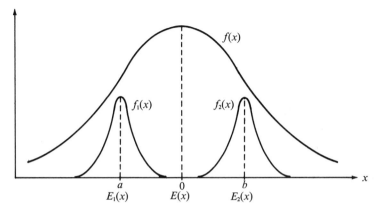

FIGURE 1

Let us examine, now, the candidate's problem if activists judge candidates in the same way that citizens judge them. If the mean of the activist preference density, $E_1(x)$, coincides with the mean of the citizen preference density, $E(x)$—if $E_1(x) = E(x)$—then the candidate adopts this mean common to both densities as it is his dominant strategy for each contest.

But if $E_1(x) \neq E(x)$, and if the activist, like the hypothetical citizen, judges the candidate solely on his spatial closeness, then the candidate's problem is evident. If the candidate has complete spatial mobility, he can adopt a strategy $E_1(x)$ for the nomination, followed by a strategy $E(x)$ for the general election, and do no worse than tie in both contests (if his opponents are as clever as he). For reasons that we suggested earlier, however, most candidates perceive real restraints on their spatial mobility. Most candidates have some mobility, though we abstract this mobility from our analysis and assume that the candidate must choose a single strategy to serve for both contests.

There are two additional pieces of information we need in order to deduce optimal strategies for the case of activist-like-citizen. First, we must be able to place some logical restrictions on the contestants' strategy choices. Second, we must be able to model the candidate's information about his opponents' strategies.

The strategy limitations we seek derive from the dominant character of $E_1(x)$ and $E(x)$ for their respective contests. Remembering that $E_1(x) = a$, $E(x) = 0$, and $E_2(x) = b$, let

θ = the candidate's strategy (the person for whom we seek a dominant strategy),

β = the candidate's nomination opponent's strategy,

ψ = The candidate's general election opponent's strategy.

We find limitations on strategies, by proving with two lemmas, dominance for restricted ranges of candidate competition.

LEMMA 1. Each strategy in the intervals $(-\infty, a)$ and (b, ∞), for the strategies θ and β (nomination contest strategies) is dominated by at least one strategy in the interval $[a, b]$.

PROOF. Consider figure 1, the position a, and a strategy $\theta^* < a$. Since $a = E_1(x)$, a dominates θ^* with respect to the nomination contest. Additionally, since a is closer to $E(x)$ than is θ^*, a dominates θ^* with respect to the general election contest. Hence, a dominates θ^* with respect to $f_1(x)$ and $f(x)$. A candidate prefers $a \in [a, b]$, therefore, to any $\theta^* < a$. A parallel proof can be constructed for $\theta^* > b$.

Q.E.D.

LEMMA 2. Each strategy in the interval $[0, b]$, for the strategies θ and β, is dominated by at least one strategy in the interval $[a, 0]$.

PROOF. Consider figure 1, the position 0, and a strategy $\theta^* > 0$. Since $0 = E(x)$, 0 dominates θ^* with respect to the general election contest. Hence, 0 dominates θ^* with respect to $f(x)$ and $f_1(x)$. The nomination candidates of party 1, whose activist preference density is $f_1(x)$ and whose strategies are θ and β, prefer strategies in the interval $[a, 0]$, or $a \leq \theta \leq 0$ and $a \leq \beta \leq 0$. Assuming that the general election opponent must also worry about nomination, a parallel proof shows his interval for ψ is $[0, b]$.

Q.E.D.

The thrust of lemmas 1 and 2, *ceteris paribus*, is that a rational candidate chooses a strategy in the closed interval $[a, 0]$ if he is a candidate for party 1's nomination and in the closed interval $[0, b]$ if he is a candidate for party 2's nomination. Our first piece of information, then, is that no candidate should leave the interval bounded by the mean of his party's activist preference density, $E_i(x)$ and the mean of the citizen preference density, $E(x)$.

Having restricted all strategies to one of two permissible intervals, we wish to know if there is some way to characterize further the strategies that a candidate's nomination opponent and general election opponent might adopt. Many scholars infer from observation of actual candidates, though, that unambiguous platforms and decisive issue stands are political rarities. There are theoretical and practical reasons, moreover, why this should be true. Shepsle (chap. 13 in this volume) demonstrates that under certain conditions, a candidate whose strategy is uncertain to the citizen might be victorious over a candidate whose strategy is unambiguous.

V. O. Key, Jr. (1964, p. 421) argues from more practical considerations that, in American presidential nominating conventions, "a desideratum . . . is the maintenance of coalitions inclusive enough to contend for the presidency . . . [consequently] platforms must conform with that necessity." There is "no simpler way . . . to destroy an electoral coalition than for its majority to insist on precise, forthright, and advanced policy positions unacceptable to other elements of the coalition." The candidate not only must win the nomination, but also, as Polsby and Wildavsky (1968, p. 74) suggest, he must "regard . . . the nominating convention as the first part of the campaign." Parties, moreover, "tend . . . to nominate candidates who at the least are not obnoxious to, and ideally are attractive to as many interest groups and state party leaders as possible."

We infer, from both the theoretical and observational studies, that there are sufficient reasons for a candidate's nomination and general election opponents to mask their exact strategies. We have reason to believe, of course, that the nomination opponent's strategy, β, is in the interval $[a, 0]$, and that the general election opponent's strategy, ψ, is in the interval $[0, b]$. Though we can place this restriction on β and ψ, we can do little more at this juncture than to speak of β and ψ's probable *location* in each strategy's interval of permissible strategies.

We assume, therefore, that β and ψ, rather than denoting exact strategies or positions along an issue space, are random variables with expected values. These strategies, hence, are the candidate's (whose position is θ) subjective estimates of where his opponents' strategies are likely to be and, as such, are subjective probability estimates. And we posit the candidate's task as the choice of a strategy, prior to nomination, that gives him the best chance of succeeding in both the nomination and the general election contests.[8]

We assume, more formally, that β and ψ are random variables whose density functions are $g_1(\beta)$ and $g_2(\psi)$ respectively, such that

$$g_1(\beta) \geq 0, \ (a \leq \beta \leq 0) \quad \text{(follows from lemmas 1 and 2)}$$
$$= 0, \text{ otherwise}$$
$$g_2(\psi) \geq 0, \ (0 \leq \psi \leq b) \quad \text{(follows from lemmas 1 and 2)}$$
$$= 0, \text{ otherwise}$$
$$E(\beta) = E_\beta$$
$$E(\psi) = E_\psi.$$

---

[8] The careful reader might well ask why the candidate himself does not attempt to create uncertainty about his strategy. We respond that this is a proper question for further research that demands a different and far more complicated model.

A. General Information Sources

There are, of course, several different ways in which the candidate might estimate his nomination and general election opponents' probable strategy choices. Though the candidate's estimates of his opponents' strategies are probability estimates, he does have *some* information on which to base his guesses.

First, the candidate may estimate each opponent's likely strategy from a knowledge of the opponent's past choices. The contender may know, for example, that either his nomination opponent or his general election opponent believes himself to be ideologically constrained to a certain position. This personal constraint can derive from a long held belief or from a matter of principle. It is not necessary for an opponent to utter that he "would rather be right" than be president; in a political context, the long held beliefs of various politicians are usually known to those around them—even known to their opponents.

Second, the candidate may judge his opponent to be attached to a particular position because of former commitments or loyalties. It is not necessary that an opponent be willing to honor these commitments for his position on the issue that the commitment entails to be fixed. Lyndon Johnson's vote against the anti-lynching bill, as well as his southern origin, for example, may have influenced several people's estimate of his position on civil rights legislation, though he attempted to redefine his position later in terms of a national constituency (Evans and Novak, 1966, pp. 119-40). Hence, even if the candidate has no idea about an opponent's former commitments and ideological tenacity, he may still estimate the likely competing strategy's location from his opponent's past choices.

1. Nomination Opponents. Let us examine some theoretical estimates a candidate might hold of his nomination opponent's possible strategy. We construct in figure 2 four possible subjectively estimated probability functions, $g_h(\beta)$, $g_i(\beta)$, $g_j(\beta)$, and $g_k(\beta)$.

A probability function like $g_h(\beta)$ occurs if the candidate has no knowledge of his nomination opponent's probable strategy choice. Every strategy in the interval of permissible strategies $[a, 0]$ is equiprobable, generating a uniform density function. This kind of estimate, a function of complete uncertainty, is most likely to occur in contests with dark horse candidates, especially those with apparent issue commitments neither to groups nor to principle.

The subjective probability estimates $g_i(\beta)$, $g_j(\beta)$, and $g_k(\beta)$ exhibit a greater information content than the estimate $g_h(\beta)$ in that they specify more exactly the candidate's judgment of his nomination opponent's likely strategy choice.

The distribution $g_i(\beta)$, for example, might find its genesis in the candidate's knowledge that his nomination opponent has ideological or organi-

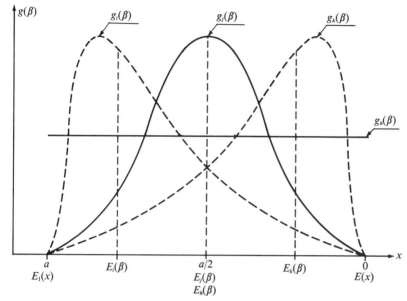

FIGURE 2

zational commitments to a position (a strategy) considerably to the left of the general electorate's mean preference and quite close to the mean preference of the party activists. John Kennedy might have made such an estimate of Hubert Humphrey's probable strategy during the 1960 West Virginia primary. The important characteristic of this distribution is that the candidate estimates his nomination opponent's probable strategy choice to be closer to the activists' mean preference than to the general electorate's mean preference.

The opposite pattern arises from a subjectively estimated probability distribution such as $g_k(\beta)$. Here the candidate estimates his nomination opponent's likely strategy to be closer to $E(x)$, the general electorate mean preference, than to $E_1(x)$, the activist mean preference. The candidate may infer such a strategy, as with $g_i(\beta)$, from his opponent's traditional loyalties as well as from his policy pronouncements.

Finally, the candidate might estimate his nomination opponent's likely strategy to fall half way between $E(x)$ and $E_1(x)$ at the position $a/2$. As we construct such an estimate's functional equivalent, $g_j(\beta)$ the probability estimate is symmetric about the point $a/2$.

2. General Election Opponents. The candidate might make the same kinds of subjective probability estimates about his general election opponent's likely strategy choice. We construct four such estimates in figure 3.

The varieties of inferences the candidate can draw about the general election opponent's strategy, though, differ from those he makes about

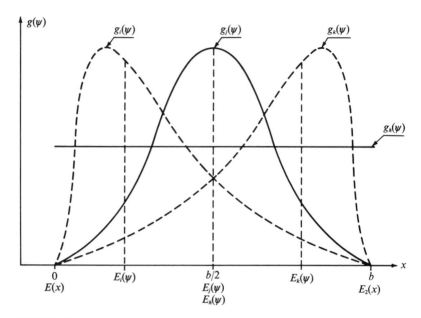

FIGURE 3

his nomination opponent's strategy. First, the opposing party may have completed its nomination or the winner of the opposing party's nomination may be known unambiguously even before the nomination process is terminated. One important example of this phenomenon is the likely renomination of a strong incumbent to the office sought. Such a candidate may receive his party's nomination ritually and traditionally. A strong incumbent has considerable spatial mobility, in which case the candidate who hopes eventually to face this incumbent can expect his general election opponent's strategy to be close to the general electorate mean preference, $E(x)$. Summarily, then, the estimate of strategy is $g_i(\psi)$.

Second, should a strong incumbent not be available to the opposing party, and should its nomination not be a foregone conclusion, the candidate might be able to estimate the location of the strategies that will compete against his own from the opposing party's past performance. The previous platforms of an opposing party's candidate may offer some information about the kind of positions that its present candidate (or likely candidate) shall advocate. This information may stem from the activists' ideological tenacity, especially in the case of parties whose activists refuse to nominate a candidate whose position differs greatly from the activist mean preference, $E_2(x)$. Should these considerations hold, the candidate might estimate that his general election opponent will choose a strategy close to $E_2(x)$. Summarily, then, the estimate of strategy is $g_k(\psi)$.

Third, the candidate might judge his expected general election opponent to hold a strategy that balances the ideological demands of both the opposing party's activists and the general electorate. Such an opponent's strategy may be described by the subjective probability function $g_j(\psi)$.

Finally, should the opposing party's nominee be completely unpredictable, either by name or by position, then every strategy in the interval $[0, b]$ is equiprobable. As with his nomination opponent who offers no information, the candidate infers a subjective probability function, $g_h(\psi)$, a uniform density function.

B. Certainty of Estimates

Though our characterizations of subjective probability estimates of the opponent's likely strategies do depend upon political information, this analysis centers around the *location* of the opponents' likely strategies and not the *certainty* with which the candidate holds those estimates. Consider, for example, the subjective probability estimates that we construct in figure 4. All four of these estimates are symmetric. All four functions assume that the opponent's strategy is as likely to be as close to $E_1(x)$ as to $E(x)$. All four have an expected value $E_\beta = a/2$. The major difference is the certainty of the estimates. For example, $g_h(\beta)$ reflects a total lack of information about the opponent's likely strategy, while $g_k(\beta)$ offers an estimate with much greater information content.

While there is some reason to suspect that the subjective probability estimate collapses about some point as the candidate gathers more information about his opponent's strategy choice, the opposite effect is also possible; his opponent can act to mask his exact strategy hence inducing considerable uncertainty.

C. Deduction of Strategies

We can now deduce optimal strategies for the candidate who must win a nomination contest judged by activists who seek to minimize spatial loss and a general election contest judged by citizens who seek also to minimize spatial loss. We define an optimal strategy as one that maximizes the joint probability of nomination and election. More formally, let

P_1 = the probability that the candidate is nominated if he uses the strategy θ.

P_2 = the probability that the candidate is elected if he uses the strategy θ.

P = the joint probability of nomination and election if the candidate uses the strategy θ.

$P = P_1 P_2$.

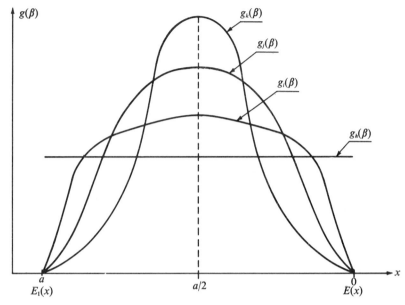

FIGURE 4

The statement of the probabilities P_1 and P_2 follows directly from the earlier conceptualization of the candidate's subjective probability estimate of his opponents' likely strategy choices.[9]

Consider the two subjective probability estimates, $g_1(\beta)$ and $g_2(\psi)$ in figure 5. The probability of nomination, P_1, is the probability that θ

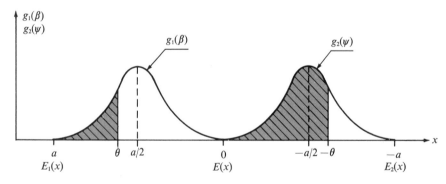

FIGURE 5

---

[9] P_2 is, of course, conditional on nomination. We could expand P as $P = $ [the probability of nomination $| \theta$] [the probability of election | nomination $| \theta$]. This is equivalent to $P = P_1 P_2$.

is closer to $E_1(x)$ than is β, or

$$P_1 = Pr[\theta < \beta].$$

P_1, then, is the probability that the nomination opponent's strategy, β, falls to the right of θ, or

$$P_1 = Pr[\theta < \beta] = \int_\theta^0 g_1(\beta) \, d\beta.$$

This is equivalent to the unshaded area under the function $g_1(\beta)$.

The probability of winning the general election is the probability that $-\theta$ is closer to $E(x)$ than is ψ, or

$$P_2 = Pr[\psi > -\theta].$$

P_2 then, is the probability that the general election opponent's strategy, ψ, falls to the right of $-\theta$, or

$$P_2 = Pr[\psi > -\theta] = \int_{-\theta}^b g_2(\psi) \, d\psi.$$

This is equivalent to the unshaded area under the function $g_2(\psi)$.

The objective function that we wish to maximize, then, is:

$$P = P_1 P_2 = \int_\theta^0 g_1(\beta) \, d\beta \int_{-\theta}^b g_2(\psi) \, d\psi. \tag{1}$$

The necessary condition for maximizing P with respect to θ is:

$$\frac{\partial P}{\partial \theta} = 0 = -g_1(\theta) \int_{-\theta}^b g_2(\psi) \, d\psi + g_2(-\theta) \int_\theta^0 g_1(\beta) \, d\beta. \tag{2}$$ [10]

Rearranging terms, the necessary condition for a maximum becomes: [11]

$$\frac{g_1(\theta)}{g_2(-\theta)} = \frac{\int_\theta^0 g_1(\beta) \, d\beta}{\int_{-\theta}^b g_2(\psi) \, d\psi}. \tag{3}$$

We can place restrictions on the limits of integration and on $g_1(\beta)$ and $g_2(\psi)$ in order to prove a modest theorem about the location of an optimal strategy if activists wish solely to minimize spatial loss.

---

[10] This assumes that there are no corner solutions; i.e., $\partial P/\partial \theta > 0$, $\forall \theta$, and $\partial^2 P/\partial \theta^2 < 0$, $\forall \theta$. Also, we can "eyeball" and eliminate the need to examine the second order condition, $\partial^2 P/\partial \theta^2 < 0$.

[11] We assume that $g_2(-\theta) \neq 0$ and $\int_{-\theta}^b g_2(\psi) \, d\psi \neq 0$.

ASSUMPTION 1. $-a = b$

ASSUMPTION 2. $g_1(\theta) = g_2(-\theta)$

THEOREM. If assumptions 1 and 2 hold, the strategy that meets the necessary condition for a maximum (i.e., the strategy that maximizes the joint probability of nomination and election) as stated by equation (3), is the median of the subjective probability estimate of the nomination opponent's likely strategy, $g_1(\beta)$.

PROOF. By assumption 2, the left side of equation (3), $g_1(\theta)/g_2(-\theta)$ equals 1, as $g_1(\theta) = g_2(-\theta)$. Hence,

$$\frac{g_1(\theta)}{g_2(-\theta)} = 1 = \frac{\int_\theta^0 g_1(\beta)\, d\beta}{\int_{-\theta}^b g_2(\psi)\, d\psi} \tag{4}$$

or,

$$\int_{-\theta}^b g_2(\psi)\, d\psi = \int_\theta^0 g_1(\beta)\, d\beta. \tag{5}$$

Consider figure 6 and a strategy, θ.

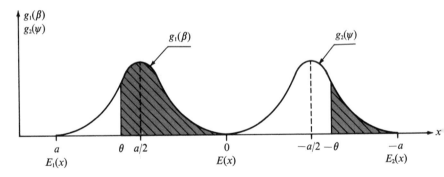

FIGURE 6

Clearly, $\int_{-\theta}^{-a} g_2(\psi)\, d\psi$ is the shaded area, bounded by $-\theta$ and $-a$ that we interpret as the probability of winning the general election. $\int_\theta^0 g_1(\beta)\, d\beta$, the probability of winning the nomination, is the shaded area bounded by θ and $E(x) = 0$. Because of the equality deduced in equation (5), an optimal strategy, θ_{max}, must insure that $P_1 = P_2$. We know by definition that

$$\int_a^0 g_1(\beta)\, d\beta = \int_0^{-a} g_2(\psi)\, d\psi = 1. \tag{6}$$

Hence, since $g_1(\theta) = g_2(-\theta)$ (by assumption 2), for $\theta = \theta_{max}$,

$$\int_{-\theta}^{-a} g_2(\psi)d\psi = 1 - \int_{\theta}^{0} g_1(\beta)\,d\beta. \tag{7}$$

Substituting equation (7) into equation (5)

$$1 - \int_{\theta}^{0} g_1(\beta)\,d\beta = \int_{\theta}^{0} g_1(\beta)\,d\beta$$

$$1 = 2\int_{\theta}^{0} g_1(\beta)\,d\beta \tag{8}$$

$$\frac{1}{2} = \int_{\theta}^{0} g_1(\beta)\,d\beta.$$

Equation (8) states, therefore, that for $\theta = \theta_{max}$, one-half of the cumulative probability of the nomination opponent's strategy occuring must fall to the left of θ_{max} and one-half to the right. This is a θ exactly at the median of $g_1(\beta)$.

Q.E.D.

COROLLARY. If assumptions 1 and 2 hold, and if $g_1(\beta)$ is symmetric about the point $a/2$ (i.e., if $g_1(a/2 + \epsilon) = g_1(a/2 - \epsilon)$), then the dominant strategy $\theta_{max} = a/2$.

This corollary follows directly from the coincidence of mean and median for symmetric distributions.

It is evident that the theorem and corollary define strategies for an infinite number of possible distributions. But the assumptions needed to deduce these optimal strategies are sufficiently restrictive to warrant their examination before discussing further empirical import.

Assumption 1, that $-a = b$ (alternatively that $E_1(x) = -E_2(x)$ or that the mean preferences of the two groups of activists are symmetric about $E(x)$, the citizen mean preference), appears heroic. We regard it, nevertheless, as a necessary *initial* assumption that greatly simplifies our analysis. It will be possible in future studies to relax this assumption; here, though, we analyze cases for which the intervals of permissible strategies are of equal length and symmetric about $E(x)$.[12]

Assumption 2, that $g_1(\theta) = g_2(-\theta)$, appears equally restrictive. This assumption states that the two subjective probability estimates are isomorphic (mirror images): $g_1(x) = g_2(-x)$. There are an infinite number of functions that satisfy assumption 2, despite its restrictiveness. We

---

[12] This assumption assures, similarly, that $E_2(x) > 0$; hence, we lose a modest amount of generality by placing $E_1(x)$ and $E_2(x)$ on different sides of $E(x)$.

might attempt to give some of these functions substantive meaning, therefore, choosing distributions by reasonable empirical criteria.

First, if the candidate has knowledge about neither his nomination opponent's nor his general election opponent's strategy, then the two resultant subjectively estimated probability distributions, $g_1(\beta)$ and $g_2(\psi)$, are uniform distributions (straight line segments) as we depict in figure 7.

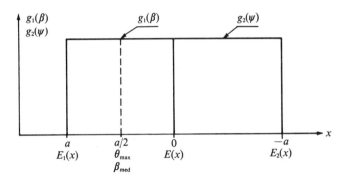

FIGURE 7

The strategy $\theta_{max} = a/2$, which maximizes the joint probability of nomination and election, falls under the deduction of the corollary, since $g_1(\theta) = g_2(-\theta)$ and $g_1(\beta)$ is symmetric about $a/2$. This result—our ability to deduce a single optimal strategy—is encouraging, as it occurs under conditions of total uncertainty about opponent strategies.

Second, if the candidate has *some* knowledge about his opponents' likely strategies, and if this knowledge suggests that both opponents wish to strike a balance between the party activists and the general electorate, then he estimates his opponents' likely strategies to be described by unimodal probability functions $g_1(\beta)$ and $g_2(\psi)$, symmetric about $a/2$ and $-a/2$ respectively. Hence, the candidate's optimal strategy is $\theta_{max} = a/2$.

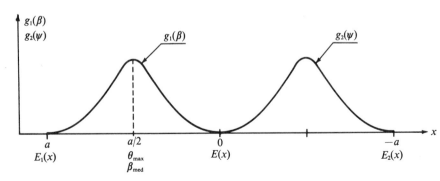

FIGURE 8

This case, which we represent in figure 8, also falls under the deduction of the corollary, since $g_1(\theta) = g_2(-\theta)$ and both functions are symmetric about their midpoints. More importantly, this case, as does the previous one in the extreme sense, assures equal information about both opponent's strategies: var β = var ψ.

Third, the candidate might confront a sequential challenge of a nomination opponent and a general election opponent each of whom adopts a strategy that he estimates to fall close to the mean citizen preference, $E(x)$. This example, which we illustrate in figure 9, has its empirical referent in candidates whose supporters and advisors are political machine leaders—Wilson's professionals—men for whom winning general elections compels adopting positions that are close to the general electorate's mean preference. Hence, the candidate adopts the strategy that the theorem selects, $\theta_{max} = \beta_{med}$.

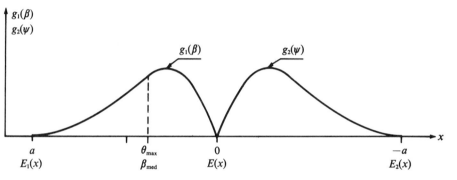

FIGURE 9

Fourth, if the candidate's opponents are attached, traditionally or ideologically, to the activists of their respective parties, then he might guess β to be closer to $E_1(x)$ and ψ to be closer to $E_2(x)$, than either strategy is to $E(x)$. This example, which we illustrate in figure 10, has its empirical reference in candidates whose supporters and advisors are ideologically and policy oriented activists—Wilson's amateurs—men for whom the clear espousal of policy is as important as electoral victory. The candidate again selects an optimal strategy $\theta_{max} = \beta_{med}$, as the theorem states, though now β_{med} is more distant from $E(x)$ than in the previous case.

There are two additional empirically reasonable sequential challenges that do not fall under the deductions of the theorem. Consider the distributions we construct in figure 11. This is the particularly nasty situation of a nomination opponent who adopts a probable strategy near the mean activist preference and a general election opponent who adopts a probable strategy near the mean citizen preference.

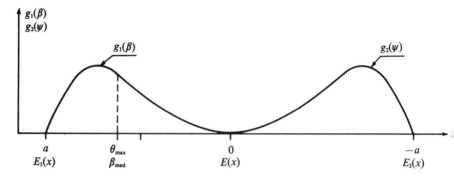

FIGURE 10

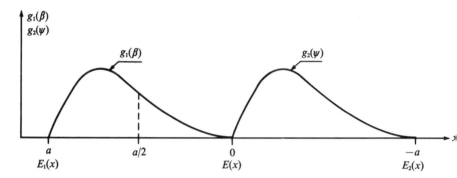

FIGURE 11

Even if we assume that $g_1(\beta)$ and $g_2(\psi)$ are identical in every respect save that $E_\beta \neq E_\psi$ (i.e., the distribution $g_2(\psi)$ is equivalent to $g_1(\beta)$ except that it is shifted over), we can deduce no single optimal strategy without specifying exact mathematical equivalents for the functions. We can demonstrate, however, that the strategy $\theta = a/2$ meets the necessary condition for a maximum, $\partial P/\partial \theta = 0$; we cannot eliminate any other permissible strategy, even by examining second order conditions for a maximum. Stated formally, let the following assumptions hold:

ASSUMPTION 3. $a = -1$, $b = 1$ (no generality lost)

ASSUMPTION 4. $g_1(-x) = g_2(-x + 1)$

THEOREM. If assumptions 3 and 4 hold, the strategy $-1/2$ meets the necessary condition for a maximum, $\partial P/\partial \theta = 0$.

PROOF. Consider $-x = -1/2$. By assumption 4, $g_1(-x) = g_2(-x + 1)$, or $g_1(-1/2) = g_2(-1/2 + 1) = g_2(1/2)$. Hence, for $\theta = -1/2$, $g_1(\theta)$

$= g_2(-\theta)$. Recalling equation (3), the necessary condition for a maximum is:

$$\frac{g_1(\theta)}{g_2(-\theta)} = \frac{\int_\theta^0 g_1(\beta)\, d\beta}{\int_{-\theta}^1 g_2(\psi)\, d\psi}.$$

At the point $\theta = -1/2$, as we demonstrate, $g_1(\theta) = g_2(-\theta)$. Hence, we must ascertain if the equality of equation (9) is true, namely that

$$\frac{g_1(-1/2)}{g_2(1/2)} = 1 = \frac{\int_{-1/2}^0 g_1(\beta)\, d\beta}{\int_{1/2}^1 g_2(\psi)\, d\psi} \tag{9}$$

or

$$\int_{1/2}^1 g_2(\psi)\, d\psi = \int_{-1/2}^0 g_1(\beta)\, d\beta. \tag{9'}$$

Observe that

$$\int_{1/2}^1 g_2(x)\, dx = \int_{1/2}^1 g_1(x-1)\, dx. \tag{10}$$

Let $t = (x - 1)$, in which case if $x = 1$, $t = 0$, and if $x = 1/2$, $t = -1/2$. Of course, $dt = dx$. Hence,

$$\int_{1/2}^1 g_1(x-1)\, dx = \int_{-1/2}^0 g_1(t)\, dt. \tag{11}$$

Therefore,

$$\int_{-1/2}^0 g_1(x)\, dx = \int_{1/2}^1 g_2(x)\, dx, \tag{12}$$

by a simple identity of calculus.

Q.E.D.

We can construct an identical proof to show that $\theta = -1/2$ meets the necessary condition for a maximum if $g_1(\beta)$ and $g_2(\psi)$ are skewed in the opposite direction (i.e., if β falls close to $E(x)$ and ψ to $E_2(x)$). Because of our earlier statement that we cannot eliminate any other $-1 \leq \theta \leq 0$, even by examining the second order condition, $\partial^2 P/\partial\theta^2 < 0$, our tentative identification of $\theta_{max} = -1/2$ (or $a/2$) is only reasonable conjecture.[13]

---

[13] $\theta = -1/2$ could also be a relative minimum, while the mode of $g_1(\theta)$ and its symmetric position about $-1/2$ could be maxima.

IV. SEQUENTIAL STRATEGY PROBLEM: ACTIVISTS JUDGE BY ISSUE STRATEGY—ELABORATION

The careful reader must note that there are countless probability functions that fulfill both theorems and the corollary and that there are some very reasonable functions with solid empirical credentials that clearly do not. Consider the distributions that we picture in figure 12. We are not able to make any simplifying assumptions about these distributions that allow us to deduce a unique strategy, though it is possible to select a range of strategies that contain the optimal strategy.

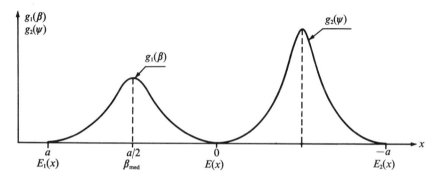

FIGURE 12

We need not be discouraged, however, by our inability to deduce exact optimal strategies in all cases from subjectively estimated probability functions that are only very generally specified. If we can specify $g_1(\beta)$ and $g_2(\psi)$, then further analysis and some stronger deductions are possible.

Consider, for example, the subjective probability estimates in figure 7 (above). We discussed this case of perfect ignorance about each opponent's strategy in the previous section. Let us continue to assume (without loss of generality) that $E_1(x) = a = -1$, and that $E_2(x) = -a = 1$. Thus,

$$P = \int_{\theta}^{0} g_1(\beta)\, d\beta \int_{-\theta}^{1} g_2(\psi)\, d\psi.$$

It is simple to show that these two cumulatives describe, for the two uniform distributions in figure 7, two straight line segments of equal but opposite slopes defined for $-1 \leq \theta \leq 0$. We know that if the candidate is totally uncertain about both opponents' likely strategies,

$$P_1 = -\theta,$$

$$-1 \leq \theta \leq 0$$

$$P_2 = \theta + 1.$$

Consequently,

$$P = P_1 P_2 = (\theta + 1)(-\theta) = -\theta^2 - \theta$$

$$\frac{\partial P}{\partial \theta} = -2\theta - 1 = 0$$

$$\theta_{max} = -1/2,$$

as we deduced earlier from the corollary.[14]

We can ask, however, what happens if knowledge about one opponent, for example the nomination foe, is superior to information about the other opponent. Let us keep the general symmetric and rectangular characteristics of P_1, while improving information by collapsing the distribution about the point $E_\beta = -1/2$. The effects of this operation on θ_{max} are not at all apparent, even should we continue to define $g_2(\psi)$ as uniform over the interval $0 \le \psi \le 1$. We know that P_2, then, is $\theta + 1$, but we need a more general statement for P_1.

P_1 must conform to the linear equation,

$$P_1 = \alpha_1 \theta + \alpha_2, \tag{13}$$

for which α_1 is the slope of P_1 (over the region for which $g_1(\beta) > 0$) and α_2 is the intercept.

We note from figure 13 that $g_1(\beta)$ is collapsed symmetrically about $-1/2$. The extent of this collapse is a measure of improved information about the nomination opponent's likely strategy. Hence, we introduce a new parameter, w, that is inversely proportional to the extent of this information. When $w = 0$, information is perfect; when $w = 1$, all strategies for $-1 \le \beta \le 0$ are equiprobable. Thus $0 \le w \le 1$.

We wish to express equation (13) as a function of w and θ. Consider α_1, the slope of P_1. We know that

$$\int_{-(w+1)/2}^{(w-1)/2} k \, dx = 1,$$

or $k = 1/w$. At $-(w + 1)/2$, $P_1 = 1/w$ and at $(w - 1)/2$, $P_1 = 0$. Thus $\Delta P_1 = -1/w$ and $\Delta \theta = w$. As $\alpha_1 = \Delta P_1 / \Delta \theta$, for $g_1(\beta) > 0$,

$$\alpha_1 = -1/w^2. \tag{14}$$

We can calculate α_2 by the ratio of sides of similar triangles. (In figure 13, the angles of the two triangles are appropriately marked.) It is simple to show that

$$\alpha_2 = \frac{w - 1}{2w^2}. \tag{15}$$

---

[14] The second order condition also holds, as $\partial^2 P / \partial \theta^2 < 0$.

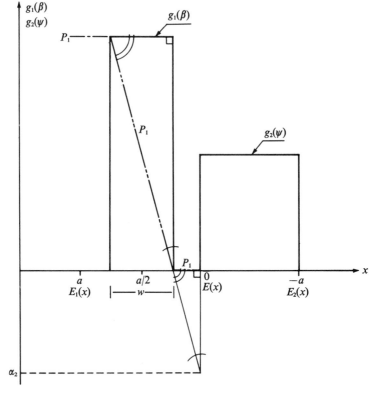

FIGURE 13

Substituting equations (14) and (15) into equation (13),

$$P_1 = \frac{-\theta}{w^2} + \frac{w - 1}{2w^2}. \tag{16}$$

Since $P_2 = \theta + 1$, we can express P (for $g_1(\beta) > 0$) as

$$P = P_1 P_2 = (\theta + 1)\left(\frac{w - 1}{2w^2} - \frac{\theta}{w^2}\right). \tag{17}$$

Differentiating P with respect to θ and setting equal to zero

$$\frac{\partial P}{\partial \theta} = 0 = \frac{1}{2w} - \frac{3}{2w^2} - \frac{2\theta}{w^2}. \tag{18}$$

Solving for θ,

$$\theta_{max} = \frac{w - 3}{4}. \tag{19}$$

But this solution is applicable only if $\theta \geq -(w+1)/2$. Hence, we must know when the solution of equation (19) satisfies this condition. It does so if

$$\frac{w-3}{4} \geq -\frac{w+1}{2}.$$

Solving this inequality for w, we find that it is true for $w \geq 1/3$. We know that $P_1 = 1$ and $P_2 = \theta + 1$ for $w \leq 1/3$. Hence $P_{w<1/3} = \theta + 1$, and $\partial P/\partial \theta = 1$. For $w \leq 1/3$, then, the candidate adopts a strategy at the left side of $g_1(\beta)$.

We illustrate the relationship between θ_{max} and w in figure 14. The interpretation of our findings suggests that the candidate's best strategy, θ_{max}, is clearly a function not only of the shape of the subjective probability estimates, but also of their variance. Collapsing $g_1(\beta)$, in this case, draws the candidate off the position $-1/2$ slowly and in a linear fashion as w decreases and moves his strategy closer to $E_1(x)$. But as w becomes smaller than $1/3$, the candidate's strategy returns more rapidly to $-1/2$.

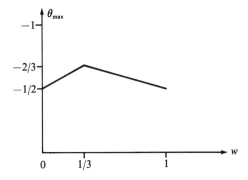

FIGURE 14

The satisfying part of this analysis is not only in the deduction of an unexpected relationship between strategy and information, as stated in equation (19). This analysis shows also that by specifying surrogate, though plausible, functions, we can deduce optimal strategies under a wide variety of very general circumstances. We can move E_β around and collapse $g_1(\beta)$ about any point we choose; a similar operation is possible, of course, for $g_2(\psi)$.

V. CANDIDATE'S NOMINATION PROBLEM IF ACTIVISTS JUDGE BY MIXED MOTIVES

The search for optimal strategies if activists use either candidate (viability) or citizen (ideological) decision-rules is reasonably simple compared to the problems that occur if activists employ a mix of these criteria. Our research on this problem is incomplete in that we develop here only the nomination strategy part of the problem, without considering the general election strategy. We believe, though, that this case is sufficiently interesting to warrant the reporting of only partially formulated results.[15]

The problem is to deduce optimal strategies for nomination contests in which the judges of those contests—the activists—evaluate a candidate not only on the ideological satisfaction they derive from his position but also on his probable viability as a general election candidate.

We continue with our earlier notation:

θ = the candidate's strategy;
β = his nomination opponent's strategy;
ψ = his general election opponent's strategy.

We add to this notation:

$L(\theta)$ = the loss that the activist associates with the candidate's position;

$L(\beta)$ = the loss that the activist associates with the position of the candidate's nomination opponent;

$L(\psi)$ = the loss that the activist associates with the position of the candidate's general election opponent (the opposing party's nominee);

P_θ = the probability that, if nominated, the candidate will win the general election;

P_β = the probability that, if nominated, the candidate's nomination opponent will win the general election.

The *expected* losses that the activist associates with θ and β, respectively, are:

$$E_\theta = P_\theta L(\theta) + (1 - P_\theta)L(\psi), \text{ and}$$
$$E_\beta = P_\beta L(\beta) + (1 - P_\beta)L(\psi).$$

---

[15] James Coleman analyzes the problem from a game theoretic view in chapter 15.

The activist prefers θ to β if and only if

$$E_\theta < E_\beta, \text{ or}$$
$$P_\theta L(\theta) + (1 - P_\theta)(L\psi) < P_\beta L(\beta) + (1 - P_\beta)L(\psi),$$

which is equivalent to

$$L(\theta) < \frac{P_\beta}{P_\theta}L(\beta) + \left(1 - \frac{P_\beta}{P_\theta}\right)L(\psi). \tag{20}$$

This inequality has the reasonable property that if $P_\beta = 0$ (i.e., the candidate's nomination opponent has no chance of winning the general election), then (20) reduces to

$$L(\theta) < L(\psi).$$

The activist, hence, prefers his own party's candidate if the loss he associates with θ is less than the loss he associates with ψ.

But we cannot ascertain the location of some θ that satisfies (20) unless we include more information. Specifically, we assume that the loss function, L, is quadratic, of the form

$$L(\theta) = A(x - \theta)^2; \; L(\psi) = A(x - \psi)^2; \; L(\beta) = A(x - \beta)^2;$$

such that x is the activist's most preferred position and A is a positive constant (Davis and Hinich, 1966). Substituting the appropriate identities into (20),

$$A(x - \theta)^2 < A\frac{P_\beta}{P_\theta}(x - \beta)^2 + A\left(1 - \frac{P_\beta}{P_\theta}\right)(x - \psi)^2. \tag{21}$$

Cancelling and rearranging terms,

$$2x[P_\theta(\psi - \theta) - P_\beta(\psi - \beta)] < P_\beta(\beta^2 - \psi^2) - P_\theta(\theta^2 - \psi^2). \tag{22}$$

We assume, now, a minimax-like property, that the candidate's opponents adopt the worst possible strategies for him, namely $\beta = -1$ and $\psi = 0$. This is a calculation that seeks a security level strategy. Hence, (22) becomes

$$x(P_\beta + P_\theta\theta) > \frac{P_\theta\theta^2 - P_\beta}{2}. \tag{23}$$

Unlike our earlier assumptions, we adopt here the convention that uncertainty arises not from locations of β and ψ, but from the location of $E(x)$, the citizens' mean preference, since β and ψ are known and equal to -1 and 0 respectively.

Let $\mu = E(x)$

$$g(\mu) = \frac{1}{2k}, \quad -k \le \mu \le k$$

$$= 0, \quad \text{otherwise.}$$

This assumption argues that $f(x)$ might have a mean, $\mu = E(x)$, anywhere between $-k$ and k, as we note in figure 15.

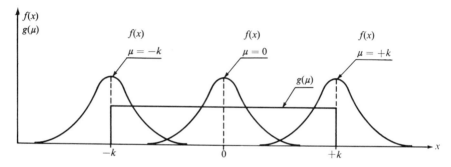

FIGURE 15

We can express P_θ, then, as

$$P_\theta = \frac{1}{2k} \int_{-k}^{\theta/2} d\mu = \frac{\theta + 2k}{4k}. \tag{24}$$

Similarly, P_β becomes

$$P_\beta = \frac{\beta + 2k}{4k}. \tag{25}$$

Substituting (24) and (25) into (23),

$$x[\beta + 2k + \theta^2 + 2\theta k] > \frac{\theta^3 + 2k\theta^2 - \beta - 2k}{2}. \tag{26}$$

By the assumption that $\beta = -1$,

$$x[2k - 1 + \theta^2 + 2\theta k] > \frac{\theta^3 + 2k\theta^2 + 1 - 2k}{2}. \tag{27}$$

(If $\theta = 0$, (27) reduces to $x > -1/2$; i.e., all activists who prefer policies greater than $-1/2$ prefer θ to β ($k > 1/2$, or $P_\beta = 0$).)

We can plot the relationship between x and θ for alternative values of k. For any k, all activists whose most preferred positions fall to the right or above the curve prefer the position β, while others prefer θ. Our computations, as described by figure 16, suggest that creating uncertainty about the mean of the electorate preference distribution may be a useful strategy, in itself, for candidates in various circumstances. A candidate who is fixed at a position close to $E(x)$ (assuming he *knows* its location) might attempt to convey his certainty to his party's activists. For as k approaches zero, assuming that $\beta < \theta$, P_β (his nomination opponent's viability) also approaches zero. The candidate distant from $E(x)$ might employ an opposite strategy, inducing considerable uncertainty about μ (by making k large), as it increases his expected viability.[16]

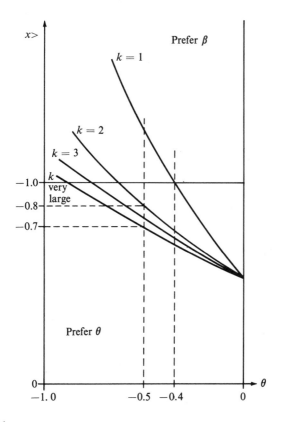

FIGURE 16

---

[16] Hence, assuming that opinion polls are accurate, for θ close to $E(x)$ the candidate advertises them. For θ far from $E(x)$ the candidate scoffs at them.

VI. CONCLUSION

The spatial model of electoral competition is a clear target for many writers who regard it as an unsatisfactory oversimplification of real world choice. We believe that this judgment is extraordinarily premature, though we welcome suggestions about areas in which the theory remains incomplete.

We stake out a small political problem in this paper: how to choose a campaign strategy that maximizes the joint probability of nomination and election, given constituencies with different preferences and possibly different motivations. Although the territory we explore is limited, we believe that this exploration exhibits three properties that are major strengths of formal theory.

First, formal theory is parsimonious. We deduce optimal campaign strategies with the smallest number of variables possible, extracting all but the essential forces that operate in sequential elections. There is little virtue in charting the entire political world, as the resulting map would be no more comprehensible than the uncharted world itself. A physicist who wishes to understand the effects of gravity, for example, does not consider at first the effects of wind resistance that a falling body encounters. Nor should we begin our investigation by including all political phenomena.

Second, formal theory permits the building of further theory on previously deduced findings. There is no need to begin anew here to deduce dominant strategies for single election campaigns. The use of previous results greatly simplifies our task. More importantly, we use these results with a greater confidence than was formerly possible in political science; these earlier studies progress with unambiguous and precise referents and progress to deductions that are theoretically unquestionable (though empirically falsifiable) because of their axiomatic structure.

Third, formal theory aids in the deduction of nonobvious relationships—a task nearly impossible for "common sense" thinking. It is not immediately obvious, for example, that in the face of total uncertainty about the opponents' likely strategies, that an optimal strategy exists, gainsay that we can locate it.

Though these three virtues are persuasive, we believe that the best answer to critical reviews of the spatial model is in the active seeking after greater explanatory and predictive power. The clearest answer to Stokes's (1963) argument that Downs's single-issue discussion oversimplifies vastly a multidimensional world is Davis and Hinich's (1966) development of the model to include the multidimensional case.

In this spirit, we believe that Froman's (1966) major objections to the theory of rational electoral choice are no longer valid. Froman suggests, "that the model itself does not even serve as a useful ideal because of its inability to cope with the problems confronted by the electorate as well as the candidates. . ." (p. 2). We cannot answer here all of Froman's arguments; our analysis, though, clearly contradicts two major propositions he advances.

First, Froman argues that the imperative of the candidate's seeking the support of groups in the electorate, "conflicts with the assumptions of the rationality model of campaigns," since, "most groups are not politically neutral" (p. 4). Expanding on this theme, Froman remarks that, "groups. . .must balance their preferences for a candidate with the candidate's chances of winning. They are not likely to maximize the former when such behavior may result in supporting a loser" (p. 5).

We answer this criticism since the group "behavior" that Froman cites is identical to the choices of activists with mixed motives. These people, whom we consider in section 5, choose voting strategies in a way that balances spatial loss against candidate viability. Should a candidate find the support of some group imperative, he can calculate an optimal strategy by substituting the group's (politically not neutral) preferences for the activist mean preferences.

Second, Froman argues that a minority party nomination candidate has "institutional factors" to overcome (p. 13). These include the problem of getting nominated if activists seek only minimal spatial loss. Froman concludes, therefore, that, "another powerful restraint is operating on the party in choosing its best candidate: the candidate with the best chance of winning is difficult to find, and, if found, is difficult to nominate" (p. 14). But our analysis shows that spatial models can incorporate this problem. (The minority question is irrelevant.) Indeed, we devote sections 3 and 4 to deducing strategies for just such a contingency.

Summarily, our results offer an explanation for the failure of candidates to converge, even if $f(x)$ is symmetric and unimodal. But the importance of this study lies not only in the specific deductions, but also in the demonstration of theory constructed on previous theory, all based on a single paradigm.

15. The Positions of Political Parties in Elections

JAMES S. COLEMAN

The positions that political parties present to constituents at an election may be conceived as similar to products which are marketed to a set of consumers. Anthony Downs systematically presented this perspective in 1957, and it has since been pursued by a number of authors (e.g., Chapman, 1967; Hinich and Ordeshook, 1969, 1970). Since, in a two-party system, both parties have the aim of capturing a majority of the electorate, there is a tendency for both parties to gravitate toward the center, to capture a greater share of the market. Downs shows, using earlier work on spatial competition by Hotelling, that the platform positions will converge at the median voter, if party platforms differ along a single dimension, if there is no entrance of third parties, if there is no nonvoting among constituents who are far removed from either party's position (and thus disaffected from both), and if certain other simplifying assumptions hold. It has also been shown (Harris, 1966) that when voters differ in two dimen-

This paper was prepared with the aid of NSF Research Grant GS25–26, for work on problems of collective decisions. It was stimulated by an approach to the problem of parties' positions taken by Robert Harris and Gudmund Hernes in a seminar on collective decisions at Johns Hopkins in early 1970. Harris and Hernes pointed out that the usual mathematical approach to optimum party position neglects the fact of competition for leadership within the party, and assumes party leaders are completely free to respond to the larger electorate. Aranson and Ordeshook (chap. 14 in this volume) also begin to adopt this more organizationally sophisticated approach.

sions, parties' behavior will not differ substantially; and Davis and Hinich (1966, 1967) examine a similar model in n dimensions. It has also been shown that when there is nonvoting among voters far removed from either party's position, there will be a movement out from the median voter, in a way that is straightforwardly dependent on the strength of this effect. Entrance of third parties into the market has also been shown to upset the equilibrium at the median voter, again following the work in spatial competition.

However, all this work proceeds from certain assumptions that appear to be overly naive, thereby reducing a complex and interesting problem to a relatively uninteresting one, and in the process failing to mirror the forces which actually do shape party platforms.

In particular, I suggest that all this work has followed too directly the analogy to economic competition in a market.[1] It has erred in treating "the party" as a wholly autonomous producer of political positions, which is constrained in those positions solely by the expected response of the electorate.[2] But parties are not this at all. They are instead collectivities with constituencies of their own; and the positions that these collectivities take is the outcome of a struggle for leadership in the party. Nearly all political parties have elections in which candidates are nominated by the party. These elections are in the United States termed "primary" elections if they are elections by the party constituency as a whole, and "nominating conventions" if they are elections by delegates. In parliamentary systems, party platforms and candidates are selected in various ways, but nearly always in a way that involves competition for leadership and selection by an electorate from among the competitors.

One might at first suppose that the problem of party positions could be treated in a way that is analogous to that of Downs, *et al.*, except that instead of the party's seeking out the median voter of the electorate as a whole, it would locate itself at the median voter *within* the party's elector-

---

[1] There are examples in the mathematical treatment of parties' positions which do not err in this fashion. MacRae (1958), who did not start from the analogy of parties as producers and voters as consumers, developed a model for the emergence of parties as coalitions, starting with an undifferentiated set of voters, located along a continuum, and with each voter attempting to maximize his utility by supporting those closest to him. This is a problem more ambitious than mine, for mine assumes party constituencies as given; and its general solution is beyond any of the work done to date. More recently, Tullock (1967) has taken some interesting steps away from the models discussed earlier. Neither of these efforts led in the present direction.

[2] Models of market competition among firms probably would also do well to modify their assumption that product changes and price changes are made wholly in response to market forces. As in the case of political parties, there are internal processes involved in gaining and holding organizational power. The outcomes of these processes constrain the changes that may be made in response to consumer demands—not in the same way, of course, as is true for political parties, because of the different organizational structure of firms.

ate, thus making itself safe from potential competitors within the party. Because the party constituencies are not representative of the population as a whole, but are concentrated toward one end of the continuum (in a two-party system), either the "left" or the "right," the party positions would be to the left or the right, the distance depending upon the ideological polarization between the two parties.

But this is too simple an approach as well, because party electorates are not merely expressive voters, electing that candidate as their nominee whom they themselves find most appealing. Instead, they elect a candidate with some view toward the final election. If their interest is in maximizing their gains in the main election, they would certainly not be doing so if they nominated an extreme candidate who had no chance of election, no matter how fully he satisfied their tastes.

These considerations are clearly voiced in primary elections, and the importance of this as an issue in primary elections indicates that those elections are different in this fundamental way from the final election.

This places the candidate running in a primary election in a rather odd position. He must present a platform that will be preferred by the majority of voters within the party (assuming for the present that he has only one competitor for the nomination), but the voters' preferences are not simply given by their positions on a continuum. They are instead determined by what they believe will be most beneficial for them in the long run, that is, after the outcome of the main election. (From this point on, we will treat the voters as rational actors, maximizing their expected gain from the election. The degree to which empirical voters correspond to these purely rational actors will not be taken in question here. It may be conjectured, however, that they differ from the rational actors not principally in what they *try* to do, but mainly in the calculating skill with which they are able to shape a strategy.) In other words, they will be voting to maximize an expected gain, and the expected gain is a product of two factors: the gain from this candidate if elected and the probability that this candidate will be elected. Since the probability in general declines as the candidate's position is shifted away from the overall population mean, while the gain from the candidate if elected increases as this position is shifted away from the population mean toward the party voter's more extreme position, the party voter whose own preference is extreme is under a cross-pressure: a candidate who is highly acceptable to the electorate as a whole is likely to be elected, but he will not be much preferable to the opposing party's candidate. Yet a candidate who fully represents his position is unlikely to be elected. (Parties when faced with concrete alternatives that have a fixed position because of prior actions sometimes choose one type of candidate, and sometimes another. The Republican party in 1952 chose Eisenhower, the generally popular center candidate, and rejected Taft, the one better representing the delegates' positions but less likely to be elected. In 1964, they chose Goldwater, the candidate representative of the delegates' positions, and rejected Rockefeller and others, who were more likely to be elected. In this work, however, it is assumed that a candidate can and will shift his position to the optimal position for primary election.) It seems possible, then, that the party members, in attempting to maximize their expected gain from the election, will find the maximum at neither extreme: at one, the expected gain would be near zero because the probability of election is near zero; at the other, the expected gain would be near zero because the candidate if elected would be no better than the opponent.

We might thus expect to find candidates of parties neither having identical platforms nor having platforms as different as the positions of the party members as a whole. There should be a tendency toward convergence, but not full convergence, so long as the members of the two parties who elect their respective candidates differ, on the average, in their own preferred political platforms.

There is one additional complication which the party voters are faced with. They would like to select a candidate with a position that maximizes their expected gain; but they do not know the position that the other party's elected candidate will have. Only if they can form some kind of expectation about the position that candidate can have will they be able to estimate what position on the part of their own candidate maximizes their expected gain.

The problem as stated appears somewhat like that of a two-person game as treated in theory of games, and it will turn out that our treatment will use the ideas behind that theory. But at this point we can state heuristically the kind of considerations that a rational actor will take (according to a definition of rationality that we will defend later). A given member of my party will want to vote for that position which will maximize his expected gain under the assumption that the other party's position will be that which maximizes the expected gain of that party's voters (which particular voters will be discussed later) when my party's position is as dictated by our maximization behavior. The reasoning sounds complicated and is, because it is like the minimax reasoning of zero-sum two-person game theory. It will be treated in detail later. At this point, it is sufficient to recognize that there is in this case more than the usual double contingency that is involved in the reasoning of game theory: a party candidate acts on the basis of assumptions about his voters' behavior. They, in turn, are acting on assumptions about the other party's position. The other party's position is taken on the basis of assumptions about their voters' behavior; and their voters' behavior is made on assumptions about my position.

The situation can perhaps be made clearer by a diagram. If we assume that there are two candidates competing for nomination in each party, A_1, A_2 in party 1, and B_1, B_2 in party 2, and that there are m party voters in party 1 labelled $a_1, \ldots, a_m$, r party voters in party 2, labelled $b_1, \ldots, b_r$, and s voters in the general election, labelled $c_1, \ldots, c_s$, which include the party voters, then the structure of direct effects is like this:

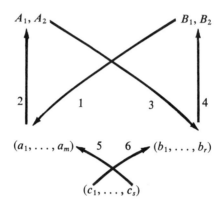

Via arrows 1 and 5, voters in party 1 are affected by the perceived or assumed positions of B_1, B_2, and by their perception of the electorate in the general election, in calculating the position they desire their own candidates to take. Via arrow 2, the candidates in party 1 are affected by the desires of $a_1, \ldots, a_m$, leading them to adjust their positions accordingly. Via arrows 3 and 6, the voters in party 2 are affected by their perception or assumptions concerning the positions of A_1, A_2, and by their perception of the electorate in the general election, and finally, via arrow 4, B_1, B_2 adjust their positions according to their voters' desires. It is assumed, in accordance with the Hotelling-Downs results, that A_1 and A_2 both locate at the same point which will maximize their probability of winning the primary, and B_1, B_2 behave similarly.[3] There may be non-voting in either primaries or the general election, but it is not assumed that nonvoting is conditional upon the candidates' positions. Obviously, by making assumptions about nonvoting conditional upon candidate positions, one could manage to create any of a variety of equilibrium positions for the candidates.

These are the general considerations that are behind the model. With these in mind, it is possible to turn to more specific considerations.

---

[3] This assumption that the candidates pay attention only to the primary may seem self-evident. However, it holds only under certain circumstances, which will be discussed below.

I. TO WHAT VOTERS DOES THE PARTY CANDIDATE NEED TO ATTEND?

The first question to be examined concerns the behavior of the party candidate: who shall he pay attention to among his voters? We assume that there is only one other challenger for the party's nomination, that all party members will vote, that the vote is a majority rule, and that voters differ along a single dimension. Each party voter will prefer that candidate position which will maximize his expected utility from the final election. That expected utility may be defined as follows:

$$E(u) = p_1 u_1 + (1 - p_1)u_2$$
$$= u_2 + p_1(u_1 - u_2)$$

where p_1 is probability of party 1's candidate winning, u_i is utility if party i wins, and the convention that will be adopted is that index i is 1 for the left party and 2 for the right party.

Before proceeding, it is useful to define more precisely how u_1 and u_2 are determined. Consider that the subsequent actions of the party while in office will involve n issues. These issues all lie along the same dimension, but differ in the extremity of the position. Issues are labelled with the most extreme left issue labelled 1, and the rest labelled in order of decreasing extremity. If a person agrees to issue 1, he agrees to all others. If he does not agree to issue i, then he does not agree to any of the first i-1 issues. If he agrees to issue i, he agrees to those labelled $i + 1$ to n. Thus the issues are like a Guttman scale. His position can be located along a continuum from 0 to n, with his position on the continuum representing the proportion of issues he rejects.[4] Dividing through by n gives a continuum from 0 to 1. This assumption of a Guttman scale of issues implies that all issues fall on the same left-right continuum. How restrictive this assumption is for the results which follow is not known. However, since the earlier approach to this problem, referred to above, shows that higher dimensions behave similarly to lower ones, it is possible that the same result will hold in the present approach as well.

A candidate's position lies on the same continuum, and a party with position at x will, in its actions, reject a proportion of actions equal to x, and these will be the leftmost xn actions.

If a voter's utility is identical for every issue on which the government takes the same position as he, then his utility is merely a constant times

---

[4] The situation is obviously symmetric. By reversing the definitions of passage and failure of the bills, the rightmost position represents acceptance of the most extreme bill.

the proportion of issues on which he and the government agree.[5] If his position, for example, is at α_i, and the government's position is to the right of α_i at x, then the utility is arrived at as follows:

a. they both prefer to reject the leftmost $\alpha_i n$ issues, which are to the left of α_i;

b. they both prefer to accept the rightmost $(1 - x) n$ issues, which are to the right of x;

c. they disagree on those issues to the right of α_i and the left of x.

This voter's utility from that government is thus proportional to $\alpha_i + 1 - x$. If α_i is to the right of x, then his utility is proportional to $x + 1 - \alpha_i$, based on similar reasoning to that above.

Thus for a voter to the left of the position of both his own party (the "left" party, labelled no. 1) and that of the opponent, his expected utility will be (disregarding here and elsewhere a scale constant):

$$E(u) = p_1(\alpha_i + 1 - x_1) + (1 - p_1)(\alpha_i + 1 - x_2)$$
$$= \alpha_i + 1 - x_2 + p_1(x_2 - x_1) \tag{1}$$

where $\alpha_i < x_1 < x_2 < 1$.

For a voter to the right of his party (party no. 1) but the left of the other party, his expected utility is:

$$E(u) = p_1(x_1 + 1 - \alpha_i) + (1 - p_1)(\alpha_i + 1 - x_2)$$
$$= \alpha_i + 1 - x_2 + p_1(x_2 - x_1) - p_1(2\alpha_i - 2x_1) \tag{2}$$

where $x_1 < \alpha_i < x_2 < 1$.

Equation (2), put in the same form as (1), shows that the two quantities differ by a term $-p_1(2\alpha_i - 2x_1)$, which without the sign is positive. The total proportion of issues on which this voter agrees with the government is not necessarily less than that of the more left voter: for a given x_1 and x_2, his α_i is larger than the first voter, and thus the first term, α_i, may be enough larger in this equation to offset the last term, $-p_1(2\alpha_i - 2x_1)$.

Returning to (1), it becomes possible to see how the candidate's position exerts a cross pressure on the voter to his left. The quantity $x_2 - x_1$

---

[5] This seems to imply equal importance of all issues, an assumption which is obviously not realized in actual political systems. However, this apparent restriction is no restriction at all, because the metric on the continuum could equally well be defined by letting each issue occupy a length proportional to its importance. The assumption then reduces to a less restrictive one: that all voters impose the same metric. Relaxation of this assumption is beyond the scope of the present paper.

increases as x_1 decreases (i.e., moves to the left). But the probability of winning, p_1, decreases as x_1 decreases. (The only assumption necessary here about the distribution of the overall electorate is that the median voter is to the right of x_1, which will be true in the region of the continuum under discussion here.) Thus the expected utility may not increase as x_1 decreases to come closer to α_i. It may, for example, reach a maximum at a point still to the right of α_i. In particular, if the probability of winning drops at first slowly and then very sharply as the candidate's position moves to the left from the center, while the utility given a win increases moderately slowly, there will be a point at which the expected utility is maximum—and if the voter is far to the left, this point of highest expected utility for him will be to his right.

This maximum point for x_1 (if it exists in the range $\alpha_i < x_1 < 0.5$) may be found by setting to zero the derivative of $E(u)$ with respect to x_1; from (1)

$$\frac{d[E(u)]}{dx_1} = \frac{-dx_2}{dx_1} + (x_2 - x_1)\frac{dp_1}{dx_1} + p_1\frac{dx_2}{dx_1} - p_1 = 0.$$

It is useful to focus attention briefly on what (1) represents. It is intended to represent the subjective estimates of a voter at position α_i. Consequently the structure of the equation is intended to reflect the way that subjective estimate is made. The first derivative with respect to x_1, in the equation above, represents the individual's assumptions about changes in the factors affecting his expected utility as his own party's position, x_1, increases. One must then ask what are the individual's assumptions about dp_1/dx_1 and dx_2/dx_1. The rational party voter will see the probability p_1 of winning the general election increasing as x_1 moves closer to the median voter in the general election, given the assumption made earlier that voters in the general election choose the candidate closer to their own position. Thus dp_1/dx_1 is not zero; and in a later section we will make some specific assumptions about how the individual estimates dp_1/dx_1. What is more problematic is the individual's estimate of dx_2/dx_1, that is, what change the other party candidate will make in response to his candidate's position. The assumption here is simple: the party voter, knowing that his own candidates (x_1) are responding solely to their own party voters' desires, assumes that the other party's candidates will do the same, and will not respond to changes in x_1. This means that dx_2/dx_1 will be zero. The equation thus becomes:

$$(x_2 - x_1)\frac{dp_1}{dx_1} = p_1, \quad \text{or}$$

$$\frac{dp_1}{dx_1} = \frac{p_1}{x_2 - x_1}. \tag{3}$$

Equation (3) shows that the maximum occurs at the point at which the ratio of the probability of winning, p_1, to the gain from winning, $x_2 - x_1$, is equal to the increment in probability with change in x_1, that is, the probability density function.[6]

Equation (3) shows that for all voters to the left of x_1 (that is, those voters for which the equation holds) the optimum position for x_1 (the position at which $E(u)$ is maximized) does not depend on their own position, if this optimum exists in the range from α_i to 0.5. In other words, by increasing x_1 (moving to the right) to the point at which the increase in $E(u)$ due to increased probability of winning balances the decrease in $E(u)$ due to decreased returns if there is a win, an optimum point is found. That optimum point is the same for all persons i with positions α_i to the left of x_1. Or to put it still another way: suppose we calculate the optimum x_1 from (3), for a hypothetical voter i at a point α_i to the left of x_1 and thus governed by (3). The maximum will be independent of α_i. Thus for all individuals to the left of that point, that position will be optimum, independent of their own position.

Suppose, however, that for a given individual i with position α_i, this maximum is not reached to the right of α_i. That is, the probability of winning is still declining more slowly than the rate of increase of utility given a win. In that case, if the candidate's position moves to the left of α_i, *both* the probability of winning and the utility given a win will decline. In this case, then, the maximum expected utility is at the individual's own position α_i. This can be seen from (2) by putting it in slightly different form:

$$E(u) = \alpha_i + 1 - x_2 + p_1(x_2 + x_1 - 2\alpha_i). \qquad (2')$$

---

[6] The fact that (3) gives a maximum rather than a minimum can be seen from the following considerations. Note that in (1), the only term which changes is $p_1(x_2 - x_1)$. As x_1 moves to the right, whatever the position of x_2 (so long as it remains to the right of x_1 as assumed), then p_1 will increase and $x_2 - x_1$ will decrease. At the starting point, when $x_1 = 0$, then p_1, and consequently $p_1(x_2 - x_1)$, will have some non-negative value, and when x_1 has moved all the way to x_2, $x_2 - x_1 = 0$, and thus $p_1(x_2 - x_1) = 0$. Since the value of $p_1(x_2 - x_1)$ can never be less than zero and must be positive at some point between 0 and x_2 (assuming that there is some subjective probability that the median voter lies to the left of x_2) then if $d[p_1(x_2 - x_1)]/dx_1$ equals zero at some point between $x_1 = 0$ and $x_1 = x_2$, this point must be a maximum. Heuristically, one can see that as x_1 moves to the right, bringing an increase in p_1 and a decrease in $x_2 - x_1$, there will be a maximum at that point at which the decrement $p_1 dx_1$ due to a further decrease, dx_1, in $x_2 - x_1$, becomes equal for the first time to the increment $dp_1(x_2 - x_1)$ due to the increase in p_1 resulting from the movement of x_1 to the right. This does not imply that there will be such a maximum for any position of x_1; and with curious types of subjective probability distributions for the location of the median voter in the general election, there may be two or more local maxima. The latter might occur when there is, for example, a subjective probability distribution of the median vote which is bimodal; but that would be a rather curious psychological phenomenon.

As x_1 decreases (moves to the left), p_1 decreases, and also the factor $(x_2 + x_1 - 2\alpha_i)$ decreases. Thus both factors in the last term on the right decrease, while all other terms on the right remain constant. The result is that $E(u)$ necessarily decreases as x_1 decreases everywhere that x_1 is to the left of α_i.

The qualitative results based on the above examination can be described as follows:

1. If for a party voter at the extreme left, there is a maximum point for x_1, labelled x_1^*, where the decline in probability of winning with further movement of x_1 to the left exactly balances the increase in utility given a win, then the following proposition holds:
   a. For all individuals to the left of this point x_1^*, the optimum candidate position will be the same point, x_1^*.
   b. For all individuals i to the right of this point, the optimum candidate position will be their own positions, α_i.
2. If for the party voter at the extreme left there is no point x_1^* which maximizes the expected utility, then this implies that the decline in probability is so slow that the maximum for the extreme voter is not yet reached when $x_1 = 0$. In this case, the optimum for the extreme voter is $x_1 = 0$, and the optimum for any voter with position α_i is $x_1 = \alpha_i$. In this case, probability of winning plays no effective part in the calculations, and voters' maxima are at their own positions. The party position in this case would be at the median party voter.

Altogether, then, there are three cases for the left party:

1. A majority of party voters is to the left of x_1^*. In this case, the optimum candidate position is at x_1^*.
2. A majority of party voters is to the right of x_1^*. In this case, the optimum candidate position is the position α_i of the median voter.
3. There is no point x_1^*, and all party voters prefer their own positions. In this case, the optimum candidate position is the position α_i of the median voter.

To return to the original question with which this section began—Who should the party candidate pay attention to?—the answer differs in different cases. First of all, he should pay attention to his voters with the most extreme positions. If they prefer their own (extreme) position, he is in case no. 3, and he then should take the position of the median party voter. If they prefer a position x_1^* to their right, but to the left of 0.5, he is in case no. 1 or 2. He then must see whether a majority of voters are to the left of x_1^*. If so, he is in case no. 1, and his position is x_1^*. If not, he in case no. 2, and his position is that of the median voter, somewhere to the right of x_1^*.

Before proceeding to examine how the party voters determine their optimum, it is useful to reexamine the assumption which has been made that the party candidate will seek to maximize his probability of winning the primary, with no consideration of the question of how this will affect his chances in the general election. This of course does not immediately follow from the assumption that he wants to maximize his expected utility. It is possible by a simple calculation to find the conditions under which he will maximize his probability of winning the primary in order to maximize his expected utility.

First, we assume that he prefers winning the general election to losing it, and prefers winning the primary to losing it, even if he fails to win the general election. There are three outcomes, with utility labelled u_{11} for winning the general election, u_{10} for winning the primary but losing the general, and u_0 for losing the primary. The assumption is that $u_{11} > u_{10} > u_0$. Then if the probability of winning the primary election is p and his probability of winning the general election given a win in the primary is r, his expected utility is $p[ru_{11} + (1 - r)u_{10}] + (1 - p)u_0$. If he seeks to maximize this by increasing p, his probability of winning the primary election, and if in increasing p he also hurts his chances in the general election, reducing r, then what are the conditions under which there will be a maximum of p that is less than 1 ?

Taking the first derivative of his expected utility with respect to p will show the conditions under which an increase in p will not lead to an increase in expected utility. The expected utility first becomes negative when $dr/dp + (1/p)[r + (u_{10} - u_0)/(u_{11} - u_{10})]$ becomes negative. Since both terms in the brackets are positive, then this means he will fail to maximize p only if dr/dp comes to be below a certain upper bound that is less than zero. The bound is

$$\frac{dr}{dp} < -\frac{1}{p}\left(r + \frac{u_{10} - u_0}{u_{11} - u_{10}}\right).$$

The ratio on the right can be expressed as the ratio of the gains he would experience from winning the primary to the gains he would experience from winning the general election. Thus the condition can be expressed qualitatively as follows: the party candidate will fail to maximize p only when the product of his probability of winning the primary times the loss in probability of winning the general election per unit gain in probability of winning the primary ($-pdr/dp$) is larger than the sum of the probability of winning (r) and the utility of winning the primary compared to winning the general election ($(u_{10} - u_0)/(u_{11} - u_{10})$). Thus when he doesn't care about winning the primary, when his chances of winning the general election are small and the chances of winning the primary are large, and when a move which increases his chance of winning the primary hurts his chances of winning the general election, he will begin to pay attention to his chance of winning the general election, in establishing his position. Unless these conditions occur, he will pay attention only to his chance of winning the primary, and take his position solely with that consideration in mind.

It will be assumed here that these conditions do not occur, and that as a consequence the party candidate takes his position on issues with the sole aim of maximizing his chance of winning the primary election. Since the primary election is assumed to be by majority vote, this means he and his competitor within the party will take the position desired by the median party voter.

II. HOW DO PARTY VOTERS DECIDE THEIR OPTIMUM?

Game Theoretic Considerations

It is useful to consider briefly the fundamental ideas in the theory of zero-sum games (or games of pure conflict, as they are better called) for two persons which led to the minimax principle of action. Von Neumann and Morgenstern conceive of a player, A, as playing a "majorant game" and a "minorant game." In the first, his opponent, B, must act first. Then he looks to see what action B took, and takes that action which maximizes his return under B's action. We consider this for all possible actions that B might take, and it is possible then to list A's best response to all these possible actions. Where B's and A's actions are continuous in gradation, the curve of best responses for A might look like that in figure 1.[7] So long as there are no actions of B which lead to two best responses on A's part, the function is single-valued, as shown in the figure (though possibly discontinuous at some points).[8] The curve may be thought of as a mountain ridge whose height varies but is everywhere higher than any other peaks in the north-south direction. The height at any point represents A's payoff when he and B take actions represented by the coordinates of that point.

Then A plays a minorant game in which he must go first, and B can choose any action he pleases after looking at A's action, that is, a best response to A's action, which will maximize B's payoff. For all possible

---

[7] This concept of "best response" is similar to the "best reply" concept of Harsanyi (1966).

[8] The points of discontinuity may make the resulting map consist of line segments, but these will be so arranged that there is always exactly one value of a for each value of b.

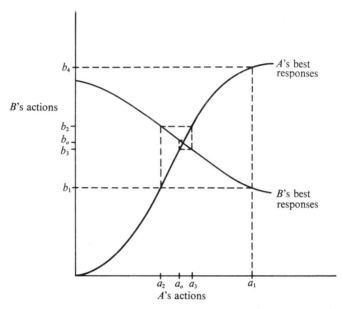

FIGURE 1

actions of A, the curve of best responses for B might be as shown in figure 1. This might be conceived as a second contour map, with the height this time representing the size of B's payoff, and the ridge shown in figure 1 being the maximum height in an east-west direction.

Von Neumann and Morgenstern reasoned as follows: the actual game should be somewhere "between" the majorant and the minorant game. In the majorant game he can do as well or better than in the real game, because B had to make his move first, and give A the benefit of that information; in the minorant game, he can at most do as well as in the real game, because B can act with information about the move he made. Thus if we select the minimum height (i.e., minimum payoff to him) along the ridge in the majorant game, this is the highest payoff that he can guarantee, independent of B's action. But in the minorant game (which for B is the majorant game), B can similarly select the point of minimum height along his ridge as a guarantee. A's payoff, then, should be between the highest payoff that he can guarantee (his minimax) and the payoff he gets when B chooses the highest payoff that he can guarantee (B's minimax). The fundamental theorem of zero-sum two-person game theory states that A's payoff in these two cases is the same. The reason is simple and straightforward: since the game is zero-sum, B's contour map is identical to A's, except that it has depressions where A's is raised. The two maps are merely two sides of the same relief map. Consequently, B's mountain ridge is a valley for A; and the point at which the two lines in figure 1 cross is simultaneously the lowest point in A's ridge and the highest point in the valley represented by B's best-response line. If we take A's perspective, the line representing his own best response is a line of maximum payoff, and the point of crossing is a minimum along that line, or a minimax. The line representing B's best responses is a line of minimum payoff to A (because of zero-sum), and the point of crossing is a maximin. In zero-sum game theory, then, the minimax point of A equals his maximin (which is B's minimax). This point will be, following von Neumann and Morgenstern, the game's equilibrium point; it is the only point between the majorant and the minorant games; and in fact they touch at this point. (Trivially, there may be other points, but they are equivalent, by giving the same payoff.)

This reasoning is useful when we depart from a zero-sum game, although the fundamental theorem no longer holds. We now have two *different* contour maps, one for B's best responses to A, and one for A's best responses to B. It is no longer the case that A's gain is unalterably B's loss, and vice versa.

Certain things do remain true. The point of intersection of the two ridges is an equilibrium point, in the sense that if A chooses action a_o, then B's best response is action b_o, at the equilibrium point. It does not, however, have the self-enforcing properties that the equilibrium point in games of pure conflict have. For A may choose action a_1, knowing that B will choose action b_1—because the position (a_1, b_1) is better for A than is position (a_o, b_o). It may be better or worse for B than position (a_o, b_o); but since there is no longer a direct inverse link between A's return and that of B, it may be either.

It does appear possible, however, to extend the ideas behind the solution of a zero-sum game to non-zero-sum games, that is, games of partial conflict, such as the one under examination here.[9]

Solution for Certain Classes of Non-zero-sum Two-person Games

The conditions of the games to be considered are like those in zero-sum games except for these:

a. The payoffs to A and B need not be zero- or constant-sum;
b. Only those games are considered in which actions are continuously variable and best response curves have no points of discontinuity.

---

[9] None of the ideas in the next section are really new. The problem of a "solution" to non-zero-sum games has been discussed by many authors. See, for example, Luce and Raiffa (1957, chap. 5), who discuss the equilibrium concept in non-zero-sum games, but who do not distinguish between stable and unstable equilibria as defined here. Y. C. Ho (1970) in a discussion of differential games, shows some of the properties of equilibrium solutions in non-zero-sum games, and discusses other solution concepts.

Then it is possible to specify the conditions under which there will be a stable equilibrium point. The sense in which an equilibrium point can be considered a "solution" to the game is discussed below.

We first consider, as do von Neumann and Morgenstern, "virtual moves" on the part of each player. This shows the best response of each player to all the other players' actions. This will generate two curves of best response as in figure 1. Then each player notes what a sequence of best responses would produce. In figure 1 it would generate a converging spiral moving toward the equilibrium point (a_o, b_o). In another figure, with the best response lines differently located, such as figure 2, the best responses would produce a diverging spiral. Still other figures could result in best response lines that would produce various patterns—but each either converging to the point at which the lines cross, or diverging from it.

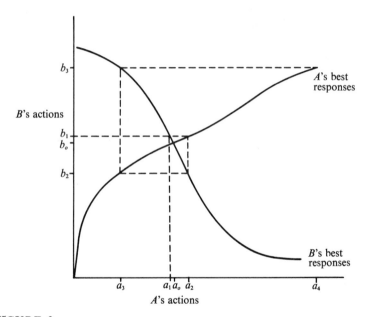

FIGURE 2

In the games with convergence to a point, one can describe a solution for the game in a weaker sense than in zero-sum games, but still in a nontrivial sense: a solution exists if the sequence of best responses in a sufficiently long series of virtual moves in majorant and minorant games leads to a single point. This solution is stable in the sense that if one player makes virtual moves away from this point, the other player's best response will be such as to lead back, through a sequence of virtual best responses, to the same point.

In figure 1, the point (a_o, b_o) is a solution point to the game in the sense under discussion; in figure 2, however, the point (a_o, b_o) is not a solution, since virtual moves away from the point would lead to moves farther and farther from it.

Several points should be noted:

1. In contrast to the solution of a zero-sum game, there may be more than one solution, or none. In the case where there is more than one, the solution achieved in any play of the game will depend on the starting point. Geometrically, such games may be represented by figures in which the curves of best response cross more than twice. (If they cross exactly twice, one point is a solution, i.e., stable, and the other is not.)

2. The solution may not be Pareto-optimal: both players might find it to their advantage to move to another (nonsolution) point. But if they did so, there would be no agreement on which point, because of differential advantages accruing to each player from different nonsolution points. By remaining at the solution point, they are giving up possible benefits for stability or predictability of return.[10]

3. The non-Pareto-optimality of the solution raises certain difficult questions of strategy which should be made explicit. Assume, in figure 1, that the utility to A at the point (a_1, b_1) is greater than that at the equilibrium point (a_o, b_o), even though it is (as it must by definition be) less than that at (a_1, b_4). This condition could not exist in a zero-sum game, but can exist in a non-zero-sum game. Then if A knew that B was going to play as described above (i.e., use the best response to A's action), he will prefer a_1 to a_o, since this would give him the utility associated with (a_1, b_1) rather than that associated with (a_o, b_o). More generally, assume that A finds the point (a^*, b^*) on B's best response curve, which constitutes the highest payoff to him, A. Then it is to his advantage (if he knows that B will make his best response) to take the action a^* associated with this point, so as to maximize his payoff.

The only fault in this reasoning is that it assumes that B is using a different kind of strategy from his own, a "reactive" strategy. If he were to assume that B would use a strategy like the one he is contemplating, then B would select that point (a^{**}, b^{**}) on A's best response curve which gives him maximum utility. Then, however, they would be at the point (a^*, b^{**}), which would be on neither best response curve, and would likely have a lower payoff than (a_o, b_o).[11]

---

[10] Some analysts might be unwilling to accept a non-Pareto-optimal point as a solution to a game. I believe this is one of those cases in which Pareto-optimality considerations are not overriding. As it will turn out in the present situation, however, the equilibrium is also Pareto-optimal.

[11] There is a class of non-zero-sum games in which these considerations would still lead to the equilibrium point, (a_o, b_o). This is the class of games in which there is no point (a^*, b^*) on B's best response curve that has a higher utility for A than an equi-

If assumptions are to be made about the other player using a strategy different from one's own, on which the above strategic considerations depend, then prior information about the other player is necessary. In the absence of such information, the action, assuming another player like himself, which gives highest utility, is that described as the solution above.

These considerations may be summed up as three levels of stability of equilibrium:

  i. An equilibrium point (a_o, b_o) may exist which is unstable in that a succession of best responses of "reactive" players would move away from it if there were initially a small move away from it.

 ii. An equilibrium point (a_o, b_o) may exist which is stable in the sense that a succession of best responses of reactive players would move toward it and remain at it; but which provides less utility to a nonreactive player A than another point (a^*, b^*) which will be attained if the second player is reactive. This I have described as a solution above. In doing so, I am rejecting that strategy which must assume that the opposing player is using a different strategy from one's own.

iii. An equilibrium point (a_o, b_o) may exist in which there is no point (a^*, b^*) as described in (ii) above. In this case, the equilibrium point is strongest, and can hardly be argued against, even though the game may not be zero-sum.[12]

4. The conditions under which a solution (in the sense of (ii) above) exists are identical to those for the existence of a stable equilibrium point in a system of two nonlinear differential equations, in which the variables in the equations are a (A's action) and b (B's action). The curves of best response of A and B are the loci of points in which $da/dt = 0$ and $db/dt = 0$, respectively, Those conditions may be found in any text on nonlinear differential equations (see Davis, 1961).

The interpretation of those conditions in the present context can be put in terms of best responses as described earlier: if the sequence of best responses to virtual actions leads to actions that are increasingly closer together, there is a solution at the point of convergence. If the sequence of best responses leads to actions that are increasingly farther apart, there is no solution. There may be several kinds of convergences or divergences, which subject to substantive interpretations. We will consider, however, only those that are relevant to the problem at hand.

---

librium point (a_o, b_o), and no point (a^{**}, b^{**}) on A's best response curve that has a higher utility for B than this same equilibrium point (a_o, b_o). Such a game becomes in effect a zero-sum game.

[12] I am grateful to James Buchanan for raising the points discussed in this section after reading an earlier draft, and to Erling Schild, for discussions in which these points were clarified.

Application to the Optimum Position of Voters

The above ideas may be applied to the present problem by a sequence of four steps:

1. Find the best response of a party no. 1 voter located at the most extreme left position for each of the possible positions of party no. 2. This will describe a curve of best responses of this voter, conditional upon party no. 2's position being at any possible point. A "best response" in this context is an ideal position for his candidate to assume.

2. Carry out the same calculation for party no. 2, giving a curve of best responses of a hypothetical party no. 2 voter located at the extreme right.

3. Find any points of intersection of these two curves, and examine each to determine whether it is a solution (i.e., convergent).

4. Determine whether the solution (or solutions, if they are multiple) are at a point (x_1^*, x_2^*) such that a majority of party no. 1 voters can be expected to be to the left of x_1^* and a majority of party no. 2 voters can be expected to be to the right of x_2^*. If so, this is the solution to the over-all game (since a majority of each side's voters will have x_1^* and x_2^* as their optima, respectively). If not, further analysis is necessary.

Calculation of Best Responses for Extreme Member of Party No. 1

If an equilibrium position x_1^* exists for any voter of party no. 1 for a given position x_2 of party no. 2, it will exist for the most extreme voter. Thus we will carry out a calculation of equilibrium assuming that it exists to the right of the most extreme voter; the assumption will be tested by the existence or nonexistence of an equilibrium point x_1^* greater than 0.

The position at which the expected utility is maximum is given by

$$\frac{dp_1}{dx_1} = \frac{p_1}{x_2 - x_1}.$$

It is necessary to express p_1 as a function of x_1 and x_2 if this equation is to be used to calculate the value x_1^* which gives this equality for a given value of x_2. The value of p_1 is the probability of side 1's winning. It can be approximated for real political systems by the following considerations:

1. It has long been noted that in two-party political systems in which there is an overall vote and a vote in separate constituencies, then if the overall proportion in favor of a given is $\bar{p}$, the proportion in each district, p_k, is normally distributed around this mean with variance 0.0187 (see Kendall and Stuart, 1950; March, 1957; Coleman, 1964, p. 350). Approximately the same variance has been found to hold in widely divergent political units.

2. Suppose each individual i in a political unit k favors a proportion of bills γ_{ik}, and the median proportion of bills favored in that unit is γ_k. Then if this median, γ_k, is distributed over political units in the same way that the proportion p_k has been found to be distributed in constituencies, it will have a mean around 0.5 and a variance of 0.0187. It will then be assumed that all individuals in a political unit have this information about γ_k; that is, they asume it to be normally distributed with mean 0.5 and variance 0.0187.

3. If party no. 1 is at position x_1 and party no. 2 is at position x_2, then in the final election, all voters (who now simply vote for the closest position, which maximizes their utility in the final election) to the left of $(x_1 + x_2)/2$ vote for party no. 1, and all to the right vote for party no. 2. Consequently, if the median γ_k is less than $(x_1 + x_2)/2$, party no. 1 will win. If it is greater, party no. 2 will win.

4. Thus the probability (as estimated by all individuals in the political unit) that the majority of voters are closer to party no. 1 (i.e., that γ_k is less than $(x_1 + x_2)/2$ is the value of the cumulative normal distribution from 0 to $(x_1 + x_2)/2$. That is,

$$p_1 = \int_0^{(x_1 + x_2)/2} \frac{1}{\sqrt{2\pi.0187}} e^{-(v - 0.5)^2/2(.0187)} \, dv.$$

5. At this point, the density function, dp_1/dx_1 is given by the normal density function,

$$\frac{dp_1}{dx_1} = \frac{1}{2} \frac{1}{\sqrt{2\pi.0187}} e^{-[(x_1 + x_2)/2 - 0.5]^2/2(.0187)}.$$

The form of the cumulative probability function makes it impossible to substitute the functions from considerations (4) and (5) above into (3) and solve the equation explicitly for x_1 as a function of x_2. What is possible is to use consideration (5) to evaluate dp_1/dx_1 for a number of values of x_1 for a fixed value of x_2; and to use consideration (4) to evaluate $p_1/(x_1 + x_2)$ for a number of values of x_1 for this same fixed value of x_2. The point at which these functions (treated as functions of x_1) intersect is the best response, x_1^*, for that value of x_2. Alternatively, it is possible to use (1) to evaluate $E(u)$ directly for a number of values of x_1 and a given value of x_2, and finding the maximum from a graph. This has the advantage of giving direct estimates of $E(u)$, so that the value of $E(u)$ for any values of x_1 and x_2 can be found. It has the disadvantage of having a relatively flat maximum, making difficult the location of the maximum with any precision. Thus the first-mentioned method will be used.

This has been done for eight values of x_2, 0.5, 0.55, 0.6, 0.7, 0.8, 0.85, 0.9, and 1.0. The points of intersection of the curves for dp_1/dx_1 and

$p_1/(x_2 - x_1)$ for each of these values of x_2 were found graphically. Each intersection gives a point on the "best response" curve for the extreme party no. 1 voter, given various positions x_2 of party no. 2. These have been plotted and joined by a curve in figure 3.

As figure 3 shows, these points are all between 0.22 and 0.33, and describe a curve of best response which lies in this range for all values of x_2 between 0.5 and 1.0. This means that for all party no. 1 voters to the left of (i.e., with α_i smaller than) about 0.22, the optimum position x_1^* for all party no. 2 positions, x_2, is given by the best response curve shown in figure 3.

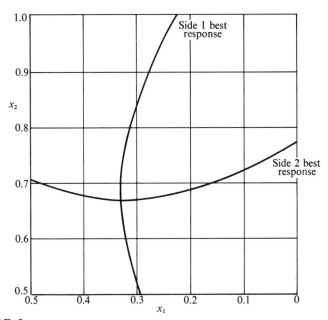

FIGURE 3

A completely analogous calculation can be carried out for the voter at the extreme right in party no. 2. Assuming symmetry in the parties, this will give results which are identical to those for party no. 1, except that the best response for party no. 2's voter is $x_2^* = 1 - x_1^*$ for values of x_1 that are one minus values of x_2. Thus for values of x_1 that are $x_1 = 0.5, 0.45, 0.4, 0.3, 0.2, 0.15, 0.1, 0.0$ respectively, the best responses x_2^* are given by eight points that describe the best response curve for party no. 2 shown in figure 3.

Geometric or numerical analysis will show that a sequence of best responses would converge to the point of intersection at about (0.33, 0.67), so that it is stable, and thus a solution. For these data, it appears to be the only solution.

The solution can be stated as follows: for a symmetric electorate in a two-party two-stage election system, if the majority of party voters in the left party is below 0.22 on the left-right continuum (that is, the majority favors less than 0.22 of the bills) and the majority of voters in the right party is above 0.78, then the only equilibrium party positions, which cannot be successfully overthrown in the party primaries, are at 0.33 and 0.67 respectively. This is a somewhat surprising and rather interesting result: the party primary results in party positions which are less extreme than would be representative of the party voters, yet are not at the center.

It is useful to see just how the equilibrium is assumed to be reached, and how any positions other than (0.33, 0.67) can be successfully overthrown. We will consider a sequence of moves beginning with a party no. 1 position at 0.1 and proceeding to a stable point. Figure 3 is used to calculate the responses.

1. A party no. 1 candidate takes a position at $x_1 = 0.1$.

2. Voters of party no. 2 calculate their (tentative) optimal candidate by reference to figure 3. This position is 0.725 for all voters to the right of 0.725, obtained as the x_2-coordinate of the intersection between $x_1 = 0.1$ and the curve of best response for side 2.

3. A party no. 2 candidate examines the preference of the median party no. 2 voter. If the median voter is to the right of 0.725 (as we will assume for the moment) there will be a majority of voters in favor of position 0.725. He thus takes position 0.725.

4. Voters of party no. 1 calculate their (tentative) optimal candidate as did voters of party no. 2 in (2) above. For voters to the left of 0.33, this preferred position is 0.33.

5. The party no. 1 candidate examines the preference of the median party no. 1 voter, and finds this to be 0.33 (if, as we shall assume, the median party no. 1 voter's own position is to the left of 0.33). He then changes his position from 0.1 to 0.33, or is replaced, in preliminary party votes, by someone who does take that position.

6. Voters of party no. 2 reassess their preferred positions in the light of the new party no. 1 candidate position (0.33 in place of 0.1). For all voters to the right of 0.67, this position is 0.67.

7. This is about the end of the sequence, which converges, as shown, very rapidly to the point (0.33, 0.67). If a candidate moves from one of those positions, he will not be able to gain a majority of votes within his party.

A few further considerations are in order. First, it is possible to go back to the questions raised in the discussion of non-zero-sum games, and try to see whether either party might find a point on the *other's* best response curve better for him than (x_1^*, x_2^*), and thus attempt to move the other party to that point. To do this, it is useful to restate the expected utility for a party voter of party no. 1 whose own position is at α_i, to the left of his party, and the expected utility for a party voter of party no. 2 whose own position is at β_j, to the right of his party. These expected utilities from (1) and from an analogous equation for an extreme right voter in party no. 2, are (again disregarding scale constants to scale each person's utility):

$$E(u_i) = 1 + \alpha_i - p_1 x_1 - (1 - p_1)x_2, \tag{4}$$

$$E(u_j) = 1 - \beta_j + p_1 x_1 + (1 - p_1)x_2. \tag{5}$$

Examination of these equations shows that there is pure conflict between these two members of the opposing parties: the only terms which vary with x_1 and x_2 appear with opposite signs in the two equations. The process considered as a whole is not one of pure conflict (i.e., a zero-sum game), because (4) and (5) express the expected utility only for those party voters more extreme than the party positions. For those party voters less extreme than their party, their expected utility is not totally in conflict. For example, a party no. 1 voter and a party no. 2 voter who are less extreme than their current party positions, lying between the parties, have expected utilities as follows:

$$E(u_i) = 1 + \alpha_i(1 - 2p_1) + p_1 x_1 - (1 - p_1)x_2, \tag{6}$$

$$E(u_j) = 1 + \beta_j(1 - 2p_1) + p_1 x_1 - (1 - p_1)x_2. \tag{7}$$

These voters have interests that wholly coincide. Both of these members gain, for example, if both parties move toward the center in a way that leaves p_1 unchanged.[13]

However, so long as the median party voters to which the two candidates are responding are more extreme than the candidates' positions, so that the candidates are governed by best response curves like those shown in figure 3, the game is effectively one of pure conflict or zero-sum. This means that the equilibrium point is a strong solution in the sense of point 3-iii. in the earlier game theoretic discussion, and is self-enforcing.

---

[13] This suggests the possibility of other possible strategies by these center members of the two parties. In the present analysis, each party member is assumed not to be able to affect the other party's activities (except through their perception of his candidate's position). However, if this is not the case, new strategies are possible, such as a coalition of the center to pull each party's candidates to the center. Some such activity occurs in states such as California, where a voter can vote in both primaries if he desires. However, these strategies will not be considered in the present paper, for we assume that the costs of coalition formation in the electorate prohibit it.

What if the Median Voter is not Outside the Best Response Curve?

The above solution assumes that median voter in both parties will lie outside the best response curves. (The actual position of those curves in the estimates of party voters may differ from that shown in figure 3. The figure gives only their location for a plausible subjective probability distribution for the position of the median voter in the collectivity.) Suppose the median voter does not lie outside—that is, not below 0.22 or above 0.78 in the present case. What is the optimum party position then. Is there an equilibrium, and what are its properties?

As an earlier section of the paper indicated, if the median voter is less extreme than *any* position on the best response curve (i.e., in party no. 1, greater than 0.33 or in party no. 2, less than 0.67), then the party candidates need respond only to the median voter's position—since the value of x_1 which maximizes his expected utility is at his own position. In this case, party no. 1's best response curve will simply be a vertical line in figure 3 somewhere between 0.33 and 0.5, while party no. 2's will be a horizontal line somewhere between 0.5 and 0.67, with the equilibrium point as their intersection.

Thus the question reduces to one in which the median voter is within the range of the best response curve: for party no. 1, between 0.22 and 0.33. In this case, the best response curve of the extreme voters will for

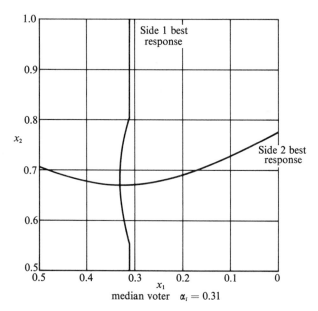

FIGURE 4

some positions of the other party candidate (values of x_2) be closer to the center than the median voter, and will thus be his best response curve; and for other values of x_2 it will be farther from the center, in which case his own position maximizes his expected utility. Suppose the median voter of party no. 1 has $\alpha_t = 0.31$. Then the best response curve to which the party no. 1 candidates should attend are not as given in figure 3, but as shown in figure 4: for values of x_2 greater than 0.8 and less than 0.55, the median voter's own position of 0.31 is optimum, and for values of x_2 between 0.55 and 0.8, a value greater than 0.31, taken from figure 3. The sequence of best responses in this case would, however, still lead to an equilibrium at (0.33, 0.67).

III. ASYMMETRY

In the above analysis, it was assumed that both parties were a priori identical with regard to size and chances of final success, with the only difference being that party no. 1's voters were concentrated toward the left side of the ideological continuum, while party no. 2's voters were concentrated toward the right side. In many systems, however, there is asymmetry of some sort.

One kind of asymmetry is that in which one party has an a priori higher probability of winning the final election in all voters' minds. Such an asymmetry in favor of party no. 1 can be mirrored by assuming that if p_1 is calculated as in the analysis of the preceding section, the overall probability of side 1 winning is $y + (1 - y)p_1$, rather than p_1, where y is between 0 and 1, 0 for no asymmetry and 1 for complete assurance that party no. 1 will win.[14] Party no. 2's probability of winning as perceived by both sides is $(1 - y)(1 - p_1)$. The probability density function, dp_1/dx_1, becomes $(1 - y)dp_1/dx_1$.

Best response curves analogous to those of figure 3 can be calculated for given values of y. They have been calculated for $y = 0.33$ and $y = 0.1$. In the first of these cases, the a priori probability of party no. 1's winning is $0.33 + (1/2)(0.67)$, or 0.67; in the second, it is $0.1 + (1/2)(0.9) = 0.55$.

For party no. 1, the advantaged party, the maximum for a given value of x_2 is given by:

$$(1 - y)\frac{dp_1}{dx_1} = \frac{y + (1 - y)p_1}{x_2 - x_1},$$

---

[14] A different kind of asymmetry could be examined by assuming that the subjective probability distribution of the median voter's position has a mean greater or less than 0.5. Other variations might also be examined—for example, a different perception on the part of voters in the two parties, with those in party no. 1 assuming the mean at, say 0.45, and those in party no. 2 assuming a mean of 0.55.

or
$$\frac{dp_1}{dx_1} = \frac{y}{(1 - y)(x_2 - x_1)} + \frac{p_1}{x_2 - x_1} \tag{8}$$

and for party no. 2, the disadvantaged party, the maximum is:

$$-(1 - y)\frac{dp_1}{dx_2} = \frac{(1 - y)(1 - p_1)}{x_1 - x_2}$$

or
$$\frac{dp_1}{dx_2} = \frac{1 - p_1}{x_2 - x_1},$$

just as in the case where the party has no disadvantage.

Thus the first result is that the responses of the voters of the disadvantaged party to positions of the candidates of the advantaged party are no different than in the symmetric case. This is not true, however, for the advantaged party. The increased probability of winning means that the optimum position for a given position x_2 of the second party candidate is more extreme (assuming that his median party voter is still more extreme).

The more extreme positions can be found much as before, by use of (8), first finding that value of x_1 which makes the equation hold for a given value of x_2, and then varying x_2. The points thus obtained are points on a best response curve for the asymmetric case of the type considered here.

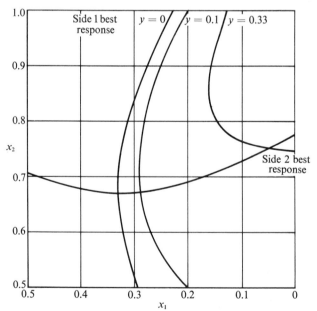

FIGURE 5

These curves, for $y = 0.1$ and 0.33, along with the symmetric case where $y = 0$, are presented in figure 5. At $y = 0.1$, the solution lies at $(0.29, 0.67)$: the advantaged party has become slightly more extreme, while the disadvantaged one has remained about the same. For $y = 0.33$, the solution lies at about $(0.05, 0.75)$: the advantaged party is very extreme, and the disadavantaged one somewhat more so than in the symmetric case. However, in this case, the existence of such a solution occurs only under very unlikely circumstances: that the median party no. 1 voter is to the left of 0.05 (i.e., between 0 and 0.05). If this is not the case, the best response point is independent of x_2, and is at the median party no. 1 voter's own position.

There are other kinds of asymmetry that could exist as well. For example, the population may be distributed unevenly along the continuum of issues, with more persons toward one end of the continuum. But investigation of such variations must await further work.

IV. CONCLUSION

The above analysis opens up a Pandora's box of possibilities. It suggests, most broadly, means of analyzing behavior of social organizations that have been until now impermeable to mathematical analysis. The most direct application is to other processes of conflict between two sides, where there is a symbiosis of leaders and led similar to that of candidates and party voters here, but where the second stage of the process is not a vote of the total collectivity, as was assumed here. In such systems, the best response curves of the followers on each side might be very different from figure 3, and might, in particular, not lead to a solution point but to instability. Similarly, it appears possible to consider applications to formal bureaucratic organizations, in which the structure determines that A must respond to B and C to A, and so on until the system is closed—but without a direct mutual contingency by any two parties. However, these analyses must await further work.

16. Spatial Competition under Constrained Choice

OTTO A. DAVIS   MELVIN J. HINICH

I. INTRODUCTION

Serious students of politics probably can agree that in national elections
there are certain issues that seem to be always with us. Thus every serious
presidential candidate can be expected to demonstrate concern over such
economic issues as the rates of inflation, unemployment and growth of
disposable incomes. Other issues, such as the war in Indochina, may be
important for several elections but surely must sometimes disappear.
Finally, there are some issues of only momentary importance.

Seasoned pollsters and political commentators probably would argue
that almost every national election has certain "special circumstances"
associated with it. Yet, while one might agree with the observation, it is
certainly true that these special circumstances vary in importance and may
be safely neglected in some elections while they may be of critical importance in others.

What implications do the above observations hold for the development

---

The authors are indebted to Resources for the Future for providing support for the
research reported here. Obviously, the usual disclaimer applies. The authors are
indebted to Professor William H. Riker, University of Rochester, for bringing to our
attention one of the two examples which serve as the inspiration for section 3 of this
paper. We also thank Professor Richard McKelvey, University of Rochester, for his
comments on this paper.

of mathematical models of the electoral process? We argue that there are two implications. First, a general model should be developed and explored in an effort to answer some of the traditional questions associated with elections. Second, this model must be capable of extensions and modifications which can take special circumstances into account.

In accordance with the above argument, this chapter first presents a general model and indicates certain of its properties. The basic model of voter behavior is similar to the economic theory of consumer behavior in the sense that the preferences of the individual (here defined over political issue space) are represented by a utility function. Of special interest for this part of the paper are statements of sufficient conditions for the existence of dominant platforms—positions which, if adopted by a party (candidate), insure that it will not lose the election. Obviously, if there is dominance, the possibly of the paradox of voting is of little concern.

The major part of the paper is devoted to a particular specialization of this general model to accommodate it to the particular political circumstances of having part of the decision space of feasible party platforms become no longer feasible because of some external event. We will discuss two examples of this phenomenon later. The discussion is not centered upon how the parties themselves react, since it is assumed that parties always adjust their platforms and remain feasible. Instead, attention is devoted to determining how this externally imposed constraint affects what would have otherwise been a situation with a dominant strategy.

II. THE GENERAL MODEL

Imagine a society in which each of the issues relevant to any given election can be measured along one of the axes of some n-dimensional space. Presume that issues are continuously measurable. Then the political issue space can be viewed as being nothing more than n-dimensional Euclidean space E_n. Let Y denote the social decision space of feasible party platforms. Since there is little loss of generality by presuming that platforms infinitely far out are never proposed, we shall assume that Y is a closed subset of E_n. For example, suppose that $n = 1$ as in the traditional Downsian (Downs, 1957) analysis. Then Y would be an arbitrarily long, but closed, interval of the line E_1. Since infinities traditionally have not entered into models of this kind, there is no loss in the assumption that Y is a closed subset of E_n.

Clearly, individuals must have preferences about policy. We adopt the convention of representing each individual voter by his utility function. Hence, let $u(c, y)$ denote the utility for the position y in Y of an arbitrarily chosen voter c in the electorate. We shall assume that for each individual

c, his utility function $u(c, y)$ is a strictly concave function of y. Although this assumption is somewhat stronger than is absolutely necessary, at least for some results, it is convenient and generally in accordance with the traditions of mathematical economics.

Since Y is a closed compact set, there exists a unique point $x(c)$ in Y which maximizes $u(c, y)$ for a fixed c. This bliss point $x(c)$ is called the ideal point (or most preferred point) for individual c. Since for our purposes here there will be no necessity to identify individuals, it is convenient to simply identify individuals by means of their own ideal points. Hence, if $x(c)$ is voter c's ideal point, as a matter of convenience we shall simply drop the identification tag and write x so that the utility function $u(c, y)$ will be written $u(x, y)$.

Assume that there are two political parties which compete in the elections. These parties have plans of action or platforms which they are supposed to enact if elected. For our purposes here the parties can be identified by their respective platforms θ and χ which, by assumption, are in Y. The citizens are presumed to have accurate perceptions of the platforms θ and χ, and the platforms themselves must be clearly defined. On the other hand, citizens need not believe that the winning party will actually enact its platform if elected. All that is required is that, for the purpose of voting, citizens evaluate the two parties on the basis of their platforms as if the platforms would be enacted. Then the belief about whether the party might or might not actually enact its platform can be incorporated into the probability of voting.

Let $h_\theta[u(x, \theta), u(x, \chi), x]$ denote the probability that a citizen with ideal point x will vote for the party with platform θ given that the opposition party has platform χ. Similarly, let $h_\chi[u(x, \chi), u(x, \theta), x]$ denote the probability that the same citizen will vote for the party with platform χ given the platform θ of the other party. These functions are assumed to have the following properties.

$$h_\theta[u(x, \theta), u(x, \chi), x]\left\{\begin{matrix}\geq\\=\\\leq\end{matrix}\right\}0 \qquad \text{if } u(x, \theta)\left\{\begin{matrix}\geq\\\leq\end{matrix}\right\}u(x, \chi)$$

$$h_\chi[u(x, \chi), u(x, \theta), x]\left\{\begin{matrix}\geq\\=\\\leq\end{matrix}\right\}0 \qquad \text{if } u(x, \chi)\left\{\begin{matrix}\geq\\\leq\end{matrix}\right\}u(x, \theta).$$

(1)

In other words, a citizen will not vote for the party with platform θ unless θ promises greater utility than platform χ. Similarly, the party with platform χ will not get a given citizen's vote unless platform χ yields greater utility than platform θ. Note that, under these assumptions, a citizen does not vote when he is indifferent between the two parties—i.e., when $u(x, \theta) = u(x, \chi)$. Also note that the probability that a citizen abstains from voting, given θ and χ, is just $1 - h_\theta - h_\chi$.

Note that in general $h_\theta \neq h_\chi$ due to party loyalty or a belief that one party may be more or less likely than the other to enact and execute their platform. If the probability of voting for either party depends only upon the respective platforms, and not party labels, then the two functions have the same form and identical parameters.

In order to characterize the distribution of preferences in the society, let $f(x)$ denote the density function of ideal points of all voters in the society. For convenience it is desirable to presume that $f(x)$ is a continuous rather than a discrete density. In other words, for the purpose of the model, but really without loss of generality, the population is viewed as if it were infinitely large.

Given these definitions, it is now possible to define the proportion of the vote going to one party or the other. Hence,

$$V_\theta(\theta, \chi) = \int h_\theta[u(x, \theta), u(x, \chi), x] f(x)\, dx \qquad (2)$$

is the proportion of the vote which is cast for the party with platform θ given that the opposition has platform χ. Similarly,

$$V_\chi(\theta, \chi) = \int h_\chi[u(x, \chi), u(x, \theta), x] f(x)\, dx \qquad (3)$$

is the portion of the vote received by the party with platform χ given the other platform θ. Clearly, the proportion of the citizens abstaining is $1 - V_\theta - V_\chi$.

A few more assumptions related to the probability of voting are needed in order to obtain a rather general result. Let us state the following definitions:

$$\begin{aligned} q_\theta &= u(x, \theta) \\ q_\chi &= u(x, \chi). \end{aligned} \qquad (4)$$

Then the functions for the probability of voting for one party or the other can be rewritten in the following form:

$$\begin{aligned} h_\theta[u(x, \theta), u(x, \chi), x] &= h_\theta(q_\theta, q_\chi, x) \\ h_\chi[u(x, \chi), u(x, \theta), x] &= h_\chi(q_\chi, q_\theta, x). \end{aligned} \qquad (5)$$

We assume that h_θ is a *monotonically increasing concave* function of q_θ and a *monotonically decreasing convex* function of q_χ for $q_\theta > q_\chi$. We assume the same form for h_χ but with q_θ and q_χ reversed. In order to demonstrate just what these assumptions mean, consider the following example. Let $n = 1$ and assume that the utility function $u(x, y)$ is quadratic in

$(y - x)$. In other words,

$$u(x, y) = \alpha_x - \beta_x(y - x)^2 \tag{6}$$

where α_x and β_x are constants which vary across individuals. Then for some given individual the general form for h_θ as a function of θ for two values of χ designated χ^* and χ^{**} is given in figure 1. Similarly, the general form for h_θ as a function of χ for two values of θ designated by θ^* and θ^{**} is given in figure 2. Obviously, the slope of h_θ can vary from individual to individual. Finally, the difference is shown in figure 3.

For any given election, a positive plurality is a requirement for winning in a two party contest. Consider the following definitions:

$$W_\theta(\theta, \chi) = V_\theta(\theta, \chi) - V_\chi(\theta, \chi)$$
$$W_\chi(\theta, \chi) = V_\chi(\theta, \chi) - V_\theta(\theta, \chi). \tag{7}$$

Then the party with platform θ will win the election if and only if $W_\theta > 0$, and the party with platform χ will win if and only if $W_\chi > 0$.

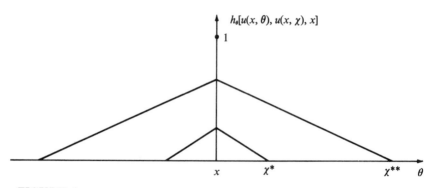

FIGURE 1

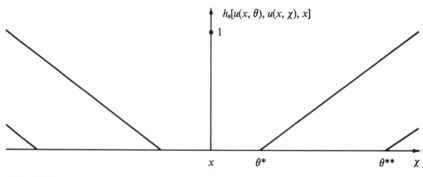

FIGURE 2

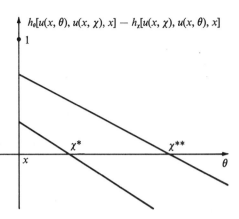

$h_\theta[u(x, \theta), u(x, \chi), x] - h_\chi[u(x, \chi), u(x, \theta), x]$

FIGURE 3

Consider the electoral process to be a two-person zero-sum noncooperative game. The two parties are viewed as the players in this game and are assumed to have the respective objective functions W_θ and W_χ as defined above. The parties compete by selecting platforms and voters choose between the two according to their platforms as described previously. The following theorem is proved in Hinich, Ledyard and Ordeshook (1972).

THEOREM 1. Assume that each party continually adjusts its platform according to the following rules:

$$d\theta_i/dt = \partial W_\theta/\partial \theta_i \qquad i = 1, \ldots, n$$
$$d\chi_j/dt = \partial W_\chi/\partial \chi_j \qquad j = 1, \ldots, n. \tag{8}$$

Then from any initial platforms (θ^o, χ^o), the solution to (8)—$[\theta(t), \chi(t)]$ —exists and converges to a unique equilibrium (θ^*, χ^*) so that $\theta(t) \rightarrow \theta^*$ and $\chi(t) \rightarrow \chi^*$ as $t \rightarrow \infty$. Moreover, $\theta^* = \chi^*$ and

$$W_\theta(\theta^*, \chi) > W_\theta(\theta^*, \chi^*) = 0 \qquad \text{if } \chi \neq \chi^*$$
$$W_\chi(\theta, \chi^*) > W_\chi(\theta^*, \chi^*) = 0 \qquad \text{if } \theta \neq \theta^*. \tag{9}$$

Let us consider the interpretation of this theorem. Clearly, the point $\theta^* = \chi^*$ is a dominant platform since, if one party chooses that platform and the other does not, then the one choosing it wins the election. Under the assumptions, a unique dominant point exists. Further, the existence of this point does not depend on the form of $f(x)$. Neither does it require the same functional form for the utility functions of the various individuals. It may be, of course, that some may object to the particular mathematical mechanism which is utilized to demonstrate the existence of this unique solution. Clearly, there is no real world counterpart to the continuous adjustment of platforms and the continuous and instantaneous voting which is incorporated into the theorem. Yet, such a criticism misses the basic point of the existence of a dominant platform under a fairly general set of assumptions. It is existence which is important here, and whether or not parties in the real world adjust as do those in the theory is irrelevant.

For the remainder of the chapter it will be convenient to restrict the form of the individual utility functions in order to more easily explore the properties of dominant positions. Hence, for any given individual whose ideal point is x, the class of utility functions is given by

$$u(x, y) = \alpha_x - \beta_x \sum_{i=1}^{n} \sum_{j=1}^{n} a_{ij} (x_i - y_i)(x_j - y_j) \tag{10}$$

where (a_{ij}) is a positive definite matrix which is the same for each individual in the society. The constants α_x and β_x, however, can vary among individuals. With no loss of generality we can set $a_{ii} = 1$ for each i and $a_{ij} = 0$ for each $i \neq j$ since there exists a linear transformation of the dimensions such that for x and y measured in the transformed dimensions

$$u(x, y) = \alpha_x - \beta_x \|x - y\|^2 \tag{11}$$

where

$$\|x - y\|^2 = \sum_{i=1}^{n} (x_i - y_i)^2 \tag{12}$$

so that all utility functions are quadratic in $\|x - y\|$, which is the Euclidean distance between x and y. Moreover, $u(x, \theta) > u(x, \chi)$ if and only if $\|x - \theta\| < \|x - \chi\|$. In other words, for this class of utility functions the differences in the utilities which an individual might assign to two different platforms can be adequately approximated for our purposes here by the differences in the Euclidean distances between that citizen's ideal point and those platforms.

The distribution of ideal points is adequately described by the density function $f(x)$. If $f(x)$ is radially symmetric about its mean μ—i.e., if for all x in Y we have $f(x + \mu) = f(-x + \mu)$—then Hinich, Ledyard and Ordeshook (1972) prove (theorem 3) that $\theta^* = \chi^* = \mu$ is the dominant platform to which the parties converge. Thus, under the assumed conditions including the allowance for abstentions, radial symmetry is a sufficient condition for the mean of the distribution of ideal points to be the dominant platform.

If everyone votes with probability one for their most preferred candidate,—i.e., if $h_\theta + h_\chi = 1$ and

$$\begin{aligned} h_\theta[u(x, \theta), u(x, \chi), x] = 1 && \text{if } \|x - \theta\| < \|x - \chi\| \\ h_\chi[u(x, \chi), u(x, \theta), x] = 1 && \text{if } \|x - \theta\| > \|x - \chi\| \end{aligned} \tag{13}$$

then Davis, DeGroot and Hinich (forthcoming), prove that radial symmetry of $f(x)$ is a sufficient condition for $\theta^* = \chi^* = \mu$ to be a dominant platform.

Thus, although the existence of the paradox will undoubtedly remain a troublesome fact for students of social choice, there is a rather general class of circumstances under which unique dominant platforms exist. Further, the unique platform often turns out to be the mean of the distribution of ideal points.

III. THE SPECIAL SITUATION OF A LINEAR CONSTRAINT

Having outlined and developed a rather general model, and having discussed some of its properties, it is appropriate to see whether it can be adopted to take into account the particular circumstances associated with a special political phenomenon. While two examples from American politics inspire this extension of the general model, it is undoubtedly true that the modification proposed here does not adequately describe the entire set of phenomena associated with either of the two examples, nor is it designed to do so. Instead, all that is claimed is that the modification may be plausibly suggestive of certain of the phenomena that may be associated with the two suggestive examples.

The first example concerns the entry of the United States into World War II. Prior to Pearl Harbor there was a considerable "peace movement" in the country. In the halls of Congress as well as in other places such as the media there was considerable debate and discussion between the hawks and doves over whether this country should "become involved." The Japanese attack on Pearl Harbor clearly undermined the position of the doves and made it infeasible. After the attack, there was no doubt but that the U. S. had no choice but to become involved. In terms of the model, the attack made infeasible part of the political issue space as well as the social decision space of feasible platforms. We represent this situation by saying that a constraint has been imposed upon these spaces and that both ideal points and platforms must satisfy the constraint. Clearly, the mere imposition of a constraint cannot represent the full psychologically traumatic event associated, say, with the attack convincing a former dove to volunteer for combat duty in the army. Our interest here is not devoted to the explanation of such dramatic changes but is centered, instead, upon the fact that part of the space is no longer feasible.

The second example concerns school desegregation. Clearly, there existed (and probably still exist) in the U. S. significant numbers of persons with varied opinions which range from the extremes of "complete integration now" to "segregation forever" even before the Brown case in 1954 accelerated the process of making clear that one of these extremes is completely unconstitutional and infeasible. While the mere imposition cannot possibly explain, and is not directed toward, such historical events as efforts to impeach Justice Warren, it is possible to argue that this approach is an adequate representation (although far too dramatic) of what can reasonably be expected to occur over a long period of time as more and more voters become convinced that the Supreme Court is here to stay and that its rulings do constitute an important part of the law of the land. At least in this long run sense, one can expect ideal points to shift so that they do conform to accepted law.

In the developments below, the sharpness of the imposed shift should be recognized as a clear exaggeration of reality, and probably an indication that the war is a better example than desegregation for the phenomena reflected in the model, although the latter is used as the major device of exposition. Accordingly, the example below should be viewed as a device to explain the theoretical idea rather than a description of a real historical phenomenon.

Imagine that $n = 2$ so that there are only two issues in our imaginary political world. Suppose that one axis is labeled "busing effort to achieve integration." Then one extreme of the horizontal axis (say, the left) would represent significant busing to achieve integrated schools while the opposite extreme (the right) would represent significant busing to achieve segregated schools. Thus the middle part of the horizontal axis represents positions where little busing is done to achieve either integration or segregation. For our purposes here we can imagine that the vertical axis is labeled "the only other issue around."

Now imagine that the Court, in a decision similar to the Brown decision, ordered that busing effort to achieve segregated schools must be kept below some specified minimum. In symbols let the amount d represent this minimum. Then the combination of policies $y = (y_1, y_2)'$, with the prime denoting the transpose of the column vector representation of y in E_2, satisfies the constraint imposed by the Court if and only if $y_1 \leq d$.

Consider an individual who is sympathetic toward the segregationist doctrine and whose ideal point $x = (x_1, x_2)'$ has the characteristic that $x_1 > d$. In other words, this citizen desires that busing effort be expended toward the achievement of segregation in the schools in an amount that the Court has declared to be unconstitutional. What does this person do? We shall assume for our purposes that this individual, and all such citizens, take the Court seriously and believe that its orders will ultimately have to be carried out. For the sake of simplicity, assume that the citizens believe that the ultimate has arrived and that the Court's orders will be carried out immediately. Hence, all citizens such as the one above are faced with the task of "correcting" their "illegitimate" ideal points. We assume that any individual whose ideal point does not satisfy the constraint selects a new ideal point in the constrained feasible space which is closest to his original preferred position. For the above example, the individual with ideal point x whose component $x_1 > d$ would choose the point $x^* = (d, x_2)'$ as his feasible ideal point. Then given a choice between any two feasible platforms, he will prefer the one closest to his new ideal position x^* (figure 4).

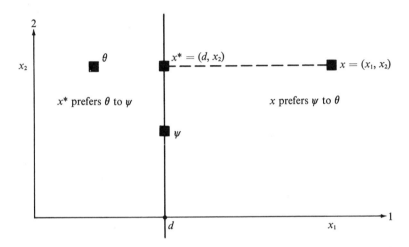

FIGURE 4

Clearly, if $n = 1$ so that politics can be analyzed in the one-dimensional Downsian world, then the imposition of a constraint would be of little interest. After all, a not necessarily unique dominant position always exists in such a world. Further, if one began with a constraint which was continually made more strict, then it would have no effect (if everyone continued to vote as usual) until the dominant position was reached and thereafter the constraint would be dominant. If $n \geq 2$, however, not only is dominance no longer insured, unless conditions such as those discussed in the previous section are satisfied, but we shall show that even when dominance does exist the imposition of a constraint of the kind discussed here can create additional difficulties for social choice. Specifically, the constraint itself can cause the paradox to come into existence when it otherwise would have been absent.

The general form for a *linear constraint* on Y involves all the dimensions. Given a column vector $\alpha = (\alpha_1, \alpha_2, \ldots, \alpha_n)'$ and a constant d, a point $y = (y_1, y_2, \ldots, y_n)'$ in Y satisfies the constraint if and only if

$$\alpha'y = \sum_{i=1}^{n} \alpha_i y_i \leq d \tag{14}$$

and if $\alpha_i = 0$ for a particular i, then the ith dimension is not constrained. With no loss of generality we can scale the α_i and d such that

$$\| \alpha \|^2 = \sum_{i=1}^{n} \alpha_i^2 = 1$$

is always true.

As in the above example, consider an individual whose ideal point x does not satisfy the constraint so that $\alpha'x > d$. Then we assume that this individual will select as a new ideal point the point in the constrained space which is closest to his old most preferred point x. The point x^*,

$$x^* = x - (\alpha'x - d)\alpha \qquad (15)$$

minimizes the distance $\| x^* - x \|$ subject to the constraint $\alpha'y \leq d$ and thus the point x^* is assumed to be the new ideal point for the citizen whose old most preferred position was x. Note that x^* lies on the hyperplane $\alpha'y = d$.

Clearly, if x^* is to be feasible we must assume that it lies in Y for each x in Y. For our purposes here we can safely assume that Y is sufficiently large that given the density $f(x)$ of ideal positions, the probability that any x is not in Y is negligible. In other words, for our purpose here we need not distinguish between E_n and Y.

In order to show that the imposition of a constraint in a situation where dominance is known to exist can result in a situation where dominance does not exist, let us assume that $f(x)$ is the n-dimensional normal density function

$$f(x) = (2\pi\sigma^2)^{-n/2} \exp \left[-\frac{1}{2\sigma^2}(x - \mu)'(x - \mu)\right]$$

and for simplicity, without loss of generality, we can assume that the origin of E_n has been chosen so that the mean ideal point $\mu = 0$. It is well known that when the distribution of ideal points $f(x)$ is normal, the mean μ is a dominant platform. See, e.g., Davis and Hinich (1968), and Davis, Hinich and Ordeshook (1970).

Suppose moreover that $d = 0$ so that the mean ideal point $\mu = 0$ lies on the hyperplane $\alpha'x = 0$ of the constraint. Thus one half of the citizens in the society do not have preferred positions which satisfy the imposed constraint. Clearly, these assumptions mean that the constraint splits the society at the center.

Suppose that the two parties have the respective platforms θ and χ and that both have the property that $\alpha'\theta \leq 0$ and $\alpha'\chi \leq 0$ so that the constraint is satisfied. Consider some citizen whose ideal point x does not satisfy the constraint, i.e., $\alpha'x > 0$. We assume that this individual will prefer the party with platform θ over the party with platform χ if and only if $\|x^* - \theta\| < \|x^* - \chi\|$. In other words this citizen will choose the party whose platform is nearest to his new ideal point. By some simple algebra it follows that the individual with preferred position x will choose θ over χ if and only if

$$2(\chi - \theta)'x^* < \|\chi\|^2 - \|\theta\|^2$$

and as a consequence of (15), if and only if

$$2(\chi - \theta)'x < \|\chi\|^2 - \|\theta\|^2 + 2\alpha'(\chi - \theta)(\alpha'x) \qquad (16)$$

which will be useful in the following discussion.

Let us restrict θ to lie on the line spanned by α. We will use the following lemmas to show the existence of voting intransitivity.

LEMMA 1. Suppose that $\theta = a\alpha$ where $a \leq 0$. The proportion of the citizens whose ideal points do not satisfy the constraint and who prefer $\theta = a\alpha$ over χ if $\|\chi\|^2 > a^2$ is

$$\frac{1}{2}\Phi\left(\frac{\|\chi\|^2 - a^2}{2\sigma\sqrt{1 - \rho^2}\|\chi - a\alpha\|}\right) > \frac{1}{4}$$

where

$$\Phi(t) = (1/\sqrt{2\pi})\int_{-\infty}^{t} \exp\left(-\frac{1}{2}z^2\right) dz$$

and, assuming $\rho \neq 1$,

$$\rho = \frac{\alpha'(\chi - a\alpha)}{\|\chi - a\alpha\|}.$$

If $\rho = 1$ all those individuals whose ideal point x satisfies $\alpha'x > 0$ vote for the party with platform $\theta = a\alpha$ if $\|\chi\| > |a|$ or for the party with platform χ if $\|\chi\| < |a|$.

PROOF. Let $z_1 = \alpha'x$ and $z_2 = x'(\chi - a\alpha)/\|\chi - a\alpha\|$. Since $\|\alpha\| = 1$, then we have from (16) that a citizen with ideal point x prefers the party with platform $\theta = a\alpha$ to the one with platform χ if and only if

$$z_2 < \frac{\|\chi\|^2 - a^2}{2\|\chi - a\alpha\|} + \rho z_1. \qquad (17)$$

Since the ideal points x are assumed to have a multivariate normal distribution, z_1 and z_2 have a bivariate normal distribution where $E(z_1) = E(z_2) = 0$ because $E(x) = 0$. The variances of z_1 and z_2 are equal to σ^2 and the correlation between z_1 and z_2 is ρ since

$$E(z_1 z_2) = E\frac{\alpha' xx'(\chi - a\alpha)}{\|\chi - a\alpha\|} = \sigma^2 \frac{\alpha'(\chi - a\alpha)}{\|\chi - a\alpha\|}.$$

Thus the conditional density of z_2 given z_1 is a normal density function whose mean is

$$E(z_2 | z_1) = \rho z_1 \tag{18}$$

and whose variance is

$$V(z_2 | z_1) = (1 - \rho^2)\sigma^2. \tag{19}$$

Thus from (17) it follows that the proportion of the citizens whose ideal points lie on the hyperplane $\alpha' x = z_1 > 0$ who prefer the party with platform $\theta = a\alpha$ over the party with platform χ is given by

$$Pr\left(z_2 - \rho z_1 < \frac{1}{2}\|\chi - a\alpha\| \Big| z_1\right) = \Phi\left(\frac{\|\chi\|^2 - a^2}{2\sigma\sqrt{1 - \rho^2}\|\chi - a\alpha\|}\right) > \frac{1}{2}$$
$$\text{if } \|\chi\|^2 > a^2 \tag{20}$$

assuming $\rho \neq 1$. The result follows since one-half of the society has ideal points such that $\alpha' x = z_1 > 0$.

Suppose that $\rho = 1$. Then χ and α are colinear and thus there exists some number $b < 0$ such that $\chi = b\alpha$. Substituting $b\alpha$ for χ in (16), we have

$$(b - a)\alpha' x < b^2 - a^2 + (b - a)\alpha' x$$

which is satisfied for all ideal points x if $b < a$, or for no ideal point x if $b > a$. We have thus formally proven the geometrically obvious result that $a\alpha$ is closer than all points on the hyperplane $\alpha' x = 0$ if $|a| < |b|$.

Let us now deal with the part of the society whose ideal points satisfy the constraint or, to put it another way, those citizens whose ideal points x satisfy $\alpha' x \leq 0$. For these individuals, $\theta = a\alpha$ is preferred to χ if and only if $\|x - a\alpha\| < \|x - \chi\|$, or equivalently by some straightforward algebra, if and only if

$$z_2 < t = \frac{\|\chi\|^2 - a^2}{2\|\chi - a\alpha\|}. \tag{21}$$

We have now proven the following result.

LEMMA 2. The proportion of the citizens whose ideal points x satisfy the constraint and who prefer the party with the platform $\theta = a\alpha$ over that with platform χ is given by

$$Pr(z_1 < 0, z_2 < t) = \int_{-\infty}^{0} \int_{-\infty}^{t} \frac{1}{2\pi\sigma^2 \sqrt{1 - \rho^2}} \exp\left(\frac{-x^2 + 2\rho xy - y^2}{2\sigma^2(1 - \rho^2)}\right) dxdy$$

assuming $\rho \neq 1$. If $\rho = 1$, there exists a negative constant b such that $\chi = b\alpha$, and thus the proportion of the citizens preferring the party with platform $\theta = a\alpha$ over the platform $\chi = b\alpha$ is given by

$$\frac{1}{2}\Phi\left(-\frac{a + b}{2}\right) \qquad \text{if } b < a < 0$$

$$\frac{1}{2}\Phi\left(\frac{a + b}{2}\right) \qquad \text{if } a < b < 0.$$

We will now use lemmas 1 and 2 to show that even in this world which was defined to be perfect from the point of view of having a dominant platform and a social preference ordering defined by majority rule (see Davis, DeGroot and Hinich, forthcoming), the mere imposition of a constraint in the social decision space can upset the ordering and cause intransivity in it if everyone in this constrained society votes. Our plan is to show that the platform $\mu = 0$ dominates all other platforms on the line $a\alpha$, $a < 0$, and that for each platform $\chi \neq a\alpha$ for some negative a, there exists a platform $a_o\alpha$, $a_o < 0$, which dominates χ. Thus if majority rule were transitive, it would follow that the mean $\mu = 0$ is the dominant platform in the constrained social decision space as might be intuitively plausible. However, we shall give an example where the mean $\mu = 0$ is dominated by a platform which does satisfy the constraint.

Consider the platforms $\theta = a\alpha$ and $\chi = b\alpha$ where $b < a < 0$. Thus $\rho = 1$ and from the second parts of lemmas 1 and 2, the proportion of the citizens in the society who prefer the party with platform $\theta = a\alpha$ over the party with platform $\chi = b\alpha$ is

$$\frac{1}{2}\left[1 + \Phi\left(-\frac{a + b}{2\sigma}\right) - \frac{1}{2}\right].$$

Since

$$\Phi\left(-\frac{a + b}{2\sigma}\right) > \frac{1}{2}$$

for $a + b < 0$, we have established the following result.

THEOREM 2. If θ and χ both lie on the line $\{a\alpha : a < 0\}$, the point closer to the mean $\mu = 0$ of the distribution of ideal points will be preferred by a majority of the citizens of the society. Consequently, the mean $\mu = 0$ dominates any platform $a\alpha$ for $a < 0$.

Let us now consider a platform χ which does not lie on the line $\{a\alpha : a < 0\}$. Further, suppose that χ satisfies the constraint so that $\alpha'\chi \leq 0$. We now state the following theorem.

THEOREM 3. Given a feasible platform $\chi \neq a\alpha$ for any $a < 0$, the feasible platform $\theta = a_o\alpha$, $a_o = \alpha'\chi$, is preferred by a majority of the citizens of the society.

PROOF. Since $\alpha'\chi \leq 0$, $\theta = (\alpha'\chi)\alpha$ satisfies the constraint. Moreover, by the Schwarz inequality, $(\alpha'\chi)^2 < \|\chi\|^2$. The inequality is strict since χ and α are not colinear by definition. Thus from lemma 2 and inequality (21) the proportion of the citizens whose ideal points satisfy the constraint and who prefer the party with platform $\theta = a_o\alpha$ over the party with platform χ is $Pr(z_1 < 0, z_2 < t)$ where $t > 0$. The variables z_1 and z_2 are jointly normal with zero means, variances equal to σ^2, and correlation

$$\rho = \frac{\alpha'(\chi - a_o\alpha)}{\|\chi - a_o\alpha\|} = 0.$$

Since $\rho = 0$ and $t > 0$,

$$Pr(z_1 < 0, z_2 < t) = Pr(z_1 < 0)Pr(z_2 < t) > \tfrac{1}{4}.$$

Moreover, from lemma 1, the proportion of the citizens whose ideal points satisfy the constraint and who prefer the party with platform $\theta = a_o\alpha$ over that with platform χ is $\tfrac{1}{2}\Phi[(\|\chi\|^2 - (\alpha'\chi)^2)/(2\sigma\sqrt{1 - \rho^2}\|\chi - (\alpha'\chi)\alpha\|)] > \tfrac{1}{2}\cdot\tfrac{1}{2} = \tfrac{1}{4}$ since $\|\chi\| > |\alpha'\chi|$. Thus a majority of the citizens prefer the party with platform $\theta = a_o\alpha$ over the party with platform χ.

If we knew that majority rule would lead to a transitive preference ordering, then these two theorems would imply that the mean of the distribution of ideal points $\mu = 0$ would be preferred to any other platform $\chi \neq 0$, $\alpha'\chi \leq 0$, by a majority of the citizens in the society. Perhaps somewhat unfortunately, we shall now show that there exists a platform $\chi \neq 0$, but "near" the mean $\mu = 0$ and with a ρ "near" 1, such that the party with platform χ will be preferred to the party with platform $\theta = \mu$ by a majority of the citizens of the society. Consequently, majority rule is not transitive in this situation when voters do not abstain.

Consider a platform χ which is near the mean $\mu = 0$ but which does not lie on the line spanned by α. Let χ be such that it satisfies $\alpha'\chi \leq 0$. Then we know from the first parts of lemmas 1 and 2 that the proportion of the citizens who prefer the party with platform $\mu = 0$ over the one with platform χ is given by

$$\tfrac{1}{2}\Phi(\|\chi\|/2\sigma\sqrt{1 - \rho^2}) + Pr(z_1 < 0, z_2 < t) \qquad (22)$$

where

$$p = \alpha'\chi/\|\chi\| \quad \text{and} \quad t = \|\chi\|/2.$$

By Taylor's series approximation

$$Pr(z_1 < 0, z_2 < t) = Pr(z_1 < 0, z_2 < 0) + o(\|\chi\|) \quad (23)$$

where $o(\|\chi\|)$ is a function of $\|\chi\|$ which goes to zero as $\|\chi\|$ goes to zero, i.e., $o(\|\chi\|)$ is small when $\|\chi\|$ is small. Setting $\sigma = 1$, it is well known that for jointly normal zero mean variables,

$$Pr(z_1 < 0, z_2 < 0) = \frac{1}{2\pi} \arcsin \sqrt{1 - p^2}. \quad (24)$$

Moreover, by Taylor's series approximation for small $\|\chi\|$

$$\Phi(\|\chi\|/2\sqrt{1 - p^2}) \leq \tfrac{1}{2} + o\|\chi\|. \quad (25)$$

Applying (23), (24) and (25) to (22), the proportion of the citizens who prefer the party with platform $\theta = \mu = 0$ to the one with platform χ is

$$\frac{1}{4} + o\|\chi\| + \frac{1}{2\pi} \arcsin \sqrt{1 - p^2}. \quad (26)$$

Let $\|\chi\| = N^{-2}$ and $\sqrt{(1 - p^2)} = N^{-1}$ so that $p = \sqrt{(1 - N^{-2})}$. These can be assumed for large N. For small values of x, $\arcsin x \approx x$. Thus for N sufficiently large the proportion of the citizens who prefer the party with platform $\theta = \mu = 0$ over the party with platform χ is *less than*

$$\frac{1}{4} + \frac{1}{N2\pi} < \frac{1}{2} \quad (27)$$

so that a majority of the citizens prefer the party with platform χ to the party with platform $\theta = \mu = 0$.

The plurality of the party with platform χ over the party with platform $\theta = 0$ is small if χ is near $\mu = 0$. If there was no constraint the basic symmetry of the density of ideal points assures dominance of the mean $\mu = 0$. Given that χ is near $\mu = 0$, and if there were no constraint, the party with platform $0 = \mu$ could command a majority, but with only a small plurality. When the linear constraint is applied and those citizens whose original ideal points do not satisfy the constraint are forced to choose a new ideal point on the hyperplane, some individuals find that χ is closer to their newly selected ideal position than is the mean $\mu = 0$ of the original density of ideal points.

In an effort to understand the switching which is caused by the imposition of the constraint, let us assume that $\sigma = 1$ for simplicity and examine that part of the population which is affected by the constraint. From (18), (19) and (20) we know that if there were no constraint, the proportion of the individuals whose ideal points lie on the hyperplane $\alpha'x = z_1 > 0$ who prefer the party with the platform $\theta = \mu = 0$ over the party with platform χ is given by

$$Pr(z_2 < t \,|\, z_1) = \Phi\left(\frac{t - \rho z_1}{\sqrt{1 - \rho^2}}\right) \qquad (28)$$

where $t = \|\chi\|/2$. Given the constraint and (20), the proportion whose ideal points lie on the hyperplane $\alpha'x = z_1$ who prefer the party with platform $\theta = 0$ over the party with platform χ is

$$\Phi\left(\frac{t}{\sqrt{1 - \rho^2}}\right).$$

Thus the proportion of the citizens whose ideal points lie on the hyperplane who switch to the party with platform χ due to the imposed constraint is the area under the standard normal density

$$f(z) = \frac{1}{\sqrt{2\pi}} \exp\left(-z^2/2\right)$$

for z between $t/\sqrt{(1 - \rho^2)}$ and $(t - \rho z_1)/\sqrt{(1 - \rho^2)}$. Also note that the correlation $\rho = \alpha'\chi/\|\chi\| < 0$ since χ satisfies the constraint and is negative.

For a given platform χ, this area increases as z_1 increases. For a given $z_1 > 0$, this area increases as $t = \|\chi\|/2 \to 0$ and $\rho \to 1$. Thus the following result has been established.

THEOREM 4. Let the set H contain those citizens whose ideal points lie on the hyperplane $\alpha'x = z_1$ and the set H^* contain those citizens whose ideal points lie on the hyperplane $\alpha'x = z_1^*$ where $z_1^* > z_1 > 0$. The proportion of H^* who switch to prefer the party with platform χ instead of the party with platform $\theta = \mu = 0$ as a result of the constraint is greater than the proportion of H who switch. Moreover, the proportion of H who switch increases as $\chi \to 0$.

Thus this theorem establishes that there is proportionately more switching among citizens who hold extremist positions on the constrained issue than there is among those whose ideal points are nearer to the mean and thus must be classified as moderates on that issue. In addition, the ability of the party with platform χ to induce citizens to switch increases as its platform gets closer to the mean $\mu = 0$ of the original density of ideal points. :

All of the above, of course, assume that everyone votes with probability one for their most preferred candidate. The general convergence theorem discussed in the previous section can be made to apply to the situation after the imposition of the constraint if abstentions are allowed in the manner required by that theorem. If abstentions are allowed in the specified manner, then a dominant platform will exist within the constrained space since the theorem does not depend upon any particular distribution of ideal points. While that result is an existence theorem and thus does not itself identify the dominant platform, it is possible for us here to identify the dominant strategy in the halfspace $\alpha'x \leq 0$ if the functional form of the abstention function is specified.

THEOREM 5. Suppose that there is no party loyalty as such and that the abstention functions are given as follows:

$$h_\theta(q_\theta, q_x, x) = \begin{cases} A(q_\theta - q_x) & \text{if } q_\theta \geq q_x \\ 0 & \text{if } q_\theta < q_x \end{cases}$$

$$h_x(q_x, q_\theta, x) = \begin{cases} A(q_x - q_\theta) & \text{if } q_x \geq q_\theta \\ 0 & \text{if } q_x < q_\theta \end{cases} \tag{29}$$

where A is a positive constant and thus abstention is related to indifference. Also assume that the density of ideal points is given by

$$f(x) = (2\pi\sigma)^{-n/2} \exp(-x'x/2\sigma^2)$$

which is the multivariate normal with mean $\mu = 0$. The dominant platform is $\theta^* = \chi^* = -(\sigma/\sqrt{[2\pi]})\alpha$.

PROOF. Given the forms of the abstention functions specified above, theorem 4 of Hinich, Ledyard and Ordeshook (1972) applies so that the dominant strategy is uniquely the mean of the density of ideal points. Given the constraint, the mean of the relevant density here is the average of the mean of the ideal points which lie on or have been projected onto the hyperplane $\alpha'x = 0$ and the mean of the ideal points which lie in the halfspace $\alpha'x \leq 0$. By symmetry, the mean on the hyperplane is zero. In order to obtain the other mean, rotate the coordinate system about zero so that in the new coordinate system $\alpha' = (1, 0, \ldots, 0)$. Thus the constraint becomes $x_1 \leq 0$. The mean in question is then $(-2\sigma/\sqrt{[2\pi]}, 0, \ldots, 0)'$ in the new space. By rotating back to the original system, the mean becomes $-(2\sigma\sqrt{[2\pi]})\alpha$. The overall mean is clearly one-half of this.

Some of the implications of this theorem may be of interest, Under the assumption that there were no abstentions, the imposition of the constraint opened the possibility that nontransitivities could be introduced into the social ordering and there might be no dominance in a situation where it otherwise would have existed. Yet the area of nontransitivity was clearly superior to platforms outside the area and it was located close to the mean of the unconstrained density, which would have been the dominant platform. Thus in this situation one might infer that the imposition of the constraint does not greatly alter the platform which a party intent upon winning the election might otherwise adopt.

When abstentions of the specified type are introduced into the analysis, then a unique dominant platform again exists, but it is much further from the old platform which was dominant prior to the introduction of the constraint. Thus under these assumptions the introduction of the constraint drives the dominant platform away from the area which was made infeasible by the constraint.

IV. CONCLUDING REMARKS

It is appropriate to review the major conclusions of this chapter. First, the chapter itself serves as an example of how a general model can be adopted to take into account special phenomena which may be important for some given election but do not generally merit attention. The special phenomenon investigated here, which was modelled by the imposition of a linear constraint, related to external events which tend to make part of the social decision space no longer feasible. Clearly, the imposition of such external events must have an effect upon electoral behavior and the authors argue that some of the results are certainly not obvious.

The results reported in the second section indicate the strength of the assumption of symmetry. This assumption is sufficient for the existence of dominance whether or not abstentions are allowed in the model. Yet, when the symmetric n-dimensional normal density of ideal points was constrained in the prescribed manner, it was shown that an area of intransitivity could arise so that dominance could disappear. Yet, the necessity of resorting to limiting arguments probably means that the area of intransitivity is not very large and it is in the neighborhood of the previously dominant position, the mean μ of the distribution of ideal points. Hence, the mean remains an important concept for this type of model.

Another somewhat surprising result is that the constraint causes a greater number of changes in the platform or party preference of those more distant from the center. Those nearer to the center appear to exhibit more stability in their choices.

When abstentions of the proscribed type are allowed, however, there is a unique dominant position. It is no longer the mean μ of the original density although it is much closer to the mean than would be the case if those whose ideal points were located in the infeasible region decided to abstain in mass.

While this chapter has demonstrated how one type of spatial circumstance can be accommodated within a general model of electoral behavior, it clearly has not exhausted the possibilities. While our inspiration had its source in two examples in our recent political experience, other examples also deserve exploration. We know, for example, that there are numerous occasions when a candidate has chosen to emphasize only one issue in a campaign and leave the voters in the dark in regard to his position on all other issues. Similarly, the effects of campaigning and fund raising need to be incorporated into models of the type examined here. These extensions, however, are beyond the scope of the present effort and await the attention of researchers in the future.

Conclusion: A Critique of Probability Modelling

The preceding chapters have touched on a number of important aspects of probability modelling. We should, however, discuss some of these matters directly. Three avenues of inquiry must be explored. The first is to consider some of the advantages and disadvantages of probability models, particularly emphasizing the gains and losses over deterministic versions. Secondly, we must consider the uses and interpretations of the probabilities—to whom or what they apply and whether they are literal descriptions of behavior. Finally, some comments are directed toward the future development of probability models, with particular emphasis on problems that need to be overcome in order for major new advances to be made.

I. ADVANTAGES AND DISADVANTAGES OF PROBABILITY MODELS

At the risk of putting the cart before the horse, it may be wise to begin by responding to two gross objections that have been made to probability modelling. Both of these objections miss the point by far, but they are so fundamental that they must be laid to rest at once.

An initial objection to probability models is that "people just don't behave that way—they make responsible, reasoned choices, and not the capricious choices that would result from coin-flipping and other random procedures." Our response to this objection is two-fold. First, there are some situations in which it is likely that people behave in a probabilistic way. This is spelled out at greater length in the uses and interpretation section below. However, even if people do not behave probabilistically, it may still be useful to model their behavior in this fashion. Bartholomew (1967, p. 6) comments that "it is a fact of experience that 'choice may mimic chance,'" so that individuals behave *as if* they employed random devices. Thus our models might usefully contain probabilistic components even if people behave deterministically. This argument, as many readers will recognize, is only a specific application of the more general position that the assumptions of models will not necessarily be realistic. The proper test of such models lies not in the correspondence of their assumptions to reality, but in the validity of assertions derived from the model.

A second objection to probabilistic models is that to suggest that people behave in a random way (or even as if they were acting randomly) dehumanizes people, lowering them to a status of mechanistic creatures who have no freedom of choice. This argument, too, misses the point as Bartholomew indicates:

> This objection rests on a misunderstanding of the role of probability theory in model-building. It is precisely because man is a free agent that his behavior is unpredictable and hence must be described in probabilistic terms. The only alternative is to adopt a deterministic point of view; it is this and not the stochastic approach which is open to the charge of making man an automaton. (1967, p. 5)

Thus, probability models, if anything, accent rather than deny the human capacity to make free choices.

These two objections aside, we can now turn to the advantages of probability models. Since several of these advantages were discussed by way of example in the introduction and substantive chapters, detailed discussions are not necessary here.[1] The first advantage that we would point to is the ability of probability formulations to deal with situations which may not otherwise be amenable to treatment. The seeming inability of deterministic models to handle these situations may arise from several sources. First, as we illustrated in the introduction by the comparison of Buchanan and Tullock with the later probabilistic formulations, deterministic models are woefully inadequate to predict events and behavior in the future.

---

[1] The advantages and disadvantages that we will cite do not apply equally to all uses of probability. However, it does not seem worthwhile at the present to spell this out in more detail.

A second point emerges from the same comparison, namely that it may not be possible to provide deterministic measures for some concepts. Third, there is sometimes an appropriate deterministic form, but the empirical data to use with it are unavailable. This is the situation with regard to the paradox of voting. In all these situations probabilistic models circumvent the problems involved and, in our opinion, provide a meaningful operationalization of the fundamental concepts. They do not necessarily solve the problems facing the deterministic models, e.g., they cannot supply missing data. But they do alter the problems sufficiently to make them tractable, while preserving the essential features of the underlying question.

A second major advantage is the ability of probability models to deal with uncertainty on the part of actors in the model. Sufficient note has been made of decision making under risk and uncertainty (in discussions of game theory, for example) and little needs to be said here. We stress, however, that uncertainty and attitudes toward uncertainty play a major role in political life, as Shepsle, Aranson and Ordeshook, Coleman, and others amply demonstrate. Therefore the ability to incorporate this aspect of political life into our models is of considerable value. There is one use of probabilities in dealing with uncertainty to which we wish to call special attention—that by Rae, Curtis, Badger, and Schofield to represent an individual's own preferences at a future time. We noted earlier that this may be one way around the problem of making decisions about future preferences. Here the important point is that it suggests another way in which probability components can be used to deal with uncertainty.

A third advantage of a probabilistic approach derives from the ability to handle models that lack total specification. It is usually the case that all sorts of variables that affect the system cannot be specified and employed in the model. A good example is found in the prediction of rain. All the variables which affect the occurrence of rain in a city on a given day are not known and predictions of rain cannot be made with certainty. Yet there is sufficient information to allow good statements of the probability of rain, so that one's activities can be affected by a prediction of a probability of rain of 0.6 on a given day. An adequate deterministic formulation cannot be provided under the present state of knowledge, but a probabilistic model can take into account the known elements while making allowances for the lack of complete specification.

A good political example is the analysis by Stokes (1962) of the probability of deviating elections. While he clearly cannot predict just when deviating elections will occur, the likelihood of their occurrence is a very useful bit of information. In this collection the paper by Niemi and Weisberg (chap. 6) provides another illustration. While we know some of the factors influencing the size of winning majorities, it is presently very difficult to predict just what size coalitions will form. Yet their analysis provides a tentative conclusion about the relative frequency of various size coalitions in groups of differing sizes. In general, this ability to provide meaningful information when specific outcomes cannot be predicted is one of the advantageous features of probability models.

The advantages of using probabilities that we have just discussed are particularly important in formal (specifically rational choice) modelling. This is somewhat ironic since formal modellers have tended to overreact to the problems they perceived in empirical modelling by discarding the probabilistic aspects of such models as they moved to increased formalism. Instead we would argue that the above-mentioned advantages in probabilistic formulations are especially important in formal modelling because probability components help overcome the difficulty of relating formal models to empirical phenomena.

Rational choice models typically take the over-simplified approach that individuals try to maximize a single variable, where that variable might be utility (in which case the theory is tautological and of limited value), power (which is itself unmeasurable at present), or votes. None of these variables plays the universal role in the study of political processes that money plays in economic theory. The possibility of adding further variables to rational choice models offers no real panacea. Instead, a Pandora's box of possible variables is opened by this possibility, with many of these variables being difficult to formulate in a rigorous (let alone quantitative) manner. And it was precisely in order to get away from the inclusion of numerous, nonrigorous, unquantified variables that provided the impetus for formal modelling in the first place. But because probabilistic elements are parsimonious and by definition quantified, and yet have the advantages cited earlier of allowing uncertainty and less than total specification, the incorporation of probabilistic features into formal models allows them to focus on single variables, e.g., power, money, winning, or whatever is maximized, without caricaturing real behavior.[2]

Having now pointed out some virtues of probability models, it is incumbent upon us to discuss some possible disadvantages of this approach. One disadvantage associated with probability models is the inability to predict exact outcomes. This is by its very nature the case when the predictions are probabilities (other than 0 or 1). A good example is the contrast between Riker's theory of minimal winning coalitions and Niemi and Weisberg's probabilistic predictions of coalition size. In Riker's theory (assuming complete information), there is no equivocation —only one result will occur. In the Niemi-Weisberg formulation, on the

---

[2] We are not suggesting that probability components should be allowed to be substituted for all the uncertainty and lack of specification in models. One must take care that probabilistic parameters are not adjusted *ad hoc* to fit all empirical phenomena.

other hand, any size coalition can reasonably form (although with varying probabilities). In a similar way, Stokes's (1962) probabilities of deviating elections leave us in the dark about exactly when to expect them. While the lack of total specification of outcomes is clearly a disadvantage, it is precisely our inability to provide such exact theories that leads to the use of probability models.

A second disadvantage of probability models is that they are often more complex than deterministic ones. Thus, in order to make progress it is sometimes advantageous or necessary to substitute deterministic models for more complex probabilistic versions. It is also the case that deterministic models sometimes achieve a satisfactory degree to fit to reality and provide good approximations to more complex probability models. However, we have argued that probabilistic models are essential for accurately portraying collective behavior. Moreover, we feel that a *completely accurate* deterministic model would be even more complex. In any case the real test of a model is how useful it is. Ultimately, the use of probability models must be judged on this basis.

A third disadvantage of probability models is that they can be difficult to disconfirm. Some models can predict virtually any results if appropriate values for their probabilistic parameters are chosen. This means that the only way to test the composition of the model may be to determine independently the values of the probabilities. On the other hand, probabilistic components are an advantage in that they are not subject to disconfirmation from a single exception or from the effects of random forces. Thus a probability model need not be a complete specification of reality.

Several other matters—the assumption of independence, the inability to justify particular probability assumptions, and the static as opposed to dynamic quality of the models—can be cited as possible disadvantages of probability models. However we feel that they are surmountable problems rather than inherent defects, and furthermore, they frequently characterize deterministic models as well as probabilistic ones. These problems and several others are briefly discussed after considering the uses and interpretations of the probabilities.

II. USES AND INTERPRETATIONS OF THE PROBABILITIES

It has been our experience that probability models are subject to a number of misunderstandings, primarily having to do with the meaning of the probabilities themselves. In anticipation of such problems, we will briefly review the variety of ways in which probabilities have been used in this book and elsewhere, giving emphasis to the interpretations placed on the probabilities.

The uses of probabilities can be classified according to a number of distinctions. Probabilities are sometimes used to model a process while in other cases probabilities are resorted to as a null model against which actual behavior can be compared. Probabilities may be objective as in many gambling situations or they may be subjective estimates by the actors or outsiders. Probabilities may refer to changes over time (as in Markov processes) or to variables at a single time point. The probabilities may refer to the results of an actual sampling process or they may relate to properties of the total population. The real world may be conceived of as probabilistic or it may be regarded as deterministic but modelled as probabilistic.

The number of possible distinctions relating to the use of probabilities may be endless, but we shall find it useful to concentrate on two further distinctions. First, some uses of probabilities involve the likelihood of *events* and their outcomes while others refer to the distribution and behavior of the *individuals*. Second, some uses involve *distributions* of events or individuals while others pertain to a specific *single* event or individual. We shall rely on these distinctions between events and individuals and between distributions and single elements in organizing our treatment of probability uses in formal modelling.

The discussion of different uses of probabilities is not intended to imply that every probability use must be classified into a single category of these distinctions and combinations of distinctions. As a matter of fact, a major point of this section is that the same probabilities are often subject to two or more meaningful interpretations. The wide variety of potential interpretations should be emphasized. One of its most important implications is that probability models should not be prematurely condemned because a given interpretation is inappropriate, since alternative interpretations may often justify the models. As we discuss the uses of probability assumptions in formal models, we shall begin with those least subject to misinterpretation and then proceed to the more problematic ones.

Uncertainty of Events

The occurrence of events is frequently unpredictable, even at the level of the individual concerned with the outcomes of his actions. The use of probabilities is well-justified in this instance since probability components capture what information is available as well as the uncertainty that remains.

Individuals are often uncertain as to future situations they will confront and as to the outcomes which would follow upon the actions from which they are choosing. The individuals may behave deterministically (though this is not necessary), but they take probabilities into account in the determination of their behavior—namely, the probabilities that alternative actions would result in the outcomes they desire. These probabilities may be objective, as when a gambler is aware of the mathematical probability of his winning a game. Or these probabilities may be subjective, as when subjects are unaware of the mathematical probabilities in an experimental situation but employ their best estimates. There may not be enough information for the assignment of probabilities, but "the rule of insufficient reason" may be employed to treat all possible outcomes as equally likely so that probabilities can still be used as, for example, in expected value or expected utility calculations.

In collective decision-making situations specifically, the individual may be uncertain how to achieve his goals, so his behavior depends on the probabilities with which he expects each possible action to successfully attain those goals. This is the situation faced by a voter when candidates purposely state their positions with ambiguity; the voter can at most estimate the probability with which a vote for a given candidate will result in the achievement of his policy goals. An individual also cannot know with certainty how he will feel on the issues which will arise in society over an indefinite period of time; at the constitutional choice stage he is limited to using his understanding of present and future societal cleavages to estimate his probability of favoring future measures. Similarly, in choosing an election strategy, a candidate may be uncertain as to his opponent's issue position (partly because of uncertainty as to the identity of his opponent); he must therefore choose his strategy on the basis of his probabilistic estimate of his opponent's position. In each of these instances there is uncertainty in the system, and the rational actor would react to this uncertainty by resorting to probability calculations.[3] Thus, so long as decision making occurs within an arena of uncertainty as to future states of the system and as to the consequences of given actions, probability assumptions are appropriate.

Events themselves are often treated *as if* they were random, even when they do not really happen randomly. In simulating legislative behavior, for example, Cherryholmes and Shapiro (1969) make use of the probabilities of given conversations occurring. Simulation of electoral systems through time can also introduce probabilities for "inevitable" events, such as wars and depressions, which occur at unpredictable intervals (Carlsson, 1965). These events are presumably not random, but their causes are so complex that specific occurrences are presently unpredictable. Nonetheless we often know some useful things about the events, such as their usual frequency and the variation in the frequency. Proba-

---

[3] A discussion of the rationality assumption would take us too far afield, but at least we would argue that it is reasonable to model the individuals as if they were acting rationally.

bility elements capture what we do know about these events while preserving the aspect of uncertainty as to precisely how and when specific occurrences are caused. The combination of knowledge and uncertainty gives meaning to probability statements about events. We might note in passing that exactly what probability values should be used is as much open to question and discussion here as for any other use of probability, but the interpretation is not usually disputed.

Random events are sometimes assumed in a probability model only for the purpose of constructing a null model against which the actual behavior of the system can be judged. An example of this use is the Stokes and Iversen (1962) random walk of historical election outcomes. It models how one would expect the elections over a century to have turned out if vote changes between elections were totally random. Empirical disproof of the implications of this model is used to imply the existence of non-random forces which would be inconsistent with a random equilibrium process. The comparison of empirical data with the null model based on random events provides a means of judging the validity of the proposed theory. Null models incorporating random events pose few interpretation problems since there is no suggestion that these processes really are random, though the construction of a suitable null model may prove difficult.

Probabilities of events are also used in modelling a process in a descriptive sense, obtaining the sets of probabilities which best predict the outcomes of the system. The Cherryholmes and Shapiro (1969) simulation of legislative voting could be used in this way. Probabilities of various events are specified in the simulation, such as the probability of conversations between congressmen from the same state. These probabilities could be altered to maximize the successful prediction of individual votes. The probabilities which maximize the predictive level of the model would then serve as the parameters describing the legislative voting process. Cherryholmes and Shapiro did not adopt this option, feeling that their original estimates of the probabilities were based on the best research in the literature so that adjustment of those estimates to better predict votes in a single issue area would be inappropriate. Yet the amount of research on some of the probability values is so slight that knowledge of the prediction maximizing probabilities might itself be useful. If the best fit values of the probabilities were sought, however, an independent test of their predictive success should be made on data which were not used in the estimation of those values.[4]

---

[4] Harsanyi (1970, p. 520) notes that this type of procedure is common in the natural sciences and in economics. He points out that it is not circular "so long as the number of theoretical parameters estimated from the empirical facts is significantly smaller than the number of independent empirical facts that the theory can explain."

Distribution of Individuals

Minimal interpretation problems also result when the probabilities are used to describe a *distribution of individuals* across the range of alternatives.[5] Under such circumstances each individual may be totally deterministic (though that need not be the case), but the frequency distribution of individuals is described by a probability distribution. The probability component of such models is not subject to serious problems of interpretation and justification, but the choice of which probability distribution to use can be a matter of contention.

The probability distribution (which is to say the particular probability assumption) can be selected on the basis of theoretical concerns. The probability distribution of voters constitutes the main use of probability in the early spatial modelling literature, with particular emphasis having been given to special classes of probability distributions (such as symmetric, unimodal, and bimodal distributions) which have particular theoretical interest. This interpretation of probabilities has been much less useful where it has not been possible to determine interesting classes of probability distributions. The latter has been the case when the probability assumptions in the paradox of voting literature have been regarded as referring to the distribution of individuals across the possible preference orders. Different probability distributions would lead to probabilities of the paradox ranging all the way from 0 to 1 so that the choice of distribution has a major effect. A uniform distribution of individuals has received some special attention in this context as it refers to an "impartial culture" (Garman and Kamien, 1968), but only recently has work begun on a meaningful classification of probability distributions (Weisberg and Niemi, 1971).

The probability distribution can also be selected on the basis of a sampling process. Rather than obtaining the full empirical population distribution, a sample can be taken and used as the best estimate of the distribution for the universe. The probability problem then becomes one of statistical inference, inferring from the sample distribution to the population distribution and deriving the implications that follow from that estimated population distribution. The choice of a probability distribution does not pose a problem when an actual sample provides the basis for the initial probability assumption. However when this interpretation is employed as an abstract justification for a probability model without any actual sampling,[6] it would again be helpful to have attention focused on some broad classes of probability distributions.

---

[5] This usually means the distribution of individual preference ideals, although other interpretations are possible.

[6] For example, this is the case when a set of elections is viewed as a sample from a hypothetical universe of all possible elections.

The probability distribution could also be given a Bayesian subjective interpretation. The subjective probabilities refer to estimates of the likely distribution of the actors. This interpretation can be used, for example, when the coalition builder must estimate the distribution of legislators on an issue. It is also appropriate when an outside investigator estimates the distribution of legislators on votes which were not taken but which could reveal such features as the paradox of voting. As much information as is available can be used in specifying the probability distribution, with the uniform probability distribution being appropriate when there is no prior information.

Probabilistic Choice Behavior

While reference to the distribution of individuals constitutes an important use of probabilities, we would reject the argument that randomness is only a property of aggregates which "carries no implications for individual human behaviour" (Bartholomew and Bassett, 1971, p. 277). Rather, *probabilistic choice behavior* is another important use of probabilities. To emphasize a point made in the previous section, this assumption does not suggest that people make decisions irresponsibly or by literally flipping a coin; the models take into account the behavioral fact that psychological mechanisms controlling judgments of alternatives and preferences can vary over time in a more or less random fashion.[7] Three different psychological mechanisms can lead to such behavior.

First, the individuals may indeed be indifferent with decisions made at random. This includes the possibility that the person does not care enough about the decision to evaluate the alternatives on a rational basis. It also includes the possibility that the individual may be indifferent between two or more alternatives that are judged highly (but equally) acceptable. This viewpoint is quite restricted as it does not extend to the case in which individuals have well-defined complete preference orders.

A second reason for probabilistic behavior is that an individual may have difficulty discriminating between a pair of alternatives, and this would result in his not always having the same choice between them. His perceptions of the alternatives may vary sufficiently that at times he finds one more attractive and at times another.[8]

The third reason for probabilistic choice is that an individual's preference point (or ideal point) may also vary over time as he evaluates a pair of alternatives, and this results in his not always responding the same way to that pair of alternatives. According to this view, an individual's attitude can be represented by a distribution of preference points, from which the

---

[7] "Random" may mean equally likely, but this is not necessarily the case.

[8] The reasons discussed in this paragraph and the next are elaborated in the appendix to chap. 6.

individual picks one at random each time he judges the alternatives. Which alternative he prefers at a given time may depend on the precise preference point that has been drawn.[9]

The distinction between these three psychological mechanisms resulting in random choice behavior is somewhat less important in practice than in theory. In a given voting situation, it may be very difficult to determine which mechanism is at work. However the major point is that the exact reason for random individual decision making is less important than the fact that it can occur and frequently does. A legislator, for example, may make an essentially random choice when he finds he must vote on a bill which does not concern his interests and on which he has not formed preferences, when he finds it difficult to understand the differences between the alternative amendments which have been proposed, and when he is not sure of his exact preference point which is somewhat unstable over time. Thus the precise reason for random voting may be unclear, but that it does occur is to be emphasized.

Even if individual choice behavior is not probabilistic, it often is useful to model it as if it were. Individuals may behave as if they were acting randomly, even though their behavior is indeed deterministic. A model can be judged by the deductions made from it rather than the assumptions on which it is based, so how realistic the assumption of random behavior is may be regarded as a peripheral issue. Whether models should be judged by their assumptions as well as their predictions is an epistemological question that goes well beyond the scope of this essay. Whether probability models yield better deductions and predictions than deterministic models, thereby justifying the use of the probability assumptions if models are to be judged solely on the quality of their deductions, is a critical question; we offer in answer to this question the sixteen articles in this volume.

We have emphasized that individuals under some circumstances behave probabilistically. Equally important, however, is that it usually makes no difference whether people are assumed to behave probabilistically or are assumed only to act as if they did. When individuals are said to behave probabilistically, the individual probabilities usually lend themselves to both the probabilistic and the deterministic (the "as if") interpretation. Only rarely does which interpretation is adopted make any difference.[10] Thus if one feels that people rarely behave probabilistically, that interpretation can be disregarded without losing more than a very few derivations from the present models.

---

[9] Coombs (1964, pp. 106–18) explains this notion and gives some experimental support for it.

[10] For one case in which it does make a difference, see the appendix of Niemi and Weisberg (chap. 6).

Three particular "as if" interpretations of probability assumptions warrant special mention. The probability assumptions of a model can frequently be interpreted as Bayesian subjective probabilities. According to this interpretation, the probabilities are personal, individual estimates of the likelihood of the behavior in question. Even if legislative voting were totally deterministic, legislative leaders, lobbyists, and outside investigators would still often resort to providing probabilistic estimates of how a given legislator would vote. This logic can be applied to estimating how legislators will act on an actual vote which is to be taken (as when coalition builders seek to construct a winning coalition) and to estimating how they would have voted on a vote which was not taken (as when scholars try to reconstruct a missing vote in order to determine whether the paradox of voting might have occurred). The problem of finding the probability assumptions which yield the most reliable results is still with us when the Bayesian viewpoint is adopted. However it should be noted that the solution for the "equally likely" assumption is of particular importance under the Bayesian interpretation for it corresponds to the case of no prior knowledge—no a priori basis by which to choose one probability assumption over another. The Bayesian interpretation of probability models has received little explicit attention in the literature, but we would regard it as one of the most important.

Another "as if" interpretation of probability assumptions escapes the usual criticisms of those assumptions in that it explicitly seeks to reject them. Probability assumptions can be used to construct a null model, specifying the results of a random process against which actual behavior can be compared. Rohde's treatment of minimal winning coalitions is an excellent example of this usage. He wishes to evaluate the empirical frequency of minimal winning coalitions on the Supreme Court. To do so, he determines the probability that they occur by chance and then compares the actual empirical probability against that expected value. There is no serious suggestion in this model that individual behavior is actually random, but comparison of empirical data with the null model employing random elements provides a gauge by which to judge the validity of the proposed theory.[11] The theory is supported (i.e., not disproved) in the measure to which predictions based on it are an improvement over random estimates. Conversely, if random estimates are equally good, the theory is eminently powerless.

One further "as if" interpretation is commonly employed when treating change processes. The investigator may know, or may be able to estimate, the proportion of individuals with a given attitude (or behavior) who change to another position between successive time periods. Indi-

---

[11] Another kind of test, obviously, is a competing theory.

vidual change may be governed by a totally deterministic process, but the likelihood of an individual changing can best be specified in a probabilistic manner if the investigator cannot specify in advance which exact individuals will change.

We have now discussed three main uses of probabilities for modelling collective decision making—for the uncertainty of events, the distribution of individuals, and probabilistic choice behavior. Our distinction between these uses of probabilities should not be taken as an indication that these uses are mutually exclusive. Often a single probability use in a model can be given several different interpretations. The probability assumptions in the work on the paradox of voting, for example, can generally be interpreted as either referring to a probability distribution of the voters or to random behavior by the individuals. The interpretation of the results of such models may occasionally depend on which specific use is intended, but generally the choice between the uses does not affect the results.

Additionally, more than one use of probabilities can be made by a single model. The Hinich, Ledyard, and Ordeshook (1972) work on spatial models, for example, uses both a probability distribution of the electorate and probabilistic behavior on the part of the individual voters. Simulations can introduce events on a random basis and then employ a probabilistic rule for individual behavior when the events occur. The specific uses of probabilities in such models should be distinguished, but otherwise the use of probabilities in several different ways in the same model poses no difficulty.

The variety of different uses and interpretations of probabilities in probabilistic modelling reflects favorably on the vitality of this approach to formal modelling. Probabilistic work is based on numerous interpretations, all of which we consider valid. Some of the uses may be more open to debate than are others, but we have argued that each is legitimate. In the end, the utility of this approach to scholarship must be judged on its results, so the ultimate test is the quality of the work which has been done in the area.

III. FUTURE DEVELOPMENT OF PROBABILITY MODELS

Most models are developed first in deterministic terms. Once it becomes apparent that a general solution cannot be obtained from the deterministic version, the model is translated into a probabilistic form. For example, the spatial modelling of candidate and voter behavior began with the deterministic work of Downs (1957) and was not given a probabilistic formulation until it became evident that such a formulation would be essential for the solution of the multidimensional case. As another example, the probability of the paradox of voting was sought only once it was realized that empirical data could not indicate how serious a problem the paradox was for normative democratic theory.

The further development of a probability model is usually a process of generalization. The initial version of a probability model tends to be highly constrained, both in terms of its probability usage and in terms of its substantive range. The first breakthrough in solving the problem can then be followed by relaxing the probability assumptions and broadening the substantive topic being modelled. We shall now detail the several aspects of such model generalization, indicating both the forms of generalization which have been employed and likely future directions.

Probability Usage

Once a probabilistic formulation is chosen, the initial probability assumptions are usually very restrictive. The paradox of voting, for example, was first studied only in terms of each possible social ordering being equally likely, and later only in terms of each possible individual preference ordering being equally likely. Similarly, when Rae (1969) first solved the problem of choosing the decision-rule which minimizes the probability of the individual member being disappointed, he used the assumption that each member is equally likely to favor or oppose each proposal. In general, the first formulation of a probability model employs probability assumptions which make the solution relatively easy, and only later is the model generalized to handle different assumptions.

One form of generalization involves moving away from an "equally likely" assumption to permit any arbitrary set of probabilities. The probability of the paradox of voting, for example, can theoretically now be solved for any set of initial probability assumptions. The work on constitutional design has been generalized to permit members to have probabilities other than one-half of voting for a proposal so long as every member has the same probability (Taylor, 1969). And, as Badger and Curtis show in this volume, even this common probability requirement may be dropped, though this may change the interpretation of the problem.

Where probability distributions are assumed in a model, the dependence on a specific distribution can be relaxed and a wide variety of possible distributions can be investigated. One level of generality is attained when the model can be used to derive results for any of a class of distributions with similar shapes. Substantial developments of this type have already taken place, but further work on additional classes of probability distributions could certainly be used. Models, for example, have tended to emphasize unimodal distributions which lead to convergence rather than U-shaped distributions which result in polarization. A likely direction, then, for future work on probability models is toward the attainment of models which can be used with any set of initial probabilities and any probability distribution.

Unfortunately, even this high level of generalization does not solve all the problems associated with the probability assumptions. Cases in point are work on the paradox of voting and the constitutional design problem. While solutions are known for any set of initial probabilities, the resulting probabilities of the paradox or this optimal decision fraction range from 0 to 1 depending on what these assumptions are. If no set or limited sets of initial assumptions can be justified as representative of some political setting, the solutions provide us relatively little information.[12] The availability of empirical data becomes especially useful at this juncture, so that the likely values of the parameters of the model can be estimated through a best-fit criterion. However as we noted previously, a resort to empirical evidence for determination of appropriate initial assumptions serves to emphasize the need to withstand empirical tests with predictions about data other than that used to estimate the parameter values.

A second way out of this problem may be to rely less on particular probabilistic results and more so on the direction in which the results move as other features of the model are altered. Thus, for example, an important result in the work on the probability of the paradox of voting is that the likelihood of the paradox increases as the number of alternatives rises, almost without regard to the initial probability assumptions. The specification of legislative conditions under which the paradox is facilitated or hindered may speak as much to the empirical frequency of the paradox as do elaborate probability calculations. Hence, even though some problems are encountered, generalization of models to allow for a wide variety of probability assumptions is a necessary direction for future development.

Another problem related to the probability assumptions is the nemesis of independent actors. One direction of relaxing the independence assumption is to divide the groups into blocs, where each bloc is entirely cohesive (and therefore its members do not vote independently of one another) but the different blocs vote independently. This translation of the problem into independent voting among blocs corresponds to Bjurulf's approach.

---

[12] There is perhaps some truth in the argument that an "equally likely" assumption properly expresses our ignorance of the real assumption, but this is a fairly weak justification.

Coleman (1970) has employed a similar solution, though with the votes of members of a bloc constrained to conform to the position of the bloc's majority. We might add here that solutions to the problem may come from within probability models. Interdependence of actors is not likely to be an absolute thing; complete dependence of one individual's behavior on that of another is likely to be the exception rather than the rule. But if dependence is not complete, it should fall naturally within the province of probability models. Thus although independence is presently a very restrictive assumption, we are confident that a probabilistic framework can be developed in which this assumption can be eliminated.

A final issue related to the use of probability terms in formal models involves the choice between mathematical solutions and simulation approaches. Simulation has been used to the exclusion of other approaches in the process modelling area and has been used along with mathematical evaluation in dealing with the probability of the paradox of voting. One view is that simulation provides a simplified evaluation procedure which is necessary only until higher-powered mathematics can be brought to bear. Another view is that some probability models are sufficiently complex that mathematical evaluation is impossible so simulation is essential. We feel that the availability of simulation should not be used to avoid simplification of a model, including the removal of redundancies. Given this caution, however, it seems best to admit that simulation approaches will continue to be useful in their own right and should not be treated as sloppy shorthand.[13]

Substantive Breadth

Generalizations of a model do not simply involve using less restrictive probability assumptions but also include increasing the generality of the event for which the probability is being sought. Rather than just focusing on the probability of a coalition winning, the probability of a minimal winning coalition can be obtained as in the work of Koehler, Rohde, and Niemi and Weisberg. Rather than just focusing on the spatial strategy for winning a general election, Aranson and Ordeshook and Coleman seek the spatial strategy for a candidate attempting to secure the nomination of his party and then to win the general election.

Models can also be generalized by seeking to optimize a function of more than one quantity. Frequently there is more than one type of loss involved in a problem and the modeller might permit a differential weighting of these losses. An example involves the constitutional design problem.

---

[13] Additional caveats about simulation are found in Bartholomew (1967, p. 7) and Coleman (1964, p. 529). A good discussion of simulation, including its probabilistic components and collective decision-making aspects, is found in Abelson (1968).

This problem has been formulated in terms of minimizing the likelihood of being disappointed. But there are two different types of disappointments—having a bill passed that one opposes and having a bill defeated that one supports. Curtis and Badger prove that the optimal decision-rule depends directly on how these two losses are weighted. Another example is the problem treated by Aranson and Ordeshook concerning the attempt of a candidate to win both his party's nomination and the final election. The candidate and the activist can be seen as attempting to minimize a loss function which equals the sum of the losses associated with being disappointed in the two contests, each weighted by an indication of how seriously the actor views that loss. This would admit the likelihood that a candidate might be so concerned with avoiding the loss of his party's nomination that he would take policy positions which would hurt his campaign for the general election. A third example involves the probability of winning coalitions as treated by Niemi and Weisberg. Instead of only attempting to maximize the probability of victory or of attempting to maximize the probability of a minimal winning coalition, a coalition builder might weight the loss to him associated with losing as opposed to the loss associated with constructing a larger than minimal coalition. Such behavior is sometimes seen in the relations between the president and Congress. When the president decides against further compromising on the contents of a bill (such as the Anti-Ballistic Missiles dispute in 1970) as a means of constructing a larger than minimal winning coalition, then he accepts a large risk of losing altogether.

Yet another way in which models can be generalized is in terms of the complexity of substantive problems they address. Many topics have first been modelled in fairly simple terms, but further work on them has increased the substantive verisimilitude of the model. Several examples and suggestions can be offered. Models involving a voting process should be generalized to allow for decision-rules other than majority rule. Probability work on the paradox of voting, for example, has typically assumed majority rule, but solutions can be extended to other decision fractions. Models involving a choice between two or three alternatives should be generalized to allow for more alternatives. The original probability work on the paradox, for example, only considered the case of three alternatives, but it became apparent that probability solutions could be extended to handle more alternatives. Models involving political parties (Aranson and Ordeshook; Coleman) or coalitions (Brams) should be generalized to allow more than two alternatives. Models assuming certain knowledge might be generalized to permit uncertainty, as Shepsle has demonstrated for the study of the paradox of voting and spatial modelling of party competition.

One further generalization of probability models is in the direction of dynamic rather than static models. Probability models, like all formal models, have tended to neglect dynamic aspects of political behavior even though it seems clear that they are a crucial part of political life. Fortunately we see in this volume and elsewhere an increase in attention to dynamic elements. Brams (chap. 5) and Coleman (1968), for example, are concerned not only about decision-making outcomes, but about the process by which coalitions are built up. The basic problem confronted by Aranson and Ordeshook and by Coleman is that a static model of electoral competition fails to take into account multiple elections. The whole constitutional design problem is one of concern with future decisions.

We do not suggest that the models cited here solve all the problems of dynamic political processes. But they do suggest that probability models are an appropriate means of attacking those problems. More generally, the uncertainties associated with time-related phenomena are a reason for suspecting that probability models will be particularly useful in making headway in this area.

In addition to directly taking dynamic elements into account in formal models, process mechanisms should receive more explicit attention as models are generalized. A large number of models have process implications, but probabilistic models are particularly well-suited to deal with them. Process mechanisms of coalition processes have already received some attention, but further work on the simulation of individual level process mechanisms and their implications for the behavior of aggregate populations would be appropriate.

A final point relates to the role of empirical work in formal models of collective decision making. The papers in this volume employ formal models, yet these models do have direct empirical applications. We concentrated on theoretical work in soliciting these papers, but we also made special attempts to obtain papers applying these models. In particular, applications are emphasized in the papers by Bowen and by Weisberg and Niemi on the probability of the paradox of voting in legislatures and in the papers by Koehler and Rohde on coalition size in Congress and the Supreme Court. Additionally several of the papers involve generalizing existing models to better cope with empirical phenomena, including Bjurulf's treatment of multiparty systems, Brams's consideration of the consequences of defection for coalition building, Shepsle's allowance for uncertainty, Davis and Hinich's considerations of constrained preferences, and Aranson and Ordeshook's and Coleman's treatment of the nomination process together with the election process. In the future we would expect the continued generalization of models to handle more complex features of reality. We also regard a concern with applications as a key feature of modelling, particularly as the models are extended and refined. It is our belief that probability models will provide the stimulus for a greater interaction between formal models and real world applications.

Bibliography

Abelson, Robert. "Simulation of Social Behavior." In *The Handbook of Social Psychology*, edited by Gardner Lindzey and Elliot Aronson. 2d ed. Vol. II. Reading: Addison-Wesley, 1968.

Abelson, Robert, and Alex Bernstein. "A Computer Simulation Model of Community Referendum Controversies." *Public Opinion Quarterly* 27 (1963): 92–122.

Adrian, Charles, and Charles Press. "Decision Costs and Coalition Formation." *American Political Science Review* 62 (1968): 556–63.

Anderson, Lee, Meredith Watts Jr., and Allen Wilcox. *Legislative Roll Call Analysis*. Evanston: Northwestern University Press, 1966.

Aranson, Peter. "Essays in the Theory of Political Participation." Unpublished Ph. D. dissertation, University of Rochester, forthcoming.

Arrow, Kenneth. *Social Choice and Individual Values*. 2d ed. New York: Wiley, 1963.

Atkinson, David, and Dale Newman. "Toward a Cost Theory of Judicial Alignments: the Case of the Truman Bloc." *Midwest Journal of Political Science* 13 (1969): 271–83.

Aumann, Robert, and Michael Maschler. "The Bargaining Set for Cooperative Games." In *Advances in Game Theory*, edited by M. Fresher, L.S. Shapley, and A.W. Tucker. Princeton: Princeton University Press, 1964.

Axelrod, Robert. *Conflict of Interest*. Chicago: Markham, 1970.

Bachrach, Peter, and Morton Baratz. "The Two Faces of Power." *American Political Science Review* 56 (1962): 947–53.

Bartholomew, David. *Stochastic Models for Social Processes.* New York: Wiley, 1967.

Bartholomew, David, and E. E. Bassett. *Let's Look at the Figures: The Quantitative Approach to Human Affairs.* Harmondsworth, England: Penguin Books Ltd., 1971.

Black, Duncan. *The Theory of Committees and Elections.* Cambridge: Cambridge University Press, 1958.

_____. "On Arrow's Impossibility Theorem." *Journal of Law and Economics* 12 (1969): 227–48.

Black, Duncan, and R. A. Newing. *Committee Decisions with Complimentary Valuation.* London: William Hodge, 1951.

Blackstone, Sir William. *Commentaries on the Laws of England.* Philadelphia: Lippincott, 1862.

Blalock, Hubert. *Social Statistics.* New York: McGraw-Hill, 1960.

Blydenburgh, John. "The Closed Rule and the Paradox of Voting." *Journal of Politics* 33 (1971): 57–71.

Borch, Karl. *The Economics of Uncertainty.* Princeton: Princeton University Press, 1968.

Bowen, Bruce. "The Paradox of Voting: A Theoretical and Empirical Examination." Unpublished Ph.D. dissertation, University of Kentucky, 1969.

Brams, Steven. "Positive Coalition Theory: The Relationship Between Postulated Goals and Derived Behavior." In *Political Science Annual: Conflict, Competition, and Coalitions, IV*, edited by Cornelius Cotter, *et al.* Indianapolis: Bobbs-Merrill, forthcoming, 1972a.

_____. "Three Equilibrium Models of Coalition Formation in Voting Bodies." In *Theories of Collective Behavior*, edited by Julius Margolis and Henry Teune, forthcoming, 1972b.

Brams, Steven and John Heilman. "When to Join a Coalition, and with How Many Others, Depends on What You Expect the Outcome to Be," forthcoming, 1972.

Brams, Steven, and Michael O'Leary. "An Axiomatic Model of Voting Bodies." *American Political Science Review* 64 (1970): 449–70.

_____. "Comment on Mayer's 'A Note on an Axiomatic Model of Voting Bodies.'" *American Political Science Review* 65 (1971): 766.

Brams, Steven, and William Riker. "Models of Coalition Formation in Voting Bodies." In *Mathematical Applications in Political Science, VI*, edited by James Herndon. Charlottesville: University Press of Virginia, 1972.

Brams, Steven and William Sensiba. "The Win/Share Principle in National Party Conventions." In *Democracy and Presidential Selection*, edited by Donald Matthews. Washington, D. C.: Brookings Institution, 1972.

Buchanan, James. "An Individualistic Theory of Political Process." In *Varieties of Political Theory*, edited by David Easton. Englewood Cliffs: Prentice-Hall, 1966.

Buchanan, James, and Gordon Tullock. *The Calculus of Consent*. Ann Arbor: University of Michigan Press, 1962.

Campbell, Angus, Philip Converse, Warren Miller, and Donald Stokes. *The American Voter*. New York: Wiley, 1960.

_____. *Elections and the Political Order*. New York: Wiley, 1966.

Campbell, Colin, and Gordon Tullock. "A Measure of the Importance of Cyclical Majorities." *Economic Journal* 75 (1965): 853–57.

Carlsson, Gosta. "Time and Continuity in Mass Attitude Change: The Case of Voting." *Public Opinion Quarterly* 29 (1965): 1–16.

Chapman, David. "Models of the Working of a Two-Party Electoral System, I." *Papers on Non-Market Decision Making* 3 (1967): 19–37.

_____. "Models of the Working of a Two-Party Electoral System, II." *Public Choice* 5 (1968): 19–37.

Cherryholmes, Cleo, and Michael Shapiro. *Representatives and Roll Calls: A Computer Simulation of Voting in the Eighty-Eighth Congress*. Indianapolis: Bobbs-Merrill, 1969.

Churchman, C. West. *Prediction and Optimal Decision*. Englewood Cliffs: Prentice-Hall, 1961.

Cochran, William. *Sampling Techniques*. 2d ed. New York: Wiley, 1963.

Coleman, James. *Introduction to Mathematical Sociology*. New York: Free Press, 1964.

_____. "The Marginal Utility of a Vote Commitment." *Public Choice* 5 (1968): 39–58.

_____. "The Benefits of Coalition." *Public Choice* 8 (1970): 45–62.

Coombs, Clyde. *A Theory of Data*. New York: Wiley, 1964.

Coombs, Clyde, Robyn Dawes, and Amos Tversky. *Mathematical Psychology: An Elementary Introduction*. Englewood Cliffs: Prentice-Hall, 1970.

Coombs, Steven, Michael Fried, and Stewart Robinovitz. "An Approach to Election Simulation Through Modular Systems." In *Simulation in the Study of Politics*, edited by William Coplin. Chicago: Markham, 1968.

Curry, R. L., Jr., and L. L. Wade. *A Theory of Political Exchange: Economic Reasoning in Political Analysis*. Englewood Cliffs: Prentice-Hall, 1968.

Danelski, David. "Values as Variables in Judicial Decision-making: Notes Toward a Theory." *Vanderbilt Law Review* 19 (1966): 721–40.

Davis, Harold. *Introduction to Nonlinear Differential and Integral Equations*. Washington, D.C.: U. S. Government Printing Office, 1961.

Davis, Otto. "Notes on Strategy and Methodology for a Scientific Political Science." In *Mathematical Applications in Political Science, IV*, edited by Joseph Bernd. Charlottesville: University Press of Virginia, 1969.

Davis, Otto, Morris DeGroot, and Melvin Hinich. "Social Preference Orderings and Majority Rule." *Econometrica* 40 (1972), forthcoming.

Davis, Otto, and Melvin Hinich. "A Mathematical Model of Policy Formation in a Democratic Society." In *Mathematical Applications in Political Science, II,* edited by Joseph Bernd. Dallas: Southern Methodist University Press, 1966.

_____. "Some Results Related to a Mathematical Model of Policy Formation in a Democratic Society." In *Mathematical Applications in Political Science, III,* edited by Joseph Bernd. Charlottesville: University Press of Virginia, 1967.

_____. "On the Power and Importance of the Mean Preference in a Mathematical Model of Democratic Choice." *Public Choice* 5 (1968): 59–72.

Davis, Otto, Melvin Hinich, and Peter Ordeshook. "An Expository Development of a Mathematical Model of the Electoral Process." *American Political Science Review* 64 (1970): 426-48.

DeGroot, Morris. *Optimal Statistical Decision.* New York: McGraw-Hill, 1970.

DeMeyer, Frank, and Charles Plott. "The Probability of a Cyclical Majority." *Econometrica* 38 (1970): 345–54.

_____. "A Welfare Function Using 'Relative Intensity' of Preference." *Quarterly Journal of Economics* 85 (1971): 179–86.

Dixon, Wilfrid, and Frank Massey, Jr. *Introduction to Statistical Analysis.* New York: McGraw-Hill, 1957.

Downs, Anthony. *An Economic Theory of Democracy.* New York: Harper and Row, 1957.

Dummett, Michael, and Robin Farquharson. "Stability in Voting." *Econometrica* 29 (1961): 33–42.

Duverger, Maurice. *Political Parties.* London: Methuen, 1965.

Edwards, Ward. "Probability Preferences in Gambling." *American Journal of Psychology* 66 (1953): 349–64.

Eldersveld, Samuel. *Political Parties: A Behavioral Analysis.* Chicago: Rand McNally, 1964.

Evans, Rowland, and Robert Novak. *Lyndon B. Johnson: The Exercise of Power.* New York: New American Library, 1966.

Farquharson, Robin. *Theory of Voting.* New Haven: Yale University Press, 1969.

Fishburn, Peter. "The Theory of Representative Majority Decision." *Econometrica,* forthcoming.

Friedman, Milton, and L. J. Savage. "The Utility Analysis of Choices Involving Risk." *Journal of Political Economy* 56 (1948): 279–304.

Froman, Lewis, Jr. "A Realistic Approach to Campaign Strategies and Tactics." In *The Electoral Process,* edited by M. Kent Jennings and L. Harmon Zeigler. Englewood Cliffs: Prentice-Hall, 1966.

Garman, Mark, and Morton Kamien. "The Paradox of Voting: Probability Calculations." *Behavioral Science* 13 (1968): 306–16.

Garvey, Gerald. "The Theory of Party Equilibrium." *American Political Science Review* 60 (1966): 29–39.

Gleser, Leon. "The Paradox of Voting: Some Probabilistic Results." *Public Choice* 7 (1969): 47–64.

Groennings, Sven, E. W. Kelley, and Michael Leiserson. *The Study of Coalition Behavior.* New York: Holt, Rinehart & Winston, 1970.

Haefele, Edwin. "Coalitions, Minority Representation, and Vote Trading Probabilities." *Public Choice* 8 (1970): 75–90.

Harris, T. Robert. "Politics on the Unit Circle." Unpublished paper, Johns Hopkins University, 1966.

Harsanyi, John. "A General Theory of Rational Behavior in Game Situations." *Econometrica* 34 (1966): 613–34.

_____. "Rational-Choice Models of Political Behavior Versus Functionalist and Conformist Theories." *World Politics* 21 (1969): 513–38.

Hays, William. *Statistics for Psychologists.* New York: Holt, Rinehart, & Winston, 1965.

Herring, Pendleton. *The Politics of Democracy.* New York: Norton, 1940.

Hildreth, Clifford. "Alternative Conditions for Social Orderings." *Econometrica* 21 (1953): 81–94.

Hinich, Melvin, John Ledyard and Peter Ordeshook. "A Theory of Electoral Equilibrium: A Spatial Analysis Based on the Theory of Games." Unpublished Paper, School of Urban and Public Affairs, Carnegie-Mellon University, 1971.

_____. "Non-voting and the Existence of Equilibrium under Majority Rule." *Journal of Economic Theory*, forthcoming, 1972.

Hinich, Melvin, and Peter Ordeshook. "Abstention and Equilibrium in the Electoral Process." *Public Choice* 7 (1969): 81–106.

_____. "Plurality Maximization vs. Vote Maximization: A Spatial Analysis with Variable Participation." *American Political Science Review* 64 (1970): 772–91.

_____. "Social Welfare and Electoral Competition in Democratic Societies." *Public Choice* 11 (1971): 73–87.

Ho, Y. C. "Differential Games, Dynamic Optimization, and Generalized Control Theory." *Journal of Optimization Theory and Applications* 6 (1970): 179–209.

Holt, Robert, and John Turner. *The Methodology of Comparative Research.* New York: Free Press, 1970.

Hotelling, Harold. "Stability in Competition." *Economic Journal* 39 (1929): 41–57.

Huntington, Samuel. "Conservatism as an Ideology." *American Political Science Review* 51 (1957): 454–73.

Inada, Ken-Ichi. "Alternative Incompatible. Conditions for a Social Welfare Function." *Econometrica* 23 (1955): 396–99.

_____. "A Note on the Simple Majority Decision Rule." *Econometrica* 32 (1964): 525–31.

Johnson, Richard. *The Dynamics of Compliance: Supreme Court Decision-Making from a New Perspective.* Evanston: Northwestern University Press, 1967.

Kalvern, Harry. *The Negro and the First Amendment.* Chicago: University of Chicago Press, 1965.

Kaplan, Abraham. *The Conduct of Inquiry.* San Francisco: Chandler, 1964.

Keech, William. *The Impact of Negro Voting.* Chicago: Rand McNally, 1968.

Kendall, Maurice, and Alan Stuart. "The Law of Cubic Proportions in Election Results." *British Journal of Sociology* 1 (1950): 193–97.

Key, V. O., Jr. *Politics, Parties and Pressure Groups.* 5th ed. New York: Crowell, 1964.

Kielson, J., and H. Gerber. "Some Results for Discrete Unimodality." *Journal of the American Statistical Association* 66 (1971): 386–89.

Klahr, David. "A Computer Simulation of the Paradox of Voting." *American Political Science Review* 60 (1966): 384–90.

Kramer, Gerald. "A Decision-Theoretic Analysis of a Problem in Political Campaigning." In *Mathematical Applications in Political Science, II,* edited by Joseph Bernd. Dallas: Southern Methodist University Press, 1966.

Krislov, Samuel. "Power and Coalition in a Nine-man Body." *American Behavioral Scientist* 6 (1963): 24–26.

Laing, James and Richard Morrison. "Coalition Formation in Certain Sequential Three-Person Games: II. Interdependent Choice in Hyperopic Considerations." Unpublished paper, Graduate School of Industrial Administration, Carnegie-Mellon University, 1971.

Lindblom, Charles. *The Policy Making Process.* Englewood Cliffs: Prentice-Hall, 1968.

Luce, R. Duncan, and Howard Raiffa. *Games and Decisions.* New York: Wiley, 1957.

McClosky, Herbert, Paul Hoffman, and Rosemary O'Hara. "Issue Conflict and Consensus Among Party Leaders and Followers." *American Political Science Review* 54 (1960): 406–29.

Machiavelli, Niccolo. *The Prince and the Discourses.* Translated from the Italian by Luigi Ricci, revised by E.R.P. Vincent, with an introduction by Max Lerner. New York: Modern Library, 1950.

McKelvey, Richard, and Peter Ordeshook. "A General Theory of the Calculus of Voting." In *Mathematical Applications in Political Science, VI,* edited by James Herndon. Charlottesville: University Press of Virginia, 1972.

McPhee, William, and Jack Ferguson. "Political Immunization." In *Public Opinion and Congressional Elections,* edited by William McPhee and William Glaser. New York: Free Press, 1962.

McPhee, William, and Robert Smith. "A Model for Analyzing Voting Systems." In *Public Opinion and Congressional Elections*, edited by William McPhee and William Glaser. New York: Free Press, 1962.

MacRae, Duncan, Jr. "Dimensions of Congressional Voting." *University of California Publications in Sociology and Social Institutions* 1, No. 3 (1958).

Madison, James. *Journal of the Federal Constitution*. Edited by E. H. Scott. Chicago: Albert, Scott, 1893.

Madison, James. No. X of *The Federalist or the New Constitution*, Introduction by W. J. Ashby. London, 1922.

March, James. "Party Legislative Representation as a Function of Election Results." *Public Opinion Quarterly* 21 (1957–58): 521–42.

Matthews, Donald, and James Stimson. "Decision-Making by U.S. Representatives: A Preliminary Model." In *Political Decision-Making*, edited by S. Sidney Ulmer. New York: Van Nostrand-Reinhold, 1970.

May, Kenneth. "A Set of Independent Necessary and Sufficient Conditions for Simple Majority Decision." *Econometrica* 20 (1952): 680–84.

May, Robert. "Some Mathematical Remarks on the Paradox of Voting." *Behavioral Science* 16 (1971): 143–51.

Mayer, Lawrence. "A Note on 'An Axiomatic Model of Voting Bodies.'" *American Political Science Review* 65 (1971): 764–65.

Meltz, David. "Competition and Cohesion: A Model of Majority Party Legislative Bargaining." Unpublished Ph.D. dissertation, University of Rochester, 1970.

Muir, William. *Prayer in the Public Schools: Law and Attitude Change*. Chicago: University of Chicago Press, 1967.

Murakami, Yasusuke. *Logic and Social Choice*. New York: Dover, 1968.

Murphy, Walter. *Congress and the Court*. Chicago: University of Chicago Press, 1962.

_____. *Elements of Judicial Strategy*. Chicago: University of Chicago Press, 1964.

Niemi, Richard. "Majority Decision-Making with Partial Unidimensionality." *American Political Science Review* 63 (1969): 488–97.

_____. "The Occurrence of the Paradox of Voting in University Elections." *Public Choice* 8 (1970a): 91–100.

_____. "An Alternative to the Equilibrium Model of Coalition Formation in Voting Bodies." Unpublished paper, University of Rochester, 1970b.

Niemi, Richard, and Herbert Weisberg. "Communications." *American Political Science Review* 61 (1967): 761.

_____. "A Mathematical Solution for the Probability of the Paradox of Voting." *Behavioral Science* 13 (1968): 317–23.

Olson, Mancur, Jr. *The Logic of Collective Action*. New York: Schocken Books, 1965.

Ordeshook, Peter. "Theory of the Electoral Process." Unpublished Ph.D. dissertation, University of Rochester, 1969.

_____. "Extensions to a Mathematical Model of the Electoral Process and Implications for the Theory of Responsible Parties." *Midwest Journal of Political Science* 14 (1970): 43–70.

_____. "Pareto Optimality in Electoral Competition." *American Political Science Review* 65 (1971): 1141–45.

Phillips, Kevin. *The Emerging Republican Majority.* New Rochelle: Arlington House, 1969.

Plott, Charles. "A Notion of Equilibrium and Its Possibility Under Majority Rule." *American Economic Review* 57 (1967a): 787–806.

_____. "A Method for Finding 'Acceptable Proposals' in Group Decision Processes." *Papers on Non-Market Decision Making* 2 (1967b): 45–59.

_____. "Recent Results in the Theory of Voting." In *Frontiers in Quantitative Economics,* edited by Michael Intriligator. Amsterdam: North Holland, 1971.

Polsby, Nelson, and Aaron Wildavsky. *Presidential Elections.* 2d ed. New York: Scribners, 1968.

Pomeranz, John, and Roman Weil, Jr. "The Cyclical Majority Problem." *Communications of the ACM* 13 (1970): 251–54.

Pool, Ithiel de Sola, Robert Abelson, and Samuel Popkin. *Candidates, Issues, and Strategies.* Cambridge: MIT Press, 1965.

Pratt, John. "Risk Aversion in the Small and in the Large." *Econometrica* 32 (1964): 122–35.

Pritchett, C. Herman. *The Roosevelt Court: A Study in Judicial Politics and Values.* New York: Macmillan, 1948.

Rabushka, Alvin, and Kenneth Shepsle. *Politics in Plural Societies: A Theory of Democratic Instability.* Columbus: Charles Merrill, 1972.

Rae, Douglas. "Decision-rules and Individual Values in Constitutional Choice." *American Political Science Review* 63 (1969): 40–56.

Riker, William. "The Paradox of Voting and Congressional Rules for Voting on Amendments." *American Political Science Review* 52 (1958): 349–66.

_____. "A Test of the Adequacy of the Power Index." *Behavioral Science* 4 (1959): 120–31.

_____. "Voting and the Summation of Preferences: An Interpretive Bibliographic Review of Selected Developments During the Last Decade." *American Political Science Review* 55 (1961): 900–11.

_____. *The Theory of Political Coalitions.* New Haven: Yale University Press, 1962.

_____. "Arrow's Theorem and Some Examples of the Paradox of Voting." In *Mathematical Applications in Political Science,* edited by John Claunch. Dallas: Southern Methodist University Press, 1965.

Riker, William, and Peter Ordeshook. "A Theory of the Calculus of Voting." *American Political Science Review* 62 (1968): 25–42.

Rohde, David. "Comments on 'A Cost Theory of Judicial Alignments'." *Midwest Journal of Political Science* 14 (1970): 331–36.

Rose, Arnold. "A Study of Irrational Judgments." *Journal of Political Economy* 65 (1957): 394–402.

Rosenthal, Howard, and Subatra Sen. "Electoral Participation in the French Fifth Republic." Paper presented at the American Political Science Association Convention. Los Angeles, 1970.

Rothenberg, Jerome. *The Measurement of Social Welfare*. Englewood Cliffs: Prentice-Hall, 1961.

_____. "A Model of Economic and Political Decision Making." In *The Public Economy of Urban Communities*, edited by Julius Margolis. Baltimore: Johns Hopkins University Press, 1965.

Scammon, Richard, and Ben Wattenberg. *The Real Majority: An Extraordinary Examination of the American Electorate*. New York: Coward-McCann, 1970.

Schattschneider, E. E. *The Semisovereign People*. New York: Holt, Rinehart and Winston, 1960.

Schelling, Thomas. *The Strategy of Conflict*. New York: Oxford University Press, 1963.

_____. "Strategy, Tactics and Non-Zero Sum Theory." In *Theory of Games: Techniques and Applications*, edited by A. Mensch. New York: American Elsevier Publishing Company, 1966.

Schmidhauser, John. "Judicial Behavior and the Sectional Crisis of 1837–1860." *Journal of Politics* 23 (1961): 615–40.

Schoenberger, Robert. "Campaign Strategy and Party Loyalty: The Electoral Relevance of Candidate Decision-Making in the 1964 Congressional Elections." *American Political Science Review* 63 (1969): 515–20.

Schubert, Glendon. *Quantitative Analysis of Judicial Behavior*. Glencoe: Free Press, 1959.

_____. "The 1960–61 Term of the Supreme Court: A Psychological Analysis." *American Political Science Review* 56 (1962): 90–107.

_____. "The Power of Organized Minorities in a Small Group." *Administrative Science Quarterly* 9 (1964): 133–53.

_____. *The Judicial Mind*. Evanston: Northwestern University Press, 1965.

Sen, Amartya. "A Possibility Theorem on Majority Decisions." *Econometrica* 34 (1966): 491–99.

_____. "Quasi-Transitivity, Rational Choice and Collective Decisions." *Review of Economic Studies* 36 (1969): 381–93.

Shapley, L. S., and Martin Shubik. "A Method for Evaluating the Distribution of Power in a Committee System." *American Political Science Review* 48 (1954): 787–92.

Shepsle, Kenneth. "Essays on Risky Choice in Electoral Competition." Unpublished Ph.D. dissertation, University of Rochester, 1970a.

_____. "A Note on Zeckhauser's 'Majority Rule with Lotteries on Alternatives'." *Quarterly Journal of Economics* 84 (1970b): 705–9.

Smithies, Arthur. "Optimum Location in Spatial Competition." *Journal of Political Economy* 49 (1941): 423–29.

Spaeth, Harold. "Judicial Power as a Variable Motivating Supreme Court Behavior." *Midwest Journal of Political Science* 6 (1962): 54–82.

Steiner, Peter. "The Public Sector and the Public Interest." In *The Analysis and Evaluation of Public Expenditures,* edited by Robert Haveman. Vol. 1. Washington, D.C.: U.S. Government Printing Office, 1969.

Stokes, Donald. "Party Loyalty and the Likelihood of Deviating Elections." *Journal of Politics* 24 (1962): 689–702.

_____. "Spatial Models of Party Competition." *American Political Science Review* 57 (1963): 368–77.

_____. "Some Dynamic Elements of Contests for the Presidency." *American Political Science Review* 60 (1966): 19–28.

Stokes, Donald, and Gudmund Iversen. "On the Existence of Forces Restoring Party Competition." *Public Opinion Quarterly* 26 (1962): 159–71.

Tables of the Binomial Probability Distribution. Appl. Math. Series 6. Washington, D.C.: U.S. Government Printing Office, 1949.

Tables of the Bivariate Normal Distribution Function and Related Functions. Appl. Math. Series 50. Washington, D.C.: U.S. Government Printing Office, 1959.

Tables of the Cumulative Binomial Probability Distribution. Cambridge: Harvard University Press, 1955.

Tanenhaus, Joseph. "Supreme Court Attitudes Toward Federal Administrative Agencies." *Journal of Politics* 22 (1960): 502–24.

Taylor, Michael. "Proof of a Theorem on Majority Rule." *Behavioral Science* 14 (1969): 228–31.

Thomas, George. *Calculus and Analytic Geometry.* Reading: Addison-Wesley, 1960.

Tullock, Gordon. *The Politics of Bureaucracy.* Washington: Public Affairs Press, 1965.

_____. *Toward a Mathematics of Politics.* Ann Arbor: University of Michigan Press, 1967.

Tullock, Gordon, and Colin Campbell. "Computer Simulation of a Small Voting System." *Economic Journal* 80 (1970): 97–104.

Ulmer, S. Sidney. "Toward a Theory of Sub-Group Formation in the United States Supreme Court." *Journal of Politics* 27 (1965): 133–52.

Vickrey, William. "Utility, Strategy, and Social Decision Rules." *Quarterly Journal of Economics* 74 (1960): 507–35.

Von Neumann, John, and Oskar Morgenstern. *Theory of Games and Economic Behavior.* 3rd ed. Princeton: Princeton University Press, 1953.

Ward, Benjamin. "Majority Rule and Allocation." *Journal of Conflict Resolution* 5 (1961): 379–89.

_____. "Majority Voting and Alternative Forms of Public Enterprise." In *The Public Economy of Urban Communities*, edited by Julius Margolis. Baltimore: Johns Hopkins University Press, 1965.

Weisberg, Herbert and Richard Niemi. "Limiting Probabilities for the Paradox of Voting." Unpublished paper, University of Michigan, 1971.

White, J. D. *Decision Theory*. Chicago: Aldine, 1970.

Williamson, Oliver, and Thomas Sargent. "Social Choice: A Probabilistic Approach." *Economic Journal* 77 (1967): 797–813.

Wilson, James. *The Amateur Democrat*. Chicago: University of Chicago Press, 1962.

Wilson, Robert. "An Axiomatic Model of Logrolling." *American Economic Review* 59 (1969): 331–41.

_____. "Stable Coalition Proposals in Majority Rule Voting." *Journal of Economic Theory*, forthcoming.

Zeckhauser, Richard. "Majority Rule with Lotteries on Alternatives." *Quarterly Journal of Economics* 83 (1969): 796–803.

NAME INDEX

407

SUBJECT INDEX

411